Lecture Notes in Computer Science 15274

Founding Editors

Gerhard Goos
Juris Hartmanis

Editorial Board Members

Elisa Bertino, *Purdue University, West Lafayette, IN, USA*
Wen Gao, *Peking University, Beijing, China*
Bernhard Steffen, *TU Dortmund University, Dortmund, Germany*
Moti Yung, *Columbia University, New York, NY, USA*

The series Lecture Notes in Computer Science (LNCS), including its subseries Lecture Notes in Artificial Intelligence (LNAI) and Lecture Notes in Bioinformatics (LNBI), has established itself as a medium for the publication of new developments in computer science and information technology research, teaching, and education.

LNCS enjoys close cooperation with the computer science R & D community, the series counts many renowned academics among its volume editors and paper authors, and collaborates with prestigious societies. Its mission is to serve this international community by providing an invaluable service, mainly focused on the publication of conference and workshop proceedings and postproceedings. LNCS commenced publication in 1973.

M. Emre Celebi · Mauricio Reyes · Zhen Chen ·
Xiaoxiao Li
Editors

Medical Image Computing and Computer Assisted Intervention – MICCAI 2024 Workshops

ISIC 2024, iMIMIC 2024, EARTH 2024, DeCaF 2024
Held in Conjunction with MICCAI 2024
Marrakesh, Morocco, October 6–10, 2024
Proceedings

Editors
M. Emre Celebi ⓘ
Department of Computer Science
and Engineering
University of Central Arkansas
Conway, AR, USA

Zhen Chen ⓘ
Yale School of Medicine, Yale University
New Haven, CT, USA

Mauricio Reyes ⓘ
University of Bern
Bern, Switzerland

Xiaoxiao Li ⓘ
University of British Columbia
Vancouver, BC, Canada

ISSN 0302-9743   ISSN 1611-3349 (electronic)
Lecture Notes in Computer Science
ISBN 978-3-031-77609-0   ISBN 978-3-031-77610-6 (eBook)
https://doi.org/10.1007/978-3-031-77610-6

© The Editor(s) (if applicable) and The Author(s), under exclusive license
to Springer Nature Switzerland AG 2025, corrected publication 2025

This work is subject to copyright. All rights are solely and exclusively licensed by the Publisher, whether the whole or part of the material is concerned, specifically the rights of translation, reprinting, reuse of illustrations, recitation, broadcasting, reproduction on microfilms or in any other physical way, and transmission or information storage and retrieval, electronic adaptation, computer software, or by similar or dissimilar methodology now known or hereafter developed.
The use of general descriptive names, registered names, trademarks, service marks, etc. in this publication does not imply, even in the absence of a specific statement, that such names are exempt from the relevant protective laws and regulations and therefore free for general use.
The publisher, the authors and the editors are safe to assume that the advice and information in this book are believed to be true and accurate at the date of publication. Neither the publisher nor the authors or the editors give a warranty, expressed or implied, with respect to the material contained herein or for any errors or omissions that may have been made. The publisher remains neutral with regard to jurisdictional claims in published maps and institutional affiliations.

This Springer imprint is published by the registered company Springer Nature Switzerland AG
The registered company address is: Gewerbestrasse 11, 6330 Cham, Switzerland

If disposing of this product, please recycle the paper.

ISIC 2024 Preface

The Ninth International Skin Imaging Collaboration (ISIC) Workshop on Skin Image Analysis was held at the Palmeraie Conference Centre, Marrakesh, Morocco on October 10, 2024, in conjunction with the 27th International Conference on Medical Image Computing and Computer-Assisted Intervention (MICCAI).

Skin is the largest organ of the human body, and the first area of a patient assessed by clinical staff. The skin delivers numerous insights into a patient's underlying health: for example, pale or blue skin suggests respiratory issues, unusually yellowish skin can signal hepatic issues, or certain rashes can be indicative of autoimmune issues. In addition, dermatological complaints are the most prevalent reason that patients seek primary care. Images of the skin are the most easily captured form of medical image in healthcare, and the domain shares qualities with standard computer vision datasets, serving as a natural bridge between standard computer vision tasks and medical applications. However, significant and unique challenges still exist in this domain. For example, there is remarkable visual similarity across disease conditions, and compared to other medical imaging domains, varying genetics, disease states, imaging equipment, and imaging conditions can significantly change the appearance of the skin, making localization and classification in this domain unsolved tasks.

This workshop served as a venue to facilitate advancements and knowledge dissemination in the field of skin image analysis, raising awareness of and interest in these socially valuable tasks. Invited speakers included major influencers in computer vision and skin image analysis, and authors of accepted papers.

Authors were asked to submit full-length manuscripts for double-blind peer review. A total of 24 submissions were received, and with a Program Committee composed of 26 experts in the field, reviewed by at least three reviewers. Based on the feedback and critiques, five of the best papers (21%) were selected for oral presentation at the workshop, and included in this LNCS volume published by Springer.

We thank the authors for submitting their excellent work, our reviewers for their timely and detailed reviews, our invited speakers, and all our attendees. We sincerely hope that the efforts coming together to make this workshop possible will help advance the field and have a positive impact on health care worldwide.

October 2024

M. Emre Celebi
Catarina Barata
Allan Halpern
Philipp Tschandl
Marc Combalia
Yuan Liu

The original version of the book has been revised. The affiliation of the volume editor M. Emre Celebi has been updated. A correction to this book can be found at https://doi.org/10.1007/978-3-031-77610-6_24

ISIC 2024 Organization

Steering Committee

Noel C. F. Codella	Microsoft, USA
Anthony Hoogs	Kitware, USA
Yun Liu	Google Health, USA
Dale Webster	Google Health, USA

Workshop Chairs

M. Emre Celebi	University of Central Arkansas, USA
Catarina Barata	Instituto Superior Técnico, Portugal
Allan Halpern	Memorial Sloan Kettering Cancer Center, USA
Philipp Tschandl	Medical University of Vienna, Austria
Marc Combalia	Kenko AI, Spain
Yuan Liu	Google, USA

Program Committee

Kumar Abhishek	Simon Fraser University, Canada
Euijoon Ahn	James Cook University, Australia
Sandra Avila	University of Campinas, Brazil
Nourhan Bayasi	University of British Columbia, Canada
Lei Bi	University of Sydney, Australia
Alceu Bissoto	University of Campinas, Brazil
Siyi Du	University of British Columbia, Canada
Matthew Groh	Northwestern University, USA
Ghassan Hamarneh	Simon Fraser University, Canada
Joanna Jaworek-Korjakowska	AGH University of Science and Technology, Poland
Jeremy Kawahara	AIP Labs, Hungary
Jinman Kim	University of Sydney, Australia
Sinan Kockara	Rice University, USA
Kivanc Kose	Memorial Sloan Kettering Cancer Center, USA
Tim K. Lee	University of British Columbia, Canada
Carlos Santiago	Instituto Superior Técnico, Portugal

Yuheng Wang — University of British Columbia, Canada
Eduardo Valle — University of Campinas, Brazil
Moi Hoon Yap — Manchester Metropolitan University, UK

iMIMIC 2024 Preface

The Seventh International Workshop on Interpretability of Machine Intelligence in Medical Image Computing (iMIMIC) was held on October 6, 2024, in conjunction with the 27th International Conference on Medical Imaging and Computer-Assisted Intervention (MICCAI).

iMIMIC was a single-track, half-day workshop consisting of high-quality, previously unpublished papers, presented either oimage computing and rally or as a poster, intended to act as a forum for research groups, engineers, and practitioners to present recent algorithmic developments, new results, and promising future directions in interpretability of machine intelligence in medical image computing.

Machine learning systems are achieving remarkable performance at the cost of increased complexity. Hence, they become less interpretable, which may cause distrust, potentially limiting clinical acceptance. As these systems are pervasively being introduced to critical domains, such as medical image computing and computer-assisted intervention, it becomes imperative to develop methodologies allowing insight into their decision making. Such methodologies would help physicians to decide whether they should follow and trust automatic decisions. Additionally, interpretable machine learning methods could facilitate defining the legal framework of their clinical deployment. Ultimately, interpretability is closely related to AI safety in healthcare.

This year's iMIMIC was held on October 6, 2024 in Marrakesh, Morocco. There was a very positive response to the call for papers for iMIMIC 2024. We received 12 full papers and 7 were accepted for presentation at the workshop, where each paper was reviewed by at least three reviewers. The accepted papers focused on introducing the challenges and opportunities related to the topic of interpretability of machine learning systems in the context of medical imaging and computer-assisted intervention.

The high quality of the scientific program of iMIMIC 2024 was due first to the authors who submitted excellent contributions and second to the dedicated collaboration of the International Program Committee and the other researchers who reviewed the papers. We would like to thank all the authors for submitting their contributions and for sharing their research activities. We are particularly indebted to the Program Committee members and to all the reviewers for their precious evaluations, which permitted us to set up this publication. We were also very pleased to benefit from the participation of the invited speaker Michael Kampffmeyer, University of Tromsø (UiT) - The Arctic University of Norway. We would like to express our sincere gratitude to this world-renowned expert.

October 2024

Mauricio Reyes
Jaime S. Cardoso
Mara Graziani
Pedro Abreu
Wilson Silva
José Amorim
Amith Kamath

iMIMIC 2024 Organization

Steering Committee

Mauricio Reyes	University of Bern, Switzerland
Jaime Cardoso	Universidade do Porto, Portugal
Jayashree Kalpathy-Kramer	MGH Harvard University, USA
Nguyen Le Minh	Japan Advanced Institute of Science and Technology, Japan
Mara Graziani	IBM Research Zürich, Switzerland
Pedro Abreu	CISUC and University of Coimbra, Portugal
Hao Chen	Hong Kong University of Science and Technology, China
Wilson Silva	Utrecht University, the Netherlands
José Amorim	CISUC and University of Coimbra, Portugal
Amith Kamath	University of Bern, Switzerland

Workshop Chairs

Mauricio Reyes	University of Bern, Switzerland
Jaime Cardoso	Universidade do Porto, Portugal
Pedro Abreu	CISUC and University of Coimbra, Portugal

Program Committee

Matan Atad	Technical University of Munich, Germany
Catarina Barata	Instituto Superior Técnico, Portugal
Alex	BuerleUlm University, Germany
Jaime Cardoso	Universidade do Porto, Portugal
Pedro Celard	Universidade de Vigo, Spain
Valentina Corbetta	Netherlands Cancer Institute, Netherlands
Ines Domingues	ISEC, Portugal
Bettina Finzel	University of Bamberg, Germany
Tiago Goncalves	INESC TEC, Portugal
MaraGraziani	IBM Research, Switzerland
Syed Nouman Hasany	University of Rouen Normandy, France
Dwarikanath Mahapatra	Inception Institute of Artificial Intelligence, UAE

Fabrice Meriaudeau	University of Burgundy, France
Nataliia Molchanova	Lausanne University Hospital, Switzerland
Helena Montenegro	Universidade do Porto, Portugal
Axel Mosig	Ruhr University Bochum, Germany
Henning Mueller	HES-SO, Switzerland
Angus Nicolson	University of Oxford, UK
Cristiano Patricio	Universidade da Beira Interior, Portugal
Caroline Petitjean	University of Rouen Normandy, France
Mauricio Reyes	University of Bern, Switzerland
Tillmann Rheude	Technische Universität Darmstadt, Germany
Isabel Rio-Torto	FEUP, Portugal
Susu Sun	University of Tübingen, Germany
Luis Teixeira	University of Porto, Portugal

EARTH 2024 Preface

The First Embodied AI and Robotics for HealTHcare (EARTH) Workshop was held at the Palmeraie Conference Centre, Marrakesh, Morocco on October 6, 2024, in conjunction with the 27th International Conference on Medical Image Computing and Computer-Assisted Intervention (MICCAI).

The integration of cutting-edge technologies like Artificial Intelligence (AI) and robotics has been pivotal in advancing medical interventions and improving patient care. The EARTH workshop aimed to further this progress by focusing on embodied AI and its synergy with robotic systems, leveraging the latest breakthroughs in general-purpose AI models like Large Language Models (LLMs). Embodied AI systems demonstrate advanced reasoning, planning, and environment interaction capabilities crucial for intelligent surgical robots. The workshop fostered the development of autonomous and semi-autonomous robotic assistants that can learn, adapt, and support complex surgical decision-making.

Authors were invited to submit full-length manuscripts on embodied AI and robotics for healthcare, such as AI-driven robotics, intelligent surgical assistants, surgical robotic systems, human-robot interaction, and operating room AI integration. A total of 6 high-quality submissions were received, and with the Workshop Chairs and the Program Committee composed of 16 experts in the field, each submission was reviewed by at least three reviewers. Each reviewer scored the papers from 1 (lowest) to 5 (highest), with an average score above 2.5 considered acceptable. Based on the feedback and critiques, 5 of the best papers were selected for oral presentation at the workshop and included in this LNCS volume published by Springer. The accepted papers covered a diverse range of topics, including deformable tissue reconstruction, surgical video synthesis, 3D reconstruction techniques, CAD-free 3D instrument tracking, and holistic operating room sensing and inference.

We thank the authors for their excellent contributions, our reviewers for their valuable feedback, our invited speakers for sharing their expertise, and all attendees for their participation. We hope that the efforts coming together at this workshop will advance the field of embodied AI and robotics in healthcare, ultimately transforming medical interventions and setting new standards for patient care.

October 2024

Zhen Chen
Alejandro Granados
Xiang Li
Hongbin Liu
Nicolas Padoy
Hongliang Ren
Jinlin Wu
Yixuan Yuan

EARTH 2024 Organization

Workshop Chairs

Zhen Chen	CAIR, HKISI-CAS, China
Alejandro Granados	King's College London, UK
Xiang Li	Harvard University, USA
Hongbin Liu	CAIR, HKISI-CAS, China
Nicolas Padoy	University of Strasbourg, France
Hongliang Ren	Chinese University of Hong Kong, China
Jinlin Wu	Institute of Automation, Chinese Academy of Sciences, China
Yixuan Yuan	Chinese University of Hong Kong, China

Program Committee

Long Bai	Chinese University of Hong Kong, China
Beilei Cui	Chinese University of Hong Kong, China
Yiming Huang	Chinese University of Hong Kong, China
Haibo Jin	Hong Kong University of Science and Technology, China
Xinyu Liu	Chinese University of Hong Kong, China
Yang Liu	King's College London, UK
Guankun Wang	Chinese University of Hong Kong, China
Qiushi Yang	City University of Hong Kong, China

DeCaF 2024 Preface

Machine learning techniques have demonstrated the ability to create transformative impacts across multiple applications and industries by using large datasets to detect and understand patterns. A key challenge in the field is how to use data while maintaining user privacy. The industrial application of machine learning faces two main issues: accessing relevant user data for continuous model improvement and addressing privacy shortcomings.

There is growing focus on developing innovative methods for data acquisition, usage, and management while ensuring privacy and security. Many current approaches rely on centralized data storage, which often puts sensitive information outside users' control. In privacy-sensitive fields like healthcare, these centralized strategies can limit model development and application. Further privacy concerns arise from the underlying mathematics of machine learning, particularly in deep learning (DL) techniques, as models can retain sensitive training data in their parameters. Ongoing research aims to mitigate these issues, which are also closely tied to distributed and collaborative learning methods.

The Fifth MICCAI Workshop on Distributed, Collaborative, and Federated Learning (DeCaF 2024) aimed to foster academic discussions focused on the comparative analysis, evaluation, and exploration of methodological innovations and practical concepts in machine learning, particularly in situations where centralized data storage is not feasible. This includes cases where data privacy is a top priority, requiring strong guarantees regarding the scope and type of private information exposed during model training. Additionally, the workshop aimed to tackle environments where managing and coordinating clusters of nodes involved in collaborative learning is essential.

At the fifth DeCaF workshop, 8 submissions were carefully reviewed, resulting in the acceptance of 6 full papers for presentation, following a double-blind peer review process. Each paper was thoroughly evaluated by at least three independent reviewers, selected to avoid potential conflicts of interest or recent collaborations. These reviewers were drawn from a global pool of leading experts in the field.

Final decisions regarding acceptance, conditional acceptance, or rejection were made by the area chairs based on the feedback from the reviews, and these decisions were conclusive and binding. For conditionally accepted papers, authors were required to implement significant revisions and improvements, following the reviewers' suggestions, to enhance the scientific rigor and clarity of their work.

The double-blind review process, which involved three impartial reviewers per submission, combined with the practice of conditional acceptance and the guidance of meta-reviewers in decision-making, collectively ensured the scientific integrity and improved the quality of the contributions presented at the fifth iteration of DeCaF. This valuable effort has significantly benefited the MICCAI community, especially those researchers focused on distributed and collaborative learning.

Therefore, we must express our sincere thanks to the authors for their valuable contributions and extend our gratitude to the reviewers for their dedication and their fair assessment of their peers' work.

October 2024

Shadi Albarqouni
Spyridon Bakas
Xiaoxiao Li
Nicola Rieke
Qi Dou
Holger Roth

DeCaF 2024 Organization

Workshop Chairs

Shadi Albarqouni	University Hospital Bonn, Germany
Spyridon Bakas	Indiana University, USA
Xiaoxiao Li	University of British Columbia, Canada
Nicola Rieke	NVIDIA, Germany
Qi Dou	Chinese University of Hong Kong, China
Holger Roth	NVIDIA, USA

Program Committee

Anabik Pal	IISER Berhampur, India
Anna Banaszak	Technical University of Munich, Germany
Chamani Shiranthika Jayakody Kankanamalage	Simon Fraser University, Canada
Di Fan	University of Southern California, USA
Guangyao Zheng	Rice University, USA
Hervé Delingette	Inria, France
Jonny Hancox	NVIDIA, USA
Kevinminh Ta	Yale University, USA
Lucia Innocenti	Inria, King's College London, UK
Malte Tölle	University Hospital Heidelberg, Germany
Marawan Elbatel	Hong Kong University of Science and Technology, China
Muzaffer Özbey	Bilkent University, Turkiye
Nikhil J. Dhinagar	University of Southern California, USA
Onat Dalmaz	Stanford University, USA
Pramit Saha	University of Oxford, UK
Ralf Floca	German Cancer Research Center (DKFZ), Germany
Ruoyou Wu	Chinese Academy of Sciences, China
Shanshan Wang	Chinese Academy of Science, China
Shunxing Bao	Vanderbilt University, USA
Sourav Kumar	Massachusetts General Hospital, USA
Tolga Çukur	Bilkent University, Turkiye
Xiaoran Zhang	Yale University, USA

Zeju Li   Imperial College London, UK
Zhao Wang   Chinese University of Hong Kong, China

Outreach Committee

Chun-Yin Huang   University of British Columbia, Canada
David D. Gaviria   University Hospital Bonn, Germany
Tiantian Zhang   Chinese University of Hong Kong, China

Contents

Proceedings of the Ninth International Skin Imaging Collaboration Workshop (ISIC 2024)

I2M2Net: Inter/Intra-modal Feature Masking Self-distillation for Incomplete Multimodal Skin Lesion Diagnosis 3
  Ke Wang, Linwei Qiu, Yilan Zhang, and Fengying Xie

From Majority to Minority: A Diffusion-Based Augmentation for Underrepresented Groups in Skin Lesion Analysis 14
  Janet Wang, Yunsung Chung, Zhengming Ding, and Jihun Hamm

Segmentation Style Discovery: Application to Skin Lesion Images 24
  Kumar Abhishek, Jeremy Kawahara, and Ghassan Hamarneh

A Vision Transformer with Adaptive Cross-Image and Cross-Resolution Attention 35
  Benjamin A. K. Murray, Wei R. Tan, Liane S. Canas, Catherine H. Smith, Satveer K. Mahil, Sebastien Ourselin, and Marc Modat

Lesion Elevation Prediction from Skin Images Improves Diagnosis 45
  Kumar Abhishek and Ghassan Hamarneh

Proceedings of the Seventh International Workshop on Interpretability of Machine Intelligence in Medical Image Computing (iMIMIC 2024)

DWARF: Disease-Weighted Network for Attention Map Refinement 59
  Haozhe Luo, Aurélie Pahud de Mortanges, Oana Inel, and Mauricio Reyes

PIPNet3D: Interpretable Detection of Alzheimer in MRI Scans 69
  Lisa Anita De Santi, Jörg Schlötterer, Michael Scheschenja, Joel Wessendorf, Meike Nauta, Vincenzo Positano, and Christin Seifert

Detecting Unforeseen Data Properties with Diffusion Autoencoder Embeddings Using Spine MRI Data 79
  Robert Graf, Florian Hunecke, Soeren Pohl, Matan Atad, Hendrik Moeller, Sophie Starck, Thomas Kroencke, Stefanie Bette, Fabian Bamberg, Tobias Pischon, Thoralf Niendorf, Carsten Schmidt, Johannes C. Paetzold, Daniel Rueckert, and Jan S. Kirschke

Interpretability of Uncertainty: Exploring Cortical Lesion Segmentation in Multiple Sclerosis 89
  Nataliia Molchanova, Alessandro Cagol, Pedro M. Gordaliza, Mario Ocampo-Pineda, Po-Jui Lu, Matthias Weigel, Xinjie Chen, Adrien Depeursinge, Cristina Granziera, Henning Müller, and Meritxell Bach Cuadra

TextCAVs: Debugging Vision Models Using Text 99
  Angus Nicolson, Yarin Gal, and J. Alison Noble

Evaluating Visual Explanations of Attention Maps for Transformer-Based Medical Imaging 110
  Minjae Chung, Jong Bum Won, Ganghyun Kim, Yujin Kim, and Utku Ozbulak

Exploiting XAI Maps to Improve MS Lesion Segmentation and Detection in MRI 121
  Federico Spagnolo, Nataliia Molchanova, Mario Ocampo-Pineda, Lester Melie-Garcia, Meritxell Bach Cuadra, Cristina Granziera, Vincent Andrearczyk, and Adrien Depeursinge

Proceedings of the Embodied AI and Robotics for HealTHcare Workshop (EARTH 2024)

EndoGS: Deformable Endoscopic Tissues Reconstruction with Gaussian Splatting 135
  Lingting Zhu, Zhao Wang, Jiahao Cui, Zhenchao Jin, Guying Lin, and Lequan Yu

VISAGE: Video Synthesis Using Action Graphs for Surgery 146
  Yousef Yeganeh, Rachmadio Lazuardi, Amir Shamseddin, Emine Dari, Yash Thirani, Nassir Navab, and Azade Farshad

A Review of 3D Reconstruction Techniques for Deformable Tissues in Robotic Surgery 157
  Mengya Xu, Ziqi Guo, An Wang, Long Bai, and Hongliang Ren

SurgTrack: CAD-Free 3D Tracking of Real-World Surgical Instruments 168
  Wenwu Guo, Jinlin Wu, Zhen Chen, Qingxiang Zhao, Miao Xu, Zhen Lei, and Hongbin Liu

MUTUAL: Towards Holistic Sensing and Inference in the Operating Room 178
    Julien Quarez, Yang Li, Hassna Irzan, Matthew Elliot,
    Oscar MacCormac, James Knigth, Martin Huber, Toktam Mahmoodi,
    Prokar Dasgupta, Sebastien Ourselin, Nicholas Raison,
    Jonathan Shapey, and Alejandro Granados

Proceedings of the Fifth MICCAI Workshop on Distributed, Collaborative and Federated Learning (DeCaF 2024)

Complex-Valued Federated Learning with Differential Privacy and MRI Applications 191
    Anneliese Riess, Alexander Ziller, Stefan Kolek, Daniel Rueckert,
    Julia Schnabel, and Georgios Kaissis

Enhancing Privacy in Federated Learning: Secure Aggregation for Real-World Healthcare Applications 204
    Riccardo Taiello, Sergen Cansiz, Marc Vesin, Francesco Cremonesi,
    Lucia Innocenti, Melek Önen, and Marco Lorenzi

Federated Impression for Learning with Distributed Heterogeneous Data 215
    Atrin Arya, Sana Ayromlou, Armin Saadat, Purang Abolmaesumi,
    and Xiaoxiao Li

A Federated Learning-Friendly Approach for Parameter-Efficient Fine-Tuning of SAM in 3D Segmentation 226
    Mothilal Asokan, Joseph Geo Benjamin, Mohammad Yaqub,
    and Karthik Nandakumar

Probing the Efficacy of Federated Parameter-Efficient Fine-Tuning of Vision Transformers for Medical Image Classification 236
    Naif Alkhunaizi, Faris Almalik, Rouqaiah Al-Refai, Muzammal Naseer,
    and Karthik Nandakumar

FedGS: Federated Gradient Scaling for Heterogeneous Medical Image Segmentation 246
    Philip Schutte, Valentina Corbetta, Regina Beets-Tan, and Wilson Silva

Correction to: Medical Image Computing and Computer Assisted Intervention – MICCAI 2024 Workshops C1
    M. Emre Celebi, Mauricio Reyes, Zhen Chen, and Xiaoxiao Li

Author Index 257

Proceedings of the Ninth International Skin Imaging Collaboration Workshop (ISIC 2024)

I2M2Net: Inter/Intra-modal Feature Masking Self-distillation for Incomplete Multimodal Skin Lesion Diagnosis

Ke Wang[1], Linwei Qiu[1], Yilan Zhang[2], and Fengying Xie[1](✉)

[1] Image Processing Center, School of Astronautics, Beihang University, Beijing 100191, China
xfy_73@buaa.edu.cn
[2] King Abdullah University of Science and Technology (KAUST), Thuwal 23955-6900, Kingdom of Saudi Arabia

Abstract. Multimodal learning has demonstrated promising advantages over single-modal approaches in the diagnosis of skin lesions. However, these methods often suffer from significant accuracy degradation when encountering missing modalities, hindering their clinical deployment. In this paper, we introduce a novel and effective framework, I2M2Net, for incomplete multimodal learning, focusing on adaptively and progressively mining knowledge about modal feature-aware combinations. Specifically, one branch conducts normal classification using the original complete multimodal features extracted by heterogeneous modal encoders, while another branch shares the same structures and weights, designed to perform self-distillation with masked modality combinations. These combinations are imposed on the complete features using two masking strategies simultaneously: 1) random dropout of modality (*i.e.* inter-modal feature masking) to simulate different missing modality combinations and foster combination-invariant dependencies, and 2) randomly mask patches of the remaining modal features (*i.e.* intra-modal feature masking) to promote combination-specific representations. Additionally, we design a combination-based curriculum learning (CCL) algorithm to identify weak combinations and progressively guide our network to facilitate incomplete modality learning on challenging combinations. This is achieved by adaptively adjusting the probabilities of masking based on the consistency between the complete combination and other combinations. Experimental results on the multimodal skin disease dataset Derm7pt demonstrate that our method outperforms other state-of-the-art approaches.

Keywords: Missing modality · Multi-modal learning · Skin lesion diagnosis

---

Supplementary Information The online version contains supplementary material available at https://doi.org/10.1007/978-3-031-77610-6_1.

© The Author(s), under exclusive license to Springer Nature Switzerland AG 2025
M. E. Celebi et al. (Eds.): MICCAI 2024 Workshops, LNCS 15274, pp. 3–13, 2025.
https://doi.org/10.1007/978-3-031-77610-6_1

1 Introduction

Skin cancer is a prevalent form of cancer, and early and precise diagnosis can greatly enhance the cure and survival rates, particularly in cases of melanoma [2]. In the clinical diagnosis, dermatologists typically take into account several factors, including clinical images, dermoscopic images, and reference metadata (*e.g.* patient information and medical history), to get final diagnosis. Inspired by this, current research on automatic skin lesion diagnosis has explored various methods that leverage comprehensive multimodal information, rather than relying solely on a single modality [22,24,25], significantly enhancing classification performance [19,20,23]. However, issues such as data corruption, data acquisition failures and unclear associations of multimodal data, often result in missing clinical information. Most existing multimodal models may struggle to handle incomplete modal information, leading to a notable reduction in model classification accuracy [21]. Thus, it is necessary to develop multimodal models that are robust to incomplete modal data.

A typical solution is to use generative networks to directly synthesize missing modalities in the input data [3,15]. However, generative networks are often challenging to train, and the quality of the generated data significantly impacts the model's final performance [27]. As an alternative, methods based on knowledge distillation [4,6,14] or matrix completion [11] have been proposed to recover missing modality features. While these approaches have shown significant improvements, they necessitate training and deploying specific models for each combination of missing modalities, resulting in high time and space costs which are impractical for real-world applications. Current researches primarily focus on training a unified model to handle all potential combinations of missing modalities. For example, TATE [21] has developed a tag encoding module to address various missing modality scenarios and incorporated a new common space projection module for learning joint representations. MMIN [26] has employed a cross-modal imagination module to learn robust joint multimodal representations. Additionally, Lee *et al.* [10] have designed modality-missing-aware prompts plugged into multimodal transformers to handle general modality missing scenarios. Although the efficiency has been improved, these unified methods primarily concentrate on unified invariant features of various missing modality combinations while overlooking the mining of information in specific combination (especially the complementary modality-specific information). Consequently, unified models generally exhibit inferior performance compared to the customized models. Considering the diverse types and similar clinical presentations of skin lesions, leveraging specific details from multimodal information can aid in identifying similar categories.

To this end, we have designed a novel and effective inter/intra-modal feature masking self-distillation framework, where one branch of the self-distillation takes the complete modal features while the other branch utilizes the masked modality combination. Initially, masking occurs between modalities, which simulates various scenarios of modal absence. This inter-modal mask aims to facilitate combination-invariant features via bidirectional knowledge transfer between complete and incomplete modal information. The transfer of knowledge from complete to missing enhances the performance of the incomplete modality combinations, while the reverse transfer reinforces the specificity of modality features. Furthermore, we randomly mask certain local features within remaining available modalities. The loss of local information within modalities encourages the model to either make inferences from the same modality itself or from other available modalities, or suffer a higher penalty for the absence of critical irreplaceable information. This encourages inter/intra-modal interaction and fosters the utilization of complementary specific information, thus prompting combination-specific representations. In addition, most existing incomplete multimodal models treat various missing modality combinations equally during training [10, 21, 26]. Nevertheless, distinct combinations of absent modalities hold varying degrees of information, resulting in diverse performance (imbalanced modality combinations). Treating them equally during training hinders the further optimization and improvement of weaker modality combinations. Therefore, we propose a curriculum learning strategy grounded in modality combinations to dynamically balance the training of imbalanced modality combinations, thus improving the model's representation ability for challenging combinations.

Our contributions can be summarized as follows: 1) We propose a novel and effective framework I2M2Net for incomplete multimodal skin disease classification, which utilizes inter/intra-modal feature masking self-distillation to learn unified combination-invariant features while prompting combination-specific representations. 2) We design a combination-based curriculum learning strategy to dynamically adjust the training of imbalanced modality combinations, promoting the robustness of the network for hard modality missing circumstances. 3) Experimental results on Derm7pt dataset [7] demonstrate the superiority of I2M2Net.

2 Method

The overall framework of proposed I2M2Net is presented in Fig. 1. It consists of three modality-specific encoders (denoted as E_c, E_d, E_m), a fusion block F for merging multimodal features (including a classification head for the final output prediction), and a mask generator M_g. Moreover, another branch F' in relation to F is introduced to perform self distillation. Note that the self-distillation and curriculum learning strategy are only utilized during the training phase and can be easily applied to other traditional multimodal models. And there is no additional structure and computational costs during inference compared to original multimodal networks. The details of each component are as follows.

2.1 Inter/Intra-modal Feature Masking Self-distillation

Knowledge distillation from a complete-modal network to the customized incomplete one has been proven effective in incomplete multimodal learning [4, 6].

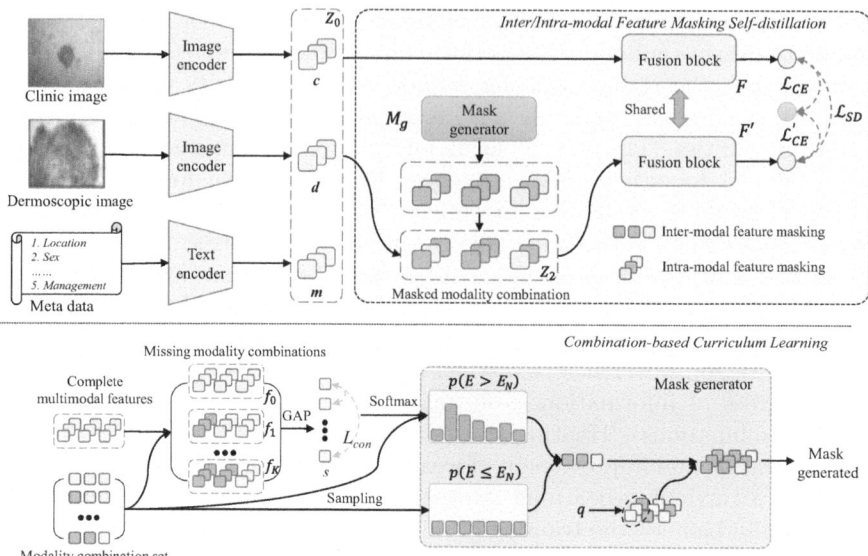

Fig. 1. The overview of the proposed framework I2M2Net. It mainly contains two important procedures, *i.e.* inter/intra-modal feature masking self-distillation and combination-based curriculum learning. F and F' share the same weights. E_N denotes the training epoch we set to start curriculum learning.

Inspired by the self-knowledge distillation strategy [1,8], which involves distilling knowledge within a model and utilizing it to train the model, we introduce an efficient self-distillation strategy which just introduces minimal parameters to implement knowledge distillation between complete and missing modality combinations within a unified model. It depends on inter-modal and intra-modal feature masking, which contributes to obtaining masked modality combinations. Self-distillation between F with complete modality information and F' with the masked modality features encourages combination-invariant/specific representations.

Concretely, F takes the original complete multimodal features (of the last stage in transformer-based modal encoders respectively) as input. Let $Z_0 = [c_1, \cdots, c_{n_c}, d_1, \cdots, d_{n_d}, m_1, \cdots, m_{n_m}] = [\mathbf{c}, \mathbf{d}, \mathbf{m}]$ be the concatenated multimodal features, where $c_i, d_i, m_i \in \mathbb{R}^C$ mean the features of clinical images, dermoscopic images, and metadata, respectively, n_c, n_d, n_m are the sequence length of each modality features, and C is the dimension (batch size is omitted for simplicity here). Another branch F' takes masked modality combinations Z_2 as input, which are obtained by employing two masking strategies concurrently on the complete Z_0.

Inter-modal Feature Masking. Random dropout of modality is utilized to simulate $2^J - 1$ different missing modality combinations (including the complete one), where J is the number of multiple modality and $J = 3$ in this paper. We first treat all combinations equally, and set the probability of each as $1/(2^J - 1)$. Let $M_{inter} = [\sigma_c, \sigma_d, \sigma_m]$ be the indicator of different missing combinations where $\sigma_i = 1$ represents the corresponding modality is existent and $\sigma_i = 0$ means not for $i \in c, d, m$. For example, if the clinical image modality feature is missing, then $M_{inter} = [0, 1, 1]$, and the masked features can be defined as:

$$Z_1 = Z_0 \odot M_{inter} = [c'_1, \cdots, c'_{n_c}, d_1, \cdots, d_{n_d}, m_1, \cdots, m_{n_m}], \quad (1)$$

where c'_i means it is masked and $\odot$ is the shape-matched dot product operation.

Intra-modal Feature Masking. Meanwhile, for a given missing modality combination, we randomly masked local patches of the remaining at a rate of q to stimulate combination-specific representation learning. *i.e.*

$$Z_2 = Z_1 \odot M_{intra} = [c'_1, \cdots, c'_{n_c}, d_1, d''_2, \cdots, d_{n_d}, m''_1, m_2 \cdots, m''_{n_m}], \quad (2)$$

where m''_i, d''_i represent masked local features.

Self-distillation. By M_{inter}, the knowledge transfers between complete and incomplete modality combination, which promotes combination-invariant dependencies. This is bidirectional: the complete to missing modality combination enhances the performances of the incomplete ones, and that in the opposite direction potentially reinforces the specificity of modality features. On the other hand, the lack of local information after applying M_{intra} within a modality encourages the model to draw conclusions from the context of the modality or other available modalities, enhancing the interaction of information both between inter- and intra-modal. Otherwise, the absence of essential and unchangeable specific details results in a higher penalty, compelling the model to enhance its use of modal-specific information. Eventually, we apply the loss of self-distillation to force the class-wise consistency between F and F'

$$\mathcal{L}_{SD} = \|F(Z_0) - F'(Z_2)\|_1. \quad (3)$$

The total loss of training is given as:

$$\mathcal{L} = \mathcal{L}_{CE}(y, F(Z_0)) + \mathcal{L}'_{CE}(y, F'(Z_2)) + \lambda \mathcal{L}_{SD}, \quad (4)$$

where y is the label, $\mathcal{L}_{CE}$ and $\mathcal{L}'_{CE}$ are cross entropy loss, and λ is the hyperparameter.

2.2 Combination-Based Curriculum Learning

The information content of missing modalities is varying. While the absence of certain modalities can lead to a significant decline in performance, the absence of others may have only a minor effect (imbalanced modality combinations). Taking it into consideration, we design a curriculum learning strategy to dynamically harmonize the training of various strong or weak masked modality combinations. The training is divided into two stages. (a) $E \leq E_N$ when our model is trained normally, and (b) $E > E_N$ when we assign different training weights to imbalanced masked modality combinations according to their degrees of capabilities. Following the normal framework of difficulty measurer and training scheduler in curriculum learning [18], a difficulty measurer to evaluate the competency level across various modality combinations is designed. Intuitively, the complete modalities, encompassing the most information within various modality combinations, is perceived to possess the highest capacity. Therefore, we utilize the consistency between complete modalities and other missing combinations as an indicator of capability, where higher consistency signifies enhanced capability. We can obtain them by

$$s_i = L_{con}(GAP(f_0), GAP(f_i)), i = 1, 2, \ldots, K, \qquad (5)$$

where f_0 is the complete modalities, K and f_i represents the num of missing modality combinations and the i-th one respectively. Here, $K = 2^J - 2$ and it is equal to 6 for three modality inputs in this paper. GAP is the global average pooling operation, and the cosine similarity is chose as L_{con}.

For training scheduler, in Sect. 2.1, we implemented self-distillation by training with randomly chosen various modality combinations as branch inputs. Here, we adjust the probabilities p_i of different missing modality combinations appearing in training based on s_i. As s_i increases, p_i decreases. *i.e.*

$$p_i = Softmax(1 - s_i), i = 0, 1, \cdots, K, s_0 = Max(s_i), \qquad (6)$$

where $Softmax$ is the Softmax function, and Max denotes acquiring the largest value from a set $\{s_i\}_{i=1}^{K}$. Let s_0 represents the consistency of complete modalities itself, set to $Max(s_i)$.

2.3 Modality Deficiency-Aware Fusion

Transformers have demonstrated significant advantages in multimodal fusion tasks [5,16]. However, because the self-attention operation is highly sensitive to missing data, the lack of modalities may result in a noticeable decrease in model performance. Inspired by [13], we adopt stacked transformer blocks in F with masked multi-head self-attention to adaptively fuse available modal information. It avoids the impact of missing modality on self-attention, and thereby we call it modality deficiency-aware fusion.

3 Experiments

3.1 Datasets and Evaluation Metrics

We evaluate the I2M2Net on the publicly available multimodal skin lesion dataset Derm7pt [7], which consists of 1011 cases in total with three modalities: dermoscopic image (der), clinical image (cli) and patient meta-data (meta).

Table 1. Comparison results on Derm7pt datasets (Acc%). # denotes complete multimodal method. ○ and ● represent missing and available modality, respectively. Avg. reports the average value of 7 modality combinations. Data format: avg (std)

der	●	○	○	●	●	○	●	Avg.
cli	○	●	○	●	○	●	●	
meta	○	○	●	○	●	●	●	
Concat #	66.58 (4.47)	52.56 (6.46)	65.82 (6.46)	67.24 (5.64)	76.86 (1.95)	72.15 (1.68)	76.45 (1.42)	69.07 (2.43)
Remixformer [19] #	63.04 (4.88)	55.95 (1.66)	57.62 (3.82)	69.16 (2.62)	77.27 (2.20)	67.24 (2.00)	79.54 (0.90)	67.12 (2.10)
Tformer [23] #	65.06 (5.14)	55.19 (1.05)	58.48 (6.14)	70.78 (3.01)	77.42 (2.78)	65.17 (6.62)	78.84 (1.85)	68.23 (0.92)
MMIN [26]	65.57 (2.25)	59.09 (3.33)	70.99 (1.10)	67.49 (3.28)	76.66 (0.79)	74.89 (0.94)	76.00 (1.18)	70.60 (1.14)
MP [10]	64.91 (1.77)	60.30 (1.94)	71.29 (1.29)	67.79 (1.10)	75.34 (1.55)	**75.85** (**1.35**)	76.20 (0.77)	70.74 (1.08)
LCKD [17]	70.18 (1.59)	66.88 (0.94)	71.14 (0.70)	71.09 (1.39)	76.86 (0.88)	75.14 (0.81)	78.23 (0.36)	72.79 (0.48)
TATE [21]	70.28 (0.65)	64.96 (1.13)	71.14 (0.42)	71.24 (1.14)	**77.92** (**1.22**)	74.78 (1.21)	78.33 (0.99)	73.16 (0.43)
I2M2Net	**71.60** (2.54)	**68.56** (**1.08**)	**71.65** (1.95)	**73.32** (1.24)	77.87 (0.63)	75.49 (0.98)	**79.64** (**0.97**)	**74.02** (**0.93**)

These 1011 cases have been officially divided into three sets: 413 cases for training, 203 cases for validation, and 395 cases for testing purposes. Larger dataset will be considered in future work. Accuracy (Acc) and F1-score (shown in supplementary material) are adopted as the evaluation metrics for evaluation.

3.2 Implementation Details

The proposed method is implemented on an NVIDIA A100 GPU with PyTorch. Our backbone for image data is a regular Swin-T/224 [12], and for text data is the typical Transformer encoder [16]. The data augmentation includes random flip, rotation, clipping, dwp [19]. We use Adam [9] as the optimizer with the weight decay 1e-4 and the initial learning rate of 0.0001 for 100 epochs. The number and dimension of the transformer blocks in Fusion module are 3 and 768. The hyperparameters q, E_N, λ are set to 0.2, 20, and 1 respectively. The model achieving the highest Acc on validation set with a 30% missing rate is selected for testing. Note that different training using the same missing dataset. Additionally, we perform experiments in 5 independent runs and present the average value and standard deviation (avg/std) in the results.

3.3 Comparison Results

To evaluate the proposed I2M2Net, we compare our method with 7 advanced methods on Derm7pt dataset. Among them, concat, Remixformer [19] and Tformer [23] are complete multimodal classification method, while MMIN [26], MP [10], LCKD [17] and TATE [21] are state-of-the-art approaches for incomplete multimodal learning. For fair comparison, we re-train all methods based on public code repositories in the same experimental environment. The results of all seven modality combinations are shown in Table 1. It can be seen that our approach significantly outperforms the other comparative methods across the majority of modal combinations (*i.e.* 5 out of 7 and Avg.). For instance, we improve the average Acc scores by 1.35% compared with TATE (p = 0.025 < 0.05) and 1.23% compared with LCKD (p = 0.003 < 0.05). Note worthy that our approach demonstrates a great gain 3.6% and 1.68% in the weakest performing modality combination(*i.e.* [der*, cli, meta*], where * represents missing) compared to Tate and LCKD, respectively. This illustrates that our combination-based curriculum learning has indeed effectively enhanced the performance of weak modal combinations. Meanwhile, in comparison to three fully modal methods, our approach still shows good enhancement (*i.e.* 3.19%, 0.1% and 0.8%, respectively) in performance when employing full multimodal data input, indicating the effectiveness of I2M2Net even for complete multimodal skin lesion classification.

Table 2. Ablation study on Derm7pt datasets (Acc%). Avg. reports the average value of 7 modality combinations. Data format: avg (std)

| der | ● | ○ | ○ | ● | ● | ○ | ● | Avg. |
| cli | ○ | ● | ○ | ● | ○ | ● | ● | |
meta	○	○	●	○	●	●	●	
Baseline	69.31 (1.15)	62.68 (1.86)	68.91 (2.28)	69.12 (1.05)	76.71 (1.10)	74.53 (1.45)	77.87 (1.09)	71.31 (0.88)
+Inter-Mask	66.38 (2.74)	65.52 (1.75)	72.50 (0.94)	70.43 (0.52)	75.75 (0.90)	74.43 (0.89)	77.17 (0.54)	71.74 (0.40)
+Intra-Mask($q = 0.2$)	71.60 (0.96)	65.77 (1.85)	65.57 (6.16)	72.30 (1.14)	76.10 (1.27)	73.31 (2.58)	77.92 (1.98)	71.80 (1.52)
+Inter&Intra-Mask($q = 0.2$)	71.45 (2.27)	65.32 (1.98)	71.95 (1.27)	72.20 (2.62)	76.00 (1.60)	75.19 (0.53)	78.99 (0.98)	73.01 (0.78)
+Inter&Intra-Mask($q = 0.1$)+CCL	**72.91** (**1.95**)	67.50 (1.10)	71.95 (0.85)	72.51 (1.61)	77.62 (1.43)	75.09 (1.40)	78.73 (0.99)	73.76 (0.43)
+Inter&Intra-Mask($q = 0.2$)+CCL	71.60 (2.54)	**68.56** (**1.08**)	71.65 (1.95)	**73.32** (**1.24**)	**77.87** (**0.63**)	75.49 (0.98)	**79.64** (**0.97**)	**74.02** (**0.93**)
+Inter&Intra-Mask($q = 0.3$)+CCL	71.65 (1.87)	68.05 (0.74)	71.90 (1.56)	72.81 (1.01)	76.81 (1.07)	75.09 (1.67)	78.73 (1.05)	73.58 (0.65)
+Inter&Intra-Mask($q = 0.5$)+CCL	70.99 (0.57)	66.02 (2.88)	**72.91** (**1.05**)	72.20 (1.64)	77.01 (1.06)	73.97 (2.23)	78.43 (1.45)	73.08 (1.13)

3.4 Ablation Study

To verify the effectiveness of each component in I2M2Net, we further conduct detailed ablation experiments, the results of which are reported in Table 2. Initially, the original single-branch network with the modality deficiency-aware fusion module is adopted as the "Baseline". We can observed that simply incorporating the inter-modal or intra-modal feature masking self-distillation alone acquires not satisfactory performance, falling short of both Tate and LCKD. The combination of these two elements enhances the combination-invariant and combination-specific representations, thereby enhancing the overall performance of classification. Furthermore, the introduction of combination-based curriculum learning strategy has remarkably improved the model's robustness to weak modality combinations. In Table 2, the Acc of 6th experiment outperforms by 3.24% in the weakest modality combinations, [der*, cli, meta*]. In addition, we investigate the impact of the hyperparameter q (*i.e.* the ratio of intra-mask). It can be seen that the model performs well in most modality combinations when q being set as 0.2. We report that a higher degree of masking complicates self-distillation training, whereas a lower level of masking does not effectively enhance combination-specific representations, resulting in a decrease in performance.

4 Conclusion

In this study, a novel and effective framework named I2M2Net is presented for incomplete multimodal learning. We first incorporate inter-modal and intra-modal feature masking self-distillation techniques to enhance combination-specific representations and promote learning of combination-invariant dependencies, thus improving overall robustness to incomplete multimodal data. Furthermore, we design a combination-based curriculum learning algorithm to assist the network in adapting to weak and challenging modality combinations. Extensive experiments conducted on the Derm7pt dataset demonstrate the effectiveness and superiority of I2M2Net compared to other contemporary approaches.

Disclosure of Interests. The authors have no competing interests to declare that are relevant to the content of this article.

References

1. Baevski, A., Hsu, W.N., Xu, Q., Babu, A., Gu, J., Auli, M.: Data2vec: a general framework for self-supervised learning in speech, vision and language. In: International Conference on Machine Learning, pp. 1298–1312. PMLR (2022)
2. Balch, C.M., et al.: Final version of 2009 AJCC melanoma staging and classification. J. Clin. Oncol. **27**(36), 6199 (2009)
3. Cai, L., Wang, Z., Gao, H., Shen, D., Ji, S.: Deep adversarial learning for multi-modality missing data completion. In: Proceedings of the 24th ACM SIGKDD International Conference on Knowledge Discovery & Data Mining, pp. 1158–1166 (2018)

4. Chen, C., Dou, Q., Jin, Y., Liu, Q., Heng, P.A.: Learning with privileged multi-modal knowledge for unimodal segmentation. IEEE Trans. Med. Imaging **41**(3), 621–632 (2021)
5. Dosovitskiy, A., et al.: An image is worth 16×16 words: transformers for image recognition at scale. arXiv preprint arXiv:2010.11929 (2020)
6. Hu, M., et al.: Knowledge distillation from multi-modal to mono-modal segmentation networks. In: Medical Image Computing and Computer Assisted Intervention–MICCAI 2020: 23rd International Conference, Lima, Peru, 4–8 October 2020, Proceedings, Part I 23, pp. 772–781. Springer (2020)
7. Kawahara, J., Daneshvar, S., Argenziano, G., Hamarneh, G.: Seven-point checklist and skin lesion classification using multitask multimodal neural nets. IEEE J. Biomed. Health Inform. **23**(2), 538–546 (2018)
8. Kim, K., Ji, B., Yoon, D., Hwang, S.: Self-knowledge distillation: a simple way for better generalization. arXiv preprint arXiv:2006.12000, vol. 3, 1 (2020)
9. Kingma, D.P., Ba, J.: Adam: a method for stochastic optimization. arXiv preprint arXiv:1412.6980 (2014)
10. Lee, Y.L., Tsai, Y.H., Chiu, W.C., Lee, C.Y.: Multimodal prompting with missing modalities for visual recognition. In: Proceedings of the IEEE/CVF Conference on Computer Vision and Pattern Recognition, pp. 14943–14952 (2023)
11. Liu, J., et al.: Self-representation subspace clustering for incomplete multi-view data. In: Proceedings of the 29th ACM International Conference on Multimedia, pp. 2726–2734 (2021)
12. Liu, Z., et al.: Swin transformer: hierarchical vision transformer using shifted windows. In: Proceedings of the IEEE/CVF International Conference on Computer Vision, pp. 10012–10022 (2021)
13. Recasens, A., et al.: Zorro: the masked multimodal transformer. arXiv preprint arXiv:2301.09595 (2023)
14. Stroud, J., Ross, D., Sun, C., Deng, J., Sukthankar, R.: D3D: distilled 3D networks for video action recognition. In: Proceedings of the IEEE/CVF Winter Conference on Applications of Computer Vision, pp. 625–634 (2020)
15. Tran, L., Liu, X., Zhou, J., Jin, R.: Missing modalities imputation via cascaded residual autoencoder. In: Proceedings of the IEEE Conference on Computer Vision and Pattern Recognition, pp. 1405–1414 (2017)
16. Vaswani, A., et al.: Attention is all you need. In: Advances in Neural Information Processing Systems, vol. 30 (2017)
17. Wang, H., et al.: Learnable cross-modal knowledge distillation for multi-modal learning with missing modality. In: International Conference on Medical Image Computing and Computer-Assisted Intervention, pp. 216–226. Springer (2023)
18. Wang, X., Chen, Y., Zhu, W.: A survey on curriculum learning. IEEE Trans. Pattern Anal. Mach. Intell. **44**(9), 4555–4576 (2021)
19. Xu, J., et al.: Remixformer: a transformer model for precision skin tumor differential diagnosis via multi-modal imaging and non-imaging data. In: International Conference on Medical Image Computing and Computer-Assisted Intervention, pp. 624–633. Springer (2022)
20. Yang, Y., et al.: Skin lesion classification based on two-modal images using a multi-scale fully-shared fusion network. Comput. Methods Programs Biomed. **229**, 107315 (2023)
21. Zeng, J., Liu, T., Zhou, J.: Tag-assisted multimodal sentiment analysis under uncertain missing modalities. In: Proceedings of the 45th International ACM SIGIR Conference on Research and Development in Information Retrieval, pp. 1545–1554 (2022)

22. Zhang, Y., Chen, J., Wang, K., Xie, F.: ECL: class-enhancement contrastive learning for long-tailed skin lesion classification. In: International Conference on Medical Image Computing and Computer-Assisted Intervention, pp. 244–254. Springer (2023)
23. Zhang, Y., Xie, F., Chen, J.: Tformer: a throughout fusion transformer for multimodal skin lesion diagnosis. Comput. Biol. Med. **157**, 106712 (2023)
24. Zhang, Y., Xie, F., Song, X., Zheng, Y., Liu, J., Wang, J.: Dermoscopic image retrieval based on rotation-invariance deep hashing. Med. Image Anal. **77**, 102301 (2022)
25. Zhang, Y., et al.: A rotation meanout network with invariance for dermoscopy image classification and retrieval. Comput. Biol. Med. **151**, 106272 (2022)
26. Zhao, J., Li, R., Jin, Q.: Missing modality imagination network for emotion recognition with uncertain missing modalities. In: Proceedings of the 59th Annual Meeting of the Association for Computational Linguistics and the 11th International Joint Conference on Natural Language Processing (Volume 1: Long Papers), pp. 2608–2618 (2021)
27. Zhou, T., Ruan, S., Hu, H.: A literature survey of MR-based brain tumor segmentation with missing modalities. Comput. Med. Imaging Graph. **104**, 102167 (2023)

From Majority to Minority: A Diffusion-Based Augmentation for Underrepresented Groups in Skin Lesion Analysis

Janet Wang[✉], Yunsung Chung, Zhengming Ding, and Jihun Hamm

Tulane University, New Orleans, USA
{swang47,ychung3,zding1,jhamm3}@tulane.edu

Abstract. AI-based diagnoses have demonstrated dermatologist-level performance in classifying skin cancer. However, such systems are prone to under-performing when tested on data from minority groups that lack sufficient representation in the training sets. Although data collection and annotation offer the best means for promoting minority groups, these processes are costly and time-consuming. Prior works have suggested that data from majority groups may serve as a valuable information source to supplement the training of diagnostic tools for minority groups. In this work, we propose an effective diffusion-based augmentation framework that maximizes the use of rich information from majority groups to benefit minority groups. Using groups with different skin types as a case study, our results show that the proposed framework can generate synthetic images that improve diagnostic results for the minority groups, even when there is little or no reference data from these target groups. The practical value of our work is evident in medical imaging analysis, where under-diagnosis persists as a problem for certain groups due to insufficient representation. Our implementation detail is available at https://github.com/janet-sw/skin-diff.

Keywords: Skin Lesion Analysis · Diffusion Models · Data Augmentation

1 Introduction

AI-assisted diagnostic systems demonstrate expert-level capability in classifying skin cancers, often identified visually [2,6,16]. These systems can potentially contribute to teledermatology as diagnostic and decision-support tools, enhancing diagnostic accessibility in rural areas [3]. However, despite such success, recent studies have highlighted their susceptibility to under-diagnosing minority groups, such as those with underrepresented skin types, hindering their ability to generalize across different demographic groups [4,11]. Although the majority group contains rich lesion information, directly training models for cross-color classification using this data is challenging due to the domain gap caused by varying skin types [24]. Prior research has suggested using synthetic images generated from majority groups to supplement the training of AI for minority groups [19].

Augmenting skin condition data with synthetic images has been explored, owing to its potential to address common challenges for skin lesion analysis, such as data privacy, imbalance, and scarcity. Notably, Generative Adversarial Networks (GANs) [10] and Diffusion Models (DMs) [5] have emerged as leading techniques for generating high-quality skin lesion images. While GANs have successfully produced photorealistic synthetic images, their generation is uncontrollable [9,18]. On the other hand, DMs pre-trained on extensive web data have enabled higher controllability over image generation through the guidance of textual prompts, allowing for the creation of diverse and high-fidelity images of target skin conditions and skin types.

Existing studies have tried diffusion models to augment minority skin types using two public datasets: Diverse Dermatology Images (DDI) [4] and Fitzpatrick17k [11]. Each image in these datasets is annotated with skin type labels based on the Fitzpatrick scoring system [7]. In their work, [21] generated multiple synthetic images for each real image using Stable Diffusion [20] and then trained the classifier on a dataset including real and synthetic data. They found that diffusion models can enhance diagnosis accuracy across skin types in binary malignancy classification on the DDI dataset, though the number of real images is the key driver in performance. Additionally, [22] sampled a small number of seed images with skin types at the ends of the Fitzpatrick spectrum (FST I-II and FST V-VI) and carefully cropped the disease pathology in them, before generating synthetic data from the seeds using OpenAI DALLůE 2's inpainting feature. They conducted class-wise data augmentation by incorporating synthetic images of the target condition and minority skin type into the real training set. Other related studies have focused on internal datasets [1,15].

Despite these advancements, the potential to leverage diffusion models' knowledge about skin variation and the rich lesion information from majority groups to benefit minority groups remains underexplored. In this work, we propose a novel diffusion-based augmentation framework capable of learning skin lesion concepts from majority groups and generating images to improve classification performance for minority groups. Unlike current works that assume the existence of data from minority groups, we hypothesize that the information gained from majority groups and the diffusion model's pre-trained knowledge is sufficient to generate useful synthetic data. We test our hypothesis in a challenging multi-condition classification task. The framework is illustrated in Fig. 1. We conduct our experiments on the Fitzpatrick17k dataset, which includes lesions that are less familiar to diffusion models than common skin cancer. This dataset has a skewed skin type distribution, with light skin types (FST I-II) being significantly more than dark skin types (FST V-VI), thus forming majority and minority groups. Our investigation focuses on images from both groups and is structured around three scenarios with increasing difficulty: **(i)** the training source includes some data from both groups; **(ii)** there is limited data from the minority group in the training source; and **(iii)** the training source lacks data from the minority group. Through extensive experiments and analysis, we found that:

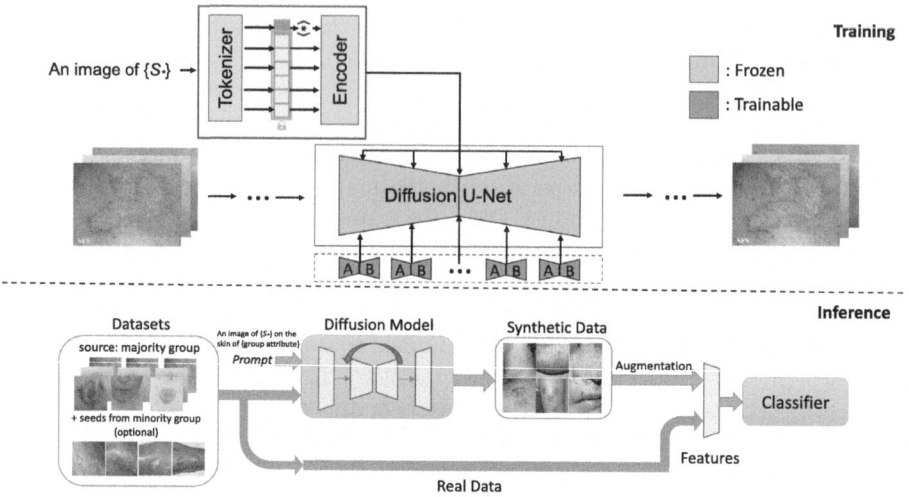

Fig. 1. Overview of the proposed augmentation framework. The framework pairs each training image with a textual prompt describing the condition as an input to train a latent diffusion model. Embeddings associated with new lesion concepts are found through Textual Inversion. Compact matrices A and B are optimized via LoRA to facilitate training with the new embeddings. During inference, the trained model produces synthetic images from the training set that mainly features the majority groups via image-to-image generation, thus conditioned on visual cues of lesions from images and textual prompts describing the target condition and group attributes.

- Our proposed method effectively leverages lesion information from the majority group to generate synthetic images that can improve classification for the minority group across all settings, even without reference data from the minority group.
- Using synthetic images generated by our method to train classifiers consistently outperforms training with real images across various architectures. Further improvement is observed when combining real and synthetic data.
- Our method is sensitive to information from the minority group. A notable improvement can be observed when even a few examples from the minority group are added to the training set.

2 Methods

In this section, we will introduce key techniques that have been adapted for skin disease datasets in our proposed augmentation framework.

Latent Diffusion Models. We implement our method using Latent Diffusion Models (LDMs) [20], a class of Denoising Diffusion Probabilistic Models

Table 1. Sample distribution across skin conditions by Fitzpatrick Skin Type.

FST	Basal Cell Carcinoma	Folliculitis	Nematode Infection	Neutrophilic Dermatoses	Prurigo Nodularis	Psoriasis	Squamous Cell Carcinoma	Total
I	85	30	15	70	7	113	100	420
II	156	97	56	115	28	232	180	864
V	24	31	32	31	29	64	40	251
VI	7	9	12	15	9	21	23	96
Total	272	167	115	231	73	430	343	**1631**

(DDPMs) [13] that operate in the latent space of an autoencoder, to enable DDPM training with limited computational resources. LDMs include two core components: a pre-trained autoencoder and a diffusion model. In our study, the encoder of the autoencoder $\mathcal{E}$ encodes skin lesion images $x \in \mathcal{D}_x$ into a latent representation $z = \mathcal{E}(x)$, while the decoder D maps the latent representations back to images, such that $D(\mathcal{E}(x)) \approx x$. The diffusion model is trained to generate representations conditioned on prompts describing skin disease and skin type, within the learned latent space. Let $c_\theta(y)$ be a model that maps a conditioning input y into a vector. We then learn the conditional LDM via

$$L_{LDM} := \mathbb{E}_{z \in \mathcal{E}(x),\, y,\, \epsilon \in \mathcal{N}(0,1),\, t} \left[\|\epsilon - \epsilon_\theta(z_t, t, c_\theta(y))\|_2^2 \right], \quad (1)$$

where t is the time step, z_t is the latent noise at time t, ϵ is the unscaled noise sample, and ϵ_θ is the denoising network.

Concept Discovery via Textual Inversion. Our proposed framework leverages Textual Inversion [8] to capture a unique embedding that accurately represents the targeted skin lesion concept from training data. Skin lesion images paired with a string containing a placeholder word (e.g., 'An image of $\{S_*\}$') are used to guide the learning of a new lesion embedding for the generative model. In particular, the optimal embedding v_* that encapsulates the lesion concept S_* is derived by minimizing the reconstruction loss,

$$v_* = \arg\min_v \mathbb{E}_{z \sim \mathcal{E}(x), y, \epsilon \sim \mathcal{N}(0,1), t} \left[\|\epsilon - \epsilon_\theta(z_t, t, c_\theta(y, S_*))\|_2^2 \right], \quad (2)$$

where the same training scheme as the original LDM model is used, with c_θ and ϵ_θ fixed.

Fine-Grained Detail Enhancement with LoRA. To enhance efficiency in fine-tuning LDM, we employ Low-Rank Adaptation (LoRA) [14] in our framework, with the discovered tokens after textual inversion. This fine-tuning strategy freezes the pre-trained model weights and introduces two compact matrices A and B, where $A \in \mathbb{R}^{n \times r}, B \in \mathbb{R}^{r \times n}$. The adaptation matrices AB are integrated into the attention layers to capture fine visual details of the skin lesion that were not initially present in the pre-trained model, with target embedding v_*. The optimization is formulated as

$$L := \mathbb{E}_{z \sim \mathcal{E}(x), y, \epsilon \sim \mathcal{N}(0,1), t} \left[\|\epsilon - \epsilon_{\theta_{AB}}(z_t, t, c_{\theta_{AB}}(y, v_*))\|_2^2 \right]. \quad (3)$$

Table 2. This table presents the results when the training set includes non-flexible images from the minority group (291 of FST V-VI) and the majority group (1228 FST I-II). The test set is a flexible subset of the minority group (56 of FST V-VI), uniformly distributed across the 7 conditions. Here, "real" indicates that the classifier is trained solely on real images, while "syn" means that it is trained exclusively on synthetic images generated by our framework. Accordingly, "real+syn" means the subsequent classifier is trained on a combination of both.

Architecture	Train Type	Train Size	Accuracy	Precision	Recall	F1 Score
VGG-16	real	1519	70.24 ± 0.12	72.49 ± 0.37	69.58 ± 0.30	70.48 ± 0.13
	syn	1519 * 5	75.00 ± 0.64	75.77 ± 0.39	73.17 ± 0.29	72.42 ± 0.61
	real + syn	1519 * 6	77.98 ± 0.40	81.51 ± 0.25	78.87 ± 0.23	77.45 ± 0.29
ResNet-18	real	1519	68.45 ± 0,42	69.42 ± 0.57	69.05 ± 0.42	67.94 ± 0.35
	syn	1519 * 5	69.05 ± 0.36	69.57 ± 0.82	69.05 ± 0.42	68.02 ± 0.33
	real + syn	1519 * 6	71.36 ± 0.69	69.02 ± 0.48	68.45 ± 0.40	67.56 ± 0.59
ViT-B-16	real	1519	70.38 ± 0.42	73.72 ± 0.69	70.82 ± 0.39	70.61 ± 0.59
	syn	1519 * 5	74.19 ± 0.37	77.89 ± 1.01	74.04 ± 0.85	73.58 ± 0.53
	real + syn	1519 * 6	78.65 ± 0.53	81.57 ± 0.47	79.17 ± 0.84	78.24 ± 0.64

3 Experiments

We conduct our experiments using the Fitzpatrick17k dataset, where each image is annotated with a condition and a Fitzpatrick Skin Type (FST) label. In line with [22], our analysis narrows down to a subset of the Fitzpatrick17k dataset, encompassing 7 conditions (Table 1). These conditions were selected because they represent the largest sample sizes at the ends of the Fitzpatrick Skin Type (FST I-II or V-VI) spectrum. Unlike [22], our study excludes intermediate skin types (FST III-IV), to explore the efficacy of our diffusion-based augmentation in a more challenging and explainable way. We randomly sample 8 images for each condition from the lightest (FST I-II) and darkest (FST V-VI) skin type groups, resulting in a **flexible subset** of 56 images for each group.

We examine three scenarios: **(i)** the training set includes images of dark and light skin types, and the test set features the uniformly distributed flexible subset across the 7 conditions; **(ii)** the training set predominantly includes light-skinned images and a few dark-skinned images, while the test set consists of dark-skin data; **(iii)** the training set lacks dark-skinned images entirely, while the test set comprises dark-skinned images. In all scenarios, we generate 5 synthetic images for each real one in the training set during inference, using the fine-tuned model, as illustrated in Fig. 1. In scenario **(i)**, to ensure a sufficient number of examples for both majority and minority groups in the training set, we designate the flexible subset of dark skin as the test set and use remaining non-flexible images for generator and classifier training. This setting also serves as the basis for hyperparameter tuning of the diffusion model, with the selected hyperparameters being fixed for subsequent experiments.

Table 3. Classification results when the training set contains a few reference images from the dark-skinned flexible subset (56 of FST V-VI) and non-flexible light-skinned images (1228 of FST I-II). The test set includes all other dark-skinned images (291 of FST V-VI) outside the flexible subset.

Architecture	Train Type	Train Size	Accuracy	Precision	Recall	F1 Score
VGG-16	real	1284	58.79 ± 0.10	58.90 ± 0.03	58.26 ± 0.05	56.98 ± 0.04
	syn	1284 * 5	62.86 ± 0.15	61.49 ± 0.15	63.32 ± 0.13	61.57 ± 0.24
	real + syn	1284 * 6	63.66 ± 0.11	62.80 ± 0.12	64.08 ± 0.08	62.72 ± 0.18
ResNet-18	real	1284	50.31 ± 0.30	50.45 ± 0.44	51.27 ± 0.30	48.23 ± 0.32
	syn	1284 * 5	56.36 ± 0.16	56.58 ± 0.13	59.78 ± 0.08	55.58 ± 0.10
	real + syn	1284 * 6	61.33 ± 0.17	59.75 ± 0,12	62.52 ± 0.17	59.94 ± 0.17
ViT-B-16	real	1284	62.03 ± 0.19	63.09 ± 0.13	62.02 ± 0.04	61.05 ± 0.04
	syn	1284 * 5	68.83 ± 0.19	70.07 ± 0.03	68.22 ± 0.25	68.34 ± 0.19
	real + syn	1284 * 6	71.20 ± 0.07	71.61 ± 0.19	71.53 ± 0.01	71.17 ± 0.13

Implementation Details. In each setting, we randomly sampled 5 flexible subsets and repeated the experiment 5 times. We used the Stable Diffusion 2.1 base [20] and the Diffusers library [17] for fine-tuning the diffusion model and generating synthetic images. For classifier backbones, we utilized pre-trained VGG-16 [23], ResNet-18 [12], and ViT-B-16 [25] and trained each classifier using the Adam optimizer with an initial learning rate of 1e-3 and transformations as in [11]. A weight-based sampler and StepLR scheduler were applied. All experiments were conducted on two NVIDIA GeForce RTX 3090 s.

4 Results

To assess the efficacy of our augmentation framework across the three settings, we train the classifier on data that includes real images only, synthetic images only, or a combination of both, respectively. Our evaluation is based on four metrics: accuracy, precision, recall, and F1. First, in the setting with some images from both majority and minority groups in the training set, we observe that synthetic data enhances performance across all architectures (Table 2). Specifically, classifiers trained on synthetic images consistently outperform those trained solely on real ones, and the combination of both types of data for training yields further improvements.

This trend of consistent improvement is also evident in the more challenging scenarios where there are little or no reference images from the minority groups (Tables 3 and 4) in the training set. Notably, significant improvement is observed when just a few reference images from the minority group are available in the training set for image generation and classification. The transformer-based classifier demonstrates a larger improvement gap over the real image baseline than the CNN-based models. In the most challenging setting, with no reference images

Table 4. Classification results when no image from the minority group is in the training set, which only has non-flexible images of the majority group (1228 of FST I-II). The test set has non-flexible images of the minority group (291 of FST V-VI).

Architecture	Train Type	Train Size	Accuracy	Precision	Recall	F1 Score
VGG-16	real	1228	55.58 ± 0.10	54.60 ± 0.11	51.84 ± 0.29	51.97 ± 0.45
	syn	1228 * 5	57.62 ± 0.09	56.62 ± 0.15	55.42 ± 0.20	55.36 ± 0.22
	real + syn	1228 * 6	58.08 ± 0.08	57.36 ± 0.13	55.78 ± 0.17	55.85 ± 0.23
ResNet-18	real	1228	49.42 ± 0.36	49.79 ± 0.44	48.30 ± 0.23	47.42 ± 0.30
	syn	1228 * 5	53.47 ± 0.32	52.39 ± 0.30	53.79 ± 0.30	51.97 ± 0.29
	real + syn	1228 * 6	56.50 ± 0.15	55.72 ± 0.15	55.10 ± 0.16	54.76 ± 0.18
ViT-B-16	real	1228	57.66 ± 0.35	61.89 ± 0.68	55.45 ± 0.36	55.96 ± 0.51
	syn	1228 * 5	58.94 ± 0.23	62.79 ± 0.20	55.62 ± 0.22	56.53 ± 0.18
	real + syn	1228 * 6	60.96 ± 0.31	64.57 ± 0.01	57.51 ± 0.29	58.92 ± 0.31

from the minority group, the improvement margin narrowed, suggesting that our pipeline effectively maximizes the use of limited information from the flexible subset of the minority group during training. Despite these challenges, the sustained improvements in the third setting validate our framework's effectiveness in transferring information across groups. Examples of real and synthetic image pairs for each condition are presented in Fig. 2. Qualitatively, the synthetic images generated by our augmentation framework introduce more diversity to the training sets, including variations in skin color and lesion patterns.

To further investigate our framework's generation capabilities, we conduct an ablation study comparing our framework with various generation strategies. This study focuses on the first setting, where the test set consists of light- or dark-skinned flexible images (56 for each type). We first examine the Stable Diffusion's vanilla text-to-image and image-to-image pipelines to generate synthetic images. Next, we leverage Textual Inversion to learn the lesion embeddings and then generate synthetic images from these embeddings, with text-to-image and image-to-image pipelines. Since image-to-image outperforms text-to-image in both vanilla SD and Textual Inversion generation, we focus on image-to-image generation after fine-tuning the diffusion model using LoRA, to investigate if optimizing the diffusion model can benefit the generation even more. We train a VGG-16 using only the synthetic images and then compare these generation strategies with ours, as shown in Table 5.

Overall, training classifiers on synthetic images generated by text-to-image models proves less effective than employing image-to-image techniques, underscoring the importance of visual cues in augmenting skin lesion classification. Additionally, using off-the-shelf models for image generation yields less improvement than training strategies such as Textual Inversion and LoRA, regardless of whether the target is a minority or majority group. Finally, the combination of Textual Inversion and LoRA results in the highest accuracy, thereby validating the practicality of our design which integrates these two strategies. This

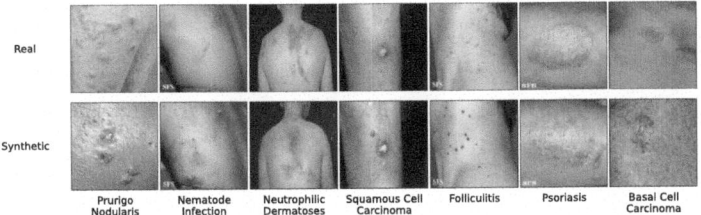

Fig. 2. Examples of synthetic images generated by a model trained exclusively on light-skinned images, using prompts describing dark skin types.

Table 5. Classification accuracy with various generation strategies for the first setting. Here, "vanilla" stands for Stable Diffusion's original text-to-image and image-to-image pipelines, "ti" for Textual Inversion, and "lora" for LoRA.

test	txt2img		img2img			
	vanilla	ti	vanilla	ti	lora	ti+lora
light (56)	18.80	35.36	48.21	46.43	52.00	53.57
dark (56)	21.22	44.64	69.64	71.43	73.21	79.57

improvement can be explained by the model's enhanced ability to associate the fine visual cues of the lesion with the learned textual tokens.

Since a direct comparison with existing related works is challenging due to the uncertain use of data, this ablation study can serve as an indirect comparison. As introduced previously, related works leveraged off-the-shelf diffusion models such as DALLûE or fine-tuned a Stable Diffusion model for text-to-image generation. Our results demonstrate that utilizing the dual guidance of visual cues and text prompts via fine-tuning diffusion models can maximize the potential of diffusion-based augmentation and enhance the diagnosis for minority groups.

5 Conclusion

In this work, we present an effective diffusion-based augmentation framework that consistently improves classification results for the minority group, even when training the classifier exclusively with synthetic images. This improvement is observed regardless of the availability of reference data from the minority group in the training set. The ablation study also validates that our framework's dual-guidance generation approach successfully learns novel lesion concepts previously unfamiliar to the diffusion models. A practical takeaway from this study is that, even in cases of data scarcity, existing data and diffusion models can still provide valuable insights, maximizing information usage and achieving better performance. In the future, we plan to apply this technique to other medical datasets characterized by significant differences in group sizes. Additionally, as we used all synthetic images generated for each setting without any filtering mechanism, we also aim to investigate which types of synthetic data are useful for lesion diagnosis and how to generate them.

Acknowledgments. This work was partly supported by the NSF EPSCoR-Louisiana Materials Design Alliance (LAMDA) program #OIA-1946231 and partly by the Harold L. and Heather E. Jurist Center of Excellence for Artificial Intelligence at Tulane University.

References

1. Akrout, M., et al.: Diffusion-based data augmentation for skin disease classification: impact across original medical datasets to fully synthetic images (2023)
2. Brinker, T., et al.: A convolutional neural network trained with dermoscopic images performed on par with 145 dermatologists in a clinical melanoma image classification task. Eur. J. Cancer **111**, 148–154 (2019). https://doi.org/10.1016/j.ejca.2019.02.005
3. Coustasse, A., Sarkar, R., Abodunde, B., Metzger, B.J., Slater, C.M.: Use of teledermatology to improve dermatological access in rural areas. Telemedicine Journal and e-Health: The Official Journal of the American Telemedicine Association (2019)
4. Daneshjou, R., et al.: Disparities in dermatology AI performance on a diverse, curated clinical image set. Science Advances (2022)
5. Dhariwal, P., Nichol, A.: Diffusion models beat GANs on image synthesis. Adv. Neural. Inf. Process. Syst. **34**, 8780–8794 (2021)
6. Esteva, A., et al.: Dermatologist-level classification of skin cancer with deep neural networks. Nature **542**, 115–118 (2017)
7. Fitzpatrick, T.B.: The validity and practicality of sun-reactive skin types I through VI. Arch. Dermatol. **124**(6), 869–871 (1988)
8. Gal, R., et al.: An image is worth one word: personalizing text-to-image generation using textual inversion. In: The Eleventh International Conference on Learning Representations (2023). https://openreview.net/forum?id=NAQvF08TcyG
9. Ghorbani, A., Natarajan, V., Coz, D., Liu, Y.: DermGAN: synthetic generation of clinical skin images with pathology. In: Dalca, A.V., et al. (eds.) Proceedings of the Machine Learning for Health NeurIPS Workshop. Proceedings of Machine Learning Research, vol. 116, pp. 155–170. PMLR (2020). https://proceedings.mlr.press/v116/ghorbani20a.html
10. Goodfellow, I., et al.: Generative adversarial networks. Commun. ACM **63**(11), 139–144 (2020)
11. Groh, M., et al.: Evaluating deep neural networks trained on clinical images in dermatology with the fitzpatrick 17k dataset. In: Proceedings of the IEEE/CVF Conference on Computer Vision and Pattern Recognition, pp. 1820–1828 (2021)
12. He, K., Zhang, X., Ren, S., Sun, J.: Deep residual learning for image recognition. In: Proceedings of the IEEE Conference on Computer Vision and Pattern Recognition, pp. 770–778 (2016)
13. Ho, J., Jain, A., Abbeel, P.: Denoising diffusion probabilistic models. Adv. Neural. Inf. Process. Syst. **33**, 6840–6851 (2020)
14. Hu, E.J., et al.: LoRA: low-rank adaptation of large language models. In: International Conference on Learning Representations (2022). https://openreview.net/forum?id=nZeVKeeFYf9

15. Ktena, I., et al.: Generative models improve fairness of medical classifiers under distribution shifts (2023)
16. Liu, Y., et al.: A deep learning system for differential diagnosis of skin diseases. Nat. Med. **26**(6), 900–908 (2020)
17. von Platen, P., et al.: Diffusers: state-of-the-art diffusion models. https://github.com/huggingface/diffusers (2022)
18. Qin, Z., Liu, Z., Zhu, P., Xue, Y.: A GAN-based image synthesis method for skin lesion classification. Comput. Methods Programs Biomed. **195**, 105568 (2020)
19. Rezk, E., Eltorki, M., El-Dakhakhni, W., et al.: Improving skin color diversity in cancer detection: deep learning approach. JMIR Dermatol. **5**(3), e39143 (2022)
20. Rombach, R., Blattmann, A., Lorenz, D., Esser, P., Ommer, B.: High-resolution image synthesis with latent diffusion models. In: Proceedings of the IEEE/CVF Conference on Computer Vision and Pattern Recognition (CVPR), pp. 10684–10695 (2022)
21. Sagers, L.W., et al.: Augmenting medical image classifiers with synthetic data from latent diffusion models (2023)
22. Sagers, L.W., Diao, J.A., Groh, M., Rajpurkar, P., Adamson, A., Manrai, A.K.: Improving dermatology classifiers across populations using images generated by large diffusion models. In: NeurIPS 2022 Workshop on Synthetic Data for Empowering ML Research (2022). https://openreview.net/forum?id=Vzdbjtz6Tys
23. Simonyan, K., Zisserman, A.: Very deep convolutional networks for large-scale image recognition. arXiv preprint arXiv:1409.1556 (2014)
24. Wang, J., Zhang, Y., Ding, Z., Hamm, J.: Achieving reliable and fair skin lesion diagnosis via unsupervised domain adaptation. In: Proceedings of the IEEE/CVF Conference on Computer Vision and Pattern Recognition, pp. 5157–5166 (2024)
25. Wu, B., et al.: Visual transformers: token-based image representation and processing for computer vision (2020)

Segmentation Style Discovery: Application to Skin Lesion Images

Kumar Abhishek[1]($\boxtimes$), Jeremy Kawahara[2], and Ghassan Hamarneh[1]

[1] School of Computing Science, Simon Fraser University, Burnaby, Canada
{kabhishe,hamarneh}@sfu.ca
[2] AIP Labs, Budapest, Hungary
jeremy@aip.ai

Abstract. Variability in medical image segmentation, arising from annotator preferences, expertise, and their choice of tools, has been well documented. While the majority of multi-annotator segmentation approaches focus on modeling annotator-specific preferences, they require annotator-segmentation correspondence. In this work, we introduce the problem of segmentation style discovery, and propose StyleSeg, a segmentation method that learns plausible, diverse, and semantically consistent segmentation styles from a corpus of image-mask pairs without any knowledge of annotator correspondence. StyleSeg consistently outperforms competing methods on four publicly available skin lesion segmentation (SLS) datasets. We also curate ISIC-MultiAnnot, the largest multi-annotator SLS dataset with annotator correspondence, and our results show a strong alignment, using our newly proposed measure AS^2, between the predicted styles and annotator preferences. The code and the dataset are available at https://github.com/sfu-mial/StyleSeg.

Keywords: inter-rater variability · image segmentation · dermatology

1 Introduction

Medical image segmentation is a critical component in medical image analysis pipelines, either as a preprocessing step for subsequent analyses or for treatment planning and image-guided human or robotic intervention. Following the seminal works of Long et al. [15] and Ronneberger et al. [21], there has been tremendous progress in deep learning (DL)-based medical image segmentation [4]. The majority of these works focus on learning to predict a single segmentation for an image. However, variability among experts when segmenting images has been well-documented, and these resulting segmentation masks are the product of latent factors such as ambiguous object boundaries and differences in tools, annotators' skill levels, criteria, and approaches to segmentation, and they capture

---

Supplementary Information The online version contains supplementary material available at https://doi.org/10.1007/978-3-031-77610-6_3.

different annotator segmentation preferences or "styles". Without accommodating these variations, a segmentation model optimized to minimize training error over a variety of human annotations may produce an "average" segmentation. This has motivated research that can be broadly categorized into two classes: methods that model and learn to predict a single "gold standard" segmentation through label aggregation [13,18,24] (SSeg) and methods that predict multiple segmentations to capture the variability of annotations [12,22,26] (MSeg).

MSeg methods rely on modeling annotator-specific preferences, and training them typically requires annotations with annotator-segmentation correspondence. Therefore, given a set of images and a set of annotators, annotator-segmentation correspondences can be represented as a bipartite graph when every image has been segmented by at least 1 annotator, e.g., LIDC-IDRI [3], or a complete bipartite graph when every image has been segmented by every annotator, e.g., RIGA [2]. However, in the absence of such a correspondence, i.e., a scenario where we have a corpus of images and corresponding annotations without any knowledge of annotator IDs, defining a segmentation style is non-trivial since the latent factors associated with each segmentation are unknown, thus making it challenging to explicitly train a segmentation model to reproduce a particular style. Since we are unable to confirm even the number of unique annotators, we hypothesize that a possible solution for modeling multi-annotator segmentations would be **discovering unique annotation styles** from the dataset alone. Such a discovery-based approach needs to ensure (1) diversity in the discovered styles, (2) segmentation plausibility across all the styles, and (3) semantic consistency of the segmentations across all the images. However, to the best of our knowledge, there is minimal prior work on the discovery and modeling of annotation styles in the absence of annotator correspondence.

We argue that since even experts can (considerably) differ in how they segment, it is only natural that automated models trained thereupon also exhibit this variety. We envision that a segmentation system should produce results that align with the expectations of its (clinical) users, and that these users can vary in their personalization preferences (e.g., a study [10] found that expert dermatologists prefer "tighter" segmentations than their inexperienced counterparts). Moreover, such a system should, with minimal supervision, continue to produce the style that a user expects, thus avoiding constant user involvement with either manual corrections or image-by-image selection of preferred segmentation style.

In this work, we tackle the problem of style discovery and personalization modeling in medical image segmentation without requiring annotator correspondence, and focus our analysis on skin lesion segmentation (SLS). Advancements in DL over the past decade as well as the availability of large publicly available annotated datasets have enabled large strides in SLS [17,23]. Therefore, in this work, we work on style discovery in the context of multiple annotators for SLS, which has not been explored extensively. The majority of previous works focus on SSeg methods: either to select training samples that have high inter-annotator agreement [20] or training ensemble models to handle annotators' variability [18]. More recently, Zepf et al. [25] presented a small-scale ($n = 300$) analysis of annotation styles in images from the ISIC 2019 dataset based on the granularity of the annotation boundaries. In this work, we make the following contributions: **(1)** we introduce the problem of segmentation style discovery in the absence of any annotator correspondence and propose a method (StyleSeg) that predicts multiple plausible, diverse, and semantically consistent segmentation styles, **(2)** we curate, to the best of our knowledge, the largest multi-annotator SLS dataset (ISIC-MultiAnnot) with annotator-segmentation mapping, and **(3)** we introduce a new measure (AS^2) for measuring the strength of alignment of the predicted styles with annotator preferences.

2 Method

Let $\mathcal{X} = \{X_i\}_{i=1}^{N}$ be a set of images and corresponding segmentation masks $\mathcal{Y} = \{\{Y_{ik}\}_{k=1}^{K_i}\}_{i=1}^{N}$, where $K_i > 0$ denotes the number of different ways X_i was segmented, without any knowledge of annotator correspondence. The goal is to discover unique annotation "styles" in this data $(\mathcal{X}, \mathcal{Y})$ such that, when given an image X_i, we predict $\{Y_{ij}\}_{j=1}^{M}$: M unique segmentations of X_i, that are diverse, plausible for X_i, and are of semantically consistent styles across all images.

To this end, we propose StyleSeg (Fig. 1(a)): a segmentation approach that learns to predict M plausible segmentations that capture a variety of styles from a corpus of images and corresponding masks without any annotator correspondence. StyleSeg consists of two deep learning models that are trained together: (i) a **segmentation model** f_s, parameterized by Θ_s, that predicts M segmentation masks from image X_i, where $M \in \mathbb{N}$ is a user-specified value,

$$\{\hat{Y}_{ij}\}_{j=1}^{M} = f_s(X_i; \Theta_s), \tag{1}$$

and (ii) a **style classifier model** f_c, parameterized by Θ_c, that predicts a vector $p_i \in \mathbb{R}^M$ of M probabilities,

$$p_i = f_c(X_i, Y_{ik}; \Theta_c), \tag{2}$$

where p_{ij} is the probability that (X_i, Y_{ik}) is of style j. Note that knowing X_i is necessary to define the styles, since the observed segmentations are a product of image content and annotation style.

Of the M predicted segmentations from f_s, we first need to identify the style that is the closest to the ground truth Y_{ik}, and then optimize it to make it even closer. Mathematically, we minimize the loss $\mathcal{L}_1$,

$$\mathcal{L}_1 = L_D(Y_{ik}, \hat{Y}_{im^*}), \tag{3}$$

$$m^* = \arg\max_j \mathrm{Dice}(Y_{ik}, \hat{Y}_{ij}), \tag{4}$$

where $L_D = 1 - \mathrm{Dice}$ and Dice denotes the Dice similarity coefficient [7]. We also require the other predicted styles to still be plausible, i.e., similar to ground truth Y_{ik}. However, requiring all styles to be equally plausible compromises the styles' diversity. Therefore, we make the strength of a style's plausibility requirement

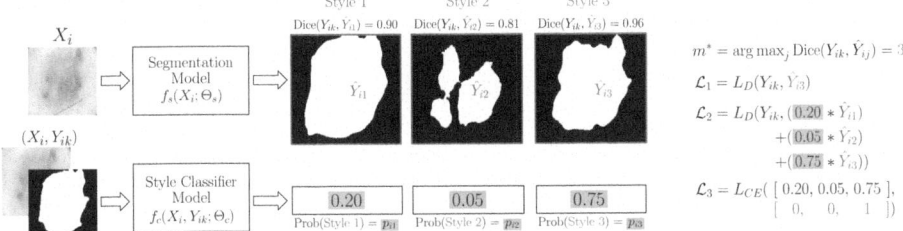

(a) StyleSeg overview with $M = 3$: the segmentation model f_s predicts 3 plausible segmentations of different styles, while the style classifier f_c predicts the style that is the most similar to the ground truth.

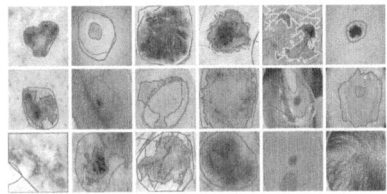

(b) Sample training images showing variability of segmentations.

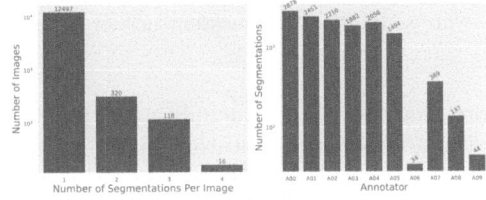

(c) Distribution of ISIC-MultiAnnot by number of annotators and segmentations.

Fig. 1. (a) An overview of the proposed method StyleSeg. (b) Inter-annotator variability in the training images. (c) An annotator-wise breakdown of the newly curated ISIC-MultiAnnot dataset.

proportional to its likelihood of being the predicted style, according to the style classifier f_c (Eq. 2). To this end, we encourage the weighted sum of predicted segmentations $\hat{Y}_{ij}$ to be similar to ground truth Y_{ik}, where the scalar weights are p_{ij}. Mathematically, we minimize the loss $\mathcal{L}_2$,

$$\mathcal{L}_2 = L_D\left(Y_{ik}, \sum_j^M p_{ij}\hat{Y}_{ij}\right). \tag{5}$$

Weighting the M segmentations by p_i ensures that when p_i has a high entropy (e.g., in the initial training epochs), all styles are encouraged to be similar to Y_{ik}, whereas when p_i has a low entropy, only a subset of the M styles are encouraged to be similar to Y_{ik}, thus enabling a coarse-to-fine style refinement.

Additionally, we employ a cross-entropy loss $\mathcal{L}_3$ to train the style classifier f_c by learning to predict the style that is the most similar to the ground truth,

$$\mathcal{L}_3 = L_{CE}(p_i, m^*). \tag{6}$$

Finally, we optimize the parameters Θ_s of f_s and Θ_c of f_c using

$$\Theta_s^*, \Theta_c^* = \arg\min_{\Theta_s, \Theta_c} \sum_i^N \mathcal{L}_{\text{total}}, \tag{7}$$

where

$$\mathcal{L}_{\text{total}} = \mathcal{L}_1 + \mathcal{L}_2 + \mathcal{L}_3. \tag{8}$$

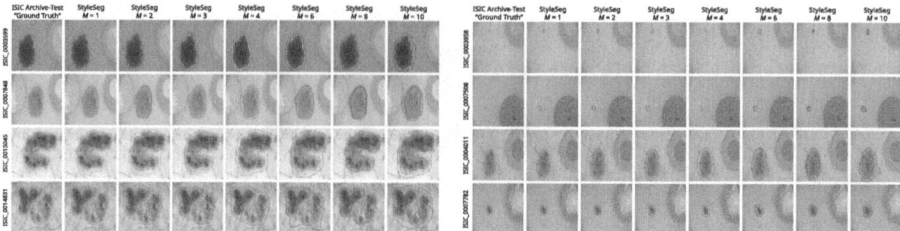

(a) Sample outputs of StyleSeg for lesions with and without distinct borders.

(b) StyleSeg produces better segmentations than even the test "ground truth".

Fig. 2. Evaluating StyleSeg on ISIC Archive-Test: diverse and plausible segmentations that are semantically consistent across styles.

Note that we do not include an explicit style distinctiveness constraint since, in the absence of annotator correspondence, the styles are entangled with the segmentations. Nevertheless, these loss terms used together (Eq. 8) implicitly encourage the styles to be different as the training progresses, as seen in our results.

3 Results and Discussion

Datasets: Similar to previous works [18,20], we train StyleSeg on images obtained from the ISIC Archive [1], specifically images with more than one "ground truth" segmentation. We select 2,261 images that meet this criterion (2,122 with two, 100 with three, 35 with four, and 4 with five segmentations), resulting in 4,704 image-mask pairs. Note that these images exhibit a vast range of inter-annotator agreement, as evidenced qualitatively (sample images with their masks in Fig. 1(c)) and quantitatively (pairwise Dice coefficients and Fleiss' kappa in Supp. Mat. Fig. SM1 (a)). We choose Fleiss' kappa [9] over Cohen's kappa [6] used by Ribeiro et al. [20] because the former can be used with multi-rater settings while the latter cannot [19]. We reserve 1,525 image-mask pairs from the ISIC Archive for our validation set. See Supp. Mat. for model architectures and training details. We evaluate on four publicly available datasets: ISIC Archive-Test containing 10,000 dermoscopic images with just one segmentation ground truth per image from the ISIC Archive, DermoFit (1,300 clinical images) [5], SCD (206 dermoscopic images) [11], and PH^2 (200 dermoscopic images) [16].

Competing Methods: We train StyleSeg with $M = \{2, 3, 4, 6, 8, 10\}$ and compare it to the following SSeg methods: NaiveTraining: a segmentation model without any annotator-specific knowledge; RandAnnotID [18]: 4 segmentation models, one optimized for each annotator randomly assigned to a mask, LessIsMore [20]: a segmentation model trained on a subset of the masks whose average pairwise Cohen's kappa is above 0.5; and D-LEMA [18]: an ensemble of Bayesian segmentation models. We also compare against an MSeg method MHP (multiple hypothesis prediction) [22] also with $M = \{2, 3, 4, 6, 8, 10\}$.

Table 1. Dice mean$_{std.dev.}$ comparing StyleSeg to SSeg [18,20] (first 4 rows) and MSeg (MHP [22]) methods. For the latter, we report the mean, median, min., max. of Dice between the ground truth and all the predicted segmentation styles. Note how StyleSeg consistently outperforms all competing methods while also producing more plausible segmentations than MHP. ⊘ denotes that the result cannot be reported since D-LEMA's [18] code is not available.

Method	ISIC Archive-Test (n = 10000)				PH² (n = 200)				DermoFit (n = 1300)				SCD (n = 206)			
	Mean	Median	Minimum	Maximum	Mean	Median	Minimum	Maximum	Mean	Median	Minimum	Maximum	Mean	Median	Minimum	Maximum
NaiveTraining	-	-	-	0.800₀.₁₄₉	-	-	-	0.880₀.₀₇₁	-	-	-	0.842₀.₁₃₉	-	-	-	0.766₀.₁₉₈
RandAnnotID [18]	-	-	-	⊘	-	-	-	0.897₀.₀₆₆	-	-	-	0.826₀.₀₆₄	-	-	-	⊘
LossInMore [20]	-	-	-	0.815₀.₁₇₈	-	-	-	0.895₀.₀₇₀	-	-	-	0.854₀.₁₆₇	-	-	-	0.804₀.₁₉₉
D-LEMA [18]	-	-	-	⊘	-	-	-	0.920₀.₀₆₄	-	-	-	0.853₀.₁₅₆	-	-	-	⊘
2-MHP	0.796₀.₁₆₆	0.727₀.₁₉₂	0.727₀.₁₉₂	0.864₀.₁₃₄	0.850₀.₁₁₄	0.786₀.₁₆₈	0.786₀.₁₆₈	0.914₀.₀₇₉	0.795₀.₁₄₉	0.707₀.₂₃₆	0.707₀.₂₃₆	0.882₀.₀₉₆	0.796₀.₁₄₉	0.713₀.₁₈₉	0.713₀.₁₈₉	0.879₀.₁₁₉
2-StyleSeg	0.814₀.₁₄₆	0.760₀.₁₆₈	0.760₀.₁₆₈	0.869₀.₁₃₁	0.878₀.₀₇₉	0.827₀.₁₂₁	0.827₀.₁₂₁	0.929₀.₀₆₂	0.824₀.₁₃₃	0.759₀.₁₄₉	0.759₀.₁₄₉	0.888₀.₀₉₆	0.824₀.₁₆₄	0.752₀.₂₁₇	0.523₀.₂₇₇	0.869₀.₁₅₆
3-MHP	0.772₀.₁₆₁	0.789₀.₁₆₄	0.652₀.₂₃₈	0.876₀.₁₃₁	0.780₀.₁₆₃	0.796₀.₁₇₉	0.625₀.₂₀₃	0.919₀.₀₇₉	0.739₀.₁₇₆	0.767₀.₁₈₆	0.562₀.₂₄₈	0.897₀.₀₉₂	0.715₀.₁₄₈	0.752₀.₁₄₅	0.523₀.₂₇₇	0.869₀.₁₅₆
3-StyleSeg	0.804₀.₁₄₆	0.819₀.₁₅₄	0.713₀.₁₉₆	0.881₀.₁₃₄	0.885₀.₀₆₉	0.900₀.₀₈₉	0.811₀.₁₃₇	0.943₀.₀₅₄	0.817₀.₁₃₂	0.835₀.₁₃₈	0.720₀.₂₀₈	0.897₀.₀₉₆	0.818₀.₁₅₁	0.837₀.₁₄₉	0.716₀.₂₁₅	0.901₀.₁₃₀
4-MHP	0.773₀.₁₇₀	0.752₀.₁₈₈	0.623₀.₂₆₈	0.886₀.₁₃₈	0.830₀.₁₃₁	0.817₀.₁₅₁	0.674₀.₂₃₄	0.933₀.₀₆₇	0.796₀.₁₃₄	0.783₀.₁₆₇	0.635₀.₂₃₀	0.904₀.₀₇₈	0.751₀.₁₈₉	0.796₀.₁₉₀	0.547₀.₂₅₁	0.896₀.₁₄₄
4-StyleSeg	0.804₀.₁₄₈	0.786₀.₁₇₇	0.693₀.₁₉₇	0.889₀.₁₄₇	0.875₀.₀₈₉	0.863₀.₁₄₇	0.776₀.₁₆₁	0.945₀.₀₄₈	0.812₀.₁₃₁	0.794₀.₁₅₄	0.681₀.₂₃₁	0.907₀.₀₇₆	0.786₀.₁₄₈	0.766₀.₁₇₉	0.632₀.₁₅₈	0.898₀.₁₃₂
6-MHP	0.647₀.₁₂₅	0.703₀.₁₅₈	0.121₀.₁₇₅	0.886₀.₁₅₁	0.790₀.₁₇₉	0.840₀.₁₆₅	0.400₀.₂₃₈	0.939₀.₀₅₃	0.749₀.₁₁₆	0.777₀.₁₃₁	0.428₀.₂₁₀	0.900₀.₀₈₉	0.649₀.₂₂₉	0.703₀.₂₀₇	0.156₀.₁₄₈	0.881₀.₁₃₉
6-StyleSeg	0.795₀.₁₇₉	0.799₀.₁₈₆	0.648₀.₂₅₀	0.889₀.₁₄₁	0.869₀.₀₉₈	0.873₀.₁₃₂	0.745₀.₁₆₇	0.948₀.₀₄₆	0.814₀.₁₃₅	0.818₀.₁₄₉	0.651₀.₂₃₈	0.911₀.₀₇₈	0.798₀.₁₄₅	0.806₀.₁₅₆	0.508₀.₂₆₄	0.906₀.₁₃₆
8-MHP	0.625₀.₁₈₆	0.658₀.₂₁₆	0.099₀.₁₄₉	0.896₀.₁₅₁	0.752₀.₁₇₉	0.801₀.₁₉₈	0.260₀.₂₁₄	0.944₀.₀₃₉	0.698₀.₁₇₇	0.708₀.₂₁₀	0.309₀.₁₈₁	0.908₀.₀₈₉	0.616₀.₁₁₇	0.627₀.₂₀₈	0.134₀.₁₁₁	0.897₀.₁₂₉
8-StyleSeg	0.790₀.₁₇₀	0.798₀.₁₉₈	0.595₀.₂₆₈	0.899₀.₁₃₆	0.875₀.₀₈₉	0.878₀.₁₃₁	0.745₀.₁₇₀	0.950₀.₀₄₇	0.810₀.₁₃₁	0.815₀.₁₃₁	0.632₀.₂₀₁	0.910₀.₀₇₈	0.798₀.₁₄₁	0.812₀.₁₇₈	0.586₀.₂₃₃	0.901₀.₁₃₄
10-MHP	0.706₀.₁₇₄	0.745₀.₁₈₅	0.281₀.₁₈₉	0.894₀.₁₃₈	0.724₀.₁₈₇	0.761₀.₁₈₈	0.339₀.₂₅₃	0.938₀.₀₄₉	0.629₀.₁₇₉	0.667₀.₂₁₉	0.181₀.₂₁₅	0.906₀.₀₉₈	0.690₀.₁₄₈	0.733₀.₂₁₅	0.223₀.₁₉₈	0.898₀.₁₃₄
10-StyleSeg	0.793₀.₁₇₉	0.805₀.₁₉₈	0.603₀.₂₁₈	0.899₀.₁₄₄	0.866₀.₁₀₁	0.880₀.₁₁₁	0.692₀.₁₇₉	0.951₀.₀₄₆	0.801₀.₁₄₇	0.813₀.₁₅₈	0.579₀.₂₂₅	0.918₀.₀₆₈	0.768₀.₁₈₁	0.791₀.₁₉₈	0.513₀.₂₄₈	0.885₀.₁₄₀

Qualitative Results of StyleSeg on ISIC Archive-Test (Fig. 2(a)) show plausibility (all segmentations cover the lesion with varying degrees of over- or under-segmentation) as well as semantic consistency across segmentations (e.g., when $M = 3$, yellow always has a tight and jagged boundary while blue always has a loose boundary). We also provide a quantitative assessment in Supp. Mat. Fig. SM1 (f). Also, observe that in lesions with well-defined borders (top two rows), the predicted styles are similar, whereas in lesions with ambiguous borders (bottom two rows), the predictions exhibit considerable diversity. It is also worth noting that several images in ISIC Archive-Test have either incorrect or imprecise "ground truth" masks (Fig. 2(b)), which leads to incorrect penalization of StyleSeg's accurate predictions during evaluation.

Quantitative Results: For SSeg methods, we report the Dice coefficient. For MSeg methods, we report $\max_j(d)$, where $d = \text{Dice}(Y_{ik}, \hat{Y}_{ij})$, to assess the highest agreement, and $\{\text{mean}_j(d), \text{median}_j(d), \min_j(d)\}$ to assess the plausibility of all M segmentations. For example, an MSeg model that produces even one poor segmentation will have low scores for $\min_j(d)$, indicating low plausibility.

Table 1 shows that predicting more than one style (StyleSeg, MHP) improves performance ($\max_j(d)$) compared to SSeg methods, and even MSeg methods that predict just two styles (2-StyleSeg, 2-MHP) consistently outperform SSeg methods. Moreover, as M increases, a larger number of diverse segmentations are produced, and the $\max_j(d)$ keeps improving. However, we observe that for three out of the four datasets, the $\max_j(d)$ performance either plateaus or starts to decline as M increases. We posit that after an optimal number of styles, generating more segmentations leads to diversity at the cost of performance, and

Table 2. StyleSeg's segmentation agreement (mean$_{std.dev.}$ of Dice$_{IASS}$ and Dice$_{ASSS}$) and style alignment (AS^2) on the 27 annotator preferences in ISIC-MultiAnnot. $\mathcal{J}$ denotes the single style that, for each row, maximizes agreement with the ground truth. As more styles are modeled, Dice$_{IASS}$, Dice$_{ASSS}$, and AS^2 all improve, and all annotator preferences consistently align with a discovered style.

Annotator + Tool + Experience	Seg. Count	1-StyleSeg	2-StyleSeg			3-StyleSeg			4-StyleSeg		
		Dice$_{ISSS}$	Dice$_{ISSS}$	Dice$_{ASSS}$	$\mathcal{J}$	Dice$_{ISSS}$	Dice$_{ASSS}$	$\mathcal{J}$	Dice$_{ISSS}$	Dice$_{ASSS}$	$\mathcal{J}$
A00+T2+E	1573	0.892$_{0.089}$	0.923$_{0.061}$	0.913$_{0.087}$	2	0.944$_{0.048}$	0.913$_{0.106}$	3	0.944$_{0.044}$	0.914$_{0.111}$	1
A00+T2+N	1305	0.716$_{0.308}$	0.761$_{0.292}$	0.728$_{0.308}$	2	0.793$_{0.287}$	0.727$_{0.313}$	3	0.790$_{0.290}$	0.726$_{0.304}$	3
A01+T1+N	6	0.559$_{0.862}$	0.766$_{0.152}$	0.766$_{0.152}$	1	0.754$_{0.138}$	0.741$_{0.185}$	2	0.819$_{0.106}$	0.767$_{0.113}$	2
A01+T3+E	297	0.900$_{0.104}$	0.915$_{0.093}$	0.897$_{0.107}$	2	0.927$_{0.075}$	0.900$_{0.097}$	1	0.931$_{0.067}$	0.904$_{0.090}$	3
A01+T3+N	2148	0.829$_{0.195}$	0.857$_{0.167}$	0.817$_{0.170}$	1	0.869$_{0.159}$	0.836$_{0.178}$	1	0.876$_{0.148}$	0.836$_{0.175}$	3
A02+T1+E	1742	0.844$_{0.177}$	0.880$_{0.140}$	0.856$_{0.159}$	1	0.886$_{0.138}$	0.854$_{0.159}$	1	0.895$_{0.112}$	0.859$_{0.148}$	4
A02+T3+E	468	0.856$_{0.172}$	0.889$_{0.167}$	0.883$_{0.175}$	2	0.899$_{0.161}$	0.874$_{0.188}$	3	0.903$_{0.146}$	0.890$_{0.160}$	1
A03+T1+E	1622	0.778$_{0.168}$	0.845$_{0.117}$	0.827$_{0.127}$	1	0.854$_{0.111}$	0.824$_{0.145}$	2	0.881$_{0.095}$	0.823$_{0.138}$	4
A03+T3+E	260	0.891$_{0.116}$	0.912$_{0.086}$	0.876$_{0.173}$	2	0.923$_{0.069}$	0.868$_{0.150}$	1	0.932$_{0.074}$	0.874$_{0.163}$	3
A04+T1+E	992	0.850$_{0.158}$	0.880$_{0.131}$	0.860$_{0.149}$	1	0.888$_{0.133}$	0.866$_{0.153}$	2	0.906$_{0.108}$	0.856$_{0.157}$	4
A04+T1+N	61	0.760$_{0.248}$	0.840$_{0.158}$	0.823$_{0.164}$	1	0.837$_{0.168}$	0.786$_{0.201}$	1	0.827$_{0.206}$	0.789$_{0.226}$	4
A04+T3+E	913	0.912$_{0.088}$	0.939$_{0.054}$	0.934$_{0.065}$	2	0.948$_{0.047}$	0.926$_{0.069}$	1	0.951$_{0.045}$	0.932$_{0.063}$	3
A04+T3+N	90	0.877$_{0.098}$	0.910$_{0.068}$	0.905$_{0.070}$	2	0.928$_{0.031}$	0.908$_{0.044}$	3	0.926$_{0.052}$	0.913$_{0.055}$	1
A05+T1+E	752	0.815$_{0.203}$	0.862$_{0.163}$	0.837$_{0.179}$	1	0.873$_{0.163}$	0.827$_{0.184}$	1	0.882$_{0.147}$	0.841$_{0.177}$	4
A05+T3+E	742	0.875$_{0.189}$	0.903$_{0.109}$	0.891$_{0.113}$	2	0.916$_{0.098}$	0.878$_{0.120}$	1	0.919$_{0.091}$	0.891$_{0.108}$	1
A06+T1+E	10	0.824$_{0.187}$	0.902$_{0.037}$	0.885$_{0.070}$	1	0.909$_{0.044}$	0.889$_{0.049}$	2	0.909$_{0.039}$	0.880$_{0.063}$	4
A06+T3+E	24	0.862$_{0.079}$	0.916$_{0.053}$	0.916$_{0.053}$	2	0.934$_{0.031}$	0.923$_{0.031}$	3	0.933$_{0.041}$	0.929$_{0.040}$	1
A07+T1+E	67	0.820$_{0.157}$	0.877$_{0.124}$	0.867$_{0.130}$	1	0.890$_{0.108}$	0.862$_{0.157}$	2	0.897$_{0.104}$	0.862$_{0.149}$	4
A07+T1+N	251	0.837$_{0.141}$	0.892$_{0.085}$	0.879$_{0.104}$	1	0.903$_{0.067}$	0.875$_{0.114}$	2	0.905$_{0.070}$	0.873$_{0.101}$	4
A07+T3+E	12	0.925$_{0.055}$	0.938$_{0.019}$	0.937$_{0.019}$	2	0.939$_{0.030}$	0.916$_{0.055}$	1	0.947$_{0.016}$	0.932$_{0.017}$	1
A07+T3+N	39	0.863$_{0.177}$	0.918$_{0.061}$	0.913$_{0.071}$	2	0.933$_{0.057}$	0.899$_{0.148}$	3	0.934$_{0.059}$	0.914$_{0.079}$	1
A08+T1+E	26	0.666$_{0.225}$	0.750$_{0.161}$	0.680$_{0.218}$	2	0.747$_{0.197}$	0.653$_{0.250}$	1	0.793$_{0.134}$	0.666$_{0.261}$	1
A08+T3+E	111	0.605$_{0.250}$	0.668$_{0.197}$	0.626$_{0.210}$	1	0.677$_{0.206}$	0.628$_{0.218}$	2	0.735$_{0.196}$	0.669$_{0.203}$	2
A09+T1+E	30	0.815$_{0.121}$	0.841$_{0.098}$	0.784$_{0.156}$	1	0.873$_{0.089}$	0.833$_{0.113}$	2	0.884$_{0.076}$	0.812$_{0.119}$	4
A09+T1+N	1	0.953$_{0.000}$	0.927$_{0.000}$	0.927$_{0.000}$	2	0.955$_{0.000}$	0.955$_{0.000}$	1	0.947$_{0.000}$	0.947$_{0.000}$	3
A09+T3+E	10	0.900$_{0.074}$	0.918$_{0.054}$	0.918$_{0.064}$	2	0.933$_{0.038}$	0.909$_{0.044}$	1	0.937$_{0.043}$	0.919$_{0.040}$	3
A09+T3+N	3	0.894$_{0.070}$	0.911$_{0.058}$	0.911$_{0.058}$	2	0.957$_{0.015}$	0.957$_{0.015}$	1	0.944$_{0.030}$	0.944$_{0.030}$	1
AS^2 (Eqn. 9)		-	0.299$_{0.308}$			0.347$_{0.337}$			0.466$_{0.396}$		

leave this investigation for future work. Interestingly, datasets that do not have a documented presence of inter-segmentation variability (DermoFit, PH^2, SCD) also benefit from learning to predict multiple segmentations, indicating style variability in the ground truth masks. A post hoc investigation of DermoFit, for example, confirms the presence of different annotation styles (difference in boundary granularity; Supp. Mat. Fig. SM1 (b)).

Finally, StyleSeg consistently outperforms MHP for all datasets and M, except $M = 10$ with SCD, and as M increases, the plausibility of MHP models across all the predictions decreases, as evident through the declining {mean$_j(d)$, median$_j(d)$, min$_j(d)$} scores. For example, when modeling 10 styles, the [min$_j(d)$, max$_j(d)$] range across 10 segmentations for 10,000 test images in ISIC Archive-Test is [0.281, 0.894] for 10-MHP and [0.603, 0.899] for 10-StyleSeg, meaning all the predicted segmentations are more plausible for the latter. We attribute this improvement to the plausibility constraint ($\mathcal{L}_2$ in Eq. 5), which penalizes predicted segmentations that considerably deviate from the ground truth.

A New Multi-annotator Dataset: Next, we propose ISIC-MultiAnnot, a new multi-annotator SLS dataset curated from the ISIC Archive that, to the best of our knowledge, is the largest such dataset to contain annotator correspondence. The annotator-segmentation mapping in ISIC-MultiAnnot forms an incomplete bipartite graph, i.e., not every image has been segmented by every annotator. ISIC-MultiAnnot contains 12,951 images segmented by 10 annotators, resulting in 13,555 image-mask pairs (breakdown in Fig. 1(c)). Unlike other multi-annotator datasets, the variability in ISIC-MultiAnnot's segmentations stems from three annotation pipeline factors: the annotator (10 annotator IDs: "A00"–"A09"), the tool used ("T1", "T2", "T3"), and the expertise of the manual reviewer ("expert" or "novice") [18], resulting in 27 unique annotator preferences, which we use for our evaluation. We measure StyleSeg performance in two settings: (i) **image-adaptive style selection (IASS)**: for every image, we find the style that maximizes the agreement with ground truth, measured as $\text{Dice}_{\text{IASS}} = \max_j(\text{Dice}(Y_{ik}, \hat{Y}_{ij}))$, and (ii) a more challenging **annotator-specific style selection (ASSS)**: we find a single style, fixed across all images, that maximizes agreement with ground truth, measured as $\text{Dice}_{\text{ASSS}} = \text{Dice}(Y_{ik}, \hat{Y}_{i\mathcal{J}})$, where $\mathcal{J} = \arg\max_j(\sum_i \text{Dice}(Y_{ik}, \hat{Y}_{ij}))$. Note that $\text{Dice}_{\text{ASSS}} \leq \text{Dice}_{\text{IASS}}$.

Quantitative results of StyleSeg on ISIC-MultiAnnot (Table 2; additional results in Supp. Mat. Fig. SM1 (c)) show that each of the discovered styles presents a high agreement with almost all the annotator preferences. A notable outlier is "A08", and upon manual inspection, we found a large number of ground truth segmentations to be incorrect to varying degrees (Supp. Mat. Fig. SM1 (e)), which explains the lower evaluation performance. Similar to Table 1, modeling even two styles yields better performance than one style. Moreover, as M increases, the newly discovered styles continue to show increasing usefulness, since all of them consistently align with one or more annotator preferences, meaning that they are able to capture the diversity in segmentations with an increasing level of granularity.

As an additional experiment to assess whether the learned styles are able to model tool-specific ("T1", "T2", "T3") latent factors, we separate the segmentations into three groups based on the tool, pass each corresponding image through a trained 3-StyleSeg model, and determine the predicted segmentation style with the highest overlap. We observe that the most commonly chosen style within a group is unique for each of the three tool groups, suggesting that differences among the three tools are learned within the three styles.

A New Style Alignment Measure: When choosing only one style to evaluate each annotator preference, it is important to note that a particular style could be assigned as the chosen style for a certain annotator even if it best fits either 100% (perfect alignment) of the images or just slightly above random chance (weak alignment). We propose to measure this Annotator-Style Alignment Strength (AS^2) as 1 − 'normalized Shannon entropy of annotator-style assignment', i.e.,

$$\text{AS}^2 = 1 - \frac{-\sum_{i=1}^{M} q_i \log_2 q_i}{-\sum_{j=1}^{M} \frac{1}{M} \log_2 \frac{1}{M}}, \quad (9)$$

where q_i is the vector of fractions of segmentations assigned to each style (e.g., $q = [0.70, 0.15, 0.15]$ for a 3-StyleSeg model that assigns 100 images from a certain annotator preference as 70:15:15 images for styles 1, 2, and 3, yielding $AS^2 = 0.255$). Note that AS^2 is 0 for uniform assignments, and increases logarithmically approaching 1 as assignments become more consistent. Our results in Table 2 show that AS^2 values do not decrease as M increases, meaning that learning to model more styles is not detrimental to segmentation quality and indeed captures more diversity. Additional results are presented in Supp. Mat. Fig. SM1 (d, g). [8,14]

4 Conclusion

We formulated the problem of segmentation style discovery in the absence of annotator correspondence. We showed how our proposed method, StyleSeg, discovers segmentation styles that are diverse, semantically consistent, and more plausible than those generated by competing methods, as evaluated on four public skin lesion segmentation (SLS) datasets. We also curated ISIC-MultiAnnot, the largest multi-annotator SLS dataset with 13,555 image-mask pairs from 10 annotators from ISIC Archive, and showed how StyleSeg consistently achieves high agreement with the annotator preferences, as measured through the Dice coefficient as well as a newly proposed measure, Annotator-Style Alignment Strength, for measuring annotator-style alignment. Future work would include an explicit "disentanglement" of annotation styles from image content and approaches to find the optimal number of styles in a segmentation dataset.

Acknowledgments. The authors are grateful for the computational resources provided by NVIDIA Corporation and Digital Research Alliance of Canada (formerly Compute Canada). Partial funding for this project was provided by the Natural Sciences and Engineering Research Council of Canada (NSERC RGPIN/06752-2020).

Disclosure of Interests. The authors have no competing interests to declare.

References

1. International Skin Imaging Collaboration: Melanoma Project. https://www.isic-archive.com/. Accessed 01 Feb 2024
2. Almazroa, A.: Agreement among ophthalmologists in marking the optic disc and optic cup in fundus images. Int. Ophthalmol. **37**, 701–717 (2017)
3. Armato, S.G., III., et al.: The lung image database consortium (LIDC) and image database resource initiative (IDRI): a completed reference database of lung nodules on CT scans. Med. Phys. **38**(2), 915–931 (2011)
4. Asgari Taghanaki, S., Abhishek, K., Cohen, J.P., Cohen-Adad, J., Hamarneh, G.: Deep semantic segmentation of natural and medical images: a review. Artif. Intell. Rev. **54**, 137–178 (2021)
5. Ballerini, L., Fisher, R.B., Aldridge, B., Rees, J.: A color and texture based hierarchical K-NN approach to the classification of non-melanoma skin lesions. In: Celebi, M.E., Schaefer, G. (eds.) Color Medical Image Analysis, vol. 6, pp. 63–86. Springer, Netherlands (2013)

6. Cohen, J.: A coefficient of agreement for nominal scales. Educ. Psychol. Measur. **20**(1), 37–46 (1960)
7. Dice, L.R.: Measures of the amount of ecologic association between species. Ecology **26**(3), 297–302 (1945)
8. Ercal, F., Chawla, A., Stoecker, W.V., Lee, H.C., Moss, R.H.: Neural network diagnosis of malignant melanoma from color images. IEEE Trans. Biomed. Eng. **41**(9), 837–845 (1994)
9. Fleiss, J.L.: Measuring nominal scale agreement among many raters. Psychol. Bull. **76**(5), 378 (1971)
10. Fortina, A.B., Peserico, E., Silletti, A., Zattra, E.: Where's the naevus? Interoperator variability in the localization of melanocytic lesion border. Skin Res. Technol. **18**(3), 311–315 (2012)
11. Glaister, J., Amelard, R., Wong, A., Clausi, D.A.: MSIM: multistage illumination modeling of dermatological photographs for illumination-corrected skin lesion analysis. IEEE Trans. Biomed. Eng. **60**(7), 1873–1883 (2013)
12. Ji, W., et al.: Learning calibrated medical image segmentation via multi-rater agreement modeling. In: Proceedings of the IEEE/CVF Conference on Computer Vision and Pattern Recognition, pp. 12341–12351 (2021)
13. Kats, E., Goldberger, J., Greenspan, H.: A soft STAPLE algorithm combined with anatomical knowledge. In: Medical Image Computing and Computer Assisted Intervention–MICCAI 2019: 22nd International Conference, Shenzhen, China, 13–17 October 2019, Proceedings, Part III 22, pp. 510–517. Springer (2019)
14. Kawahara, J., Hamarneh, G.: Fully convolutional neural networks to detect clinical dermoscopic features. IEEE J. Biomed. Health Inform. **23**(2), 578–585 (2018)
15. Long, J., Shelhamer, E., Darrell, T.: Fully convolutional networks for semantic segmentation. In: Proceedings of the IEEE Conference on Computer Vision and Pattern Recognition, pp. 3431–3440 (2015)
16. Mendonça, T., Ferreira, P.M., Marques, J.S., Marcal, A.R.S., Rozeira, J.: PH^2 - a dermoscopic image database for research and benchmarking. In: IEEE Engineering in Medicine and Biology Society, pp. 5437–5440 (2013)
17. Mirikharaji, Z., et al.: A survey on deep learning for skin lesion segmentation. Med. Image Anal. 102863 (2023)
18. Mirikharaji, Z., Abhishek, K., Izadi, S., Hamarneh, G.: D-LEMA: deep learning ensembles from multiple annotations-application to skin lesion segmentation. In: Proceedings of the IEEE/CVF Conference on Computer Vision and Pattern Recognition, pp. 1837–1846 (2021)
19. Powers, D.M.W.: The problem with kappa. In: Proceedings of the 13th Conference of the European Chapter of the Association for Computational Linguistics, pp. 345–355 (2012)
20. Ribeiro, V., Avila, S., Valle, E.: Less is more: sample selection and label conditioning improve skin lesion segmentation. In: Proceedings of the IEEE/CVF Conference on Computer Vision and Pattern Recognition Workshops, pp. 738–739 (2020)
21. Ronneberger, O., Fischer, P., Brox, T.: U-net: convolutional networks for biomedical image segmentation. In: Medical Image Computing and Computer-Assisted Intervention–MICCAI 2015: 18th International Conference, Munich, Germany, 5–9 October 2015, Proceedings, part III 18, pp. 234–241. Springer (2015)
22. Rupprecht, C., et al.: Learning in an uncertain world: representing ambiguity through multiple hypotheses. In: Proceedings of the IEEE International Conference on Computer Vision, pp. 3591–3600 (2017)

23. Tschandl, P., Sinz, C., Kittler, H.: Domain-specific classification-pretrained fully convolutional network encoders for skin lesion segmentation. Comput. Biol. Med. **104**, 111–116 (2019)
24. Warfield, S.K., Zou, K.H., Wells, W.M.: Simultaneous truth and performance level estimation (STAPLE): an algorithm for the validation of image segmentation. IEEE Trans. Med. Imaging **23**(7), 903–921 (2004)
25. Zepf, K., Petersen, E., Frellsen, J., Feragen, A.: That label's got style: handling label style bias for uncertain image segmentation. In: The Eleventh International Conference on Learning Representations (2023). https://openreview.net/forum?id=wZ2SVhOTzBX
26. Zhang, L., et al.: Learning to segment when experts disagree. In: Medical Image Computing and Computer Assisted Intervention–MICCAI 2020: 23rd International Conference, Lima, Peru, October 4–8, 2020, Proceedings, Part I 23, pp. 179–190. Springer (2020)

A Vision Transformer with Adaptive Cross-Image and Cross-Resolution Attention

Benjamin A. K. Murray[1] (✉), Wei R. Tan[2], Liane S. Canas[1], Catherine H. Smith[2], Satveer K. Mahil[2], Sebastien Ourselin[1], and Marc Modat[1]

[1] Biomedical Engineering and Image Sciences, King's College London, London SE1 7EH, UK
benjamin.murray@kcl.ac.uk
[2] St John's Institute of Dermatology, Guy's and St Thomas' NHS Foundation Trust and King's College London, London, UK

Abstract. Vision Transformers (ViTs) are the current state-of-the-art in deep learning for computer vision tasks. They are trained on vast datasets and are capable of useful downstream tasks through clever use of the attention mechanism.

The biggest limiting factor for ViTs is the number of pixels and tokens that can be processed in a given pass. Memory constraints on both patch size and the number of patches mean that ViTs are most effective at processing relatively low-resolution images.

Whilst ViTs can attend very flexibly across an image, attending across images in a naive fashion requires memory proportional to the square of the number of images. This is a further limiting factor. Given the task of automated assessment of psoriasis severity, a chronic skin condition that can affect large portions of a person's skin, it is necessary to look across multiple images and at fine detail in large images.

We present a method that adapts ViTs to a two-stage design that allows for the regression of a patient's psoriasis score across multiple images and resolutions and shows its effectiveness relative to a baseline ViT.

The implementation of our method is available at https://github.com/KCL-BMEIS/multivit.git.

Keywords: Vision Transformer · Multi-image · Multi-resolution · Psoriasis

1 Introduction

Psoriasis is a common, incurable inflammatory skin disease associated with multimorbidity and reduced life expectancy. It affects 2 million individuals in the UK, and costs the NHS over č750 million (estimated) annually. Research has successfully delivered several new psoriasis therapies over the past 2 decades [14], but disease severity and evolution over time are still monitored through clinical evaluation of skin lesions, which has well-recognised limitations.

The Psoriasis Area Severity Index (PASI) [7] is the gold standard for disease severity assessments. It integrates area of psoriasis involvement with *erythema* (redness of skin), *induration* (thickening/hardening of skin) and *scaling* of psoriasis plaques. It is measured by clinicians and ranges from 0 (no disease) to 72. A PASI of 10+ is considered severe. Physical Global Assessment (PGA) is another measure used to grade psoriasis. It is an overall assessment of all psoriasis lesions on the body according to a Likert scale, which is a 6 point score between 0 (no psoriasis) and 5 (severe psoriasis). PGA is correlated with PASI.

Both PASI and PGA are time-consuming, highly subjective and poorly reproducible (low intra- and inter-rater consistency). Assessments rely on face-to-face contact between clinician and patient, which may not be deliverable with increasingly limited healthcare resources.

Deep-learning-based computer vision has the potential to automate image-based assessment of psoriasis severity. Initially created for language processing, the state of the art transformer [12] architecture has been adapted to vision tasks [5] with great success. Vision Transformers (ViTs) use image patches converted to tokens rather than pixel values in isolation. This is done for two reasons. Firstly, a pixel conveys very little semantic information, but a patch of pixels can convey significant semantic information. Secondly, attention is $O(T^2)$ in memory usage for T tokens in a standard transformer architecture, as all pairwise patch interactions must be considered. A position encoding is added to each of the patches, and can be learned depending on the architecture, so that the network can understand the spatial relationship between patches.

Transformers use Scaled Dot-Product attention; a mechanism that allows ViTs to learn the relationship between image patches. ViTs typically use self-attention, meaning patches of the same image attend to each other and to a class token that captures image-level semantics and is typically used as the input to class-level task heads. The class token allows ViTs to be trained to pay attention to the parts of an image most important to the model task, or even to use the patch to class attentions to act as semantic segmentation with only image-level labels for training [2].

ViTs require images to be of a given resolution and trained at or fine-tuned to a desired resolution. ViTs are configured to a given number of patches that is typically constrained by memory usage, given that attention is $O(T^2)$ in memory for T patches. A typical patch size in pixels is around 16^2 to 32^2 as larger patches require larger token memory to properly capture the information in a patch. As such, ViTs generally handle image sizes between 256^2 and 512^2 pixels. Commodity cameras have resolutions in the thousands of pixels squared, so fine-grained detail may not be readily detectable by a ViT.

Given the nature of psoriasis, standard ViT architectures cannot perform at their full potential. Psoriasis tends to occur across much of a patient's body rather than being limited to a single area, and is a heterogeneous condition with the pattern of presentation varying widely between individuals. A patient's full presentation of psoriasis is not provided by a single image in the general case, and many of the images are whole body images of a high resolution that must be downsampled to a much lower resolution to fit in a ViT architecture, necessitating a dramatic drop in detail.

Skin type is a confounding factor automated psoriasis assessment. The Fitzpatrick Skin Type (FST) [6] puts skin tones into six categories. Automated assessment for people with FST V and VI is a challenge as psoriasis does not present as distinctly in images as it does for FST I to IV, and datasets tend to have few people with FST V and VI.

In order for ViTs to pay attention across multiple images, images can be packed into a single composite image. For N images having T patches each, the memory requirement is $O((NT)^2)$ as every image patch must attend to every other image patch across the images. This typically necessitates reducing the resolution of the images or using fewer patches per image. For biomedical imaging, in which fine-grained texture is generally important in the assessment of a condition, this might negate any advantage of being able to attend between images.

We present a novel method, MultiViT, with a mechanism that adaptively focuses on regions across multiple related images in order to focus on important features and thus capture a person's whole psoriasis presentation. Mechanisms to increase resolution for the most clinically relevant subsections of the images are also presented. We demonstrate its effectiveness in the prediction of PASI scores given images.

2 Related Work

Multiple Instance Learning is a technique that attempts to learn across multiple related images, and approaches such as [9] use earlier forms of attention to look across multiple images.

SparseViT [3] is a shifted window (SWIN) [10] transformer-based model developed to efficiently parse high resolution images with low latency. SparseViT is designed to skip less important regions of a high-resolution image via the $L2$ norm of each window activation to focus on key image areas (for example the detection of pedestrians for self-driving cars). SparseViT is focused on mitigating latency with minimal performance loss, whereas the goal for MultiViT is to maximise auto-diagnostic power, as latency is not a significant factor in our clinical pipeline.

NaViT [4] is a method to improve training time for large scale networks with large scale datasets during pre-training. It allows ViTs to be trained on multiple images of differing aspect ratios. During training, a set of images is packed into a set of tokens and masked to prevent attention between images. They use a novel position encoding to avoid deforming images of different aspect ratios that factorizes position in to x, y components, meaning that image patch grids can be adapted to any aspect ratio. In contrast to NaVit, MultiViT allows attention between images to exploit relationships between them. MultiViT also avoids windowed attention as we want to maximise the use of the attention mechanism on each image.

3 Method

MultiViT is a novel adaptation of the ViT architecture that enables memory-efficient adaptive attention across multiple images. It does so via two mechanisms. Firstly, MultiViT implements adaptive attention with a fixed patch budget, meaning that for N images, each having T patches, it uses $O(NT^2)$ memory, rather than $O((NT)^2)$ memory for a vanilla ViT. Secondly, MultiViT can optionally focus on critical tokens at an increased resolution, narrowing its field of focus but enabling it to better exploit fine-grained resolution where required.

MultiViT is composed of two ViT stages that are connected together by our *Attention Filter* module. Each stage of the MultiViT architecture consists of a ViT model backbone that has been pre-trained on a large, general-purpose dataset. One or more attention heads are added to the class token output of the ViT model and used to fine-tune the model on image-level labels.

The MultiViT architecture is depicted in Fig. 1 and consists of the following stages:

Stage 1 is executed on a set of N related images (from a given patient). Each image execution generates tokens and class-to-patch attentions on a per-image basis based on the task head losses for *Stage 1*.

The *Attention Filter* module ranks, selects and composes the most influential tokens from the *Stage 1* executions. It creates a composite hidden state and composite image from the image patches corresponding to the tokens kept from *Stage 1*.

Stage 2 is a slightly modified ViT that takes the composite hidden state and composite image as its inputs, and calculates a final task score using its own task heads. It has a *Token Concatenator* module that can merge the composite tokens with tokens embedded from the composite image.

3.1 Attention Filter

The *Attention Filter*, shown in Fig. 1(a) creates the composite hidden state and composite high-resolution image from the tokens output by the executions of *Stage 1* as follows:

The *Attention Scorer* ranks tokens for all N input images output by *Stage 1* by their activation strength relative to their corresponding class token. The T most highly ranked tokens are selected and the rest discarded.

The *Mapping Generator* generates a mapping for the selected tokens from their source hidden states to the composite hidden states and a mapping for the corresponding image patches that the tokens map to in the high resolution images.

The *Token Mapper* takes the *Stage 1* hidden states and the token mapping and creates a composite hidden state. Given a resolution multiplier of ratio R,

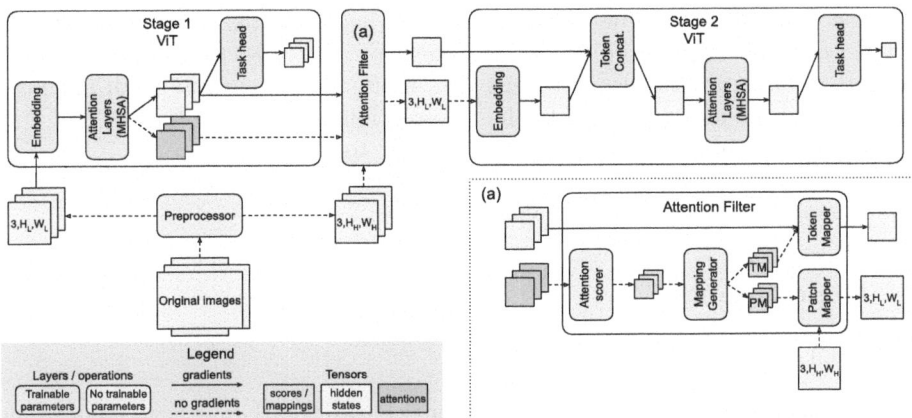

Fig. 1. The MultiVit architecture. MultiViT consists of three stages. *Stage 1* is a standard ViT that is executed on multiple images, sequentially. The *Attention Filter* (a.) takes the resulting patch tokens and attentions from *Stage 1*, ranks those tokens by importance to the *Stage 1* class token and then generates mappings for the T most important tokens. The *Attention Filter* generates a composite hidden state of surviving tokens and the corresponding compound image. These are then input to a modified *Stage 2* ViT.

each patch token from *Stage 1* maps to $R \times R$ input patch tokens for *Stage 2*. Class tokens from *Stage 1* are discarded.

The *Patch Mapper* takes the image patch mapping and uses it to select image patches from the high-resolution version of the images. The resulting composite image is passed through the *Stage 2* patch embedder to generate a set of high-resolution tokens.

Critically, because tokens selected by the *Attention Filter* are passed to *Stage 2*, gradients from *Stage 2* also inform *Stage 1*, and the overall network learns from the task heads of both stages concurrently.

The *Token Concatenator* added to *Stage 2* takes the hidden state from *Stage 1* and concatenates it with the hidden state from the embedded high-resolution image patches. This is done by concatenating the two sets of tokens along the hidden axis and then passing them through a *Linear* layer to reduce them back to the standard hidden size. These resulting tokens are then passed to the rest of the *Stage 2* ViT.

3.2 MultiViT Configurations for Ablation

MultiViT has three configuration parameters, *Mode*, *N*, and *R*.

Mode controls whether patch tokens are passed between *Stage 1* and *Stage 2*. In *Multi* mode, this is enabled, but in *Partial* mode it is disabled. N is a positive integer value that controls how many images are being attended across for each sample. R is a positive integer value that sets the resolution multiplier for *Stage 2*.

Mode and *R* determine in combination whether patch tokens and image patches are output from the *Attention Filter*. For *Multi-N-1* the *Attention Filter* outputs only composite patch tokens. For *Multi-N-2*, it outputs both composite patch tokens and a composite (high-resolution) image. For *Partial-N-1* and *Partial-N-2*, it only outputs a composite image to *Stage 2*.

The *Token Concatenator* is only used if both composite tokens and a composite image are required by the configuration.

4 Experiments

4.1 Dataset

The dataset used here is an internal clinical dataset gathered from consenting psoriasis patients. It is comprised of 1109 color images of 152 patients with demographics and clinical information. 763 images are professional medical photographs and 346 are self-taken photographs. Images are de-identified by digitally removing heads and features such as tattoos. Demographic and clinical data includes FST, PASI, and PGA.

Images range from 480 to 6016 pixels in width and 480 to 4640 pixels in height, with aspect ratios between 1 : 0.45 and 2.41 : 1. The dataset is augmented by randomly cropping up to 10% of the borders of each image. This is done before resampling the data to $(384, 384)$ for low resolution images and $(384 \times R, 384 \times R)$ for high resolution images so that the augmentation is consistent for low and high resolution images. 80% of the patients are used for the training fold and 20% kept as the test fold and never trained upon.

The dataset is heavily biased toward FSTs of *I-IV*. In the training fold, there are 104 patients with FSTs *I-IV* and 18 with FSTs *V-VI*. In the test fold, there are 24 patients with FSTs *I-IV* and 6 with FSTs *V-VI*.

4.2 Model

The model uses the HuggingFace [13] *ViTModel* as a donor architecture, with configuration and starting weights from *'google-vit-large-patch32-384'*. This model accepts images of 384×384 and has a patch size of 32, meaning there are 12×12 patches per image. Each model has 23 multi-head attention blocks with 16 channels and a hidden size of 1024. The model uses absolute positions that are learned during training. The model weights have no task heads; these are trained during our fine-tuning step.

We make use of two values from the dataset when training the model PASI and clinical severity. Two scores are provided for each patient, we use the score from the first rater throughout. The task heads are configured to be Multi Layer Perceptrons [11] with a hidden layer of size 128 or 256. The two configurations used during the experiments are (PASI(128) & PGA(128)) and (PASI(256) & PGA(128)).

The model is trained for 300 epochs. Fine-tuning is employed, with the embedding layers, the last 5 attention layers, and task heads unfrozen. Weight decay is set at 0.01 and the hidden layer dropout is set to 0.1. Learning rate is initialised to $1e-4$ and linearly decays over 300 epochs to $1.25e-7$.

5 Results and Discussion

Tables 1 and 2 show the performance of the different network configurations in terms of Mean Absolute Error (MAE) and Mean Signed Error (ME) for the PASI regression task.

Table 2 shows that *Baseline* is outperformed by all four configurations of MultiViT, coming last or second to last in all evaluation metrics.

Multi-3-1 has the best MAE for PASI and is within clinically acceptable inter-rater variance over the dataset as a whole, taken to be an MAE of 4.67 from 43 dermatologists reported by [8]. It has the second best MAE over FSTs I to IV.

All configurations tend to under evaluate PASI, although MultiViT improves this tendency over the *Baseline* configuration. Figure 2 presents this visually.

Interestingly, the MultiViT configurations with R set to 2 do not demonstrate a consistent improvement across the metrics evaluated. We note however that *Partial-3-2* significantly outperforms other configurations on FST V-VI for MAE and ME, and *Multi-3-2* has the best overall ME performance, indicating less tendency to under evaluate PASI.

Performance of all networks on FSTs V to VI indicates that more patients with these skin types are needed.

A direct comparison with the literature is complicated by lack of publicly available datasets and implementations. Current studies employ convolutional neural networks trained on professional medical photographs of clinical poses, demonstrating an MAE of 3.12 with a dataset of 14096 images from 2367 patients [8], and an MAE of 3.3 on a dataset of 2700 images of 60 patients [14] taken over treatment course.

Table 1. Mean Absolute Error (MAE) for various MultiViT configurations against the baseline ViT model. Lower scores are better. **Bold** entry indicates the best score. Entry in parentheses indicates the per-image MAE.

Task heads	Baseline	Multi-3-1	Multi-3-2	Partial-3-1	Partial-3-2
PASI(128)+PGA(128)	(5.361) 5.210	4.024	4.860	4.836	5.242
PASI(256)+PGA(128)	(5.281) 5.127	**3.877**	4.220	4.674	4.516

Table 2. MAE and Mean signed Error (ME), for the dataset as a whole and for FST I-IV vs. V-VI for Baseline and MultiViT configurations with PASI(256)+PGA(128) task heads. **Bold** indicates the best score for a given metric and *italics* indicates the second best score.

Metrics	Baseline	Multi-3-1	Multi-3-2	Partial-3-1	Partial-3-2
MAE (per-image)	5.281	—	—	—	—
MAE	5.127	**3.877**	*4.220*	4.674	4.516
MAE (I-IV)	3.968	*2.804*	**2.736**	3.402	4.283
MAE (V-VI)	9.763	*8.167*	10.158	9.761	**5.451**
ME	−3.192	*−2.402*	**−1.741**	−2.644	−2.721
ME (I-IV)	−1.717	−1.178	**0.117**	*−0.865*	−2.081
ME (V-VI)	−9.093	*−7.298*	−9.172	−9.761	**−5.281**

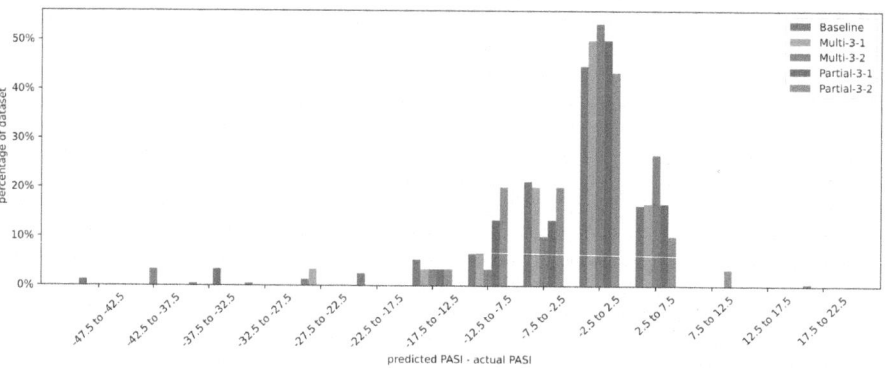

Fig. 2. Histograms of predicted PASI - actual PASI for the test fold of our psoriasis dataset. This figure highlights the tendency of all the different architectures to underestimate PASI.

6 Conclusion and Further Work

Our proof of concept method highlights that ViTs can be adapted to effectively handle the challenges posed by psoriasis. Our MAE of 3.877 is within a reported inter-rater MAE of 4.67, despite the limited size of our dataset. Critically, the ability to learn from a mixture of self-taken photos and clinical photos may open new avenues for remote app-based psoriasis monitoring.

The following are identified as limitations of this work:

Primarily, we are limited by the small size of our dataset and the lack of public psoriasis datasets with gold-standard annotations due in part to the identifiable and sensitive nature of skin photographs. We are in the process of greatly expanding our internal dataset, especially for FST $V - VI$.

We will further demonstrate this architecture on non-psoriasis datasets with public benchmarks. We are looking for other medical and non-medical tasks that benefit from efficient attention over multiple images. Additionally, many classification/regression tasks involve high resolution single images in which only small areas of the image are of importance, such as digital histopathology and dermoscopic images, and our method can be readily adapted to these.

There are a number of architectural improvements that we intend to make to MultiViT. These include but are not limited to adaptive patch geometry, attention scoring mechanism [1], a more general adaptive attention mechanism and the use of attention-based semantic segmentation to enhance token selection and model interpretability.

Acknowledgements. This research was supported by the Wellcome Engineering and Physical Sciences Research Council Centre for Medical Engineering at King's College London (WT 203148/Z/16/Z) and the UK Research and Innovation London Medical Imaging and the Artificial Intelligence Centre for Value-Based Healthcare. The Jade Consortium, funded by the Engineering and Physical Sciences Research Council (grant EP/T022205/1) provided compute for model training. The dataset was collected as part of Psoriasis Association (grant BSTOP50/5 [to CHS]), the National Institute for Health and Care Research (NIHR Advanced Fellowship NIHR302258 [to SKM] and NIHR Senior Investigator Award [to CHS]), under 20/YH/0135 ethics. Ben Murray is an affiliate of the AI Institute at KCL.

Disclosure of Interests. C. H. Smith reports departmental research funding as an investigator in the European Union's Innovative Medicines Initiative consortia involving multiple industry partners (see biomap-imi.eu and hippocrates-imi.eu for details). S. K. Mahil reports departmental income from AbbVie, Almirall, Eli Lilly, Janssen, Leo, Novartis, Pfizer, Sanofi, and UCB, outside the submitted work.

References

1. Abnar, S., Zuidema, W.: Quantifying attention flow in transformers. In: Jurafsky, D., Chai, J., Schluter, N., Tetreault, J. (eds.) Proceedings of the 58th Annual Meeting of the Association for Computational Linguistics, pp. 4190–4197. Association for Computational Linguistics, Online (2020). https://doi.org/10.18653/v1/2020.acl-main.385
2. Caron, M., et al.: Emerging properties in self-supervised vision transformers. In: Proceedings of the IEEE/CVF International Conference on Computer Vision (ICCV), pp. 9650–9660 (2021)
3. Chen, X., Liu, Z., Tang, H., Yi, L., Zhao, H., Han, S.: Sparsevit: revisiting activation sparsity for efficient high-resolution vision transformer. In: Proceedings of the IEEE/CVF Conference on Computer Vision and Pattern Recognition (CVPR), pp. 2061–2070 (2023)
4. Dehghani, M., et al.: Patch n' pack: Navit, a vision transformer for any aspect ratio and resolution. In: Oh, A., Naumann, T., Globerson, A., Saenko, K., Hardt, M., Levine, S. (eds.) Advances in Neural Information Processing Systems, vol. 36, pp. 2252–2274. Curran Associates, Inc. (2023)
5. Dosovitskiy, A., et al.: An image is worth 16×16 words: transformers for image recognition at scale. In: International Conference on Learning Representations (2021)

6. Fitzpatrick, T.B.: The validity and practicality of sun-reactive skin types I through VI. Arch. Dermatol. **124**(6), 869 (1988)
7. Fredriksson, T., Pettersson, U.: Severe psoriasis-oral therapy with a new retinoid. Dermatologica **157**(4), 238–244 (1978)
8. Huang, K., et al.: Artificial intelligence-based psoriasis severity assessment: real-world study and application. J. Med. Internet Res. **25**, e44932 (2023). https://doi.org/10.2196/44932
9. Ilse, M., Tomczak, J., Welling, M.: Attention-based deep multiple instance learning. In: Dy, J., Krause, A. (eds.) Proceedings of the 35th International Conference on Machine Learning. Proceedings of Machine Learning Research, vol. 80, pp. 2127–2136. PMLR (2018)
10. Liu, Z., et al.: Swin transformer: hierarchical vision transformer using shifted windows. In: Proceedings of the IEEE/CVF International Conference on Computer Vision (ICCV), pp. 10012–10022 (2021)
11. Rumelhart, D.E., Hinton, G.E., Williams, R.J.: Learning representations by back-propagating errors. Nature **323**(6088), 533–536 (1986)
12. Vaswani, A., et al.: Attention is all you need. In: Guyon, I., et al. (eds.) Advances in Neural Information Processing Systems, vol. 30. Curran Associates, Inc. (2017)
13. Wolf, T., et al.: Transformers: state-of-the-art natural language processing. In: Liu, Q., Schlangen, D. (eds.) Proceedings of the 2020 Conference on Empirical Methods in Natural Language Processing: System Demonstrations, pp. 38–45. Association for Computational Linguistics, Online (2020). https://doi.org/10.18653/v1/2020.emnlp-demos.6. https://aclanthology.org/2020.emnlp-demos.6
14. Xing, Y., et al.: Deep learning-based psoriasis assessment: harnessing clinical trial imaging for accurate psoriasis area severity index prediction. Digit. Biomarkers **8**(1), 13–21 (2024). https://doi.org/10.1159/000536499

Lesion Elevation Prediction from Skin Images Improves Diagnosis

Kumar Abhishek[✉][iD] and Ghassan Hamarneh[iD]

School of Computing Science, Simon Fraser University, Burnaby, Canada
{kabhishe,hamarneh}@sfu.ca

Abstract. While deep learning-based computer-aided diagnosis for skin lesion image analysis is approaching dermatologists' performance levels, there are several works showing that incorporating additional features such as shape priors, texture, color constancy, and illumination further improves the lesion diagnosis performance. In this work, we look at another clinically useful feature, skin lesion elevation, and investigate the feasibility of predicting and leveraging skin lesion elevation labels. Specifically, we use a deep learning model to predict image-level lesion elevation labels from 2D skin lesion images. We test the elevation prediction accuracy on the derm7pt dataset, and use the elevation prediction model to estimate elevation labels for images from five other datasets: ISIC 2016, 2017, and 2018 Challenge datasets, MSK, and DermoFit. We evaluate cross-domain generalization by using these estimated elevation labels as auxiliary inputs to diagnosis models, and show that these improve the classification performance, with AUROC improvements of up to 6.29% and 2.69% for dermoscopic and clinical images, respectively. The code is publicly available at https://github.com/sfu-mial/LesionElevation.

Keywords: skin lesion · lesion elevation · deep learning · diagnosis

1 Introduction

Skin cancer is highly prevalent globally and the most commonly diagnosed cancer in the USA [5] with over 5 million annual diagnoses [35]. Although it accounts for a small fraction of all skin cancers, melanoma is the deadliest form with an estimated 99,700 diagnoses and 8,290 deaths in 2024 in the USA alone, and timely diagnosis is critical as early detection results in a 99% estimated 5-year survival rate. Deep learning (DL)-based methods have proven to be successful in improving image-based clinical decision support systems with expert-level computer-aided dermatological diagnosis [10,21]. While DL-based methods have demonstrated remarkable performance, there is a considerable body of research showing that incorporating additional features, such as shape priors [33], texture [46],

Supplementary Information The online version contains supplementary material available at https://doi.org/10.1007/978-3-031-77610-6_5.

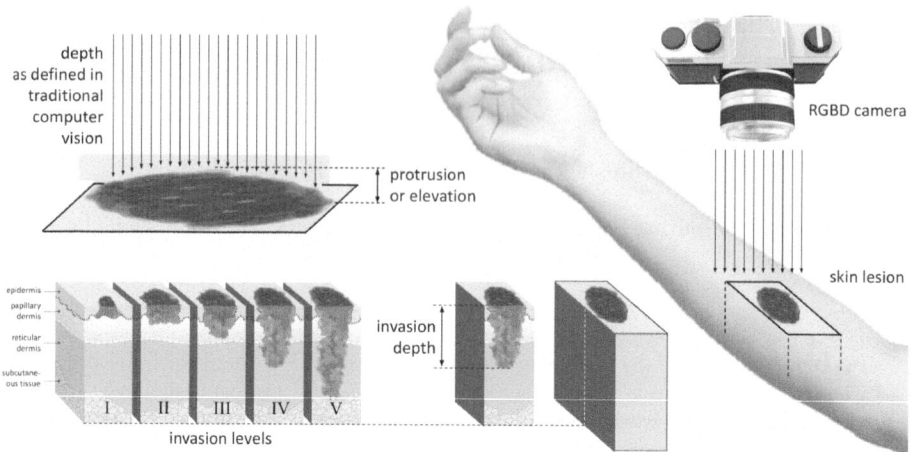

Fig. 1. Visualizing the difference between skin lesion elevation versus depth. Invasion levels inset figure courtesy of Melanoma Institute Australia [31].

color constancy [36], and illumination [2], can further improve skin lesion image analysis. Another feature that has been shown to enhance lesion diagnosis and clinical management prediction, using both classical machine learning [29] and DL methods [3,26,27,32,37], is lesion elevation. However, learning-based methods have yet to incorporate lesion elevation prediction into computerized diagnosis.

The American Cancer Society's ABCDE criteria include elevation (E) as one of the components [43]. Moreover, in the clinical setting, dermatologists often palpate the skin to examine the lesion when making a diagnosis [16]. Case in point, a study showed that palpation alone, without any visual assessment, was sufficient to correctly diagnose 14 of 16 cases [17]. With the rise of teledermatology, partly accelerated by external factors such as COVID-19 [4], one of the major reasons for dermatologists' dissatisfaction with teledermatology is the inability to palpate lesions [18,20]. This is particularly pressing for "store-and-forward" teledermatology, where images are captured and submitted alongside patient history, which has been adopted for its efficiency and low cost, is imperfect since *"even good quality photos are two-dimensional; raised lesions ... for example, may be difficult to distinguish from flat lesions of a similar colour"* [16]. Clinical and dermoscopic images of lesions do not capture elevation, and while it is recommended to capture tangential views of lesions in teledermatology, measuring elevation is not easy to do with limited camera views, making the examinations "less complete" [8,25]. Therefore, while teledermatology has the potential to improve triage, access to care for underserved communities, and patient convenience [15,24,34,40], it would greatly benefit from being able to leverage lesion elevation information as a proxy for in-person palpation. Solutions to bridge this gap could be either in the form of patient side hardware [28], which is expensive to develop, maintain, and deploy, or purely software-based approaches to estimate lesion elevation from single RGB images, which we focus on.

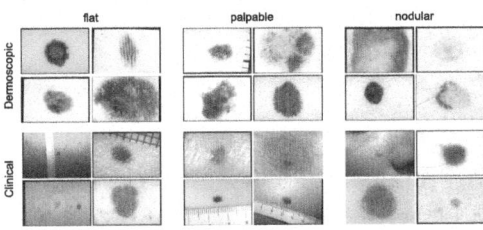 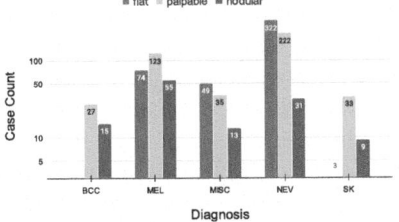

(a) Sample dermoscopic and clinical images from derm7pt showing the three image-level lesion elevation labels.

(b) Distribution of elevation. Note the absence of a clear diagnosis-to-elevation mapping.

Fig. 2. derm7pt dataset: (a) sample images categorized by elevation labels and (b) distribution of elevation labels across diagnoses.

Before proceeding, it is worth clarifying the difference in terminology vis-à-vis lesion "elevation" and "depth" (Fig. 1), and how these terms differ in their usage in dermatology compared to traditional computer vision. Lesion elevation refers to the lesion's surface and how it protrudes above the outer skin surface (epidermis). On the other hand, lesion depth or thickness, unlike the definition of depth in computer vision, refers to the depth of invasion of melanoma underneath the skin surface and is used for melanoma staging, measured using scales such as Breslow's depth [9] and Clark level [11].

While lesion elevation has been used along with other clinical metadata (e.g., gender, lesion location, and age) for skin lesion image analysis tasks and has shown to improve performance [3,26], to the best of our knowledge, there is no work that explores either the utility of elevation alone as a metadata, or the feasibility of predicting elevation from 2D RGB skin lesion images. In this work, we pose three research questions: (i) can we predict, with sufficient accuracy, lesion elevation from a single lesion image?; (ii) does lesion elevation alone, without any other metadata, improve lesion diagnosis?; (iii) can we leverage an elevation prediction model to infer elevations on datasets without ground truth elevation, thus potentially improving the diagnosis accuracies thereon? Our results show that the answer is affirmative to all these questions.

2 Method

The Dataset: Let $(\mathcal{X}, \mathcal{Y}, \mathcal{E})$ be the dataset of images, diagnosis labels, and elevation labels. Specifically, $\mathcal{X} = \{X_i\}_{i=1}^N$ is the set of skin images with corresponding diagnosis labels $\mathcal{Y} = \{Y_i\}_{i=1}^N$ and single image-level elevation labels $\mathcal{E} = \{E_i\}_{i=1}^N$, where $X_i \in \mathbb{R}^{H \times W \times 3}$, $Y_i \in \{1, 2, \cdots, N_D\}$, and $E_i \in \{1, 2, \cdots, N_E\}$, and N_D and N_E denote the total number of diagnosis and image-level elevation class labels, respectively.

A Diagnosis Prediction Model: A diagnosis prediction model f_D, parameterized by Θ_D, is trained to generate disease predictions from images,

$$\widehat{Y}_i = f_D(X_i; \Theta_D). \tag{1}$$

Leveraging Ground Truth Elevation Labels for Diagnosis Prediction: The f_D model architecture can also be modified to take the elevation label as an auxiliary input for diagnosis prediction,

$$\widehat{Y}_i = f_{DE}(X_i \oplus E_i; \Theta_{DE}), \tag{2}$$

where $\oplus$ is a combination operator.

Predicting Elevation Labels: Additionally, since we have images with corresponding image-level elevation labels, we can also train a DL-model g to predict elevation labels from an input image,

$$\widehat{E}_i = g(X_i; \Phi), \tag{3}$$

where $\widehat{E}_i \in \mathbb{R}^{N_E}$ is an N_E-element probabilistic prediction of the elevation label. We denote elevation class label with the highest predicted probability as $\widehat{E}_i^{\max} = \arg\max_j \widehat{E}_{ij}$. For example, if $N_E = 3$ and $\widehat{E}_i = [0.1, 0.7, 0.2]$, then $\widehat{E}_i^{\max} = 2$.

Leveraging Predicted Elevation Labels for Diagnosis Models: Finally, given a trained elevation prediction model g, we use this model to infer elevation labels (Eq. 3) on datasets without ground truth elevation, and use these labels as auxiliary inputs to re-train the diagnosis prediction model,

$$\widehat{Y}_i = f_{D\widehat{E}}(X_i \oplus \widehat{E}_i; \Theta_{D\widehat{E}}). \tag{4}$$

More details about exact model architectures, losses, and metrics for evaluation are discussed in the next section.

3 Results and Discussion

Datasets: Since skin lesion elevation data is expensive and difficult to acquire, there are, to the best of our knowledge, only 2 publicly available datasets with lesion elevation labels: PAD-UFES-20 [38] and derm7pt [26]. PAD-UFES-20 contains 2,298 smartphone camera images of skin lesions with binary labels indicating if a lesion is elevated or not, whereas derm7pt contains 1,011 cases with clinical and dermoscopic images with 3 elevation class labels: "flat", "palpable", and "nodular", and because of the relatively more granular elevations and the presence of two imaging modalities in the latter, we use derm7pt for our experiments. We partition the dataset with elevation label-based stratification into training, validation, and testing sets in the ratio of 70:15:15, accounting for the inherent class imbalance: "flat": 448 cases, "palpable": 440 cases, "nodular": 123 cases. See Fig. 2 (a,b) for sample images from different elevation labels and

Table 1. Results (accuracy and area under the ROC curve (for skin lesion elevation prediction from clinical and dermoscopic images of derm7pt. Reported values are the mean ± std. dev. averaged over 3 runs. Numbers in [·] present the 95% CI values. Bold values denote the best values for the metrics.

Model Architecture	# Params (M)	Clinical Images Accuracy ↑	AUROC ↑	Dermoscopic Images Accuracy ↑	AUROC ↑
MobileNetV2	2.228	0.8234 ± 0.0515 [0.7954, 0.8514]	0.7474 ± 0.0496 [0.7251, 0.7697]	0.8039 ± 0.0552 [0.7780, 0.8298]	0.7789 ± 0.0536 [0.7549, 0.8029]
MobileNetV3L	4.206	0.7969 ± 0.0561 [0.7712, 0.8226]	0.7326 ± 0.0535 [0.7111, 0.7541]	0.7908 ± 0.0576 [0.7659, 0.8157]	0.7481 ± 0.0552 [0.7260, 0.7702]
EfficientNet-B0	4.011	0.8190 ± 0.0582 [0.7914, 0.8466]	0.7444 ± 0.0570 [0.7222, 0.7666]	0.8257 ± 0.0573 [0.7978, 0.8536]	0.8088 ± 0.0563 [0.7825, 0.8351]
EfficientNet-B1	6.517	0.8013 ± 0.0604 [0.7752, 0.8274]	0.7284 ± 0.0602 [0.7071, 0.7497]	0.8344 ± 0.0604 [0.8056, 0.8632]	0.8033 ± 0.0576 [0.7774, 0.8292]
DenseNet-121	6.957	0.8146 ± 0.0589 [0.7874, 0.8418]	0.7405 ± 0.0568 [0.7186, 0.7624]	0.8301 ± 0.0589 [0.8018, 0.8584]	0.7931 ± 0.0544 [0.7680, 0.8182]
VGG-16	14.724	**0.8543 ± 0.0632** [0.8229, 0.8857]	**0.8220 ± 0.0610** [0.7941, 0.8499]	**0.8475 ± 0.0592** [0.8173, 0.8777]	**0.8152 ± 0.0582** [0.7883, 0.8421]
ResNet-18	11.178	0.8190 ± 0.0582 [0.7914, 0.8466]	0.7321 ± 0.0555 [0.7106, 0.7536]	0.7996 ± 0.0536 [0.7740, 0.8252]	0.7653 ± 0.0530 [0.7422, 0.7884]
ResNet-50	23.514	0.7660 ± 0.0607 [0.7425, 0.7895]	0.6927 ± 0.0576 [0.6732, 0.7122]	0.8083 ± 0.0576 [0.7820, 0.8346]	0.7586 ± 0.0536 [0.7359, 0.7813]

diagnosis-wise distribution of elevation labels, respectively. We group the diagnosis labels in derm7pt into 5 classes as originally proposed by Kawahara et al. [26]: BCC (basal cell carcinoma), MEL (melanoma), NEV (nevi), SK (seborrheic keratosis), and MISC (miscellaneous). Although some elevation labels appear more or less frequently with certain diagnoses, we note that there is no direct diagnosis-elevation mapping, and elevation labels are distributed across all diagnoses in our dataset (an exception is that BCC and SK have almost no "flat" elevations).

In addition, we also use five other datasets for diagnosis prediction that do not contain ground truth elevation labels: (i) ISIC 2016 [23], (ii) ISIC 2017 [13], (iii) ISIC 2018 [12], (iv) MSK [1], and (v) DermoFit [7], where (i) is a binary classification dataset and all others are multi-class classification datasets. Note that (i)-(iv) are dermoscopic image datasets while (v) contains clinical images. For (i)-(iii), we use the standard dataset partitions, and for (iv), (v), we generate training, validation, and testing partitions in 70:10:20 ratio.

Experiment 1: Can we predict skin lesion elevation labels from images alone? To test the feasibility of predicting skin lesion elevation labels directly from images, we train eight different DL model architectures on the derm7pt dataset. Specifically, we train elevation prediction models g that, given a skin lesion image X_i, predict the elevation label $\widehat{E}_i$ (Eq. 3). We choose the architectures from a variety of families, covering a large range of model sizes (see parameter counts in Table 1): ResNet-18 and ResNet-50, MobileNetV2 and

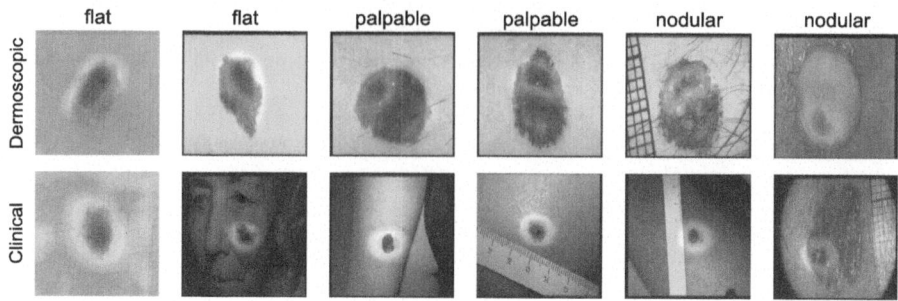

Fig. 3. Visualizing class activation maps for skin lesion elevation label prediction for dermoscopic and clinical images, generated through GradCAM. Notice how the activation areas are focused around the lesion regions, indicating that the prediction model g does not learn to rely on spurious features or "shortcuts".

MobileNetV3L, DenseNet-121, EfficientNetB0 and EfficientNetB1, and VGG-16. For all architectures except VGG-16, we modify the final layer to predict 3 classes ($N_E = 3$ for derm7pt). However, since a large number of parameters in VGG-16 emanate from the fully-connected layers, we modify the architecture by replacing these fully-connected layers with a global average pooling layer [44]. We use ImageNet-pretrained weights for initialization. All models are trained for 50 epochs with stochastic gradient descent and momentum of 0.9, weight decay of 1e-4, batch size of 32, and a learning rate of 1e-2 which was decayed by a factor of 0.1 every 10 epochs. All images are resized to 224 × 224 and we augment the images with horizontal and vertical flips and rotations in multiple of 90°. To account for the inherent class imbalance, we use the cross-entropy loss with median frequency balancing to assign class weights, i.e. class-wise weights in the loss calculation are weighted by the ratio of the median of class frequencies in the entire training set to each class's frequency [6,19]. The model with the best area under the ROC curve (AUROC) on the validation set was chosen for evaluation. All experiments were repeated 3 times for robust results.

Table 1 lists the quantitative results for elevation prediction on both clinical and dermoscopic images in the derm7pt dataset. We report mean and the std. dev. of the overall accuracy of classification as well as the AUROC across 3 repeated runs, as well as the 95% confidence intervals (CIs). We observe that while all architectures are able to predict elevation labels reasonably accurately, the VGG-16 model performs the best across both imaging modalities. To ascertain that this performance is not due to the model learning spurious features or "shortcuts" in the images to make the predictions, we generate the class activation maps (CAMs) for the VGG-16 model using GradCAM [42]. Sample CAMs for both modalities and all elevation labels are shown in Fig. 3. We observe that the CAMs are almost completely contained within and around the lesion regions, suggesting that the elevation predictions are indeed based on lesion fea-

Table 2. Leveraging inferred elevation labels (Eq. 4), either "discrete" ($f_{D\widehat{E}\text{max}}$) or "probabilistic" ($f_{D\widehat{E}}$) improves diagnosis performance over no elevation labels (f_D). Reported metrics are mean ± std. dev. over 3 repeated runs. We also report statistical significance tests (McNemar's mid-p test) and effect sizes (Cohen's d).

Dataset	Experiment	Metrics						Statistical Tests	
		Bal. Acc. ↑	Accuracy ↑	Precision ↑	Recall ↑	F1-score ↑	AUROC ↑	p-value	Cohen's d
DermoFit [7]	f_D	0.8145 ± 0.0170	0.9331 ± 0.0051	0.8121 ± 0.0194	0.8145 ± 0.0170	0.8103 ± 0.0149	0.8856 ± 0.0092	-	-
	$f_{D\widehat{E}}$	0.8586 ± 0.0003	0.9480 ± 0.0003	0.8449 ± 0.0004	0.8586 ± 0.0003	0.8511 ± 0.0002	0.9125 ± 0.0001	9.87e-03	4.1348
	$f_{D\widehat{E}\text{max}}$	0.8541 ± 0.0009	0.9497 ± 0.0010	0.8466 ± 0.0019	0.8541 ± 0.0009	0.8500 ± 0.0015	0.9108 ± 0.0007	7.08e-03	3.8626
MSK [1]	f_D	0.6004 ± 0.0010	0.8446 ± 0.0159	0.6156 ± 0.0302	0.6004 ± 0.0010	0.5843 ± 0.0091	0.7374 ± 0.0017	-	-
	$f_{D\widehat{E}}$	0.6514 ± 0.0019	0.8833 ± 0.0018	0.7228 ± 0.0037	0.6514 ± 0.0019	0.6726 ± 0.0013	0.7747 ± 0.0014	4.04e-12	23.9526
	$f_{D\widehat{E}\text{max}}$	0.6352 ± 0.0047	0.8878 ± 0.0011	0.7169 ± 0.0210	0.6352 ± 0.0047	0.6638 ± 0.0021	0.7632 ± 0.0038	4.10e-11	8.7647
ISIC 2016 [23]	f_D	0.7008 ± 0.0307	0.8100 ± 0.0474	0.7208 ± 0.0524	0.7008 ± 0.0307	0.6998 ± 0.0338	0.7008 ± 0.3070	-	-
	$f_{D\widehat{E}}$	0.7344 ± 0.0124	0.8545 ± 0.0131	0.7615 ± 0.0022	0.7344 ± 0.0124	0.7467 ± 0.0059	0.7344 ± 0.0124	7.36e-02	0.1547
	$f_{D\widehat{E}\text{max}}$	0.7574 ± 0.0183	0.8391 ± 0.0165	0.7513 ± 0.0213	0.7574 ± 0.0183	0.7515 ± 0.0045	0.7574 ± 0.0183	8.75e-02	0.2603
ISIC 2017 [13]	f_D	0.6926 ± 0.0207	0.8296 ± 0.0072	0.7303 ± 0.0160	0.6926 ± 0.0207	0.7060 ± 0.0133	0.6926 ± 0.0207	-	-
	$f_{D\widehat{E}}$	0.7417 ± 0.0030	0.8500 ± 0.0060	0.7634 ± 0.0118	0.7417 ± 0.0030	0.7513 ± 0.0036	0.7417 ± 0.0030	3.06e-02	3.3198
	$f_{D\widehat{E}\text{max}}$	0.7555 ± 0.0040	0.8583 ± 0.0044	0.7776 ± 0.0095	0.7555 ± 0.0040	0.7644 ± 0.0018	0.7555 ± 0.0040	9.80e-03	4.2192
ISIC 2018 [12]	f_D	0.7949 ± 0.0303	0.9450 ± 0.0055	0.7601 ± 0.0426	0.7949 ± 0.0303	0.7690 ± 0.0413	0.8808 ± 0.0190	-	-
	$f_{D\widehat{E}}$	0.8481 ± 0.0016	0.9668 ± 0.0021	0.8314 ± 0.0064	0.8481 ± 0.0016	0.8390 ± 0.0043	0.9132 ± 0.0014	7.54e-03	2.4051
	$f_{D\widehat{E}\text{max}}$	0.8524 ± 0.0024	0.9641 ± 0.0032	0.8250 ± 0.0102	0.8524 ± 0.0024	0.8376 ± 0.0046	0.9143 ± 0.0012	3.52e-03	2.4885

tures. Since VGG-16 most accurately predicts elevation for both modalities, we use this model architecture for all subsequent experiments.

Experiment 2: Do ground truth elevation labels help improve lesion diagnosis? For this experiment, we train lesion diagnosis models f_{DE} (Eq. 2) that leverage ground truth elevation labels as auxiliary inputs and compare their diagnosis performance to "vanilla" diagnosis models f_D trained without any elevation labels (Eq. 1). To combine the elevation labels as inputs along with the lesion image (i.e., the $\oplus$ operator in Eq. 2), we concatenate the one-hot encoded elevation labels for each image to the output of VGG-16's global-average pooling layer, which is then passed to the final classification layer, thus adding only a minimal number of parameters ($N_E \times N_D$, i.e., the number of elevation labels × the number of diagnosis classes). The training details (optimizer, loss, number of epochs, learning rate) for both f_{DE} and f_D remain the same.

We observe that for clinical images, leveraging ground truth elevation labels for diagnosis prediction (f_{DE}) improves the performance [overall accuracy, AUROC]: [0.8569, 0.6820] compared to diagnosis without elevation (f_D): [0.8464, 0.6331]. A similar improvement is noted for dermoscopic images: the performance with elevation labels: [0.9216, 0.8703] is an improvement over that of a "vanilla" diagnosis model: [0.9137, 0.8431]. This improvement in AUROC of 4.89% and 2.72% for clinical and dermoscopic images, respectively, is consistent with findings from previous works [3,26] that showed that using elevation labels along with other metadata is beneficial for lesion diagnosis prediction.

Experiment 3: Can inferred elevation labels improve lesion diagnosis? Having established that it is possible, with a reasonable accuracy, to predict elevation labels from lesion images, and that elevation labels improve lesion diagnosis, the natural next question is if we can infer lesion elevation on datasets that do not contain elevation labels, and if diagnosis prediction models trained with these inferred elevation labels also improve diagnosis accuracy. Therefore, given a trained elevation prediction model g, we infer elevation labels for all images in 5 skin lesion datasets that do not have elevation labels: ISIC 2016, ISIC 2017, ISIC 2018, MSK, and DermoFit. We note that there is a considerable domain shift between these skin lesion datasets [45], and therefore we use modality specific elevation prediction models for inferring elevation labels, i.e., the elevation prediction model g trained on derm7pt's dermoscopic images is used for the first 4 datasets, and g trained on derm7pt's clinical images is used for DermoFit. Next, for each dataset, we train three prediction models: (i) diagnosis prediction without any elevation labels (f_D), (ii) diagnosis prediction with probabilistic "soft" inferred elevation labels ($f_{D\widehat{E}}$), and (iii) diagnosis prediction with "discrete" inferred elevation labels ($f_{D\widehat{E}^{\max}}$). Model training details remain the same as Experiment 1, except the models are trained for longer (20 epochs for ISIC 2018 and 50 epochs for the other datasets), since these datasets are larger than derm7pt. We report several classification metrics: balanced accuracy, overall accuracy, precision, recall, F1-score, and AUROC, and train each model thrice for robustness. In addition to these metrics, we also perform statistical analysis: McNemar's mid-p test [22,30] and effect size (Cohen's d [14]) for comparing $\{f_{D\widehat{E}}, f_{D\widehat{E}^{\max}}\}$ AUROC predictions to those from f_D.

Quantitative results in Table 2 show that leveraging estimated lesion elevation labels consistently improves diagnosis performance across all datasets: up to 6.29% and 2.69% improvements in AUROC for dermoscopic and clinical images, respectively. Moreover, for all datasets except ISIC 2016, this improvement is statistically significant at $p < 0.05$. Similarly, Cohen's d estimates indicate "huge" effect sizes for these four datasets and "small" effect size for ISIC 2016 [41]. While both "soft" and "discrete" estimates of the elevation label appear to improve diagnosis performance, interestingly, there does not appear to be a consistent pattern of one of them outperforming the other. This is especially surprising since the "soft" labels would convey the uncertainty associated with the elevation prediction, and intuitively, they would be more informative. Nevertheless, we shelve this observation for a future investigation.

4 Conclusion

In this work, we showed that it is possible to predict image-level lesion elevation labels directly from 2D RGB skin lesion images with sufficient accuracy, and that these estimated elevation labels do indeed help improve lesion diagnosis on other datasets, improving AUROC by up to 6.29% and 2.69% on dermoscopic and clinical images, respectively. The ability to predict lesion elevation from 2D images, in addition to improving computer-aided diagnosis, offers the potential to improve teledermatology consults by offering practitioners access to useful estimates of clinical information otherwise unavailable in virtual consultations. Our experiments with off-the-shelf monocular depth prediction models [39] from natural computer vision failed to generate any usable depth maps (see Fig. SM1 in the Supplementary Material), and we postulate that this may be because of the difference in scale of depth that these models are trained on (several orders of magnitude larger than skin lesion elevation) as well as the scene anisotropy of the images they are trained on (natural images generally have a depth anisotropy where the lower parts of the image are closer to the camera plane, which is typically not true for skin lesion images). Therefore, in future work, we would like to explore the feasibility, accuracy, and utility of reconstructing dense elevation maps from single RGB images, specific to skin lesions. Another future direction would be improving the elevation prediction accuracy, which may help reach the upper bound of performance improvement achieved when using ground truth elevation labels. Finally, we would also like to explore using multiple datasets for training elevation labels' prediction models to alleviate any potential biases emanating from using a single dataset (derm7pt).

Acknowledgments. The authors would like to thank Jeremy Kawahara, Manolis Savva, and Aditi Jain for helpful discussions on this work, and are grateful for the computational resources provided by NVIDIA Corporation and Digital Research Alliance of Canada (formerly Compute Canada). Partial funding for this project was provided by the Natural Sciences and Engineering Research Council of Canada (NSERC RGPIN/06752-2020).

Disclosure of Interests. The authors have no competing interests to declare.

References

1. International Skin Imaging Collaboration (ISIC): Melanoma Project - ISIC Archive (2016). https://www.isic-archive.com/. Accessed 01 Mar 2024
2. Abhishek, K., et al.: Illumination-based transformations improve skin lesion segmentation in dermoscopic images. In: CVPRW (2020)
3. Abhishek, K., et al.: Predicting the clinical management of skin lesions using deep learning. Sci. Rep. (2021)
4. AlAbdulkareem, A.: Palpation in dermatology, will covid-19 be the last straw? Dermatol. Ther. (2021)
5. American Cancer Society: Cancer Facts & Figures 2024 (2024). https://www.cancer.org/research/cancer-facts-statistics/all-cancer-facts-figures/2024-cancer-facts-figures.html. Accessed 01 Mar 2024
6. Badrinarayanan, V., et al.: Segnet: a deep convolutional encoder-decoder architecture for image segmentation. IEEE Trans. Pattern Anal. Mach. Intell. (2017)
7. Ballerini, L., et al.: A color and texture based hierarchical K-NN approach to the classification of non-melanoma skin lesions. In: Color Medical Image Analysis (2013)
8. Bashshur, R.L., et al.: The empirical foundations of teledermatology: a review of the research evidence. Telemed. J. E Health (2015)
9. Breslow, A.: Thickness, cross-sectional areas and depth of invasion in the prognosis of cutaneous melanoma. Ann. Surg. (1970)
10. Brinker, T.J., et al.: Deep learning outperformed 136 of 157 dermatologists in a head-to-head dermoscopic melanoma image classification task. Eur. J. Cancer (2019)

11. Clark, W.H., Jr., et al.: The histogenesis and biologic behavior of primary human malignant melanomas of the skin. Cancer Res. (1969)
12. Codella, N., et al.: Skin lesion analysis toward melanoma detection 2018: a challenge hosted by the International Skin Imaging Collaboration (ISIC). arXiv:1902.03368 (2019)
13. Codella, N.C., et al.: Skin lesion analysis toward melanoma detection: a challenge at the 2017 international symposium on biomedical imaging (ISBI), hosted by the international skin imaging collaboration (ISIC). In: ISBI (2018)
14. Cohen, J.: Statistical Power Analysis for the Behavioral Sciences. Routledge (2013)
15. Coustasse, A., et al.: Use of teledermatology to improve dermatological access in rural areas. Telemed. J. E Health (2019)
16. Cox, N.H.: Palpation of the skin – an important issue. J. R. Soc. Med. (2006)
17. Cox, N.H.: A literally blinded trial of palpation in dermatologic diagnosis. J. Am. Acad. Dermatol. (2007)
18. Eedy, D., et al.: Teledermatology: a review. Br. J. Dermatol. (2001)
19. Eigen, D., et al.: Predicting depth, surface normals and semantic labels with a common multi-scale convolutional architecture. In: ICCV (2015)
20. English, J., et al.: Has teledermatology in the UK finally failed? Br. J. Dermatol. (2007)
21. Esteva, A., et al.: Dermatologist-level classification of skin cancer with deep neural networks. Nature (2017)
22. Fagerland, M.W., et al.: The mcnemar test for binary matched-pairs data: mid-p and asymptotic are better than exact conditional. BMC Med. Res. Methodol. (2013)
23. Gutman, D., et al.: Skin lesion analysis toward melanoma detection: a challenge at the International Symposium on Biomedical Imaging (ISBI) 2016, hosted by the International Skin Imaging Collaboration (ISIC). arXiv:1605.01397 (2016)
24. Hwang, J.K., et al.: Review of teledermatology: lessons learned from the covid-19 pandemic. Am. J. Clin. Dermatol. (2024)
25. Jahnke, M., et al.: Pediatric teledermatology (2022). https://www.hmpgloballearningnetwork.com/site/thederm/cover-story/pediatric-teledermatology. Accessed 01 Mar 2024
26. Kawahara, J., et al.: Seven-point checklist and skin lesion classification using multitask multimodal neural nets. IEEE J. Biomed. Health Inform. (2019)
27. Kharazmi, P., et al.: A feature fusion system for basal cell carcinoma detection through data-driven feature learning and patient profile. Skin Res. Technol. (2018)
28. Kim, K.: Roughness based perceptual analysis towards digital skin imaging system with haptic feedback. Skin Res. Technol. (2016)
29. Li, X., et al.: Depth data improves skin lesion segmentation. In: MICCAI (2009)
30. McNemar, Q.: Note on the sampling error of the difference between correlated proportions or percentages. Psychometrika (1947)
31. Melanoma Institute Australia: Melanoma diagnosis. https://melanoma.org.au/for-patients/melanoma-diagnosis/. Accessed 01 Mar 2024
32. Mendes, C.F.S.d.F., et al.: Deep and handcrafted features from clinical images combined with patient information for skin cancer diagnosis. Chaos Solitons Fractals (2022)
33. Mirikharaji, Z., et al.: Star shape prior in fully convolutional networks for skin lesion segmentation. In: MICCAI (2018)
34. Morenz, A.M., et al.: Evaluation of barriers to telehealth programs and dermatological care for American Indian individuals in rural communities. JAMA Dermatol. (2019)

35. Nagarajan, P., et al.: Keratinocyte carcinomas: current concepts and future research priorities. Clin. Cancer Res. (2019)
36. Hua Ng, J., et al.: The effect of color constancy algorithms on semantic segmentation of skin lesions. In: SPIE Medical Imaging (2019)
37. Pacheco, A.G., et al.: The impact of patient clinical information on automated skin cancer detection. Comput. Biol. Med. (2020)
38. Pacheco, A.G., et al.: PAD-UFES-20: a skin lesion dataset composed of patient data and clinical images collected from smartphones. Data Brief (2020)
39. Ranftl, R., et al.: Towards robust monocular depth estimation: mixing datasets for zero-shot cross-dataset transfer. IEEE Trans. Pattern Anal. Mach. Intell. (2022)
40. Santosa, A., et al.: Teledermatology in an emergency department: benefits and gaps. BMC Emerg. Med. (2023)
41. Sawilowsky, S.S.: New effect size rules of thumb. J. Mod. Appl. Stat. Methods (2009)
42. Selvaraju, R.R., et al.: Grad-CAM: visual explanations from deep networks via gradient-based localization. In: ICCV (2017)
43. Strayer, S.M., et al.: Diagnosing skin malignancy: assessment of predictive clinical criteria and risk factors. J. Fam. Pract. (2003). https://www.mdedge.com/familymedicine/article/60122/diagnosing-skin-malignancy-assessment-predictive-clinical-criteria-and
44. Yan, Y., et al.: Melanoma recognition via visual attention. In: IPMI (2019)
45. Yoon, C., et al.: Generalizable feature learning in the presence of data bias and domain class imbalance with application to skin lesion classification. In: MICCAI (2019)
46. Zhang, L., et al.: Automatic skin lesion segmentation by coupling deep fully convolutional networks and shallow network with textons. J. Med. Imaging (2019)

Proceedings of the Seventh International Workshop on Interpretability of Machine Intelligence in Medical Image Computing (iMIMIC 2024)

DWARF: Disease-Weighted Network for Attention Map Refinement

Haozhe Luo[1], Aurélie Pahud de Mortanges[1], Oana Inel[2], and Mauricio Reyes[1(✉)]

[1] ARTORG Center for Biomedical Engineering Research, University of Bern, Bern, Switzerland
haozhe.luo@uzh.ch
[2] University of Zurich, Zurich, Switzerland

Abstract. The interpretability of deep learning is crucial for evaluating the reliability of medical imaging models and reducing the risks of inaccurate patient diagnoses. This study addresses the "human-*out*-of-the-loop" and "trustworthiness" issues in medical image analysis by integrating medical professionals into the interpretability process and model guidance. We propose a disease-weighted attention map refinement network (DWARF) that leverages expert feedback to enhance model relevance and accuracy. Our method employs cyclic training [13] to iteratively improve diagnostic performance, generating precise and interpretable feature maps. Experimental results demonstrate significant improvements in interpretability and diagnostic accuracy on three publically-available multi-label chest X-ray datasets. The proposed DWARF approach fosters effective collaboration between AI systems and healthcare professionals, ultimately aiming to improve patient outcomes. The code is available on https://github.com/Roypic/DWARF.

1 Introduction

Machine learning (ML) techniques, especially deep learning (DL) have significantly expanded in both research and industrial sectors, particularly with the advancements in deep neural networks (DNN). The impact and potential repercussions of these technologies have become too significant to overlook. In certain applications, failure is unacceptable; for example, a temporary malfunction in a computer vision algorithm for autonomous vehicles can result in fatalities. In the medical field, the stakes are even higher as human lives are directly affected. Early detection of diseases is crucial for patient recovery and for preventing the progression of illnesses to more severe stages. Despite recent promising results from machine learning methods [3,11,12,18,27–29], current methods are not without imperfections [7,14,23]. Specifically, many medical AI systems

Supplementary Information The online version contains supplementary material available at https://doi.org/10.1007/978-3-031-77610-6_6.

still struggle with issues such as short-cut learning [5] and misattribution [6], which can hamper the reliability of a medical AI system.

The significance of interpretability in medical imaging arises from the crucial need for transparency, trust in healthcare applications of AI, and ultimately ensuring patient safety. Traditionally, medical imaging analysis prioritized accuracy, but with the increasing integration of AI, the emphasis has shifted towards creating robust, understandable and explainable AI systems. The goal of explainable AI (XAI) is to make AI decision-making processes in medical imaging more comprehensible, thereby enhancing reliability and enabling healthcare professionals to effectively integrate AI tools into clinical practice while ensuring patient safety [1,24]. Current XAI methods interpret model outputs through various means, but due to the inherent uncertainty and complexity of deep learning patterns, translating these into intuitive interpretations for users remains difficult. This situation demands transparency and active involvement of medical professionals to ensure accuracy and relevance [4,17].

Saliency map-based techniques are extensively utilized in XAI for medical imaging due to their capability to highlight critical regions in medical images that influence model predictions. These techniques enhance transparency and trust in AI-driven diagnostic tools by visually representing areas of interest, such as tumors or lesions [2]. Methods like Grad-CAM [20], Integrated Gradients [22], and SmoothGrad [21] provide explanations by generating class-specific localization maps and reducing noise. Consequently, saliency maps play a crucial role in making AI decisions interpretable and justifiable in clinical settings.

In this work, we tackle the "human-*out*-of-the-loop" and "trustworthiness" issues in medical image analysis by incorporating medical professionals into the interpretability process [16]. By leveraging their insights, we enhance interpretability maps, aligning deep learning explanations more closely with expert knowledge. This approach enhances the relevance and utility of deep learning interpretations in medical diagnostics through expert feedback. To be specific, in this work, we are aiming to address the imperfect alignment between expert knowledge and corresponding AI-generated visual regions [26]. In this approach, we use the clinicians' attention annotations as visual guidance during the classification model training to simultaneously optimise attention maps and classification performance. Through extensive experiments, DWARF outperforms other baselines on both classification and attention map performance across different datasets. Single-blind tests on clinicians' preferences reveal that DWARF significantly enhances the usability of AI-assisted disease classification in clinical settings.

2 Method

In this section, we introduce DWARF from three aspects: architecture and training strategy, losses and network initialization.

Architecture and Training Strategy: In medical imaging, different findings reveal distinct visual cues crucial for accurate diagnosis. For instance, in chest X-

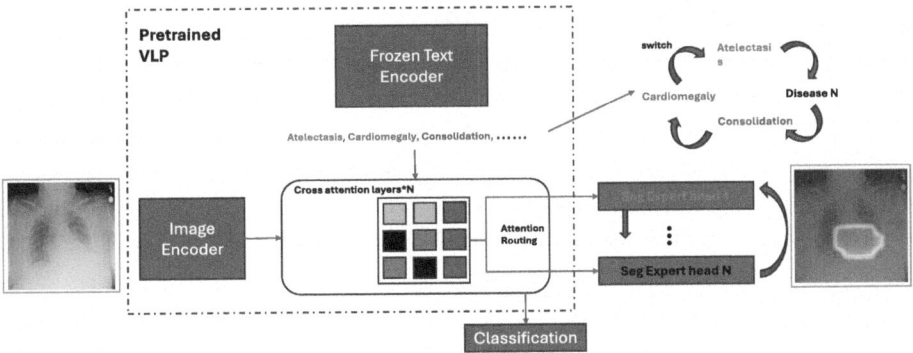

Fig. 1. Flow chart of finetuning the classification model. Our method trains single disease each epoch with disease name as prompt. For each disease, we add an additional head to map unrefined attention to refined segmentation map.

rays, Atelectasis is typically indicated by a localized reduction in lung volume and compensatory crowding of nearby ribs. To refine the saliency map with finding-related prior knowledge, we introduce our DWARF module, as shown in Fig. 1. The overall structure of DWARF consists of a pretrained Vision-Language Model (VLM), denoted as f_{vlm}, and segmentation expert heads f_{heads}. For a multi-modality model, it is hard to directly optimize cross attention maps because of the differences between human and model's attention maps human [25], as well as their different scale values. To address this, we utilize the segmentation expert heads to project the cross attention map denoted as $M_c \in \mathbb{R}^{h \times w}$ of class c where c is in a collection of different findings' labels N. Finally we obtain the segmentation map $M'_c = f_{\text{head}}(M_c)$. To accumulate finding-specific knowledge, we introduce a cyclic training process. The cyclic training mechanism is designed to iteratively refine the network's understanding and segmentation of specific findings. By incorporating cyclic training, the network can effectively refine its ability to identify and segment specific medical findings, leading to improved diagnostic performance. The overall training pseudo code is shown in Algorithm 1.

Loss Function: In our framework, we employ the cross-entropy loss, denoted as $\mathcal{L}_{cls}$, for multi-label classification tasks. Additionally, we use a modified Dice loss, $\mathcal{L}_{seg}$, optimized for attention maps. Attention maps in medical image analysis are critical for detecting disease-related markers. Training and validation typically focus on positive samples, which may cause models to overestimate certain features, leading to false positives. Our False Positive Suppression technique mitigates this by adjusting the Dice score to penalize false positives.

The standard metric, the Soft Dice Score, is mathematically represented as:

$$\mathcal{L}_{\text{Dice}} = \frac{2 \cdot |X \cap Y| + \alpha + \varepsilon}{|X| + |Y| + \alpha + \varepsilon} \quad (1)$$

Algorithm 1. Training Process for DWARF

Input: Multi-label dataset D_{multi}, backbone $N_{backbone}$, Segmentation head N_{head}, .Ground truth G
Output: Optimized network parameters θ
1: **Data Preparation:**
2: Decompose D_{multi} into single-label datasets D_{single}
3: **for** each finding f in D_{multi} **do**
4: $\quad D_{single}[f] \leftarrow$ createSingleLabelDataset(D_{multi}, f)
5: **end for**
6: **Segmentation and Classification:**
7: **for** each $D_{single}[f]$ **do**
8: $\quad$ **for** each image I in $D_{single}[f]$ **do**
9: $\quad\quad M_c[I] \leftarrow N_{head}^f(N_{backbone}(I))$
10: $\quad\quad C_{output}[I], L_{seg}, L_{cls} \leftarrow$ processImage($I, M_c[I], G[I]$)
11: $\quad\quad \theta \leftarrow$ updateParams(θ, L_{seg}, L_{cls})
12: $\quad$ **end for**
13: **end for**
14: **Iterative Refinement:**
15: **for** each epoch **do**
16: $\quad \theta \leftarrow$ refineParams($D_{single}, N_{backbone}, N_{head}, G, \theta$)
17: **end for**
18: Return θ

where X and Y are sets representing the predicted and true regions, respectively, α is a smoothing constant to prevent division by zero, and ε ensures numerical stability.

To specifically address false positives, we define:

$$\mathcal{L}_{\text{seg}} = \frac{2 \cdot |X \cap Y| + \alpha + \varepsilon}{|X| + \text{adjusted}|Y| + \alpha + \varepsilon} \quad (2)$$

$$\text{adjusted}|Y| = |Y| + (w_{\text{FP}} - 1) \cdot \text{FP} \quad (3)$$

Here, FP is the count of false positives, and w_{FP} is the weighting factor penalizing each false positive.

The combined loss function, aimed at minimizing, is expressed as:

$$\mathcal{L} = \lambda \mathcal{L}_{seg} + (1 - \lambda) \mathcal{L}_{cls} \quad (4)$$

where α adjusts the emphasis on attention annotations.

Model Initialization: We introduce a simple yet effective initialization approach, called **Identity Enhanced Initialization (IEI)** technique, to address the limitations of random or simplistic initializations in medical image segmentation. DWARF utilizes the text encoder initialized with Med-KEBERT's citech6zhang2023knowledge pretrained weights and adopts the architecture from DeViDe [12] for the image encoder and cross-attention layers. Random initialization of disease-specific segmentation heads which in our experience can lead

(a) Random initialization   (b) IEI initialization

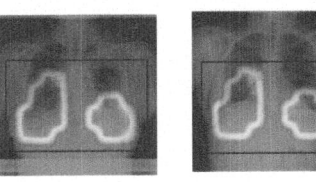 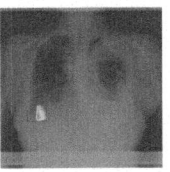 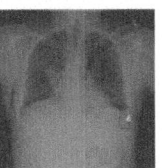

Fig. 2. With random initialization, the model outputs unspecific areas of attention. With IEI initialization the model yields more specific and focused areas of attention.

to attention map results hinting on a potential shortcut learning issue, as illustrated in Fig. 2(a). Instead, using a pretrained Visual Language Model (VLM) provides a more robust foundation for initialization. The IEI method initializes the segmentation heads with an identity matrix. We found that this improves sensitivity to specific disease structures, directing learning towards more precise features. This approach is depicted in Fig. 2.

3 Experiments and Results

To fully assess the properties of our framework, we conduct extensive experiments across quantitative metrics and qualitative indices.

Dataset: We utilized three publicly available datasets: ChestX-Det [10], CheXlocalize [19], and Vindr-CXR [15], each comprising 1,000 to 10,000 chest X-rays (CXRs) with multi-label and segmentation labels. The ChestXDet dataset is divided into three versions based on segmentation difficulty: a basic version with four common findings (Atelectasis, Cardiomegaly, Consolidation, Effusion), an expanded version with seven findings including Diffuse Nodule, Emphysema, and Mass, and a full version featuring all 13 original findings.

Baselines and Training Details: To ascertain the efficacy of the proposed DWARF method, we established several baselines for comparison. These include a pretrained vision language model without fine-tuning using DeViDe [12], and also KAD [28], a finetuned VLM employing only a multi-label classification loss, and a finetuned VLM training with classification loss and multi-label segmentation loss (extra supervision strategy of GAIN [8]). For the training procedure, we adopted ViT-B as the visual backbone and Med-KEBERT as the textual backbone. We finetune on the ChestX-Det dataset [9] on an image size of 224. We utilize the AdamW optimizer with learning rates $lr = 5 \times 10^{-5}$. We optimize on V100 16G GPUS with a total batch size of 32 for a total of 500 epochs.

3.1 Quantitative Results

DWARF Achieves SoTA Results Compared to Other Pretrained/finetuned VLM Baselines. In Table 1, we compared the performance of the proposed DWARF with various state-of-the-art models, including pretrained DeViDe, KAD and finetuned GAIN, which was trained with direct Cross-Entropy Loss and Dice Loss. These models were evaluated based on Max AUC, Max Dice, F1 Score, and MCC. Our analysis extends to various datasets including ChestX-Det, cheXlocalize and Vindr-CXR, highlighting the models' adaptability and effectiveness across different datasets. Overall, DWARF yields more robust results than the other aforementioned methods.

DWARF Achieves Enhanced Stability. To explore the scalability and stability of DWARF, we compared DWARF with GAIN [8] across different numbers of diseases (defined in Sect. 3). For 7 diseases, the Dice score improved from 0.1903 to **0.3492**, and the max AUC score increased from 0.8519 to **0.8717**. Similarly, for 4 diseases, the Dice score improved from 0.1438 to **0.3854**, and the max AUC score increased from 0.8660 to **0.8871**. These results, as shown in the Table 2, highlight the consistent enhancement provided by Dwarf across different numbers of diseases.

DWARF's Independence from Extensive Annotation: To address the challenges of obtaining dense and high-quality annotations for CXRs, we explored the feasibility of substituting human annotations with pseudo labels generated by segmentation models. The results are detailed in Table 3, and show that DWARF outperforms GAIN by **17.31** percentage on Dice metric.

DWARF Enhances Clinician Confidence in Classification Models: To test our method's effectiveness in boosting clinician confidence in classification models, we conducted a single-blind experiment. We selected 5 samples from each of four common diseases (Atelectasis, Cardiomegaly, Consolidation, and Effusion) from the ChestXDet dataset, for a total of 20 samples. Clinicians evaluated anonymized attention maps generated by DWARF and DeViDe for accuracy (precision in highlighting the finding) and specificity (focus and intuitiveness). DWARF was preferred in 15 and 18 out of 20 cases, respectively, achieving an average preference rate of 82.5.

Ablation Experiment - Disease-Specific Head Makes Attention Map Trainable: According to the analysis presented in Sect. 2, the segmentation expert heads are pivotal for projecting the cross-attention values effectively. To explore the contributions of these heads, we conducted an ablation study where we removed the projection operation, the results of which are detailed in Table 4. The inclusion of segmentation expert heads significantly enhanced the attention performance, with the metric improving from 0.2288 to a robust **0.3559**.

Qualitative Result: To enhance the clarity of the explanation regarding the visual explainability representation of DWARF, we show in Fig. 3, an example case of attention maps using the test set of the CheX-Det dataset. DWARF

Table 1. DWARF outperforms other finetuned/pretrained VLM on classification performance and attention accuracy on 4 metrics: AUC, Dice, F1 score and MCC. All models use the same transformer architecture as encoder. The best methods are indicated in bold.

Method	Dataset	AUC (%)	F1 Score (%)	MCC (%)	Max Dice (%)	Model Type
DeViDe [12]	ChestX-Det	74.24	42.46	34.29	13.66	Pretrained VLM
KAD [28]	ChestX-Det	73.81	40.04	31.84	13.89	Pretrained VLM
GAIN [8]	ChestX-Det	80.90	48.57	42.65	13.90	Finetuned VLM
DWARF	ChestX-Det	**81.94 ± 0.37**	**53.73 ± 0.29**	**49.87 ± 0.06**	**18.24 ± 0.18**	Finetuned VLM
DeViDe	cheXlocalize	78.26	41.66	59.83	11.93	Pretrained VLM
KAD	cheXlocalize	74.22	58.01	41.53	11.59	Pretrained VLM
GAIN	cheXlocalize	83.64	62.86	50.18	11.91	Finetuned VLM
DWARF	cheXlocalize	**84.93 ± 0.05**	**63.44 ± 0.21**	**50.79 ± 0.32**	**13.40 ± 0.51**	Finetuned VLM
DeViDe	Vindr-CXR	72.92	41.28	31.43	7.19	Pretrained VLM
KAD	Vindr-CXR	73.19	40.22	30.78	7.06	Pretrained VLM
GAIN	Vindr-CXR	78.51	45.20	36.48	7.23	Finetuned VLM
DWARF	Vindr-CXR	**80.01 ± 0.23**	**47.05 ± 1.14**	**39.55 ± 1.07**	**10.21 ± 0.42**	Finetuned VLM

Table 2. Comparison of DWARF and GAIN models on different numbers of selected diseases from the ChestX-Det dataset.

Backbone	Disease number	AUC (%)	F1 (%)	MCC (%)	Max Dice (%)
GAIN	4	86.80	–	–	14.38
	7	85.19	–	–	19.03
	13	80.90	48.57	42.65	13.90
DWARF	4	**88.71**	–	–	**41.47**
	7	**87.17**	60.17	52.01	**39.11**
	13	**81.94**	**53.73**	**49.87**	**18.24**

Table 3. Ablations of expert supervision - DWARF using generated pseudo-labels as guidance. Seven usual findings in ChestX-Det are used for evaluation including: Atelectasis, Cardiomegaly, Consolidation, Effusion, Diffuse Nodule, Emphysema, and Mass.

Method	Disease	AUC (%)	Dice (%)	Max Dice (%)
GAIN(cls)	7	86.80	14.38	14.38
DWARF (expert)	7	84.73	31.71	36.94
DWARF	7	**87.17**	**38.56**	**39.11**

Table 4. Ablations of disease-specific head. Seven usual findings are selected for evaluation (see Table 3). Compared to directly optimizing cross attention value, introducing additional segmentation expert head improves both the classification and attention performance.

Method	AUC	Max Dice
Directly optimize	86.63	22.88
Disease-specific head	**87.32**	**35.59**

significantly improves the focus of the classification model's attention. This enhancement allows the model to more precisely highlight the relevant areas that form the basis for its classification decisions.

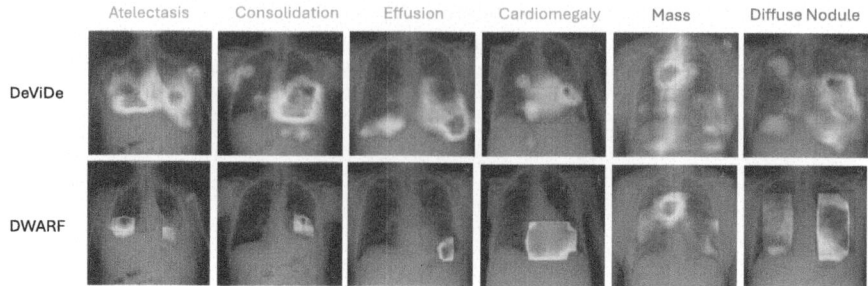

Fig. 3. Qualitative results of training with and without the DWARF architecture demonstrate that utilizing our DWARF framework consistently enhances the aggregation of feature maps and provides prior region information.

4 Conclusion

In this research, we have developed a two-stage saliency map revision strategy. This approach effectively integrates disease-related knowledge and clinicians' preferences into the generation of saliency maps. By incorporating this methodology, we are also introducing clinicians into the AI training loop. This strategy not only improves the accuracy of the AI but also makes it more user-friendly for clinicians, ensuring that their expertise and insights are reflected in the AI's learning process. Further work includes experiments on the generalization and few-shot ability of the model.

References

1. Band, S.S., et al.: Application of explainable artificial intelligence in medical health: a systematic review of interpretability methods. Inform. Med. Unlocked 101286 (2023)
2. Banerjee, S., Mitra, S., Shankar, B.U.: Automated 3D segmentation of brain tumor using visual saliency. Inf. Sci. **424**, 337–353 (2018)
3. Cao, K., et al.: Large-scale pancreatic cancer detection via non-contrast CT and deep learning. Nat. Med. **29**(12), 3033–3043 (2023)
4. Chen, H., Gomez, C., Huang, C.M., Unberath, M.: Explainable medical imaging AI needs human-centered design: guidelines and evidence from a systematic review. NPJ Digit. Med. **5**(1), 156 (2022)
5. Geirhos, R., et al.: Shortcut learning in deep neural networks. Nat. Mach. Intell. **2**(11), 665–673 (2020)
6. Hatherley, J.J.: Limits of trust in medical AI. J. Med. Ethics **46**(7), 478–481 (2020)
7. Kaviani, S., Han, K.J., Sohn, I.: Adversarial attacks and defenses on AI in medical imaging informatics: a survey. Expert Syst. Appl. **198**, 116815 (2022)
8. Li, K., Wu, Z., Peng, K.C., Ernst, J., Fu, Y.: Tell me where to look: guided attention inference network. In: Proceedings of the IEEE Conference on Computer Vision and Pattern Recognition, pp. 9215–9223 (2018)

9. Lian, J., Liu, J., Zhang, S., Gao, K., Liu, X., Zhang, D., Yu, Y.: A structure-aware relation network for thoracic diseases detection and segmentation. IEEE Trans. Med. Imaging **40**(8), 2042–2052 (2021)
10. Liu, J., Lian, J., Yu, Y.: ChestX-Det10: chest X-ray dataset on detection of thoracic abnormalities (2020)
11. Luo, H., Changdong, Y., Selvan, R.: Hybrid ladder transformers with efficient parallel-cross attention for medical image segmentation. In: International Conference on Medical Imaging with Deep Learning, pp. 808–819. PMLR (2022)
12. Luo, H., Zhou, Z., Royer, C., Sekuboyina, A., Menze, B.: DeViDe: faceted medical knowledge for improved medical vision-language pre-training. arXiv preprint: arXiv:2404.03618 (2024)
13. Ma, D., Pang, J., Gotway, M.B., Liang, J.: Foundation ark: accruing and reusing knowledge for superior and robust performance. In: International Conference on Medical Image Computing and Computer-Assisted Intervention, pp. 651–662. Springer (2023)
14. Maier-Hein, L., et al.: Metrics reloaded: pitfalls and recommendations for image analysis validation. arXiv. org (2206.01653) (2022)
15. Nguyen, H.Q., et al.: VinDr-CXR: an open dataset of chest X-rays with radiologist's annotations. Sci. Data **9**(1), 429 (2022)
16. Patrício, C., Neves, J.C., Teixeira, L.F.: Explainable deep learning methods in medical image classification: a survey. ACM Comput. Surv. **56**(4), 1–41 (2023)
17. Prentzas, N., Kakas, A., Pattichis, C.S.: Explainable AI applications in the medical domain: a systematic review. arXiv preprint: arXiv:2308.05411 (2023)
18. Ronneberger, O., Fischer, P., Brox, T.: U-Net: convolutional networks for biomedical image segmentation. In: Medical Image Computing and Computer-Assisted Intervention–MICCAI 2015: 18th International Conference, Munich, Germany, 5–9 October 2015, Proceedings, Part III 18, pp. 234–241. Springer (2015)
19. Saporta, A., et al.: Benchmarking saliency methods for chest X-ray interpretation. Nat. Mach. Intell. **4**(10), 867–878 (2022)
20. Selvaraju, R.R., Cogswell, M., Das, A., Vedantam, R., Parikh, D., Batra, D.: Grad-CAM: visual explanations from deep networks via gradient-based localization. In: Proceedings of the IEEE International Conference on Computer Vision, pp. 618–626 (2017)
21. Smilkov, D., Thorat, N., Kim, B., Viégas, F., Wattenberg, M.: SmoothGrad: removing noise by adding noise. arXiv preprint: arXiv:1706.03825 (2017)
22. Sundararajan, M., Taly, A., Yan, Q.: Axiomatic attribution for deep networks. In: International Conference on Machine Learning, pp. 3319–3328. PMLR (2017)
23. Topol, E.J.: High-performance medicine: the convergence of human and artificial intelligence. Nat. Med. **25**(1), 44–56 (2019)
24. Van der Velden, B.H., Kuijf, H.J., Gilhuijs, K.G., Viergever, M.A.: Explainable artificial intelligence (XAI) in deep learning-based medical image analysis. Med. Image Anal. **79**, 102470 (2022)
25. Yan, K., Ji, L., Wang, Z., Wang, Y., Duan, N., Ma, S.: Voila-A: aligning vision-language models with user's gaze attention. arXiv preprint: arXiv:2401.09454 (2023)
26. You, D., Liu, F., Ge, S., Xie, X., Zhang, J., Wu, X.: AlignTransformer: hierarchical alignment of visual regions and disease tags for medical report generation. In: Medical Image Computing and Computer Assisted Intervention–MICCAI 2021: 24th International Conference, Strasbourg, France, September 27–October 1, 2021, Proceedings, Part III 24, pp. 72–82. Springer (2021)

27. You, S., Wiest, R., Reyes, M.: SaRF: saliency regularized feature learning improves MRI sequence classification. Comput. Methods Programs Biomed. **243**, 107867 (2024)
28. Zhang, X., Wu, C., Zhang, Y., Xie, W., Wang, Y.: Knowledge-enhanced visual-language pre-training on chest radiology images. Nat. Commun. **14**(1), 4542 (2023)
29. Zhou, Z., Luo, H., Pang, J., Ding, X., Gotway, M., Liang, J.: Learning anatomically consistent embedding for chest radiography. arXiv preprint: arXiv:2312.00335 (2023)

PIPNet3D: Interpretable Detection of Alzheimer in MRI Scans

Lisa Anita De Santi[1,6](✉), Jörg Schlötterer[2,3], Michael Scheschenja[4], Joel Wessendorf[4], Meike Nauta[5], Vincenzo Positano[6], and Christin Seifert[2]

[1] University of Pisa, Pisa, Italy
lisa.desanti@phd.unipi.it
[2] University of Marburg, Marburg, Germany
[3] University of Mannheim, Mannheim, Germany
[4] Department of Diagnostic and Interventional Radiology,
University Hospital Marburg, Marburg, Germany
[5] Datacation, Eindhoven, Netherlands
[6] Fondazione Toscana G Monasterio, Pisa, Italy

Abstract. Information from neuroimaging examinations is increasingly used to support diagnoses of dementia, e.g., Alzheimer's disease. While current clinical practice is mainly based on visual inspection and feature engineering, Deep Learning approaches can be used to automate the analysis and to discover new image-biomarkers. Part-prototype neural networks (PP-NN) are an alternative to standard blackbox models, and have shown promising results in general computer vision. PP-NN's base their reasoning on prototypical image regions that are learned fully unsupervised, and combined with a simple-to-understand decision layer. We present PIPNet3D, a PP-NN for volumetric images. We apply PIPNet3D to the clinical diagnosis of Alzheimer's Disease from structural Magnetic Resonance Imaging (sMRI). We assess the quality of prototypes under a systematic evaluation framework, propose new functionally grounded metrics to evaluate brain prototypes and develop an evaluation scheme to assess their coherency with domain experts. Our results show that PIPNet3D is an interpretable, compact model for Alzheimer's diagnosis with its reasoning well aligned to medical domain knowledge. Notably, PIPNet3D achieves the same accuracy as its blackbox counterpart; and removing the remaining clinically irrelevant prototypes from its decision process does not decrease predictive performance.

Keywords: Deep Learning · XAI · Explainable AI · Interpretable Deep Learning · Part-prototypes · MRI · Alzheimer

1 Introduction

Alzheimer's Disease (AD) is a neurodegenerative disease resulting in a progressive decline of cognitive abilities. The diagnosis of AD is typically integrated

Supplementary Information The online version contains supplementary material available at https://doi.org/10.1007/978-3-031-77610-6_7.

with neuroimaging examinations, e.g., structural Magnetic Resonance Imaging (sMRI) [2,4,23]. Dementia patients exhibited pathological patterns in sMRI, such as gray matter atrophy and other tissue abnormalities in specific brain areas [2]. Such existing quantitative tools [5] present limited detection capabilities [2,23], Deep Learning (DL) models can facilitate the analysis of sMRI and have the potential to extract yet unknown image-based biomarkers in AD. However, the blackbox nature of DL models makes their application in high-stakes decisions controversial. Explainable Artificial Intelligence (XAI) aims to develop transparent systems while maintaining the advantages of DL [18,20,22]. For the application of XAI models in real-world scenarios, objectively assessing the quality of explanations is crucial [9]. However, evaluating explanations is considered challenging, such there is no ground truth of "good explanations" [20] and due to their multidisciplinary nature [11]. In addition, previous studies highlighted the centrality of involving domain experts in the development stage of XAI clinical supporting-decision system [1], but most of the current XAI works did not include a human evaluation approach [9]. As posthoc XAI approaches may not faithfully reflect a model's reasoning [18], there is growing interest in self-explanatory models, where the model itself inherently provides the explanation. One such type of models are part-prototype neural networks (PP-NN), which base their reasoning on the detection of machine-learned *prototypical parts* [3]. Several works applied DL for AD diagnosis [6] from sMRI. While the majority use blackbox models, a few also applied PP-NN [12,13]. However, their models can not consider spatial relationships in the 3rd dimension [12], or use non-interpretable (nonlinear) decision layers [13]. There is an increasing interest in extending PP-NN models from general computer vision tasks to 3D medical images [24,25]. However, those works are based on ProtoPNet [3], which has been shown to lack in compactness of the explanation [19] and semantic quality of prototypes [15]. Among PP-NN models, PIPNet reported appealing properties for the medical domain [14], because it learns a small number of semantically meaningful prototypes, enables human interaction and direct manual adaptation of the model's reasoning, and detects out-of-distribution data, abstaining from decisions when there is not sufficient evidence for any of the classes. As PIP-Net was designed for 2D images, and processing 3D volumes with a 2D backbone might induce information loss, we introduce PIPNet3D: an interpretable classifier able to process 3D scans.

In summary, our contributions are the following: (1) We introduce PIPNet3D, an interpretable part-prototype classifier for 3D input data, based on the PIPNet 2D model [15]. (2) We apply PIPNet3D to AD diagnosis from sMRI, and find that PIPNet3D performs equally well to its corresponding blackbox baseline. (3) We thoroughly assess PIPNet3D w.r.t. comprehensive explanation desiderata and propose *Prototype Brain Entropy* and *Prototype Localization Consistency* as novel measures for functionally grounded evaluations. (4) We proposed a domain experts' evaluation setup generalizable for the assessment of other PP-NN architectures. (5) From the domain experts' evaluation we find that i) PIPNet3D aligns well with domain knowledge and ii) removing clinically irrel-

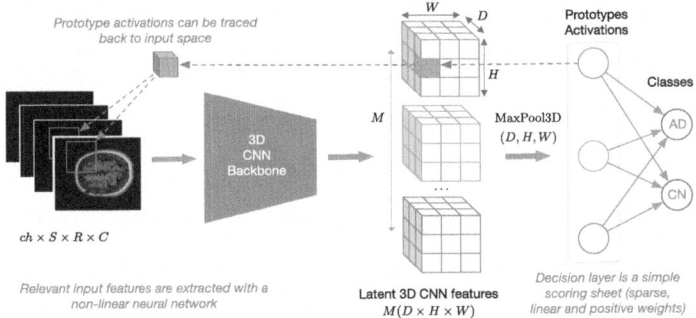

Fig. 1. Overview of PiPNet3D. 3D prototypes are learned through a CNN backbone. Representations are optimized through a contrastive pre-training step. A linear sparse decision layer computes the predictions based on prototype (VOI) activations.

evant prototypes improved the model's compactness without impacting performances. Source code and trained models are available at https://anonymous.4open.science/r/PIPNet3D-58CA.

2 Methodology

This section introduces the architecture of PiPNet3D (cf. Sect. 2.1 and Fig. 1), which enables an understandable decision structure of the model (cf. Fig. 2). We describe the evaluation, including the novel metrics *Prototype Brain Entropy* and the *Prototypes Localization Consistency*, and expert evaluation in Sect. 2.2.

2.1 PIPNet3D

We designed our PiPNet3D based on a 3D-CNN feature extractor and follow the scoring-sheet reasoning and training paradigm of Nauta et al. [15]. The architecture (cf. Fig. 1) consists of an input layer, a CNN backbone, global max pooling of the feature maps, and a linear classification layer. The **input layer** is of dimension $\mathbf{x} \in \mathbf{R}^{ch \times S \times R \times C}$ where ch, S, R, C respectively represents the number of channels, slices, rows and columns which constitutes the input volume. The **CNN backbone**, $z = f(\mathbf{x})$ extracts the latent features consisting of M 3-dim $(D \times H \times W)$ feature maps where $z_{m,d,h,w}$ represents to the one-hot encoding of patch d, h, w to the prototype m. A **global max-pooling 3D** operation extracts M prototypes and calculates the prototypes presence scores $\mathbf{p}$ where $p \in [0., 1.]^M$ and p_j measures the presence of the prototype m in the input image. The **linear classification layer** of size $\mathbf{w_c} \in \mathbf{R}_{\geq 0}^{M \times K}$ connects prototypes to the classes acting as a scoring sheet, where $w_c^{m,k}$ represents the contribution of prototype m for class k. In our use case $k = 2$ classes: AD (Alzheimer's disease) and CN (Cognitively Normal). This layer is optimized to be sparse (i.e., having as few connections as possible). The final output is a score for each of the K classes, where every **class output score** is given by the sum of the prototypes' presence score weighted by the relevance of each prototype to that class: $\mathbf{o} = \mathbf{p} \cdot \mathbf{w_c}$, where $\mathbf{o}$ is $1 \times K$ and $o_k = \sum_{d=1}^{D} p_d w_c^{d,k}$. As CNN backbones we used ResNet-18 3D pretrained on Kinetics400 [21] and ConvNeXt-Tiny 3D pretrained on the STOIC medical dataset [7], denote respectively as PIPNet$_{RN}$ and PIPNet$_{CN}$. This results in a number of initial prototypes $M = 512$ and $M = 768$. We applied data augmentation that does not alter the information content relevant to the clinical task [6] and finetuned PIPNet3D re-using the hyperparameter settings of the original PIPNet [15]. We only changed the batch size $= 12$ to adapt it to our computational capabilities. We reported the details on the data augmentation pipeline and hyperparameter setting in Suppl. Material. After training, we selected the relevant prototypes, i.e., those that have a weight connection $w_c > 10^{-3}$ for at least one class and were detected with a similarity $p > 0.1$ in the training set [15]. The global explanation (cf. Fig. 2) consists of relevant prototypes of the most similar images in the training set marked as a volume of interest (VOI). During inference, PIPNet3D returns the predicted class and the annotation of every prototype detected with similarity $p > 0.1$, together with its similarity score.

2.2 Neuroimaging Prototypes Explanation Quality

We assessed the explainability using the Co-12 evaluation framework [16, 17] (details in Suppl. Material). We designed an automated quantitative functionally-grounded evaluation setup, and an evaluation setup with domain experts. For both setups, we defined quantitative metrics to perform objective measurements relevant to the neuroimaging domain. We selected the PIPNet3D backbone which obtained the highest predictive performances and applied the evaluation to compare the quality of the prototypes from the 5 different folds (denoted as **Mx** where **x** indicates the current fold) and to study their relationship with their diagnostic performance.

Functionally Grounded Evaluation. We measured the compactness of PIPNet3D by calculating the total number of prototypes (*Global size*), the average number of detected prototypes in a test image (*Local size*), and the *Sparsity* of the decision layer following previous work [14]. Additionally, we propose two quality measures for prototypes based on brain reference standards to anatomically localize and study the composition of the extracted prototypes.

We propose *Prototype Brain Entropy* H_p to measure prototype purity. We used the Cerebrum Atlas (CerebrA) corresponding to the ICBM2009c space to annotate the prototypes with the anatomical brain regions [10]. For every prototype p_i we selected the corresponding VOI_p in the atlas, counted the voxels of every brain region, and computed the Shannon Entropy $H(.)$ over brain regions. A "pure" prototype focused on one specific brain area has an $H_p = 0$, while a higher value indicates the inclusion of multiple regions. An explanatory Figure is reported in Suppl. Material.

$$H_p = H(CerebrA_{VOI_p}) \tag{1}$$

We propose *Prototypes Localization Consistency* to measure whether the same prototype is activated in similar brain regions. We generate the local explanations for every image img in the test set, and evaluate the coordinate center (cc) of the VOI representing each prototype p, $VOI_{cc,p}|_{img}$. Next, we compute the average prototype's cc $\overline{VOI}_{cc,p}$. We then compute the Euclidean distance between $VOI_{cc,p}|_{img}$ and $\overline{VOI}_{cc,p}$ and normalize for the maximum linear dimension of the VOI (for a cubic VOI $l\sqrt{3}$, where l is the side of the cube). We define *Prototypes Localization Consistency*, LC_p of p by averaging over the test set. LC_p ranges between $0-1$ where 0 expresses the maximum localization consistency of the prototype. A prototype consistently located ($LC_p \approx 0$) can be associated with a specific brain region in the ICBM2009c standard space.

$$LC_p = \sum_{img} \frac{||VOI_{cc_p}|_{img} - \overline{VOI}_{cc}||^2}{l\sqrt{3}} \tag{2}$$

Evaluation with Experts. We collected quantitative and qualitative feedback on the prototypes from two radiologists at the University Hospital of Marburg. Our survey prompted the participants to assess the following statements.[1] "The prototype is located in a brain region typically affected in AD." (*Localization coherence*). "A prototype adding evidence to CN does not show pathological patterns, a prototype adding evidence to AD shows an abnormal pattern." (*Pattern coherence*). "The prediction returned by the model based on the VOI is correct." (*Classification coherence*). For each item we used a 6-point Likert scale (1: strongly disagree – 6: strongly agree). Additionally, we asked participants "Which clues in this VOI vote for or against each diagnosis?" (free text). The radiologists assessed 35 prototypes in total. Each prototype was shown as i) a montage of the most activated image in the training set with the prototype marked with a VOI; ii) a detailed view montage of the extracted VOI. The survey proposed is an evaluation scheme that can be used to empirically assess the consistency of the prototype with respect to domain knowledge of other PP-NN architectures. An explanatory Figure is reported in Suppl. Material. We assessed the inter-user agreement for each item using the Interclass Correlation Coefficient (ICC) [8]. We averaged the scores of the two radiologists for every prototype and binarized the scores considering a prototype with a score ≥ 3.5 as coherent. We finally evaluated the rate of coherent prototypes. Additionally, we tested a human-in-the-loop setting by suppressing the incoherent prototypes from the model (setting PIPNet$_{EK}$ in Table 1).

3 Evaluation

Data used in the preparation of this article were obtained from the Alzheimer's Disease Neuroimaging Initiative (ADNI) database[2]. The ADNI was launched in

---
[1] We performed two pre-tests, and only report on the final survey design.
[2] https://adni.loni.usc.edu.

Table 1. Performances (5 folds, in percentages) of the black-box models, and the interpretable PIPNet. PIPNet$_{EK}$ are models after pruning prototypes that do not align with expert knowledge (cf. Sect. 2.2). ⌀: averaged over 5 folds, *: best.

	Balanced Accuracy	Specificity	Sensitivity	F1
ResNet	80 ± 06	78 ± 15	82 ± 12	79 ± 07
PIPNet$_{RN}$	82 ± 02	88 ± 07	76 ± 09	79 ± 03
ConvNeXt	61 ± 07	67 ± 15	56 ± 24	54 ± 15
PIPNet$_{CN}$	69 ± 03	71 ± 07	68 ± 08	66 ± 04
AFTER ALIGNING WITH EXPERT KNOWLEDGE				
PIPNet$_{EK}$$^⌀$	82 ± 02	88 ± 07	74 ± 12	78 ± 05
PIPNet$_{EK}$*	85	84	86	83

2003 as a public-private partnership, led by Principal Investigator Michael W. Weiner, MD. The primary goal of ADNI has been to test whether serial magnetic resonance imaging (MRI), positron emission tomography (PET), other biological markers, and clinical and neuropsychological assessment can be combined to measure the progression of mild cognitive impairment (MCI) and early Alzheimer's disease (AD). Selecting the *"ADNI1 Standardized Screening Data Collection for 1.5T scans"* processed with Gradwarp, B1 non-uniformity, and N3 correction, we obtained 307 CN and 243 AD sMRI brain scans. Our data pre-processing pipeline is inspired by Mulyadi et al. [13], detailed in Suppl. Material. We performed 5-fold cross-validation with patient-wise random splits. 20% of training images are used for validation. We compared PIPNet$_{RN}$ and PIPNet$_{CN}$ to their corresponding blackbox ResNet-18 and ConvNeXt-Tiny 3D models, which we fine-tuned with dynamic data augmentation using the same augmentation pipeline of PIPNet. Prediction performances were compared using paired t-test. We report hyperparameter settings in Suppl. Material. We implemented PIPNet3D using PyTorch and MONAI[3]. We trained our models on an Intel Core i7 5.1 MHz PC, 32 GB RAM, equipped with an NVIDIA RTX3090 GPU with 24 GB of embedded RAM. The overall training process took on average 1 h and 25 min for PIPNet3D and 1 h for the blackbox.

3.1 Predictive Performance

We evaluated the classification performances using Balanced Accuracy, Specificity, Sensitivity and F1 (cf. Table 1). The ResNet-18 model obtained the highest predictive performances both as blackbox and PIPNet backbone. Paired two-tailed t-tests, $\alpha = 0.05$ showed no significant differences in performance between all 5 folds, suggesting that PIPNet3D adds interpretability to the corresponding blackbox model without reducing classification performance. We report classification results and interpretability of related works (not directly comparable to ours) in Suppl. Material.

---

[3] https://monai.io.

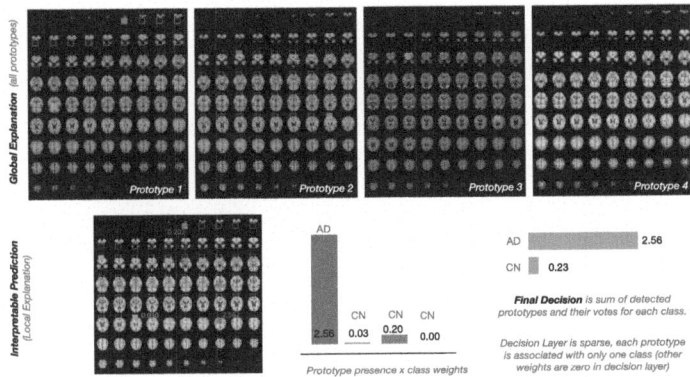

Fig. 2. Example of local and global explanation (LE and GE). The GE shows all the learned prototypes. The LE shows the model's reasoning for one particular patient.

3.2 Interpretability

Table 2 reports on the quality of prototypes. All folds of PIPNet3D have a small number of prototypes (Global size, max 11), while initially starting with a setup of 512 prototypes for PIPNet$_{RN}$. Additionally, we observed that prototypes can uniquely be assigned to one class (e.g., the connection to the other class is zeroed out), leading to compact and comprehensible models. Most of the prototypes are consistently located in the same anatomical location (small H_{p_i}, and LC_{p_i}). While all our models have a relatively small size (average 2.4 to 5.4 prototypes in local explanations), a Pearson correlation of 0.91 (± 0.03) between F1 score and Local size suggest that models with high accuracy are those with less compact local explanations (more prototypes). A Pearson correlation of -0.89(± 0.04) between F1 and Prototype Entropy H_p, shows that a model with purer prototypes also has higher accuracy. Our evaluation with domain experts showed a good reliability (ICC: 0.80, 0.76 and 0.85 for the quantitative tasks) [8]. Prototypes were found to be coherently located (coherence score 0.70, cf. Table 2), exhibit a coherent pattern (score 0.90), and classification decision (score 0.90). Most prototypes incoherently located are associated with the CN class (Localization coherence of 0.54, AD: 0.87). Incoherent CN prototypes might be due to PiPNet3D training scheme that requires finding evidence for every class; even if this class is representing absence of abnormalities. We observed that most of the prototypes showed a coherent pattern with the connected class. This indicates that most of the prototypes provide evidence coherent with the medical knowledge to support the model's decision. In this case, we observed a lower pattern coherence for the AD prototypes (0.77 vs. 0.93). We also noticed that most of the AD incoherent prototypes were observed in M3 and M4, where the model reported a lower recall for the AD class. We further analyzed the qualitative feedback for the prototypes that did not show a coherent pattern. For one CN prototype, both radiologists reported the presence of dilated ventricles as a viable sign of AD, suggesting incorrect model reasoning. For two AD proto-

Table 2. Evaluation of prototype quality for models M1, ..., M5. For the evaluation with experts, we show median rating in brackets. ↑ and ↓: tendency for better values.

		M1	M2	M3	M4	M5	Average
FUNCTIONAL EVALUATION	Global size ↓	10	11	5	5	4	7.0
	for CN	5	4	3	3	3	3.6
	for AD	5	7	2	2	1	3.4
	Local size ↓	5.4	5.2	2.7	3.0	2.4	3.8
	Sparsity ↑	0.990	0.989	0.995	0.995	0.996	0.993
	LC_p ↓	0.004	0.021	0.008	0.018	0.030	0.016
	for CN	0.009	0.003	0.000	0.015	0.030	0.017
	for AD	0.000	0.016	0.020	0.022	0.050	0.022
	H_p ↓	2.5	3.1	3.4	3.1	3.4	3.1
	for CN	2.8	3.3	3.5	3.1	2.9	3.1
	for AD	2.3	2.9	3.3	3.1	3.8	3.1
USERS	Localization Coherence ↑	0.90	0.60	0.60	0.80	0.50	0.70 (3.5)
	for CN	0.80	0.25	0.67	0.67	0.33	0.54
	for AD	1.00	0.86	0.50	1.00	1.00	0.87
	Pattern Coherence ↑	1.00	0.90	0.80	0.80	0.80	0.90 (4.5)
	for CN	1.00	1.00	1.00	1.00	0.67	0.93
	for AD	1.00	0.86	0.50	0.50	1.00	0.77
	Classification Coherence ↑	1.00	0.90	0.80	1.00	0.80	0.90 (4.5)
	for CN	1.00	1.00	1.00	1.00	0.67	0.93
	for AD	1.00	0.86	0.50	1.00	1.00	0.87

types, the VOI showed no or only mild pathological clues. This may again point to incorrect model reasoning or indicate yet unknown patterns, that may not be visible to a human observer. We suppressed the prototypes that did not show a coherent pattern and we did not observe statistically significant differences in classification performance in the adapted models w.r.t. the original ones (cf. Table 1, models PIPNet$_{EK}$). Thus, adapting to domain knowledge increased the models' compactness and coherency, without negatively impacting their accuracy.

4 Conclusion

In summary, we introduced PIPNet3D, a part-prototype model for 3D input images, applied to diagnose AD from sMRI, whose interpretability has been systematically assessed. We obtained an interpretable and compact model able to support AD diagnosis with prototypes in line with medical knowledge. Our results show, that interpretable models that align with domain-knowledge can be as effective as blackbox models. We hope to inspire their usage in the future, especially in high-risk domains, such as medical image analysis. We plan to extend PIPNet3D to a multi-modal system additionally taking patients' demographic information, introducing intermediate levels of cognitive impairments, and evaluating OoD performances with intermediate levels of dementia and patients with different age groups.

References

1. Cabitza, F., et al.: Rams, hounds and white boxes: investigating human-AI collaboration protocols in medical diagnosis. Artif. Intell. Med. **138** (2023). https://doi.org/10.1016/j.artmed.2023.102506
2. Chandra, A., Dervenoulas, G., Politis, M.: Magnetic resonance imaging in Alzheimer's disease and mild cognitive impairment (2019).https://doi.org/10.1007/s00415-018-9016-3
3. Chen, C., Li, O., Tao, C., Barnett, A.J., Su, J., Rudin, C.: This looks like that: deep learning for interpretable image recognition. In: Proceedings of the 33rd International Conference on Neural Information Processing Systems. Curran Associates Inc., Red Hook (2019)
4. De Santi, L., Pasini, E., Santarelli, M., Genovesi, D., Positano, V.: An explainable convolutional neural network for the early diagnosis of Alzheimer's disease from 18F-FDG PET. J. Dig. Imaging **36** (2023). https://doi.org/10.1007/s10278-022-00719-3
5. Fischl, B.: Freesurfer. Neuroimage **62**(2), 774–781 (2012). https://doi.org/10.1016/j.neuroimage.2012.01.021
6. Khojaste-Sarakhsi, M., Haghighi, S.S., Ghomi, S.F., Marchiori, E.: Deep learning for Alzheimer's disease diagnosis: a survey. Artif. Intell. Med. **130**, 102332 (2022). https://doi.org/10.1016/j.artmed.2022.102332
7. Kienzle, D., Lorenz, J., Schön, R., Ludwig, K., Lienhart, R.: COVID detection and severity prediction with 3D-ConvNeXt and custom pretrainings (2022). http://arxiv.org/abs/2206.15073
8. Koo, T.K., Li, M.Y.: A guideline of selecting and reporting intraclass correlation coefficients for reliability research. J. Chiropr. Med. **15**(2), 155–163 (2016). https://doi.org/10.1016/j.jcm.2016.02.012
9. Longo, L., et al.: Explainable Artificial Intelligence (XAI) 2.0: a manifesto of open challenges and interdisciplinary research directions. Inf. Fusion **106**, 102301 (2024). https://doi.org/10.1016/j.inffus.2024.102301
10. Manera, A.L., Dadar, M., Fonov, V., Collins, D.L.: Cerebra, registration and manual label correction of Mindboggle-101 atlas for MNI-ICBM152 template. Sci. Data **7** (2020). https://doi.org/10.1038/s41597-020-0557-9
11. Miller, T.: Explanation in artificial intelligence: insights from the social sciences. Artif. Intell. **267**, 1–38 (2019).https://doi.org/10.1016/j.artint.2018.07.007
12. Mohammadjafari, S., Cevik, M., Thanabalasingam, M., Basar, A.: Alzheimer's disease neuroimaging initiative: using ProtoPNet for interpretable Alzheimer's disease classification. In: anadian Artificial Intelligence Association (CAIAC) (2021)
13. Mulyadi, A.W., Jung, W., Oh, K., Yoon, J.S., Lee, K.H., Suk, H.I.: Estimating explainable Alzheimer's disease likelihood map via clinically-guided prototype learning. NeuroImage **273** (2023).https://doi.org/10.1016/j.neuroimage.2023.120073
14. Nauta, M., Hegeman, J.H., Geerdink, J., Schlötterer, J., van Keulen, M., Seifert, C.: Interpreting and correcting medical image classification with PIP-Net. In: ECAI International Workshop on Explainable and Interpretable Machine Learning (XI-ML), pp. 198–215. Springer Nature Switzerland, Cham (2023). https://doi.org/10.1007/978-3-031-50396-2_11
15. Nauta, M., Schlötterer, J., van Keulen, M., Seifert, C.: PIP-Net: patch-based intuitive prototypes for interpretable image classification. In: IEEE/CVF Conference on Computer Vision and Pattern Recognition (CVPR) (2023). https://doi.org/10.1109/CVPR52729.2023.00269

16. Nauta, M., Seifert, C.: The Co-12 recipe for evaluating interpretable part-prototype image classifiers. In: Longo, L. (ed.) Proceedings of World Conference Explainable Artificial Intelligence (XAI), pp. 397–420. Springer Nature Switzerland, Cham (2023). https://arxiv.org/abs/2307.14517
17. Nauta, M., et al.: From anecdotal evidence to quantitative evaluation methods: a systematic review on evaluating explainable AI. ACM Comput. Surv. (2023) https://doi.org/10.1145/3583558
18. Rudin, C.: Stop explaining black box machine learning models for high stakes decisions and use interpretable models instead. Nat. Mach. Intell. **1**, 206–215 (2019). https://doi.org/10.1038/s42256-019-0048-x
19. Rymarczyk, D., Struski, Ł., Górszczak, M., Lewandowska, K., Tabor, J., Zieliński, B.: Interpretable image classification with differentiable prototypes assignment. In: European Conference on Computer Vision, pp. 351–368. Springer (2022)
20. Salahuddin, Z., Woodruff, H.C., Chatterjee, A., Lambin, P.: Transparency of deep neural networks for medical image analysis: a review of interpretability methods. Comput. Biol. Med. **140**, 105111 (2022). https://doi.org/10.1016/j.compbiomed.2021.105111
21. Tran, D., Wang, H., Torresani, L., Ray, J., LeCun, Y., Paluri, M.: A closer look at spatiotemporal convolutions for action recognition (2017). http://arxiv.org/abs/1711.11248
22. van der Velden, B.H., Kuijf, H.J., Gilhuijs, K.G., Viergever, M.A.: Explainable artificial intelligence (XAI) in deep learning-based medical image analysis. J. Med. Image Anal. **79**, 102470 (2022). https://doi.org/10.1016/j.media.2022.102470
23. Vemuri, P., Jack, C.: Role of structural MRI in Alzheimer's disease. Alzheimer's Res. Therapy **2**(4) (2010). https://doi.org/10.1186/alzrt47
24. Wei, Y., Tam, R., Tang, X.: MProtoNet: a case-based interpretable model for brain tumor classification with 3D multi-parametric magnetic resonance imaging. In: Oguz, I., et al. (eds.) Medical Imaging with Deep Learning. Proceedings of Machine Learning Research, vol. 227, pp. 1798–1812. PMLR (2024). https://proceedings.mlr.press/v227/wei24a.html
25. Wolf, T.N., Pölsterl, S., Wachinger, C.: Don't PANIC: prototypical additive neural network for interpretable classification Alzheimer's disease. In: Proceedings International Conference on Information Processing in Medical Imaging. pp. 82-94. Springer, Berlin, Heidelberg (2023).https://doi.org/10.1007/978-3-031-34048-2_7

Detecting Unforeseen Data Properties with Diffusion Autoencoder Embeddings Using Spine MRI Data

Robert Graf[1,2(✉)], Florian Hunecke[1,2], Soeren Pohl[1,2], Matan Atad[1,2], Hendrik Moeller[1,2], Sophie Starck[2], Thomas Kroencke[4], Stefanie Bette[4], Fabian Bamberg[5], Tobias Pischon[6], Thoralf Niendorf[7], Carsten Schmidt[8], Johannes C. Paetzold[3], Daniel Rueckert[2,3], and Jan S. Kirschke[1]

[1] Department of Diagnostic and Interventional Neuroradiology, Klinikum rechts der Isar, TUM School of Medicine and Health, Munich, Germany
robert.graf@tum.de
[2] Institut fuer KI und Informatik in der Medizin, Klinikum rechts der Isar, TUM, Munich, Germany
[3] Biomedical Image Analysis Group, Depart. of Computing, Imperial College London, London, UK
[4] Diagnostic and Interventional Radiology, University Hospital Augsburg, Augsburg, Germany
[5] Klinik fuer Diagnostische und Interventionelle Radiologie, Universitaetsklinikum Freiburg, Freiburg im Breisgau, Germany
[6] Molecular Epidemiology Research Group, Max Delbrueck Center for Molecular Medicine in the Helmholtz Association (MDC), Berlin, Germany
[7] Berlin Ultrahigh Field Facility, Max Delbrück Center for Molecular Medicine in the Helmholtz Association (MDC), Berlin, Germany
[8] University Medicine of Greifswald, Greifswald, Germany

Abstract. Deep learning has made significant strides in medical imaging, leveraging the use of large datasets to improve diagnostics and prognostics. However, large datasets often come with inherent errors through subject selection and acquisition. In this paper, we investigate the use of Diffusion Autoencoder (DAE) embeddings for uncovering and understanding data characteristics and biases, including biases for protected variables like sex and data abnormalities indicative of unwanted protocol variations. We use sagittal T2-weighted magnetic resonance (MR) images of the neck, chest, and lumbar region from 11186 German National Cohort (NAKO) participants. We compare DAE embeddings with existing generative models like StyleGAN and Variational Autoencoder. Evaluations on a large-scale dataset consisting of sagittal T2-weighted MR images of three spine regions show that DAE embeddings effectively separate protected variables such as sex and age. Furthermore, we used t-SNE visualization to identify unwanted variations in imaging protocols, revealing differences in head positioning. Our embedding can identify samples where a sex predictor will have issues learning the correct sex. Our findings highlight the potential of using advanced embedding techniques like DAEs to detect data quality issues and biases in medical imaging datasets. Identifying such hidden relations can enhance the reliability and fairness of deep learning models in healthcare applications, ultimately improving patient care and outcomes.

Keywords: Bias detection · Data Quality · Embeddings · Large Cohorts

1 Introduction

Historically, deep learning in medicine has relied on large datasets, which have been difficult to obtain. However, in recent years, significant progress has been made. Notable examples include extensive datasets such as chest radiographs [10,11], as well as images from comprehensive epidemiological studies like the UK-Biobank [1] and the German National Cohort ("NAKO Gesundheitsstudie") [2]. Nevertheless, the sheer size of these datasets makes it difficult to detect data shifts and biases visually. Biases can occur through various sources, such as deviations from the examination protocol, the subjects themselves, changes in framing, or data processing errors [5]. Detecting biases in large data sets is a laborious and time-consuming task and would require a large survey to strongly evaluate the data [9,13]. For disease prediction, it is paramount to know what biases exist to compensate for them or at least observe them if they have an influence on a classifier. Other approaches tried to reduce biases to force disentangling [3,13,16] or use unsupervised embeddings [4,17,21]. Unsupervised clustering is a particularly promising option to overcome this hurdle. To better cluster images, we can first reduce the image to an embedding. Then, the whole dataset can be visualized with t-SNE [14]. Embeddings are representations of data generated, in our case, through an unlabeled reconstruction task. In large language models, embeddings are crucial in learning relationships between words, sentence structures, and meaning. For images, these embeddings are often used to manipulate generative networks because they reorder images so that image features, like age or skin tone, are split into individual hyperplanes. We aim to utilize this property of embeddings to gain insight into data properties and thereby identify potential biases. For instance, visualizing embeddings concerning acquisition location or date can reveal biases stemming from differences in acquisition protocols or variations in imaging equipment. Additionally, we can investigate how protected variables like sex and age correlate with the data. Generative embeddings are either generated with the VAEs [8] or StyleGAN2 [12]. In VAE, the bottleneck output is the embedding of the input. StyleGAN models use inversion networks like "encoder for editing" [22] to generate embeddings from real data. The inversion model gets the input and output pairs of StyleGAN and predicts the noise from a given image. Presently, diffusion-based techniques have outperformed GANs, and the Diffusion Autoencoder (DAE) [18] may offer superior embeddings while requiring only a single end-to-end training process.

Contributions. We propose DAE [18] embeddings as a better replacement for existing embedding models for medical images. First, we want to investigate if the improved DAE embeddings can better disentangle images than previous generative embeddings. Second, we want to highlight the ability to detect data shifts that could impact fairness by investigating two example anomalies we observed in the DAE embeddings and get an explanation for those outliers.

2 Materials and Methods

This study included 11186 [5745 male; 5441 female] subjects from the NAKO. Each subject provides sagittal T2-weighted (T2w) magnetic resonance images (MRI) of the neck, chest, and lumbar region. We used sagittal slices to train our DAE. We normalized the data to [-1, 1] for training by linear rescaling from [0, max-value] and random cropping to 256 × 256. We employed a fixed center cropping approach to create an MRI volume embedding, concatenating 12 center slices into a single embedding. 12 slices are guaranteed to be available, and the number of images must be constant. We want to avoid embedding differences through random cropping; therefore, all embeddings and predictions are made with the same fixed field of view. Three embeddings (neck, chest, lumbar) were evaluated separately for each subject. Subjects were then divided into training, validation, and test sets using an 80%, 5%, and 15% split ratio throughout. The t-SNE visualization encompassed all images. We studied two classes of bias. First, we analyzed individual characteristics like sex, age, weight, and height. These protected variables can cause the prediction to get worse; for instance, in face recognition, most models performed worse for dark-skinned women due to training and testing data imbalance and the difficulty of cameras to collect light from darker skin [15]. The second class of bias is the acquisition location and date. In an ideal scenario, we would be unable to identify the time and location where any of the scans were taken. In a multi-center study that took over three years to collect, there is a risk that we could reidentify different institutes or the time when a scan was taken. We first trained the DAE and extracted the image embeddings. Support Vector Machines (SVMs) [7] were then trained on balanced embedding data sets. We compared the classification results with other established generative modeling approaches to evaluate the performance of DAE embeddings.

3 Experiments and Results

In an initial step, we generated the DAE embeddings and visualized them in a t-SNE plot using a perplexity value of 50 (Fig. 1). We observed that the model can differentiate protected properties even though the process is fully unsupervised. The DAE especially well separates sex, weight, and age. Sex and age are something a radiologist would not be confident in estimating from a spine image alone. The acquisition year had no visible clustering, but the acquisition locations had multiple unexpected clusters in the cervical region. For StyleGAN, we

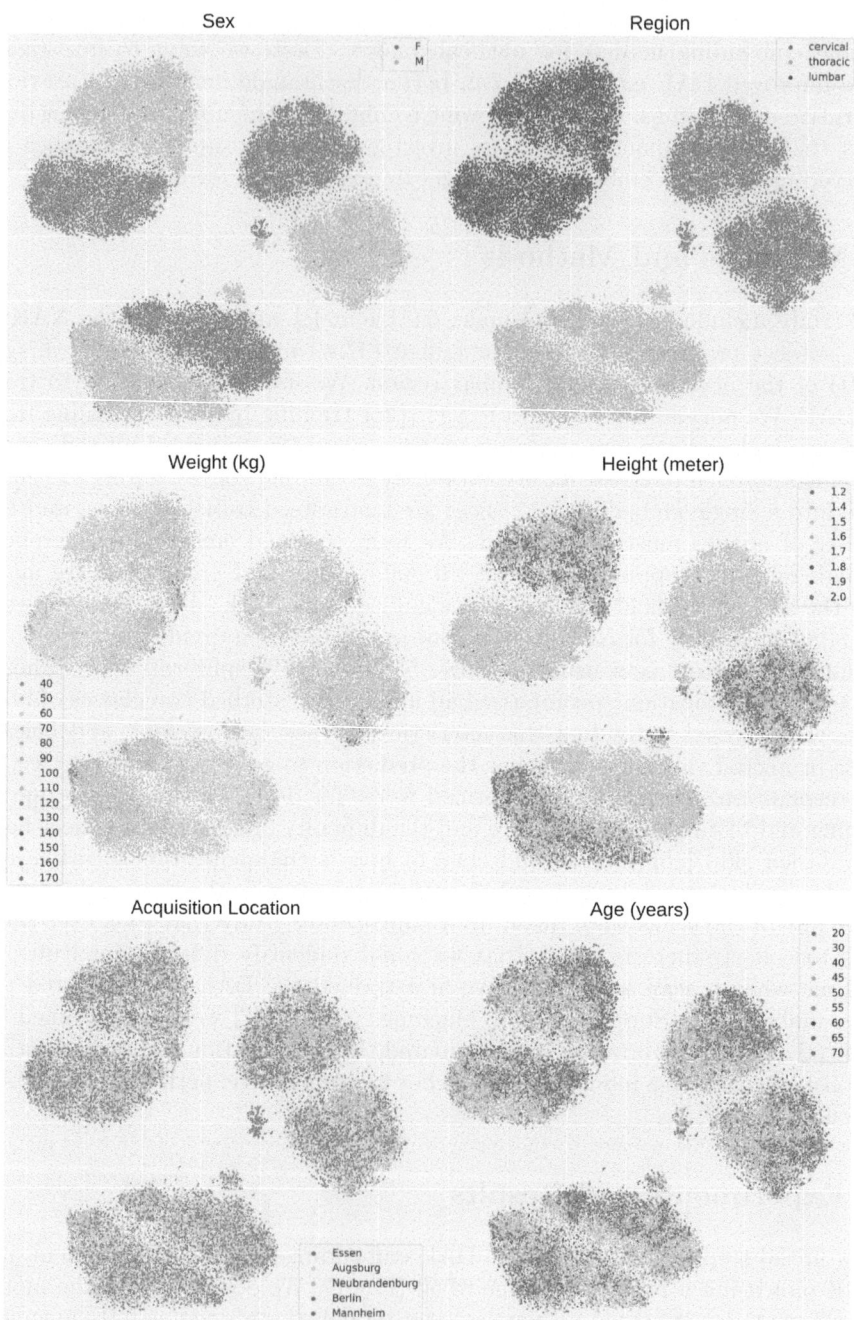

Fig. 1. t-SNE plots of our DAE embeddings. The embeddings are colored with the patient sex, height, weight, and age. The Region label describes the body region; the acquisition location is the city where the image was recorded. (Color figure online)

observe the same location-dependent clustering, but the split into sex is not as clear as the DAE embedding in the t-SNE plots.

Embedding Quality. To assess embedding quality, we employed SVMs to train a predictor and compare it with networks trained on the images and labels themselves. We used ResNet10, ResNet34, and DenseNet121 to learn the data distribution. We compared DAE with β-VAE and StyleGAN. To show that DAE outperforms other generative embedding methods, we considered age, weight, height, body region, and sex as training objectives. Body region and sex were treated as a classification task, while age, weight, and height were subject to regression analysis to minimize mean-absolute error. Optimization involved carefully rebalancing the training data to ensure equal representation across all predicted value ranges. This was especially important for age since the networks would otherwise predict the average age for all samples. Further, weight decay between 0.01 to 0.0001 can drastically improve the final prediction of the NN classifiers. Subject age ranges from 20 to 72 years, height ranges from 1.25 to 2.05 m, and weight varies from 38 to 192 kg. All participants self-reported their sex, either male or female. Our DAE embeddings outperformed StyleGAN and β-VAE by a considerable margin. Only for body regions, StyleGAN also reaches perfect accuracy. The unsupervised embedding and SVM clustering were good enough to beat ResNet10 in all but one task. The larger fully supervised models performed better. Still, the gap between DAE embeddings and supervised classification is smaller than between other embedding methods and DAE embeddings (Table 1). Our tested age models are in line with other age predictors. For example, dedicated architectures on the full-body excluding the head achieved on the UK-Biobank [1] are MAE of 2.38 [6] and 2.76 [20] with an age range of 44–82. The age range and larger 3D field of view can noticeably impact the MAE, so they are not perfectly comparable. Starck and Kini et al. [20] show that their model mainly focuses on the spine, which is the area we exclusively look at.

Table 1. Regression and classification with images and embedding.

	Supervision	Type	Body Region accuracy ↑	Sex accuracy ↑	Weight ℓ_1 kg ↓	Height ℓ_1 meter ↓	Age ℓ_1 years ↓
β-VAE + Hessian	semi	embed.	0.998	0.870	6.75	0.055	7.80
StyleGAN	semi	embed.	**1.000**	0.885	5.66	0.047	5.62
DAE (ours)	semi	embed.	**1.000**	0.988	4.32	0.032	3.84
ResNet10	fully	image	0.997	0.993	10.26	0.072	4.15
ResNet34	fully	image	**1.000**	**0.999**	**3.28**	0.029	3.12
DenseNet121	fully	image	0.997	**0.999**	4.09	**0.028**	**2.84**

3.1 Bias Detection

In order to investigate the unknown systemic biases, we first delineated clusters in the t-SNE plots. Then, we resorted to training image classifiers on the new cluster labels from the delineation and employed explainability methods to discover the feature's location causing the clustering.

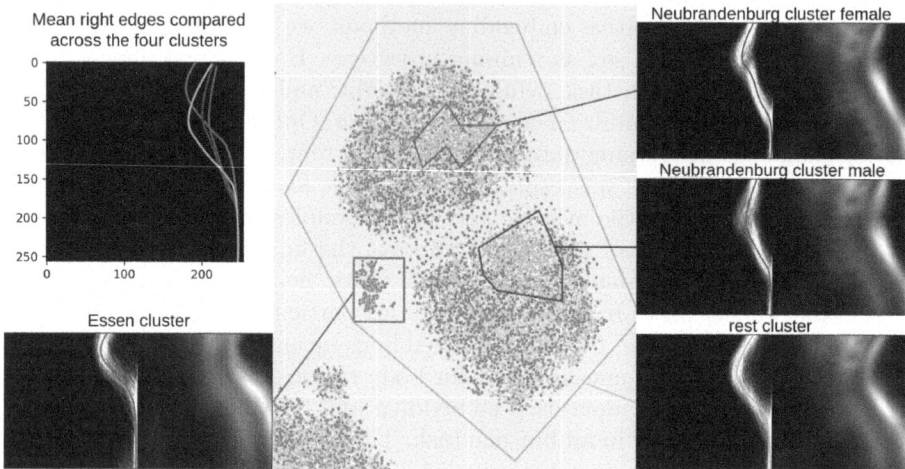

Fig. 2. Location Biases. Three clusters separate from the head images when we color them by the examination center where the MRI was taken. For each cluster and the rest class, we show two images. The left is a selection of the right edges of the images, and on the right are the images summed together. Both are made from 1000 images and are averaged. We observe that the neck curve differs in the clusters. On the top left, we visualized this by plotting the mean line of all 4 clusters.

Location. To unravel unexpected findings behind unexpected clusters, we implemented a classifier trained on images where we manually delineate cervical location clusters using t-SNE. For better explainability, we used GradCAM [19], which allowed us to visualize the salient features influencing decision-making. The GradCAM activation for the cluster in the cervical area highlighted the right edge (back of the neck). To provide a more straightforward depiction of location bias, we employed an averaging technique across 1000 images from a specific cluster, revealing common shapes and patterns (Fig. 2). We observed that the clusters have other neck curvature by printing the right edge and overlaying 1000 images. We found that the neck is shifted in a constant way in all clusters, which can only be explained by an altered physical or software setup in the scanner. For the red "Essen" cluster, we observed that the whole person is shifted in superior direction by about 50 voxels (43 mm). This could be a technical or human error, where the subjects were sent deeper into the MRI device than other centers or a software issue where the field of view selection diverged from the other scanning locations. The thoracic and lumbar regions, in contrast, are unaffected. The separated green/purple clusters from "Neubrandenburg" and "Mannheim" are created by a difference in a neck rest position determined by the MR device's neck support. The neck curve is much flatter in the "Neubrandenburg" clusters. We also checked for time-dependent clustering and found no clustering. Nonetheless, we observe that subjects in the separated "Neubrandenburg" clusters were scanned in the second and third years but not in the first year. Our embeddings unveiled framing differences in head images. For a subset of images, we can deduce the potential scanning location. In a more extreme case, this would be a privacy concern to be able to re-identify subjects.

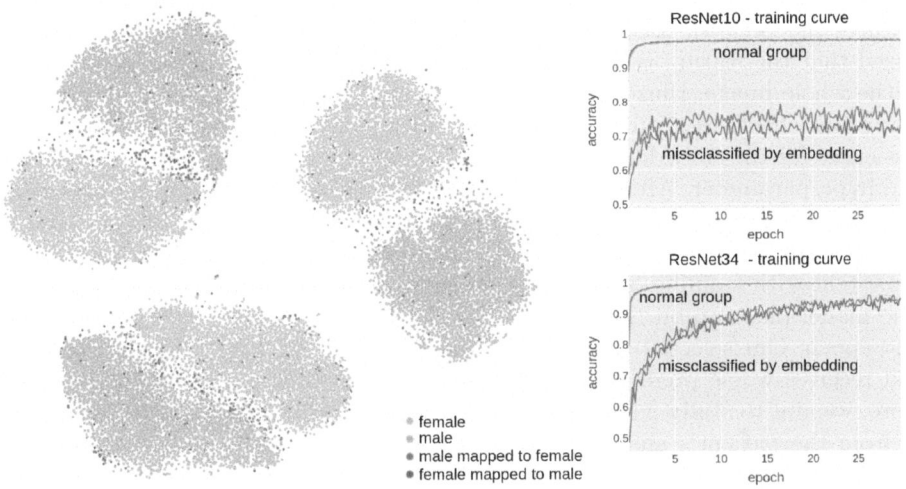

Fig. 3. Sex Biases. Left: A subset of subjects are clustered between the male and female blobs, and others are completely pushed to the opposite sex. They must have a set of features that indicate that the spine is the opposite sex. We have no further evidence of how this is reflected in the sex and gender of those persons overall. Right: The training curves of a male/female classifier of ResNet10 and ResNet34. We train only on the male/female label but measure the misclassified group separately and observe that they clearly lag behind during training.

Sex. The DAE embeddings separate the subjects by sex. We observe that a few hundred people have an embedding that puts their images into the cluster of the other sex. In cases where embeddings deviate from their true sex class, we scrutinized individual instances to detect labeling errors but found that the sexes of the patients were correctly labeled. We defined sex by their primary sex organ as visible in different full-body MRI acquisitions. 411 thoracic (3.7%), 347 lumbar (3.1%), and 211 cervical (1.9 %) images out of 11,186 subjects were classified towards the opposite sex. Out of the misclassified images, 585 (77.0

% of misclassed) had a single region misclassified, 141 (18.6 % of misclassed) subjects had two regions that were misclassified, and 34 (4.5 % of misclassed) subjects had all three regions classified as a different sex. Assuming the independent probability of separate regions, we would expect a count of 26.6 subjects with two misclassified regions and 0.24 subjects for all three regions; therefore, the number of subjects with more than one switch in sex clustering is far above random chance. Misclassifications are equally frequent in both sexes. The cervical region probably has the lowest misclassification because, unlike the other images, it has more non-spine tissue visible, especially parts of the skull. The other regions are shadowed towards the front. The back is fully visible in the images. First, we delineated clusters in the t-SNE plot and separated the misclassified images. We trained different networks and observed that the GradCAM highlights the whole spine image. This indicates that it is unclear what image features the network uses because we can not pinpoint a location. We hypothesized that the feature is a texture or structure difference that can be observed in the whole image, thus introducing a potential bias in classification tasks. To study this effect, we trained a classifier on the given sex label, but we plot the loss curve for the embedding misclassified group separately. We varied the model and hyperparameter. After one epoch, the classifiers reach 96–98% and converge to 98%–99%, but the misclassified group clearly underperforms. After one epoch, the accuracy is 40–70% and reaches a maximum of 70–95%. The validation is consistent with training or swings between overpredicting either male or female. The model picks up on the same feature as the embedding network within the first epoch. Our selected subgroup is clearly biased (See Fig. 3) by the classifier and receives worse prediction results than the rest of the population. Furthermore, we aim to study whether this effect originates from the T2w images alone or from the patient's anatomy. We replaced the T2w image with T1-weighted Dixon technique images. We received the same results with our classifier when using a similar field of view. We conclude that we observe a real phenomenon where a network picks up subtle image changes between the two sexes, which are not always reliable for all subjects. The models detect features that can identify the sex of most people, but some persons have the indication of the opposite sex for those features. We believe that this previously unknown bias is a normal variant, and after discussing it with multiple radiologists, we discussed many hormonal and growth differences that could cause this effect but are not visible to the human eye. With large datasets and longer training time, the larger supervised networks can learn additional features to distinguish some of the remaining persons into their correct sex. Still, they take longer to fit into the model, and we expect that smaller datasets do not have enough samples to provide this level of detail.

4 Conclusion

We used DAE to visualize properties of T2-weighted MR images of the neck, chest, and lumbar region based on data from the German National Cohort related to individual characteristics and detecting image acquisition abnormalities indicative of protocol violations. We compared DAE with StyleGAN and VAE and showed that DAEs yielded better embeddings. Especially sex, which is dependent on subtle image differences, is better distinguished in DAE embeddings. DAE successfully differentiated sex on spine MRI but were not 100% identical to the self-reported sex, an issue we can reproduce in a supervised setting, and found a subpopulation that was consistently difficult for a DL-Model to learn. We found inconsistent head positions in the cervical images in different examination centers. We believe that embedding can be used to find consistent data biases that may hurt learning tasks towards protected properties like sex, age, or race.

Acknowledgments. The research for this article received funding from the European Research Council (ERC) under the European Union's Horizon 2020 research and innovation program (101045128 - iBack-epic-ERC2021-COG). This project was conducted with data from the German National Cohort (NAKO) (www.nako.de). The NAKO is funded by the Federal Ministry of Education and Research (BMBF) [project funding reference numbers: 01ER1301A/B/C, 01ER1511D and 01ER1801A/B/C/D], federal states of Germany and the Helmholtz Association, the participating universities and the institutes of the Leibniz Association. We thank all participants who took part in the NAKO study and the staff of this research initiative.

References

1. Allen, N., et al.: UK Biobank: current status and what it means for epidemiology. Health Policy Technol. **1**(3), 123–126 (2012)
2. Bamberg, F., et al.: Whole-body MR imaging in the German national cohort: rationale, design, and technical background. Radiology **277**(1), 206–220 (2015)
3. Berg, H., et al.: A prompt array keeps the bias away: debiasing vision-language models with adversarial learning. arXiv preprint: arXiv:2203.11933 (2022)
4. Elnaggar, A., et al.: ProtTrans: toward understanding the language of life through self-supervised learning. IEEE Trans. Pattern Anal. Mach. Intell. **44**(10), 7112–7127 (2021)
5. Fabbrizzi, S., Papadopoulos, S., Ntoutsi, E., Kompatsiaris, I.: A survey on bias in visual datasets. Comput. Vis. Image Underst. **223**, 103552 (2022)
6. He, S., Feng, Y., Grant, P.E., Ou, Y.: Deep relation learning for regression and its application to brain age estimation. IEEE Trans. Med. Imaging **41**(9), 2304–2317 (2022)
7. Hearst, M.A., Dumais, S.T., Osuna, E., Platt, J., Scholkopf, B.: Support vector machines. IEEE Intell. Syst. Appl. **13**(4), 18–28 (1998)
8. Higgins, I., et al.: beta-VAE: learning basic visual concepts with a constrained variational framework. In: International Conference on Learning Representations (2016)
9. Hu, X., et al.: Discovering biases in image datasets with the crowd. In: Proceedings of HCOMP (2019)
10. Irvin, J., et al.: CheXpert: a large chest radiograph dataset with uncertainty labels and expert comparison. In: Proceedings of the AAAI Conference on Artificial Intelligence, vol. 33, pp. 590–597 (2019)

11. Johnson, A.E., et al.: MIMIC-CXR-JPG, a large publicly available database of labeled chest radiographs. arXiv preprint: arXiv:1901.07042 (2019)
12. Karras, T., Laine, S., Aittala, M., Hellsten, J., Lehtinen, J., Aila, T.: Analyzing and improving the image quality of StyleGan. In: Proceedings of the IEEE/CVF Conference on Computer Vision and Pattern Recognition, pp. 8110–8119 (2020)
13. Li, Z., Xu, C.: Discover the unknown biased attribute of an image classifier. In: Proceedings of the IEEE/CVF International Conference on Computer Vision, pp. 14970–14979 (2021)
14. Van der Maaten, L., Hinton, G.: Visualizing data using t-SNE. J. Mach. Learn. Res. **9**(11) (2008)
15. Najibi, A.: Racial discrimination in face recognition technology. Sci. News **24** (2020)
16. Peebles, W., Peebles, J., Zhu, J.Y., Efros, A., Torralba, A.: The hessian penalty: a weak prior for unsupervised disentanglement. In: Computer Vision–ECCV 2020: 16th European Conference, Glasgow, UK, 23–28 August 2020, Proceedings, Part VI 16, pp. 581–597. Springer (2020)
17. Petreski, D., Hashim, I.C.: Word embeddings are biased. but whose bias are they reflecting? AI Soc. **38**(2), 975–982 (2023)
18. Preechakul, K., Chatthee, N., Wizadwongsa, S., Suwajanakorn, S.: Diffusion autoencoders: toward a meaningful and decodable representation. In: Proceedings of the IEEE/CVF Conference on Computer Vision and Pattern Recognition, pp. 10619–10629 (2022)
19. Selvaraju, R.R., Cogswell, M., Das, A., Vedantam, R., Parikh, D., Batra, D.: Grad-CAM: visual explanations from deep networks via gradient-based localization. In: Proceedings of the IEEE International Conference on Computer Vision, pp. 618–626 (2017)
20. Starck, S., Kini, Y.V., Ritter, J.J.M., Braren, R., Rueckert, D., Mueller, T.: Atlas-based interpretable age prediction. arXiv preprint: arXiv:2307.07439 (2023)
21. Tommasi, T., Patricia, N., Caputo, B., Tuytelaars, T.: A deeper look at dataset bias. Domain Adaptat. Comput. Vis. Appl., 37–55 (2017)
22. Tov, O., Alaluf, Y., Nitzan, Y., Patashnik, O., Cohen-Or, D.: Designing an encoder for StyleGAN image manipulation. ACM Trans. Graph. (TOG) **40**(4), 1–14 (2021)

Interpretability of Uncertainty: Exploring Cortical Lesion Segmentation in Multiple Sclerosis

Nataliia Molchanova[1,2,3], Alessandro Cagol[4,5], Pedro M. Gordaliza[1,3], Mario Ocampo-Pineda[4], Po-Jui Lu[4], Matthias Weigel[4], Xinjie Chen[4], Adrien Depeursinge[1,2], Cristina Granziera[4], Henning Müller[2,6], and Meritxell Bach Cuadra[1,3]

[1] University of Lausanne and Lausanne University Hospital, Lausanne, Switzerland
nataliia.molchanova@unil.ch
[2] University of Applied Sciences Western Switzerland (HES-SO), Delémont, Switzerland
[3] CIBM Center for Biomedical Imaging, Lausanne, Switzerland
[4] University Hospital and University Basel, Basel, Switzerland
[5] University of Genova, Genoa, Italy
[6] University of Geneva, Geneva, Switzerland

Abstract. Uncertainty quantification (UQ) has become critical for evaluating the reliability of artificial intelligence systems, especially in medical image segmentation. This study addresses the interpretability of instance-wise uncertainty values in deep learning models for focal lesion segmentation in magnetic resonance imaging, specifically cortical lesion (CL) segmentation in multiple sclerosis. CL segmentation presents several challenges, including the complexity of manual segmentation, high variability in annotation, data scarcity, and class imbalance, all of which contribute to aleatoric and epistemic uncertainty. We explore how UQ can be used not only to assess prediction reliability but also to provide insights into model behavior, detect biases, and verify the accuracy of UQ methods. Our research demonstrates the potential of instance-wise uncertainty values to offer post hoc global model explanations, serving as a sanity check for the model. The implementation is available at https://github.com/NataliiaMolch/interpret-lesion-unc.

Keywords: Uncertainty quantification · Interpretability of uncertainty · Instance-wise uncertainty · Segmentation · Multiple sclerosis · Cortical lesions · Magnetic resonance imaging

1 Introduction

Uncertainty quantification (UQ) is gaining popularity within the field of medical image segmentation as a means to assess the reliability of artificial intelligence systems by representing the "degree of untrustworthiness" of their predictions [1,

3,8]. Higher uncertainty in a prediction indicates an increased likelihood of an erroneous prediction. Consequently, a common UQ evaluation practice involves assessing the correspondence between uncertainty and error, using methods such as uncertainty calibration measures [5], accuracy-confidence curves [7], or error retention curves [11]. Uncertainty can thus be effectively used for assessing the quality of predictions at inference time without the need for ground truth [5,7]. UQ has also been applied in other downstream tasks, including active learning and domain adaptation, among others [3,8].

While UQ is actively used for various downstream tasks, little has been done to analyze and interpret the uncertainty values themselves [2]. Additional analyses providing insights into uncertainty would be highly valuable for: i) detecting biases in deep learning (DL) model behavior; ii) performing a sanity check of the UQ methods themselves; iii) extracting information captured by uncertainty beyond errors.

In this work, we explore the interpretability of instance-wise uncertainty values in DL segmentation within the context of focal lesion segmentation from magnetic resonance imaging (MRI). Specifically, we focus on UQ in CL segmentation, a key task for differential diagnosis and prognosis in multiple sclerosis (MS) [15].

Automating CL segmentation is complicated by poor data quality. The ground-truth annotations are subject to errors and high intra- and inter-rater variability due to small lesion sizes and confusion with white matter lesions adjacent to the cortex (see examples in Fig. 1). The data is sparse and limited to private cohorts with varying data characteristics. Additionally, significant class imbalance affects machine learning solutions. These factors hinder the development of DL models, which face two main sources of uncertainty: data noise (aleatoric uncertainty) and training data scarcity and/or domain shifts (epistemic uncertainty) [3]. In this context, we propose an interpretability analysis for lesion-scale uncertainty values to provide post hoc global model explanations serving as a sanity check for both the model and the uncertainty values themselves. We validate the results of the proposed analysis through clinical feedback.

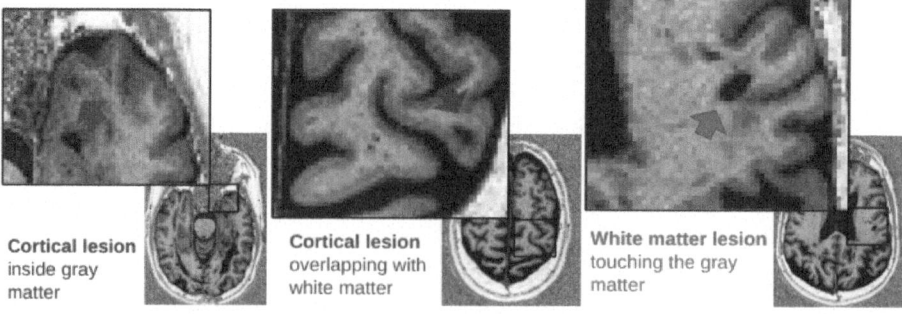

Fig. 1. Examples of several types of MS lesions visible on MP2RAGE scans, appearing as hypointense regions.

2 Materials and Methods

2.1 Data

We use a dataset obtained at University of Basel, Switzerland and previously explored in other studies [6,12]. Our cohort includes 117 patients diagnosed with MS [15] at different stages of the disease: relapsing-remitting (62), primary-progressive (39), and secondary-progressive (16). The male-to-female ratio is 0.77; the median Q2 (Q1–Q3) age: 51 (40–58) years, disease duration: 8.7 (1.7–18.2) years, and the expanded disability status scale: 3 (2–6). All brain MRI scans are obtained with a standardized acquisition protocol on a 3 T whole-body MR system (Magnetom Prisma, Siemens Healthineers), using a 64-channel phased-array head and neck coil for radiofrequency reception. The protocol includes the acquisition of 3D magnetization-prepared 2 rapid gradient-echo (MP2RAGE) images (TR/TI1/TI2=5000/700/2500 ms; resolution = $1 \times 1 \times 1$ mm^3). Brains are extracted using the HD-BET masks from FLAIR scans registered to the MP2RAGE space. The annotations are formed by consensus of two medical doctors with expertise in neuroimaging and include intracortical lesions (in gray matter) and leukocortical lesions (intersecting with white matter). The dataset was split into training, validation, and test sets in the proportion of 79:8:30 patients, corresponding to 859:69:302 CLs.

2.2 Cortical Lesion Segmentation Model

There exist few machine learning models that tackle CL segmentation [6], and they do so jointly with the identification of white matter lesions (WMLs) within the same *lesion* class. Given the clinical importance of the CL biomarker for differential diagnosis [15], we propose a model dedicated solely to CL segmentation. We adopted a 3D shallow U-Net architecture based on a baseline model from the UQ WMLs segmentation challenge (Shifts Challenge [10]). We modified this model to improve segmentation performance and address specific challenges of CLs, such as small sizes and data sparsity. Specifically, we adjusted data augmentation strategy to minimize the distortion of small lesions; replaced the Dice focal loss with focal loss with appropriate weighting; adopted a more effective training strategy (warm-up epochs, a learning rate plateau scheduler, and early stopping). The probability thresholds for all models were chosen on the 5-fold cross validation (CV) and set to 0.55.

2.3 Uncertainty Quantification

We focus on deep ensemble (DE) and Monte Carlo Dropout (MCDP), two UQ methods widely explored for medical imaging tasks in general and in MS lesion segmentation specifically [7,8,13]. DE involves training several similar networks with varied random initialization seeds, which affect random augmentation, weight initialization, training example sampling, and stochastic optimization.

This approach allows for obtaining different samples from the posterior distribution of model parameters. MCDP was initially designed as a way to perform variational inference by placing dropout layers between the neural network layers and treating different dropout masks as random variables, inducing a distribution over the model's weights. DE has been shown to provide better UQ results in terms of the relationship with errors [3].

For both methods, the final prediction is formed as the mean average across M sampled predictions, and uncertainty is quantified by assessing the spread of these predictions. Commonly, for classification tasks, information-theory-based measures like entropy and mutual information are used to quantify uncertainty. For segmentation, classification measures can be used at the pixel/voxel scale. Additionally, it is possible to quantify uncertainty associated with a set of voxel predictions, such as for segmented instances/structures or even for the entire prediction.

In this work, we aim to explore instance-scale uncertainty and its interpretability. Thus, we focus on computing uncertainty for each predicted lesion. Several approaches have been proposed: aggregation (*e.g.* averaging) of voxel-wise uncertainty values [5,13], graph neural networks [7], and disagreement in structural predictions [11]. We chose a UQ metric based on structural disagreement, which has been shown to better capture lesion detection errors compared to aggregation-based measures [11,12].

In a nutshell, given a predicted lesion L and corresponding lesions from the mth sampled prediction $L^m, m = 0, 1, 2, ..., M - 1$, the lesion structural uncertainty is defined as:

$$LSU = 1 - \frac{1}{M} \sum_{m=0}^{M-1} IoU(L, L^m).$$

The corresponding lesions are defined as the ones with maximum intersection over union (IoU).

The number of ensemble members and MCDP samples is chosen to be $M = 10$, selected from 3, 5, 7, 10, based on joint uncertainty-robustness assessment (proposed in [12]) for the DE model. We use a dropout probability of 0.1 for MCDP, chosen among 0.01, 0.05, 0.1, 0.15, 0.2, and 0.25 as the maximum dropout probability that does not yield a significant drop in model prediction quality (quality-diversity trade-off).

2.4 Interpretability Analysis for Lesion Uncertainties

The proposed interpretability analysis for lesion uncertainties consists of explaining lesion uncertainty in terms of lesion-related features.

Lesion Features - Each predicted lesion is characterized by the following features: i) intensity, ii) texture, iii) shape, iv) location in the brain, and v) segmentation quality. Radiomic features from the PyRadiomics Python Library (v3.1.0) are used to characterize the intensity, texture, and shape (i-iii). The location (iv) in the brain is characterized using the MNI atlas separated into right (R) and left

(L) hemispheres [4]. The location feature is computed as the distance between the center of a predicted lesion and the center of the brain structure it belongs to; features corresponding to the rest of the brain structures are zeroed. The belonging of a CL to the MNI brain structure is decided by the maximum overlap. The lesion segmentation quality (v) is evaluated using the adjusted intersection over union (IoU_{adj}) measure [14], which is similar to IoU but corrected for overlaps explained by other predicted instances. Recursive features elimination with the decision trees is used for feature selection.

Uncertainty Regression Model - To explain the lesion-scale uncertainty in terms of the aforementioned features, we use a linear regression model, ElasticNet, which combines L_1- and L_2-regularization. Given that all the features are normalized prior to model fitting, the coefficients of the linear model are interpreted as *feature importance*. Model selection and feature importance are computed 10 times with different random seeds to assess the standard error. A five-fold CV procedure is used to tune the parameters of the pipeline comprising feature selection and ElasticNet model (fraction of selected features, L_1/L_2 ratio, and intercept parameters) by optimizing the coefficient of determination (R^2). CV is performed on the training set with an evaluation on the test set.

3 Results

The CL detection of the DL models reaches a 0.55 F1-score (computed as in [7]), which is a good performance considering the high inter-rater variability of CL manual segmentation (Cohen $\kappa \in [0.4, 0.6]$ depending on the study) [9].

The regression quality (R^2) of the uncertainty interpretability model is shown in Table 1 for different sets of features: only IoU_{adj} (v), only radiomics and location (i-iv), and all together (i-v). For both DE and MCDP uncertainty, the R^2 improves when using all features compared to other settings. For MCDP, less variation in uncertainty can be predicted (worse quality fit) compared to DE, regardless of the features used. For both DE and MCDP uncertainty, some variability in uncertainty is unexplained in terms of chosen features.

The relative feature importance of different features is shown in Fig. 2. Overall, the model explaining the MCDP uncertainty selected more features than DE. For DE uncertainty, the prediction quality explains most of the uncertainty, indicating a strong relationship between uncertainty and error. For MCDP uncertainty, the texture features have more importance than prediction quality (greater values of linear model coefficients). Features selected for both UQ methods resemble, including a strong positive relationship of lesion uncertainty with the presence of texture (SmallDependence...Emphasis, ShortRun...Emphasis); a positive relationship with lesion elongated shape and negative with sphericity (SufaceVolumeRatio, Maximum2DDiameterColumn, Shpericity, Flatness) and lesion small sizes (SufaceVolumeRatio, LeastAxisLength); a negative relationship with features indicating high intensities in a hypointense CL (90Percentile, Energy, Maximum); a positive relationship with left brain lobes locations (Temporal and Occipital L).

Table 1. $R^2(\uparrow)$ of a linear model explaining lesion uncertainty computed on CV (averaged over 10 model fits) and on the test set (averaged across patients). Features used to fit the linear models: only prediction quality (Only IoU_{adj}); all features except for the prediction quality (No IoU_{adj}); all features (All).

	CV			Test		
	Only IoU_{adj}	No IoU_{adj}	All	Only IoU_{adj}	No IoU_{adj}	All
DE	$0.520_{\pm 0.006}$	$0.598_{\pm 0.004}$	$0.661_{\pm 0.004}$	$0.431_{\pm 0.001}$	$0.512_{\pm 0.002}$	$0.632_{\pm 0.004}$
MCDP	$0.393_{\pm 0.006}$	$0.589_{\pm 0.014}$	$0.604_{\pm 0.013}$	$0.261_{\pm 0.003}$	$0.425_{\pm 0.013}$	$0.494_{\pm 0.004}$

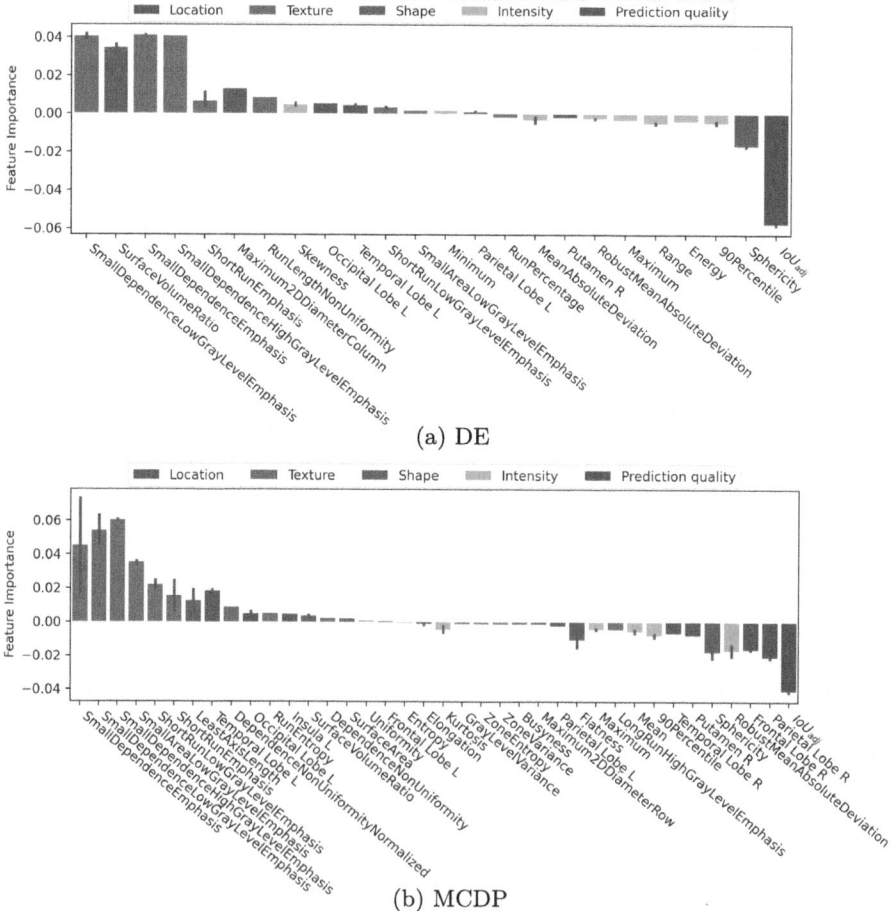

(a) DE

(b) MCDP

Fig. 2. Coefficients of a linear regression model for explaining lesion uncertainty, averaged over 10 model fits, with standard error. Positive values indicate higher uncertainty, negative - lower.

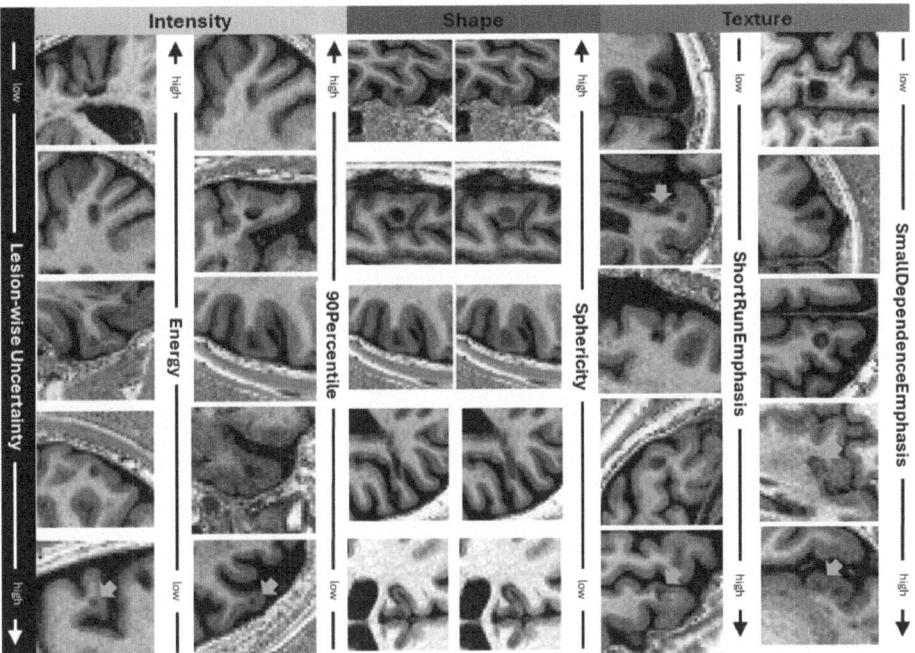

Fig. 3. Qualitative results: visualization of true positive CLs with different important feature activation. CLs are T1-hypointense regions in the center of each image, marked with blue errors in doubtful cases. Long black arrows indicate the direction of features growth (from low to high feature values), white arrow indicates the direction of uncertainty growth. (Color figure online)

4 Discussion

Explained Uncertainty - The *prediction quality* explains a significant portion of the variability in lesion uncertainty. However, the inclusion of lesion-related features provides additional information, helping to predict even more variability. This could be due to either the effect of errors in the ground truth or the fact that uncertainty carries more information than just prediction quality.

The *texture features* selected as important and associated with higher uncertainty are derived from gray level dependence matrices (GLDM) and gray level run length matrices (GLRLM) methods of quantifying texture. Higher values of GLDM SmallDependence...Emphasis and GLRLM RunLengthNonUniformity indicate the presence of textural patterns and less homogeneous textures. Some texture features are typically higher for smaller regions of interest. Both factors complicate the visual identification of lesions (see Fig. 3).

The selected *shape features* describe two different lesion profiles. Less spherical, more spiculated, elongated (low Sphericity, high SurfaceVolumeRatio, and high Maximum2DDiameter) lesion shapes are associated with higher uncertainty. SurfaceVolumeRatio also tends to be high for small lesions, which are harder to detect visually during the annotation process. The elongation and irregularity can be related to the burden of delineation due to the greater surface.

The *location features* are prioritized by the model explaining the MCDP uncertainty, rather than DE uncertainty. Both uncertainty types have an association with lesions located on the periphery of the left occipital and temporal lobes. For MCDP, the proximity to the centers of the right frontal, parietal, and temporal lobes and putamen correlated with more confidence in predictions.

The *intensity features* indicating the presence of high-intensity voxels in a lesion (90Percentile and Energy) are associated with lower uncertainty.

Clinical Perspective - Clinical feedback on the visualized lesions (Fig. 3) was provided by an expert neurologist. Lesions associated with higher uncertainty (smaller sizes, heterogeneous intensity with texture blending into the surrounding area) were candidates for lower confidence of raters and are more likely to be overlooked during the manual annotation process. Among the lesions with low sphericity feature, many likely represented subpial lesions. These lesions have a distinct pathogenesis and shape, are less evident, and thus less prevalent on 3T MRI. Subpial and inhomogeneously-shaped lesions, less common in MS, are likely under-represented in the training data.

The association between higher intensities and lower uncertainty can be due to the neighboring white matter, which has higher intensity on MP2RAGE. CLs appear hypointense on MP2RAGE, thus neighboring white matter increases contrast and visibility of lesions. Additionally, from a radiological perspective, higher intensities within a lesion-gray-matter overlap help confirm that the lesion is a true CL rather than a pure white matter lesion.

The characterization of CL locations is still poorly understood, hence the right and left hemispheric differences shown in our analysis are difficult to justify. Lesions on the periphery of the temporal and occipital lobes being more uncertain might indicate proximity to the cerebellum and brain stem, hence less common locations with worse lesion-surrounding contrast. These lesions are also likely under-represented in the training data.

Unexplained Uncertainty - The R^2 reaches 0.661, meaning that some variability in lesion uncertainty is left unexplained. There are several potential reasons. First, the fact of using a linear model to explain the non-linear relationships between uncertainty and features. We repeated the analysis with a non-linear random forest model, but this did not significantly improve the regression quality or alter the importance of the features. Second, the lack of informative features. We use lesion features that encompass characteristics of different natures and approximate the clinical perspective. However, more features could be added to describe the lesion surroundings or to introduce additional clinical context, such as patient information or MS lesion subtypes. Finally, interpretability also suffers from the noise in the UQ, related to the quality of the UQ itself. This may explain the higher R^2 of the DE uncertainty model compared to MCDP, serving as a sanity check for the UQ.

5 Conclusions

We explore the interpretability of instance-wise uncertainty within the context of cortical lesion DL-based segmentation in MS. To explain lesion uncertainty, we use an ElasticNet regression model with radiomics, location, and ground-truth overlap features. Our results demonstrate how explaining the predicted lesion uncertainty in terms of lesion-related features can: i) detect model biases towards over- or underperforming on specific types of CLs; ii) validate the sanity of UQ by assessing the unexplained variability in uncertainty; iii) facilitate the visual qualitative assessment of the model, helping to select informative lesion examples.

We observe that lesion-scale uncertainty cannot be solely explained by the quality of CL segmentation. Given the clinical feedback, we conclude that the features associated with higher uncertainty describe the lesions that are harder to annotate for radiologists and are often less common. Thus, we hypothesize that uncertainty would be better explained by the inter-rater variability or rater confidence rather than the ground-truth overlap, as it is dominated by aleatoric or label uncertainty [8]. Our future work should verify those hypotheses.

It is worth mentioning that the proposed analysis show correlations between uncertainty, not causality. Thus, it can help hypothesize about the sources of uncertainty, but they require additional validation and clinical feedback. Last but not least, the proposed analysis does not need to be limited to instance segmentation. It can be performed for structure- or patient-wise uncertainty values for any semantic segmentation task, as well as for an image classification.

Disclosure of Interests. PMG, MOP, PJL, MW, XC, AD, MBC: no competing interests to declare relevant to the content of this article. NM: funded by Hasler Foundation Responsible AI program. AC: supported by EUROSTAR E!113682 HORIZON2020, speaker honoraria from Novartis. CG: The employer, University Hospital Basel, has received research grants or speaker fees or consultancy fees from Siemens, GeNeuro, Genzyme-Sanofi, Biogen, Roche, Actelion, Novartis, and Merck. HM: mandates with Roche.

References

1. Begoli, E., Bhattacharya, T., Kusnezov, D.F.: The need for uncertainty quantification in machine-assisted medical decision making. Nat. Mach. Intell. **1**(1) (2019)
2. Bhatt, U., et al.: Uncertainty as a form of transparency: measuring, communicating, and using uncertainty. In: Proceedings of the 2021 AAAI/ACM Conference on AI, Ethics, and Society, AIES 2021, pp. 401–413. Association for Computing Machinery, New York (2021)
3. Gawlikowski, J., et al.: A survey of uncertainty in deep neural networks. Artif. Intell. Rev. 1–77 (2023)
4. Grabner, G., Janke, A.L., Budge, M.M., Smith, D., Pruessner, J., Collins, D.L.: Symmetric atlasing and model based segmentation: an application to the hippocampus in older adults. In: Larsen, R., Nielsen, M., Sporring, J. (eds.) Medical Image Computing and Computer-Assisted Intervention - MICCAI 2006, pp. 58–66. Springer, Heidelberg (2006)

5. Jungo, A., Balsiger, F., Reyes, M.: Analyzing the quality and challenges of uncertainty estimations for brain tumor segmentation. Front. Neurosci. **14** (2020)
6. La Rosa, F., et al.: Multiple sclerosis cortical and WM lesion segmentation at 3T MRI: a deep learning method based on FLAIR and MP2RAGE. NeuroImage: Clin. **27**, 102335 (2020)
7. Lambert, B., Forbes, F., Doyle, S., Tucholka, A., Dojat, M.: Beyond voxel prediction uncertainty: Identifying brain lesions you can trust. In: International Workshop on Interpretability of Machine Intelligence in Medical Image Computing, pp. 61–70 (2022)
8. Lambert, B., Forbes, F., Tucholka, A., Doyle, S., Dehaene, H., Dojat, M.: Trustworthy clinical AI solutions: a unified review of uncertainty quantification in deep learning models for medical image analysis. Artif. Intell. Med. **150**, 102830 (2024)
9. Madsen, M.A., Wiggermann, V., Bramow, S., Christensen, J.R., Sellebjerg, F., Siebner, H.R.: Imaging cortical multiple sclerosis lesions with ultra-high field MRI. NeuroImage. Clin. **32**, 102847 (2021)
10. Malinin, A., et al.: Shifts 2.0: extending the dataset of real distributional shifts (2022)
11. Molchanova, N., et al.: Novel structural-scale uncertainty measures and error retention curves: application to multiple sclerosis. In: 2023 IEEE 20th International Symposium on Biomedical Imaging (ISBI), pp. 1–5 (2023)
12. Molchanova, N., et al.: Structural-based uncertainty in deep learning across anatomical scales: analysis in white matter lesion segmentation (2024)
13. Nair, T., Precup, D., Arnold, D., Arbel, T.: Exploring uncertainty measures in deep networks for multiple sclerosis lesion detection and segmentation. Med. Image Anal. **59**, 101557 (2020)
14. Rottmann, M., et al.: Prediction error meta classification in semantic segmentation: detection via aggregated dispersion measures of softmax probabilities. In: 2020 International Joint Conference on Neural Networks (IJCNN), pp. 1–9 (2020)
15. Thompson, A.J., et al.: Diagnosis of multiple sclerosis: 2017 revisions of the McDonald criteria. Lancet Neurol. **17**(2), 162–173 (2018)

TextCAVs: Debugging Vision Models Using Text

Angus Nicolson[1,2(✉)], Yarin Gal[2], and J. Alison Noble[1]

[1] Institute of Biomedical Engineering, University of Oxford, Oxford, UK
angus.nicolson@eng.ox.ac.uk
[2] OATML, Department of Computer Science, University of Oxford, Oxford, UK

Abstract. Concept-based interpretability methods are a popular form of explanation for deep learning models which provide explanations in the form of high-level human interpretable concepts. These methods typically find concept activation vectors (CAVs) using a probe dataset of concept examples. This requires labelled data for these concepts – an expensive task in the medical domain. We introduce TextCAVs: a novel method which creates CAVs using vision-language models such as CLIP, allowing for explanations to be created solely using text descriptions of the concept, as opposed to image exemplars. This reduced cost in testing concepts allows for many concepts to be tested and for users to interact with the model, testing new ideas as they are thought of, rather than a delay caused by image collection and annotation. In early experimental results, we demonstrate that TextCAVs produces reasonable explanations for a chest x-ray dataset (MIMIC-CXR) and natural images (ImageNet), and that these explanations can be used to debug deep learning-based models. Code: github.com/AngusNicolson/textcavs.

Keywords: Interpretabilty · Concepts · Text Explanations · Chest X-rays

1 Introduction

Deep learning-based models are increasingly utilised in healthcare scenarios where mistakes can have severe consequences. One approach for creating safer, more reliable models is to use interpretability: the ability to explain or present a model in terms understandable to a human [4].

Many different interpretabilty methods have emerged, with explanations taking a variety of different forms such as individual pixels, prototypes or concepts. We focus on concept-based methods which provide explanations using high-level terms that humans are familiar with. Concept activation vectors (CAVs) are a common approach used to represent concepts within the activation space of a model and are found using a probe dataset of concept exemplars [13].

The labels required for this can be expensive to obtain in medical domains where expert clinical input is necessary. We introduce TextCAVs, a concept-based interpretability method that uses solely the text label of the concept, or descriptions of it, rather than image examples.

We demonstrate that TextCAVs give meaningful explanations for both natural image (ImageNet [3]) and chest X-ray (MIMIC-CXR [11,12]) tasks. Further, as interpretability itself is difficult to measure, we demonstrate its usefulness in debugging deep learning-based models through finding implanted dataset bias in MIMIC-CXR (Fig. 1).

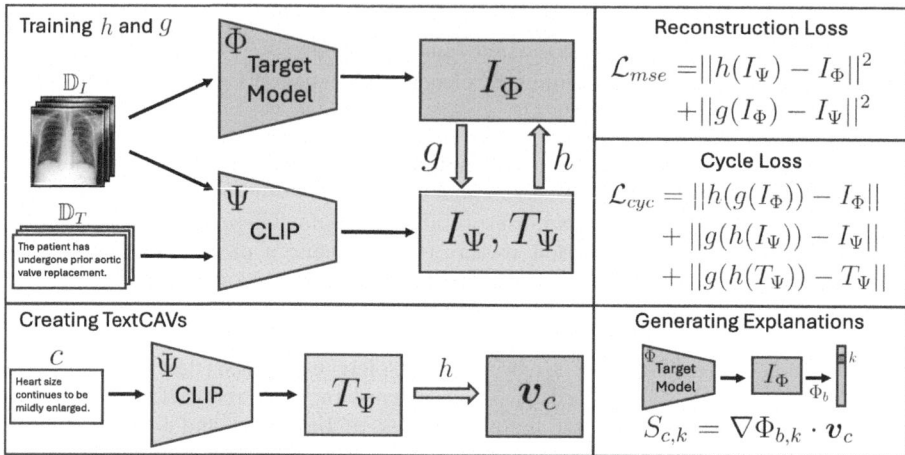

Fig. 1. Explaining models with TextCAVs. In order to move between the activations of a CLIP model and our target model, we train linear transformations, h and g, using a text dataset, $\mathbb{D}_T$, and image dataset, $\mathbb{D}_I$. The loss terms are detailed on the right with I_Φ, I_Ψ and T_Ψ representing the image features of the target model, the image features of the CLIP model, and the text features of the CLIP model, respectively. Once h is trained, TextCAVs can be created by passing text representing some concept, c, through the CLIP model and h. The model's sensitivity to c, for some logit output, k, can then be measured using the directional derivative, $S_{c,k}$: the similarity between the model gradient, $\nabla \Phi_{b,k}$, and a TextCAV, $\boldsymbol{v}_c$.

2 Related Work

Kim et al. [13] introduce Testing with Concept Activation Vectors (TCAVs) where they use probe datasets of concept examples to create CAVs and then compare the CAVs with model gradients to measure a model's sensitivity to a concept for a specific class. We also use the directional derivative (dot product between CAV and gradient) to measure model sensitivity, but our CAVs are created using a multi-modal model and so do not require a probe dataset for each concept.

In order to reduce the cost of creating concept-based explanations, a variety of different methods automate the process of finding concepts [5–7,18,22]. However, the meaning of each concept is not always readily apparent and the concept must be visually present in the dataset used to discover the concepts. Our method reduces cost using a different approach as we also do not need to collect labelled data for each concept, but our resulting CAVs have inherent meaning from their text descriptions.

CLIP models [17] have demonstrated strong performance in vision-language tasks. Their joint embedding space for text and images allows for built-in comparisons between the modalities and therefore for zero-shot classification. A variety of adaptations have been suggested for the biomedical space [24] with some models being trained for specific modalities like chest X-rays (e.g. BioViL [1]) and others more generally (e.g. BiomedCLIP [23]). We use these vision-language models in our method but, importantly, inference is performed by the target model, without placing restrictions on its architecture or method of training.

Yuksekgonul et al. [21] use multimodal models to create CAVs and then use the similarity between model activations and these CAVs to create a concept bottleneck model. Moayeri et al. [15] extend this approach to target vision models more generally by, as in our work, training a simple linear layer to transfer the features of the target model to a CLIP model. Also as in our work, Shipard et al. [19] improve the transfer of features by training a linear layer in both directions and using multimodal losses. However, these approaches focus on zero-shot classification and on changing how the model inference is performed, rather than explaining the model in its current state using gradients.

3 TextCAVs

For some target model, Φ, and a CLIP-like vision-language model, Ψ, let $I_\Phi \in \mathbb{R}^m$ and $I_\Psi \in \mathbb{R}^n$ be the extracted features for some image dataset $\mathbb{D}_I$. As Ψ contains a joint embedding space between text and images we can also extract text features: $T_\Psi \in \mathbb{R}^n$ from some text dataset $\mathbb{D}_T$. We train two linear layers $h : \mathbb{R}^n \to \mathbb{R}^m$ and $g : \mathbb{R}^m \to \mathbb{R}^n$ which can be used to convert between the features of the two models. To create TextCAVs, we only need h but to improve h's ability to convert text features we use a cycle loss term which requires g. The loss is composed of two parts: reconstruction loss and cycle loss. The reconstruction loss is simply the mean squared error (MSE) between the image features and converted features.

$$\mathcal{L}_{mse} = ||h(I_\Psi) - I_\Phi||^2 + ||g(I_\Phi) - I_\Psi||^2 \tag{1}$$

The reconstruction loss can only be calculated for image features as we need features from both models (Φ and Ψ). To include information from the text features in the loss function we use cycle loss which ensures that the features are consistent with their original form when converted back to their original space:

$$\mathcal{L}_{cyc} = ||h(g(I_\Phi)) - I_\Phi|| \tag{2}$$
$$+ ||g(h(I_\Psi)) - I_\Psi|| \tag{3}$$
$$+ ||g(h(T_\Psi)) - T_\Psi||. \tag{4}$$

Once trained, we use h, Ψ and a concept label, c, to obtain a concept vector in the activation space of the target model:

$$\boldsymbol{v}_c = h(\Psi(c)). \tag{5}$$

Φ can be decomposed into two functions: $\Phi_a(\boldsymbol{x}) = I_\Phi \in \mathbb{R}^m$ which maps the input $\boldsymbol{x} \in \mathbb{R}^N$ to its features I_Φ, and $\Phi_b(I_\Phi)$ which maps I_Φ to the output. To obtain the model's sensitivity to a concept for a specific class, as in [13], we calculate the directional derivative:

$$\begin{aligned} S_{c,k}(\boldsymbol{x}) &= \lim_{\epsilon \to 0} \frac{\Phi_{b,k}\left(\Phi_a(\boldsymbol{x}) + \epsilon \boldsymbol{v}_c\right) - \Phi_{b,k}\left(\Phi_a(\boldsymbol{x})\right)}{\epsilon} \\ &= \nabla \Phi_{b,k}\left(\Phi_a(\boldsymbol{x})\right) \cdot \boldsymbol{v}_c. \end{aligned} \tag{6}$$

If Φ_a is chosen to be the output of the penultimate layer in a model then the directional derivative can be calculated without image exemplars:

$$S_{c,k} = \nabla \Phi_{b,k} \cdot \boldsymbol{v}_c. \tag{7}$$

This is due to the lack of non-linearities between the penultimate layer and the logit output. Having solely a linear layer between the features and the output means the gradient of the activations with respect to the logit does not depend on the activations. This means we can extract gradients, and therefore model explanations, using solely the model weights. Therefore, once h has been trained, TextCAVs requires **only** the text you wish to test to be able to generate an explanation. In practice, to calculate the gradient, we input an array of zeros of the same shape as the images, but this is an arbitrary choice. In this work, we use the penultimate layer in all experiments and leave exploration of using other layers for future work.

By ranking concepts based on their directional derivative, we obtain a list of sentences/words ordered by the model's sensitivity for a specific class. If we can filter this list for concepts which we expect to be there, we can discover bugs in the model. Ideally, this would be done by a human expert who could use their domain knowledge to explore different hypotheses. The minimal overhead for testing new concepts allows the user to test words related to new hypotheses quickly and provide an interactive process to model debugging.

4 Experiments

In this section we provide a description of our training setup, our model choices, evaluation and then a discussion and analysis of our results experiments with both the ImageNet and MIMIC-CXR datasets.

4.1 ImageNet

TextCAVs achieved 3rd place at the Secure and Trustworthy Machine Learning Conference (SaTML) interpretabilty competition to detect trojans (implanted bugs) in vision models trained on ImageNet [2]. Additionally, as part of the competition, TextCAVs was used to identify all four secret trojans demonstrating its potential for interactive debugging.

In this section, however, we simply demonstrate that TextCAVs produces reasonable explanations for a standard ResNet-50 [8] trained on ImageNet.

Training Details. We use 20% of the ImageNet training dataset to train h and g and train for 20 epochs. For the target model, Φ we use the default weights for a ResNet-50 [8] in the TorchVision package in PyTorch. For the vision-language model, Ψ, we use a pretrained ViT-B/16 CLIP model [17].

Concepts. In a similar manner to Oikarinen et al. [16], in order to automate the process, we use a large language model (LLM) to obtain a list of concepts. We use three prompts asking for the "things most commonly seen around" "visual elements or parts" and "superclasses" of each class in ImageNet. We then extract and perform basic filtering of the concepts, removing: plurals of the same word; the words "an", "a" and "the"; and concepts containing more than 2 words. To obtain the final list of concepts we remove similar concepts using text embeddings from Ψ. If a set of concepts have a cosine similarity greater than 0.9, only the shortest concept is retained. This reduces the number of near synonyms in the concept list. For the LLM, we use a 4-bit quantized version of the Tulu-v2-7b model [10].

Results. In Table 1, we show the top-10 concepts for a selection of ImageNet classes. All the concepts relate to their respective class, indicating that TextCAVs can produce reliable explanations.

Table 1. Top-10 concepts ordered by directional derivative for a selection of classes in the ImageNet model.

bullfrog	albatross	orangutan	bucket	cellphone
american bullfrog	gannet	orangutan	crab buckets	mp3 player
green frog	seagull	howler monkey	diaper pail	phone
boreal toad	sea eagle	macaque	bucket	phone case
western toad	shearwater	tarsier	laundry basket	memory card
frog	gull	great ape	watering can	walkman
musk turtle	white-tailed eagle	long-nosed monkey	flower pot	cordless phone
snapping turtle	petrel	gibbon	cooking pot	bluetooth
toad	merganser	gorilla	dustbin	smartwatch
terrapin turtle	wading bird	langur	fishing basket	card reader

4.2 MIMIC-CXR

In this section we demonstrate TextCAVs ability to produce meaningful explanations for a model trained on the chest X-ray dataset MIMIC-CXR and how we can use TextCAVs to discover bias in a model trained on a biased version of the dataset.

Training Details. We train both the linear transformations, h and g, and the target model, Φ, using the MIMIC-CXR training set. The target model is a ResNet-50 [8] pretrained on ImageNet and then fine-tuned for the 5-way multi-label classification of chest X-rays with the classes: No Finding, Atelectasis (lung collapse), Cardiomegaly (enlarged heart), Edema (fluid in the lungs) and Pleural Effusion (fluid between the lungs and the chest wall). We use the Adam optimiser [14] with weight decay of $1e-4$ and initial learning rate of $1e-4$. The learning rate is halved or the training is stopped if the validation loss does not decrease within 3 or 5 epochs, respectively. Images are resized to 256×256. We use random rotation of up to 15 degrees, random horizontal flipping, random crop and resize with a minimum size of 40%, and distortion to augment the images. We use the published data splits and, after removing images with no positive class labels, there are $368,945$ training, $2,991$ validation and $1,012$ test images. We use labels from CheXpert [9] for the training and validation labels, which have been generated by a model using the text reports. Whereas, for the test dataset, we use the provided labels annotated by a single radiologist.

We train both h and g on the training set of MIMIC-CXR for 20 epochs. We use the output of the average pool operation as the features from the target model as it simplifies the extraction of model gradients (Eq. 7).

For Ψ, we use BiomedCLIP [23] – the current state of the art vision-language model for chest X-ray tasks.

Concepts. The MIMIC-CXR dataset has a clinical report associated with each image. We use these reports as a source of concepts. We extract the sentences from the "FINDINGS" and "IMPRESSION" sections of the reports and use a random subset of 5000 sentences to obtain a wide variety of concepts to test.

Biased Data. To evaluate TextCAVs as an interpretability tool we explore its usefulness in model debugging. We induced a dataset bias in the MIMIC-CXR training set by removing all participants with a positive label for Atelactesis and a negative label for Support Devices. This means that all participants with Atelactesis in the training set also had a Support Device (e.g. tube or pacemaker) as can be seen in Fig. 2.

Metrics. To provide a quantitative metric, we labelled the top-50 sentences for each class, ordered by directional derivative, on whether they relate to the class. We report this information as a concept relevance score (CRS), which is simply the proportion of concepts that were related to the class. Using Edema as an example, a sentence was labelled as related if it directly diagnosed the class, e.g., "Worsening cardiogenic pulmonary edema", or if the class was implied, e.g., "bilateral parenchymal opacities" or "there is alveolar opacity throughout much of the right lung".

Results. We are comparing two models: one trained on the standard MIMIC-CXR dataset and the other trained on the biased version. We will refer to the models as "standard" and "biased", respectively. The standard model achieved a mean area under the receiver operator characteristic curve (AUC) of 0.83 and the biased model a mean AUC of 0.81. The individual class AUCs can be found in Table 2. We expect, and see that the biased version has higher performance on a biased version of the test set since Support Devices tend to be easy to detect.

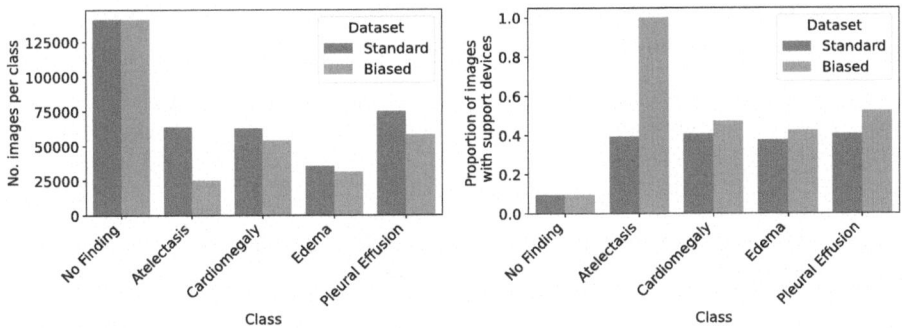

Fig. 2. MIMIC-CXR dataset characteristics. Left: The number of images per class in the training set of the target models. Right: The proportion of training images that contain a support device for each class.

Table 2. Area under the receiver operator characteristic curve (AUC) and concept relevance score (CRS) for the standard and biased MIMIC-CXR models. AUC* was calculated on the biased version of the MIMIC-CXR test set. The low CRS for Atelectasis in the biased model means almost none of the top TextCAVs are relevant to the class, demonstrating that they can be used to detect if a model is using biased features.

Model	Standard		Biased		
Metric	AUC	CRS	AUC	AUC*	CRS
No Finding	0.87	0.74	0.85	0.94	0.76
Atelectasis	0.73	0.56	0.68	0.81	0.04
Cardiomegaly	0.81	0.94	0.81	0.82	0.90
Edema	0.85	0.90	0.84	0.81	0.80
Pleural Effusion	0.89	1.00	0.88	0.88	1.00
Mean	0.83	0.83	0.81	0.85	0.70

As evidence for this, we trained a reference model separately and achieved an AUC of 0.92 for Support Devices.

In Table 3, we show the five sentences whose CAVs have the highest directional derivatives for the classes of No Finding, Atelectasis (lung collapse) and Cardiomegaly (enlarged heart). Some of these are clearly linked to the class in question (e.g. "The lungs are clear" for No Finding and "Heart size continues to be mildly enlarged" for Cardiomegaly) but there also sentences which do not relate to the classes (e.g. "Nasogastric tube extends below the hemidiaphragm" for Atelectasis or "There is a fracture of the upper most sternal wire" for No Finding). The noise present in the explanations could be due to several different causes: (1) the target model is using unexpected features in its classification; (2) the feature conversion between Φ and Ψ is not perfect (i.e., h); or (3) the inherent noise present in gradient vectors [20]. It is difficult to ascertain which of these is the cause but a tool can still be useful even with noise present. Hence, we demonstrate its ability to detect dataset bias that we induce in MIMIC-CXR.

Table 4 shows the top-5 sentences for a model trained on the biased version of MIMIC-CXR. The bias is apparent in the explanations, as the top-5 sentences

Table 3. Top-5 concepts ordered by directional derivative for the standard MIMIC-CXR model.

No Finding	Atelectasis	Cardiomegaly
The lungs are clear and the cardiac, mediastinal, and hilar contours are normal	Nasogastric tube extends below the hemidiaphragm and out of view	Marked cardiac enlargement as before and unchanged position of previously described metallic prosthesis of porcine type
Normal chest radiograph with unremarkable appearance of the lung parenchyma and normal appearance of the heart and the mediastinal and hilar contours	Interval placement of a basilar right sided pleural space pigtail catheter with improved small right pleural effusion and right medial lung base atelectasis	Heart size continues to be mildly enlarged
The trachea is slightly deviated to the right by the aortic knob, which is ill-defined	Worsening of the left retrocardiac opacity likely secondary to increasing atelectasis and/or effusion	The patient has undergone prior aortic valve replacement
This could represent a granuloma or possibly a bone island in the rib itself	There is persistent elevation of the left hemidiaphragm with evidence of Bochdalek hernia seen at the left lower hemithorax	Dense retrocardiac opacity which could represent effusion, atelectasis, consolidation or a combination thereof
There is a fracture of the upper most sternal wire, unchanged	Stable opacification of the mid and lower right lung consistent with large loculated pleural effusions and adjacent atelectasis	The heart continues to be enlarged with mild to moderate CHF

for Atelectasis all refer to Support Devices, rather than to any concepts relating to the class itself. The CRS values in Table 2 also indicate the presence of bias: a CRS of 0.04 for Atelectasis for the biased model shows that almost none of the top-50 concepts contain reference to the class. To further quantify the difference between the two sets of explanations we also labelled whether they referred to Support Devices. For the class of Atelectasis, we found that 13/50 concepts were related to Support Devices for the standard model compared to 44/50 for the biased model, demonstrating that TextCAVs are sensitive to the difference in behaviour between the two models.

Table 4. Top-5 concepts ordered by directional derivative for the biased MIMIC-CXR model.

No Finding	Atelectasis	Cardiomegaly
Bronchial wall thickening is minimal	ET and NG tubes positioned appropriately	If cardiomegaly persists, the presence of a pericardial effusion could be excluded with echocardiography
Hilar and mediastinal contours are otherwise normal	ET tube, nasogastric tube, Swan-Ganz catheter, and midline drains are all in standard placements	Worsening heart failure in the context of chronic atelectasis
This could represent a granuloma or possibly a bone island in the rib itself	Nasogastric tube extends below the hemidiaphragm and out of view	The patient has undergone prior aortic valve replacement
No discrete solid pulmonary nodule are concerning mass	Impella LVAD and transvenous atrioventricular pacer leads unchanged in their respective positions	Moderate-to-severe cardiomegaly and stigmata of previous mitral valve repair noted
There is a fracture of the upper most sternal wire, unchanged	Nasogastric tube has been placed that extends well into the stomach	The heart remains moderately enlarged and the aorta remains unfolded and tortuous

5 Conclusion

In this work we introduce TextCAVs, an interpretability method that, once two linear layers have been trained, can measure the sensitivity of a model to a concept with only a text description of the concept. We show that TextCAVs produce reasonable explanations for models trained on both natural images (ImageNet [3]) a chest X-ray dataset (MIMIC-CXR [11]). As first demonstrated in the SaTML CNN interpretability competition [2], we show that TextCAVs can be used to debug models. We generated explanations for a model trained on a biased version of the MIMIC-CXR dataset and showed that explanations for the biased class substantially changed with most (44/50) concepts referring to the bias compared to just 13/50 for the unbiased model.

Once the linear transformations, h and g, have been trained, TextCAVs enables fast feedback when testing the sensitivity of different concepts. This makes it ideally suited for interactive debugging which we aim to study in future work. Some of the concepts with a high directional derivative did not appear to be related to the class. In Sect. 4.2 we state three possible sources of this: (1) Φ, (2) h or (3) $\nabla \Phi_{b,k}$. In future work we will explore which of these have the greatest effect.

Acknowledgments. We appreciate the members of OATML and the Noble group for your support and discussions during the project, in particular Lisa Schut. We thank Shreshth Malik for organising the hackathon where we began developing TextCAVs. A. Nicolson is supported by the EPSRC Centre for Doctoral Training in Health Data Science (EP/S02428X/1). Y. Gal is supported by a Turing AI Fellowship financed by the UK government's Office for Artificial Intelligence, through UK Research and Innovation (grant reference EP/V030302/1) and delivered by the Alan Turing Institute. J.A. Noble acknowledges EPSRC grants EP/X040186/1 and EP/T028572/1.

Disclosure of Interests. The authors have no competing interests to declare that are relevant to the content of this article.

References

1. Boecking, B., et al.: Making the most of text semantics to improve biomedical vision–language processing. In: ECCV (2022)
2. Casper, Set al.: The SaTML '24 CNN interpretability competition: new innovations for concept-level interpretability. arXiv:2404.02949 (2024)
3. Deng, J., Dong, W., Socher, R., Li, L.J., Li, K., Fei-Fei, L.: ImageNet: a large-scale hierarchical image database. In: CVPR, pp. 248–255 (2009)
4. Doshi-Velez, F., Kim, B.: Towards a rigorous science of interpretable machine learning. arxiv:1702.08608 (2017)
5. Fel, T., et al.: CRAFT: concept recursive activation FacTorization for explainability. In: CVPR (2023)
6. Ghorbani, A., Wexler, J., Zou, J., Kim, B.: Towards automatic concept-based explanations. In: Advances in Neural Information Processing Systems (2019)
7. Graziani, M., O'Mahony, L., phi Nguyen, A., Müller, H., Andrearczyk, V.: Uncovering unique concept vectors through latent space decomposition. TMLR (2023)
8. He, K., Zhang, X., Ren, S., Sun, J.: Deep residual learning for image recognition. In: CVPR (2016)
9. Irvin, J., et al.: CheXpert: a large chest radiograph dataset with uncertainty labels and expert comparison. In: AAAI Conference on Artificial Intelligence, vol. 33, pp. 590–597 (2019)

10. Ivison, H., et al.: Camels in a changing climate: enhancing LM adaptation with Tulu 2. arXiv:2311.10702 (2023)
11. Johnson, A.E.W., et al.: MIMIC-CXR: a large publicly available database of labeled chest radiographs (2019)
12. Johnson, A.E.W., et al.: MIMIC-CXR-JPG - chest radiographs with structured labels (2024)
13. Kim, B., et al.: Interpretability beyond feature attribution: quantitative testing with concept activation vectors (TCAV). In: ICML (2018)
14. Kingma, D., Ba, J.: Adam: a method for stochastic optimization. In: ICLR (2015)
15. Moayeri, M., Rezaei, K., Sanjabi, M., Feizi, S.: Text-to-concept (and back) via cross-model alignment. In: ICML (2023)
16. Oikarinen, T., Das, S., Nguyen, L.M., Weng, T.W.: Label-free concept bottleneck models. In: ICLR (2023)
17. Radford, A., et al.: Learning transferable visual models from natural language supervision. In: ICLR (2021)
18. Ramaswamy, V.V., Kim, S.S.Y., Meister, N., Fong, R., Russakovsky, O.: ELUDE: generating interpretable explanations via a decomposition into labelled and unlabelled features. arXiv:2206.07690 (2022)
19. Shipard, J., Wiliem, A., Thanh, K.N., Xiang, W., Fookes, C.: Zoom-shot: fast and efficient unsupervised zero-shot transfer of clip to vision encoders with multimodal loss. arXiv:2401.11633 (2024)
20. Smilkov, D., Thorat, N., Kim, B., Viégas, F., Wattenberg, M.: SmoothGrad: removing noise by adding noise. arXiv:1706.03825 (2017)
21. Yuksekgonul, M., Wang, M., Zou, J.: Post-hoc concept bottleneck models. In: ICLR (2023)
22. Zhang, R., Madumal, P., Miller, T., Ehinger, K.A., Rubinstein, B.I.P.: Invertible concept-based explanations for CNN models with non-negative concept activation vectors. In: AAAI Conference on Artificial Intelligence (2020)
23. Zhang, S., et al.: BiomedCLIP: a multimodal biomedical foundation model pretrained from fifteen million scientific image-text pairs. arXiv:2303.00915 (2023)
24. Zhao, Z., et al.: CLIP in medical imaging: a comprehensive survey. arXiv:2312.07353 (2023)

Evaluating Visual Explanations of Attention Maps for Transformer-Based Medical Imaging

Minjae Chung[1], Jong Bum Won[1], Ganghyun Kim[1], Yujin Kim[1], and Utku Ozbulak[1,2(✉)]

[1] Center for Biosystems and Biotech Data Science, Ghent University Global Campus, Incheon, Republic of Korea
utku.ozbulak@ghent.ac.kr

[2] Department of Electronics and Information Systems, Ghent University, Ghent, Belgium

Abstract. Although Vision Transformers (ViTs) have recently demonstrated superior performance in medical imaging problems, they face explainability issues similar to previous architectures such as convolutional neural networks. Recent research efforts suggest that attention maps, which are part of decision-making process of ViTs can potentially address the explainability issue by identifying regions influencing predictions, especially in models pretrained with self-supervised learning. In this work, we compare the visual explanations of attention maps to other commonly used methods for medical imaging problems. To do so, we employ four distinct medical imaging datasets that involve the identification of (1) colonic polyps, (2) breast tumors, (3) esophageal inflammation, and (4) bone fractures and hardware implants. Through large-scale experiments on the aforementioned datasets using various supervised and self-supervised pretrained ViTs, we find that although attention maps show promise under certain conditions and generally surpass GradCAM in explainability, they are outperformed by transformer-specific interpretability methods. Our findings indicate that the efficacy of attention maps as a method of interpretability is context-dependent and may be limited as they do not consistently provide the comprehensive insights required for robust medical decision-making.

Keywords: Interpretability · Vision Transformers · Attention Maps

1 Introduction

The global population is experiencing a significant shift as advancements in modern medicine have led to increased life expectancy and a rising median age which necessitates continuous medical attention, particularly for the elderly [33].

M. Chung, J. B. Won, G. Kim and Y. Kim—Equal contribution.

Recent shortage of medical workforce in many countries exacerbated these challenges, making it difficult for healthcare systems to meet the growing demand [14,33].

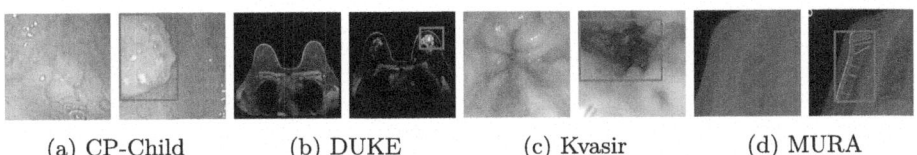

(a) CP-Child (b) DUKE (c) Kvasir (d) MURA

Fig. 1. Examples of medical images in (a) CP-Child, (b) DUKE, (c) Kvasir, and (d) MURA datasets. The left images shows benign (disease-negative) images, while the right shows malignant (disease-positive) images for each dataset. Red annotation boxes highlight the regions with diseases. (Color figure online)

An innovative solution to address the issues faced by global healthcare is the use of artificial intelligence (AI) for accurate and fast diagnosis, especially for medical imaging problems. Nowadays, such solutions often utilize the recently discovered Vision Transformer (ViT) architecture, which originates from transformers which make use of attention mechanism. As it stands, ViTs achieve state-of-the-art results in several medical imaging tasks and have the potential to be become the dominant architecture in the field, possibly replacing convolutional neural networks (CNNs) in near future [17,27,29].

Despite notable advancements in the accuracy of ViT-based medical imaging models, these models face challenges regarding explainability similar to CNNs. These explainability issues are one of the major obstacles preventing the large-scale adoption of AI-based diagnostic methods in medical institutes [9,13,20]. To enhance the trustworthiness of predictions made by ViTs and to address the aforementioned interpretability challenges, numerous methods have been proposed in the literature [11,24]. Among these methods, attention maps stand out as an explainability technique, since they are part of the ViT architecture and directly influence the predictions made by the model. However, there is an ongoing debate [3] on the usage of attention maps as explanation, with some research efforts advocating for [4,7,31] and some against it [1,26]. Complicating this issue further, recent research on self-supervised learning (SSL) for ViTs has shown that SSL pretraining improves the efficacy of attention maps for explainability [4]. However, these results are often demonstrated in the context of natural images, and it remains unclear if these findings apply to medical imaging problems with specific modalities.

In this work, we evaluate the suitability of attention maps for interpreting transformer-based medical imaging models by comparing them with other commonly used methods for explainability. Our study complements that of [15] by expanding the scope to include a wider range of datasets, including non-radiology medical images. Additionally, we also utilize state-of-the-art SSL pretrained ViTs to investigate the impact of self-supervised pretraining on explainability.

Table 1. Details for datasets used in this study, including the number of negative and positive samples, and the classification tasks, are provided.

Dataset	Training		Validation		Classification task
	Negative	Positive	Negative	Positive	
CP-Child	7,000	1,100	1,100	300	Colonic polyp
DUKE	17,642	17,546	4,350	4,446	Breast tumor
Kvasir	800	800	200	200	Gastrointestinal disease
MURA	21,935	14,873	1,667	1,530	Bone abnormality

2 Experimental Setup

2.1 Datasets

To conduct a comprehensive investigation widely applicable to medical imaging, we selected four distinct datasets differing in image modality and body part (Fig. 1). Table 1 contains the task and the number of images in the training and validation sets for each dataset. Below, we briefly describe each dataset.

CP-Child Colonic Polyp Detection Dataset – Obtained from 1,600 patients, the task of this dataset is the detection of colonic polyps in the gastrointestinal track [30].

DUKE Breast Cancer Dataset – This dataset, obtained from 922 patients with invasive breast cancers collected at Duke Hospital over 14 years, is one of the largest publicly available breast cancer 3D MRI image datasets, where the task is identifying the presence of breast tumors [23].

Kvasir Gastrointestinal Disease Detection Dataset – Part of the Kvasir dataset [19], we utilize the Z-line subcategory, where the task is to distinguish between a healthy Z-line and esophagitis at the junction between the esophagus and stomach.

MURA Musculoskeletal Radiograph Dataset – Obtained from 14,863 bone X-ray studies, Stanford's MURA dataset involves the identification of abnormalities such as bone fractures and hardware implants [21].

2.2 Models

To evaluate interpretability methods, we employ widely used Vision Transformer-Base/16 (ViT-B/16) [8]. This model processes images of size 224×224 with 16×16 image tokens, resulting in total 196 tokens. We modify the final linear layer for our two-class classification problems and use four ViT-B/16 models with different weight initializations: random (i.e., from scratch), supervised pretrained, discriminatively pretrained using DINO [4], and generatively pretrained using MAE [10]. Both supervised and self-supervised pretrained models are pretrained using the ImageNet dataset [22].

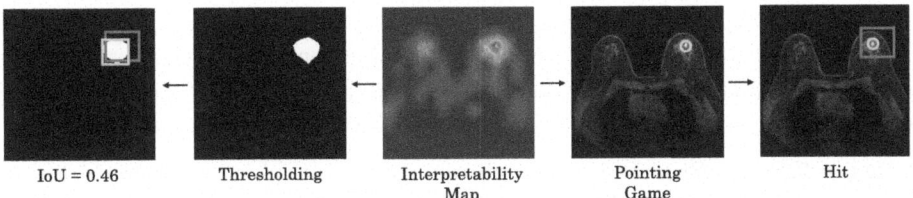

Fig. 2. Evaluation of interpretability maps is visualized. The right side illustrates the pointing game, identifying the most significant point and checking for a hit against the annotation box (red). The left part illustrates the IoU overlap, including the thresholding opeartion to create a binary mask and the calculation of IoU. (Color figure online)

2.3 Interpretability Methods

To evaluate the efficacy of attention maps and to compare it with other methods, we use GradCAM [25] and the transformer-specific interpretability method proposed in [6] (henceforth referred to as the "Chefer method" in the rest of the paper).

GradCAM – GradCAM, an extension of Class Activation Mapping (CAM), ensures interpretability for CNNs by incorporating both forward activations as well as gradients originating from the selected class [25,34]. Despite various extensions, GradCAM remains widely adopted for its robust results [5]. Following the past research efforts, we employ GradCAM on the final self-attention layer of ViT-B/16 [6].

Attention Maps – In the ViT-B/16 setup, images are tokenized and prepended with an additional [cls] token, resulting in 197 tokens [8]. The [cls] token, in conjunction with image patch tokens, are utilized to form attention maps for the self-attention mechanism. The [cls] token is presumed to encapsulate key information about the contributions of specific image patches to the model's classification decisions. Following previous research, we investigate attention map of the [cls] token at the final layer [4,8,18].

Chefer Method – [6] argue that attention maps alone are insufficient for transformer interpretability, focusing narrowly on attention scores obtained from the inner products of queries and keys, and discarding other components. To address these limitations, [6] propose a method that propagates gradient and relevance scores backward through all layers from the classification output.

2.4 Interpretability Evaluation

In order to enable a fair comparison across explainability methods, for each dataset, 50 disease-positive images from the validation set were annotated by a group of medical experts, highlighting the region with the disease using a bounding box. Given the aforementioned annotations containing a bounding box $\mathbf{b} \in \{0,1\}^p$ where $\mathbf{b}_i = 1$ denotes the regions within the bounding box and $\mathbf{b}_i = 0$ outside and an interpretability map $\mathbf{m} \in \mathbb{R}^p$ obtained via one of the methods described in Sect. 2.3, we evaluate the correctness of interpretability maps using two metrics: pointing game and Intersection over union (IoU).

Pointing Game – Proposed by [32], the pointing game measures the precision of interpretability methods [12]. It finds the position in the map with the highest activation $a = \arg\max(\mathbf{m})$. If $\mathbf{b}_a = 1$, it is a "Hit". Otherwise, it is a "Miss". Based on this, we can calculate the average pointing game accuracy by measuring $\text{Acc} = \frac{\#\text{Hit}}{\#\text{Hit}+\#\text{Miss}}$.

Intersection over Union – When the bounding box surrounding the area of interest is large, such as in the Kvasir dataset, interpretability methods may appear inflated in performance using the pointing game. To conduct a more accurate investigation, we employ IoU metric.

Based on $\mathbf{m}$, we select the pixels with activations higher than the top kth percentile (p_k) and produce a binary interpretability map denoted as $\boldsymbol{t}$ where $t_i = \begin{cases} 1 & \text{if } m_i \geq p_k \\ 0, & \text{otherwise} \end{cases}$. In this work, we use $k = 5$. Then, we estimate the tightest bounding box around $\boldsymbol{t}$ where $t_i = 1$. Given the bounding box estimation for the interpretability map $\boldsymbol{t}$ and the ground truth $\boldsymbol{b}$, we calculate $\text{IoU} = \frac{t \cap b}{t \cup b}$. Visual summary of both the pointing game and the IoU overlap are provided in Fig. 2.

3 Experimental Results and Discussion

Using a grid-search approach for finding the most-suitable hyperparameters, we train four models on the datasets described in Sect. 2.1 and present results in Table 2. Compared to the benchmark results from various studies, our models demonstrate results that are comparable to the state-of-the-art, thus making them suitable for experiments on explainability. Further details on the employed training approach and the final models can be found in this repository: https://github.com/ugent-korea/attention_maps.

Using the trained models with state-of-the-art performance, we follow the protocol detailed in Sect. 2.4 and present experimental results on interpretability in Fig. 3, Fig. 4, and Table 3. In particular, Fig. 3 illustrates several qualitative examples, while Table 3 displays pointing game accuracy and mean IoU scores. Finally, Fig. 4 represents IoU distributions represented in the form of boxplots. Based on these results, we make the observations below.

Qualitative Results can be Misleading. In Fig. 3, we present qualitative interpretability outputs for all methods considered. As can be seen, depending on the selected subset of images and the method, both accurate and inaccurate interpretability maps can be found. These findings emphasize the danger of making strong claims about interpretability methods based solely on qualitative results, including attention maps.

Table 2. Performance of ViT-B/16 models trained on datasets from Sect. 2.1 with random, supervised, and self-supervised initializations. Validation accuracies exceeding the benchmark are highlighted in bold and * denotes approximate benchmark accuracy.

Dataset	Model initialization	Validation			Benchmark validation accuracy
		Accuracy	Precision	Recall	
CP-Child	Random	96.00	92.36	88.66	
	Supervised	**99.71**	99.00	99.66	99.29 [30]
	DINO	**99.64**	99.00	99.33	
	MAE	**99.57**	99.33	98.66	
DUKE	Random	74.63	70.19	86.57	
	Supervised	**78.88**	75.60	85.96	76.00* [16]
	DINO	**78.53**	79.48	77.55	
	MAE	**79.78**	77.26	85.02	
Kvasir	Random	69.25	73.05	61.00	
	Supervised	**85.25**	89.38	80.00	77.00* [19]
	DINO	**85.00**	87.63	81.50	
	MAE	**85.50**	90.34	79.50	
MURA	Random	70.15	78.68	51.63	
	Supervised	80.63	84.90	72.41	81.20 [28]
	DINO	81.01	86.65	71.30	
	MAE	**82.23**	85.21	76.07	

Pretraining Method Influences the Interpretability Outcome. While most models achieve similar accuracies on the same dataset, their interpretability outcomes differ significantly, as seen in Table 3. This indicates that pretraining methods indeed affect interpretability outcomes. Specifically, in the majority of cases (though not all), self-supervised pretrained models yield higher performance with attention maps. However, contrasting the findings reported by [4], we find that interpretability results from DINO may not necessarily outperform those from supervised or MAE pretraining. This suggests that certain pretraining tasks may be more suitable for specific medical datasets than others.

GradCAM Interpretability for ViTs is Inadequate. In both evaluation types and across multiple models, GradCAM is significantly outperformed by both attention maps and Chefer method, revealing that both methods are more appropriate for ViT interpretability compared to GradCAM, which was originally proposed for CNNs.

Attention Maps Show Promise for Interpretability. As shown in Table 3 and Fig. 4, interpretability results of attention maps and the Chefer method are comparable. Attention maps generally perform better in the pointing game, while the Chefer method yields better IoU results. These observations hold true for the majority of models across all datasets, with the exception of CP-Child, where

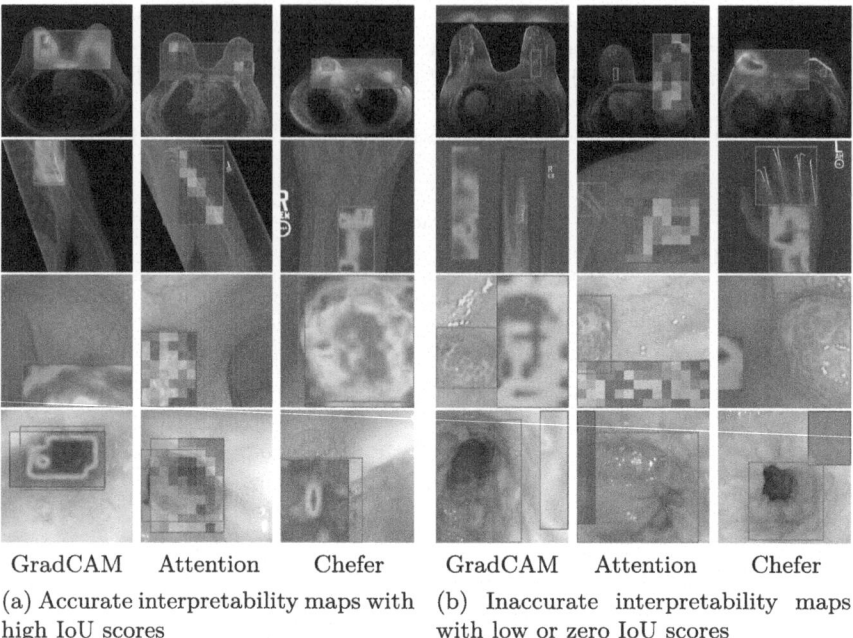

GradCAM   Attention   Chefer   GradCAM   Attention   Chefer
(a) Accurate interpretability maps with   (b) Inaccurate interpretability maps
high IoU scores   with low or zero IoU scores

Fig. 3. Qualitative examples generated using interpretability methods from Sect. 2.3 on the four datasets employed in this study. Red boxes highlight annotations made by medical experts, whereas blue boxes indicate regions with intensity levels exceeding the top 5%, as identified by the interpretability methods. When the red and blue areas overlap, it indicates a high IoU score, whereas low overlap indicates a low score. When the two boxes do not intersect, it means that the IoU is zero. (Color figure online)

the Chefer method outperforms attention maps in the pointing game. Based on these findings, we suggest that researchers employ attention maps when the goal is to identify the most important location in an image. In other scenarios, however, we recommend using the Chefer method. In summary, while attention maps show promise, we find that the Chefer method is a more appropriate choice for interpretability in medical datasets.

Bounding Box Annotations May be Inadequate for Interpretability Evaluation on Medical Datasets. In this work, we worked with expert clinicians to highlight disease-positive regions with a bounding box to evaluate the efficacy of interpretability maps. However, we discover that this approach comes with significant shortcomings. For instance, in the MURA and Kvasir datasets, regions of interest often occupy large spaces, resulting in annotation boxes that include non-target areas, and leading to inflated results regardless of the method's actual precision. Therefore, using segmentation maps, which provide detailed pixel-level annotations of the areas of interest, could offer a more precise evaluation in future research.

Table 3. Comparison of interpretability methods evaluated using the pointing game and IoU overlap for various ViT initializations across four datasets. The largest pointing game accuracy for each row is highlighted in bold font, while the highest average IoU overlap is underlined.

Dataset	Model init.	Pointing game			IoU		
		GradCAM	Attention	Chefer	GradCAM	Attention	Chefer
CP-Child	Random	0.64	**0.96**	0.54	0.36	<u>0.45</u>	0.33
	Supervised	0.38	0.36	**0.54**	0.27	0.42	<u>0.55</u>
	DINO	0.76	0.68	**0.86**	0.38	0.54	<u>0.63</u>
	MAE	0.56	0.96	**0.98**	0.41	0.67	<u>0.73</u>
DUKE	Random	0.04	**0.18**	0.12	0.03	<u>0.04</u>	0.03
	Supervised	0.00	**0.30**	0.28	0.00	0.04	<u>0.08</u>
	DINO	0.10	**0.52**	0.40	0.03	0.07	<u>0.08</u>
	MAE	0.12	**0.36**	0.36	0.01	0.07	<u>0.08</u>
Kvasir	Random	0.88	**0.98**	0.72	<u>0.54</u>	0.36	0.34
	Supervised	0.80	0.88	**0.92**	0.44	0.59	<u>0.61</u>
	DINO	0.72	**0.96**	0.90	0.32	0.43	<u>0.48</u>
	MAE	0.52	**0.82**	0.80	0.52	0.59	<u>0.62</u>
MURA	Random	0.30	**0.40**	0.34	0.18	0.19	<u>0.20</u>
	Supervised	0.56	**0.94**	**0.94**	0.36	0.47	<u>0.56</u>
	DINO	0.78	**0.90**	0.86	0.35	0.41	<u>0.52</u>
	MAE	0.30	**0.76**	0.68	0.18	0.35	<u>0.39</u>

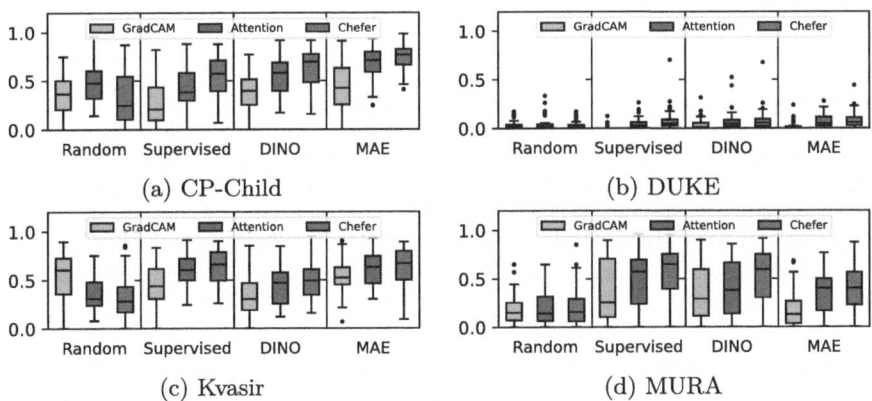

Fig. 4. Box plots showing the IoUs of evaluated interpretability methods for datasets from Sect. 2.1. Each panel illustrates the distribution of IoU values across four pre-training strategies: Random, Supervised, DINO, and MAE.

4 Conclusions and Future Perspectives

AI-assisted medical imaging holds significant potential to revolutionize medical diagnostic processes. Despite the superb performance of ViTs on various medical imaging tasks, widespread adoption of these models has been hindered by explainability issues and the opaque nature of their decision-making processes. Recently, the use of attention maps as a method of explainability has garnered significant research interest, as attention maps are an integral part of the ViT's decision-making process and directly influence its predictions. In this work, we investigated the explainability performance of attention maps and compared them to two commonly used methods: GradCAM and Chefer method. Using state-of-the-art ViT-B/16 models pretrained through various methods and applied to four medical datasets involving different imaging modalities and body parts, we found that, while attention maps show promise, the Chefer method should be preferred for explainability on medical datasets thanks to its superior results.

Throughout our investigation, we also discovered that commonly used interpretability evaluation methods relying on bounding box information have significant shortcomings in the context of medical imaging. As such, we advise future research efforts to refrain from using this type of evaluation and instead employ segmentation maps for a more precise assessment.

In this work, we evaluated the quality of visual explanations based on the annotations of experts. Recent research in this field suggests that this type of evaluation might be misleading in identifying the best-performing explainability method due to several reasons, with spurious correlations being the primary one [2]. As such, we suggest that practitioners exercise caution when selecting methods and conduct thorough analyses to assess each method's effectiveness and reliability, considering potential biases and limitations in the evaluation process.

References

1. Bai, B., Liang, J., Zhang, G., Li, H., Bai, K., Wang, F.: Why attentions may not be interpretable? In: Proceedings of the 27th ACM SIGKDD Conference on Knowledge Discovery & Data Mining, pp. 25–34 (2021)
2. Baniecki, H., Chrabaszcz, M., Holzinger, A., Pfeifer, B., Saranti, A., Biecek, P.: Be careful when evaluating explanations regarding ground truth. arXiv preprint arXiv:2311.04813 (2023)
3. Bibal, A., et al.: Is attention explanation? An introduction to the debate. In: Proceedings of the 60th Annual Meeting of the Association for Computational Linguistics (Volume 1: Long Papers), pp. 3889–3900 (2022)
4. Caron, M., et al.: Emerging properties in self-supervised vision transformers. In: Proceedings of the IEEE/CVF International Conference on Computer Vision, pp. 9650–9660 (2021)
5. Chattopadhay, A., Sarkar, A., Howlader, P., Balasubramanian, V.N.: Grad-CAM++: generalized gradient-based visual explanations for deep convolutional

networks. In: 2018 IEEE Winter Conference on Applications of Computer Vision (WACV), pp. 839–847. IEEE (2018)
6. Chefer, H., Gur, S., Wolf, L.: Transformer interpretability beyond attention visualization. In: Proceedings of the IEEE/CVF Conference on Computer Vision and Pattern Recognition, pp. 782–791 (2021)
7. Darcet, T., Oquab, M., Mairal, J., Bojanowski, P.: Vision transformers need registers. arXiv preprint arXiv:2309.16588 (2023)
8. Dosovitskiy, A., et al.: An image is worth 16×16 words: transformers for image recognition at scale. arXiv preprint arXiv:2010.11929 (2020)
9. Hatherley, J.J.: Limits of trust in medical AI. J. Med. Ethics **46**(7), 478–481 (2020)
10. He, K., Chen, X., Xie, S., Li, Y., Dollár, P., Girshick, R.: Masked autoencoders are scalable vision learners. In: Proceedings of the IEEE/CVF Conference on Computer Vision and Pattern Recognition, pp. 16000–16009 (2022)
11. Ivanovs, M., Kadikis, R., Ozols, K.: Perturbation-based methods for explaining deep neural networks: a survey. Pattern Recogn. Lett. **150**, 228–234 (2021)
12. Jung, Y.J., Han, S.H., Choi, H.J.: Explaining CNN and RNN using selective layer-wise relevance propagation. IEEE Access **9**, 18670–18681 (2021)
13. Kerasidou, C.X., Kerasidou, A., Buscher, M., Wilkinson, S.: Before and beyond trust: reliance in medical AI. J. Med. Ethics **48**(11), 852–856 (2022)
14. Kim, M., et al.: Estimation of supply and demand for cardiologists in Korea. Korean Circul. J. **54**(1), 1–12 (2024)
15. Komorowski, P., Baniecki, H., Biecek, P.: Towards evaluating explanations of vision transformers for medical imaging. In: Proceedings of the IEEE/CVF Conference on Computer Vision and Pattern Recognition, pp. 3725–3731 (2023)
16. Konz, N., Gu, H., Dong, H., Mazurowski, M.A.: The intrinsic manifolds of radiological images and their role in deep learning. In: International Conference on Medical Image Computing and Computer-Assisted Intervention, pp. 684–694. Springer (2022)
17. Matsoukas, C., Haslum, J.F., Söderberg, M., Smith, K.: Is it time to replace CNNs with transformers for medical images? arXiv preprint arXiv:2108.09038 (2021)
18. Ozbulak, U., et al.: Know your self-supervised learning: a survey on image-based generative and discriminative training. arXiv preprint arXiv:2305.13689 (2023)
19. Pogorelov, K., et al.: KVASIR: a multi-class image dataset for computer aided gastrointestinal disease detection. In: Proceedings of the 8th ACM on Multimedia Systems Conference, pp. 164–169 (2017)
20. Rajpurkar, P., Chen, E., Banerjee, O., Topol, E.J.: Ai in health and medicine. Nat. Med. **28**(1), 31–38 (2022)
21. Rajpurkar, P., et al.: MURA: large dataset for abnormality detection in musculoskeletal radiographs. arXiv preprint arXiv:1712.06957 (2017)
22. Russakovsky, O., et al.: ImageNet large scale visual recognition challenge. Int. J. Comput. Vision **115**(3), 211–252 (2015)
23. Saha, A., et al.: A machine learning approach to radiogenomics of breast cancer: a study of 922 subjects and 529 DCE-MRI features. Br. J. Cancer **119**(4), 508–516 (2018)
24. Samek, W., Montavon, G., Lapuschkin, S., Anders, C.J., Müller, K.R.: Explaining deep neural networks and beyond: a review of methods and applications. Proc. IEEE **109**(3), 247–278 (2021)
25. Selvaraju, R.R., Cogswell, M., Das, A., Vedantam, R., Parikh, D., Batra, D.: Grad-CAM: visual explanations from deep networks via gradient-based localization. In: Proceedings of the IEEE International Conference on Computer Vision, pp. 618–626 (2017)

26. Serrano, S., Smith, N.A.: Is attention interpretable? arXiv preprint arXiv:1906.03731 (2019)
27. Shamshad, F., et al.: Transformers in medical imaging: a survey. Med. Image Anal. 102802 (2023)
28. Siddiqui, A.: neXt-ray: deep learning on bone X-rays (2020)
29. Singhal, K., et al.: Towards expert-level medical question answering with large language models. arXiv preprint arXiv:2305.09617 (2023)
30. Wang, W., Tian, J., Zhang, C., Luo, Y., Wang, X., Li, J.: An improved deep learning approach and its applications on colonic polyp images detection. BMC Med. Imaging **20**, 1–14 (2020)
31. Wu, L., et al.: Demystify self-attention in vision transformers from a semantic perspective: analysis and application. arXiv preprint arXiv:2211.08543 (2022)
32. Zhang, J., Bargal, S.A., Lin, Z., Brandt, J., Shen, X., Sclaroff, S.: Top-down neural attention by excitation backprop. Int. J. Comput. Vision **126**(10), 1084–1102 (2018)
33. Zhang, X., Lin, D., Pforsich, H., Lin, V.W.: Physician workforce in the United States of America: forecasting nationwide shortages. Hum. Resour. Health **18**(1), 1–9 (2020)
34. Zhou, B., Khosla, A., Lapedriza, A., Oliva, A., Torralba, A.: Learning deep features for discriminative localization. In: Proceedings of the IEEE Conference on Computer Vision and Pattern Recognition, pp. 2921–2929 (2016)

Exploiting XAI Maps to Improve MS Lesion Segmentation and Detection in MRI

Federico Spagnolo[1,2,3,4], Nataliia Molchanova[4,5],
Mario Ocampo-Pineda[1,2,3], Lester Melie-Garcia[1,2,3],
Meritxell Bach Cuadra[5,6], Cristina Granziera[1,2,3],
Vincent Andrearczyk[4], and Adrien Depeursinge[4,7(✉)]

[1] Translational Imaging in Neurology (ThINk) Basel, Department of Medicine and Biomedical Engineering, University Hospital Basel and University of Basel, Basel, Switzerland
[2] Department of Neurology, University Hospital Basel, Basel, Switzerland
[3] Research Center for Clinical Neuroimmunology and Neuroscience Basel (RC2NB), University Hospital Basel and University of Basel, Basel, Switzerland
[4] MedGIFT, Institute of Informatics, School of Management, HES-SO Valais-Wallis University of Applied Sciences and Arts Western Switzerland, Sierre, Switzerland
[5] CIBM Center for Biomedical Imaging, Lausanne, Switzerland
[6] Radiology Department, Lausanne University Hospital (CHUV) and University of Lausanne, Lausanne, Switzerland
[7] Nuclear Medicine and Molecular Imaging Department, Lausanne University Hospital (CHUV), Lausanne, Switzerland
adrien.depeursinge@hevs.ch

Abstract. To date, several methods have been developed to explain deep learning algorithms for classification tasks. Recently, an adaptation of two of such methods has been proposed to generate instance-level explainable maps in a semantic segmentation scenario, such as multiple sclerosis (MS) lesion segmentation. In the mentioned work, a 3D U-Net was trained and tested for MS lesion segmentation, yielding an F1 score of 0.7006, and a positive predictive value (PPV) of 0.6265. The distribution of values in explainable maps exposed some differences between maps of true and false positive (TP/FP) examples. Inspired by those results, we explore in this paper the use of characteristics of lesion-specific saliency maps to refine segmentation and detection scores. We generate around 21000 maps from as many TP/FP lesions in a batch of 72 patients (training set) and 4868 from the 37 patients in the test set. 93 radiomic features extracted from the first set of maps were used to train a logistic regression model and classify TP versus FP. On the test set, F1 score and PPV were improved by a large margin when compared to the initial model, reaching 0.7450 and 0.7817, with 95% confidence intervals of [0.7358, 0.7547] and [0.7679, 0.7962], respectively. These results suggest that saliency maps can be used to refine prediction scores, boosting a model's performances.

Keywords: XAI · radiomics · segmentation · multiple sclerosis

1 Introduction

Multiple sclerosis (MS) is a demyelinating and autoimmune disease of the central nervous system, which increasingly affects the quality of life of relatively young people [1]. A crucial magnetic resonance imaging (MRI) biomarker in diagnosing and monitoring MS is the presence of plaques (or lesions) in the white matter (WM), which are visible on fluid attenuated inversion recovery (FLAIR) and T1-weighted contrasts, such as the magnetisation-prepared rapid gradient echo (MPRAGE) [2–4].

Manual or semi-automatic annotation of such lesions is a tedious process, which has been automated in many tools based on deep learning (DL) [5,6]. The "black box" nature of standard DL models [7] and the lack of clinical validation [8] have jeopardized the clinical integration of these tools. In this sense, research in explainable AI (XAI) could result as decisive to better understand and optimize the architecture and the performances of DL models [9]. An exhaustive review of XAI models and applications published before 2023 can be found in [10].

However, XAI methods were not designed for segmentation tasks and, to date, no ad-hoc methods were capable to do so [11,12]. To this end, two methods were recently developed in [14], which adapt SmoothGrad [13] and Grad-CAM++ [15] to provide instance-level explanation maps. Therefore, these two methods can generate separate (i.e., lesion-specific) explainable maps for distinct instances of a class, e.g., MS plaques. This is important to understand which parts of the image were responsible for the segmentation of a specific targeted lesion. The distribution of maximum and minimum values in explainable (saliency) maps generated with the adapted SmoothGrad for true positive (TP) predictions was compared to that of false positives (FP), false negatives (FN), and true negatives (TN). The first two groups were defined as having, respectively, a non-zero and zero overlap with ground truth (GT). FN predictions were determined as GT segmentations with zero overlap with the predicted lesions. TN examples were obtained by randomly sampling ten sphere-like shapes (with the average lesion volume of the test set), which have zero overlap with the previous groups and are located in patients' brain and skull. The study suggested that maximum and minimum values of XAI maps (with respect to FLAIR) of the four groups present different distributions, as shown in Fig. 1.

Radiomic features have been extensively used in radiology to perform a quantitative analysis of medical images [25–27]. A recent work [28] showed that the outputs of an automatic segmentation model can be used to determine the region of interest (ROI) to extract radiomic features from PET images of intraprostatic cancer lesions.

Inspired by these results, in this work we investigate the discriminatory power of radiomic features extracted from XAI maps to distinguish observations from the first two groups (TP and FP), aiming at improving the model's performance.

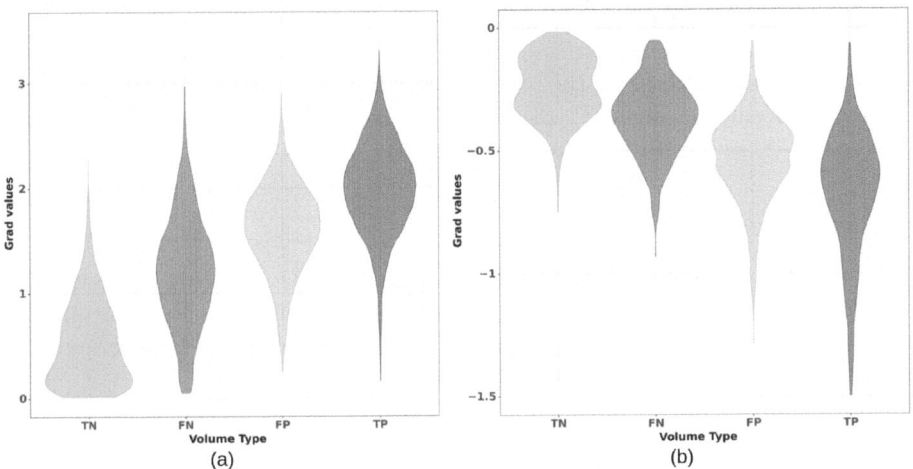

Fig. 1. Violin plots representing the distribution of saliency maps maximum (a) and minimum (b) values. The four distributions refer to true negative (TN), false negative (FN), false positive (FP) and true positive (TP) volumes. Figure retrieved from [14].

Our main hypothesis is that XAI maps contain specific signatures that are distinctive of TP versus FP. This is based on experiments in [14], which highlight the fact that TPs, FPs, and FNs presented a different distribution of values in XAI maps. The quantitative nature of those saliency maps leads us to test the aforementioned hypothesis.

2 Material and Methods

2.1 Dataset and Model

We used 4023 FLAIR and MPRAGE MRI scans (SIEMENS Avanto/Espree/Symphony 1.5T and Prisma/Skyra/Verio/MAGNETOM Vida 3T, 1mm isotropic) from 687 patients diagnosed with MS (age = 45.2 ± 12.2, 433 females, Expanded Disability Status Scale median of 2.5 [0–9]), acquired at the University Hospital of Basel, Switzerland [29]. WM lesions annotation was performed by three expert clinicians at baseline and follow-ups. Data were randomly split into training, validation and test sets, containing 560, 90 and 37 patients with 3369, 553 and 101 visits respectively (training/validation set's and test set's mean lesions number of 52.9 ± 36.4 and 42.3 ± 21.4 per patient). Datasets from a same patient were ensured to be included in the same split.

Images were pre-processed by registering FLAIR images to MPRAGE space with the *elastix* toolbox [20,21], correcting for bias field inhomogeneity [22], and standardizing intensities using z-score.

With the described data, a 3D U-Net [16] was trained and tested to segment MS plaques, using patches of dimensions 96^3 and a linear combination of normalized Dice [17] and blob [18] loss. This last choice was made to minimize the impact of instance imbalance within a class and bias towards the occurrence of positive class [19]. The trained model achieved a Dice score of 0.60, and a normalized Dice score of 0.71 on the test set, for what concerns lesion segmentation. The model predicted 3050 TP, 1818 FP, and 789 FN examples, reaching an F1 score of 0.7006 and a positive predictive value (PPV) of 0.6265.

2.2 Instance-Level Saliency

Following [14], we referred to the lesion domain as Ω: a subset of the image domain Γ, such that $\Omega \subset \Gamma \subset \mathbb{Z}^D$. Each lesion domain presents a cardinality $|\Omega|$, which is the number of voxels within the lesion. For a given Ω, the generation of explainable maps followed these steps:

1. Injecting Gaussian noise $\mathcal{N}(0, \sigma)$ with standard deviation $\sigma = 0.05$ to obtain N noisy versions of the input,
2. Generating a collection of saliency maps for all output voxels in the domain Ω of the lesion,
3. Determining the voxel-wise maximum with sign from this collection of maps,
4. Repeating steps 1–3 and combining these $N = 50$ saliency maps to obtain a single one for the target lesion.

The computation of instance-level saliency maps $M_\Omega^{\text{gradient}}[v] \in \mathbb{R}$ is summarized in Eq.(1). Originally, separate saliency maps were obtained for each input modality (FLAIR and MPRAGE) to differentiate their respective contribution. For this work we selected maps with gradients computed with respect to FLAIR, based on findings reported in [14]. The first is that MPRAGE was shown to have a lower contribution to the segmentation of lesions. Secondly, gradients with respect to MPRAGE were less sensitive to the targeted groups (TP, FP, etc.).

$$M_\Omega^{\text{gradient}}[v] = \frac{1}{N} \sum_{n=1}^{N} D_{argmax_{v'}|D_{v'}^n|}^n, \text{ where } D_{v'}^n = \frac{\partial y(x_n)[v']}{\partial x_n[v]} \quad (1)$$

2.3 Saliency Domain-Shift Verification Between Training and Test Sets

Such explainable maps were generated for TP and FP predictions in the whole test set (3050 and 1818) and a subset S of the training set (containing 11569 TP and 9434 FP from 217 and 439 visits). The mean, maximum and minimum values (and their standard deviation) of maps in the training set were compared with those in the test set, to exclude possible domain shifts. Such shifts could jeopardize the ability of the radiomics-based model to distinguish between TP and FP on the test set due to changes in the saliency maps. A Mann-Whitney U test was run over the distributions of the three measurements in the two groups.

2.4 Radiomics Feature Extraction

Standardized (z-score) explainable maps and the predicted binary lesion masks from S were used as input to a radiomic features extractor. The binary segmentation of each lesion was dilated to ensure that the computation of features was determined by the saliency values within the ROI (i.e., the lesion domain Ω and in its neighborhood). This is needed to avoid the exclusion of negative saliency map values, as described in [14]. An illustration is provided by the block diagram in Fig. 2.

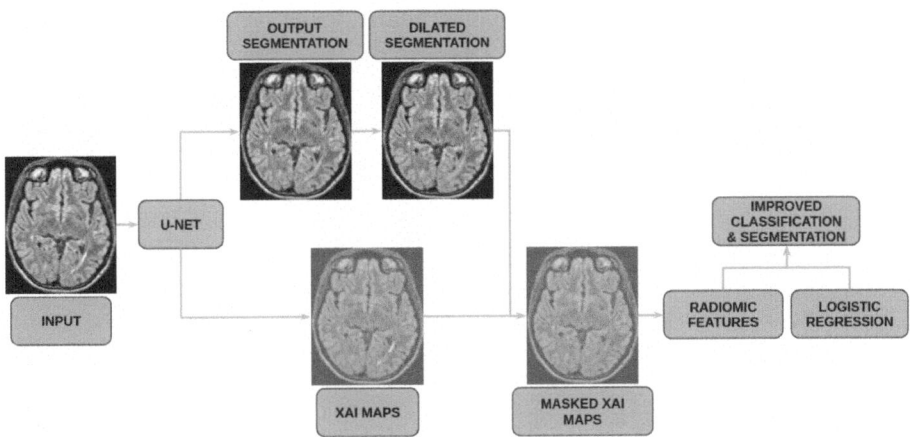

Fig. 2. Block diagram describing how an XAI map is used to extract radiomic features. In this example, a true positive lesion is shown in the axial plane.

We used the library *pyradiomics* [23], with $binWidth = 10$ and $sigma = [1, 2, 3]$. From the pool of 107 available features, those related to *shape* were not considered relevant as depending on the initial segmentation of Ω, resulting in 93 target features.

2.5 TP/FP Prediction Refinement

The radiomic features of saliency maps from the training set were standardized and used to train a logistic regression (LR) model using *scikit-learn* [24], with the following parameters: maximum number of iterations: 10000, solver: *liblinear*, penalty: *L1*, class weights: 0.29, 0.71. The class weights were selected to reflect the proportion of TP and FP examples per visit in the training set S. To investigate feature importance, we compared the normalized (0–1) regression coefficients of each feature.

The trained model was applied to the entire test set. Following a bootstrapping approach with 1000 iterations, we computed the mean and 95% confidence interval (CI) of the F1 score and PPV. The updated number of TP, FP and FN predictions was also derived for comparison with the performance of the initial U-Net model. The confusion matrix, F1 score, and PPV reported by the U-Net represent the best scores achieved on the entire test set.

3 Results

3.1 Domain-Shift of Saliency Between Training and Test Sets

The comparison between saliency maps computed on the subset S of the training set and the test set is summarized in Fig. 3. For all the metrics, mean values from both sets fell into the interval $\pm\sigma$ (one standard deviation), associated to non-significant differences.

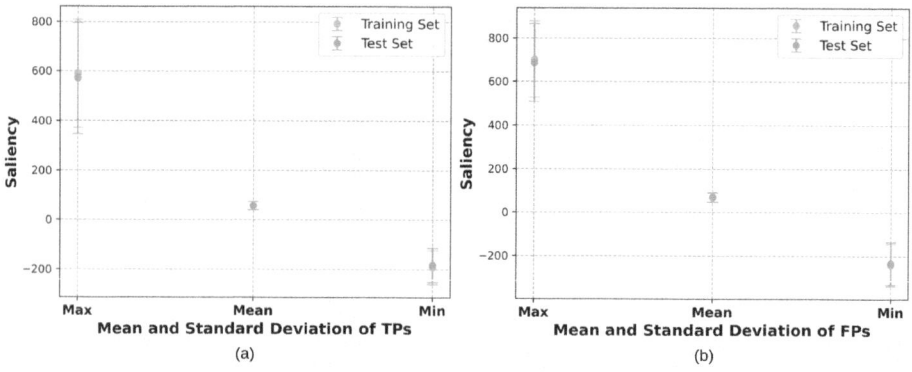

Fig. 3. Comparison between mean, maximum and minimum values of saliency maps computed on the training and test set, for TP (a) and FP (b) examples.

3.2 Refinement of TP/FP Predictions

Testing the LR model with bootstrapping we obtained an F1 score of 0.7450 with a 95% CI of [0.7358, 0.7547], and a PPV of 0.7817 with a 95% CI of [0.7679, 0.7962]. The F1 score and PPV of the non-refined U-Net were 0.7006 and 0.6265, respectively. A comprehensive performance comparison is presented in Table 1.

Examples of a slice in the sagittal plane of the 3D XAI maps generated from a TP and a FP are illustrated in Fig. 4. The LR output probability (relative to the TP class) for the TP lesion was 0.9398, and 0.0232 for the FP. The example FP candidate is located at the boundary between WM and cortex, and corresponds to one of the brain sulci.

The importance of radiomic features used by the model is presented in Fig. 5. The most important were two features based on saliency intensity, mean absolute deviation (MAD) and Root Mean Squared (RMS), and reported a normalized coefficient of 0.89 and -1.0 respectively.

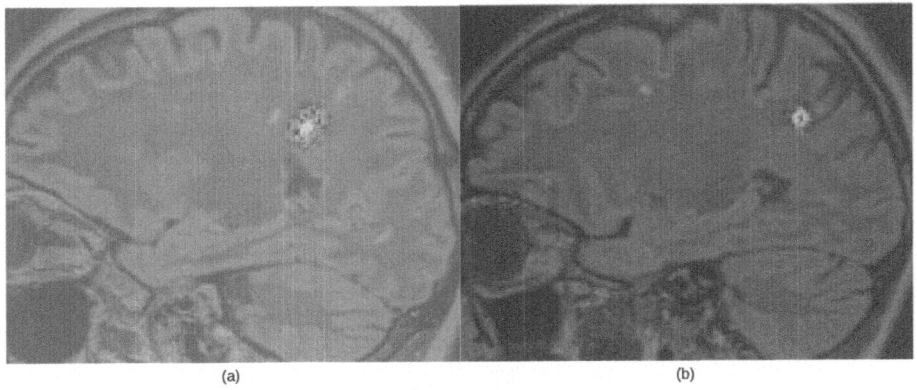

Fig. 4. An example of a slice in the sagittal plane from a saliency map computed on a true (a) and false (b) positive lesion, scoring 0.9398 and 0.0232 for the true positive class.

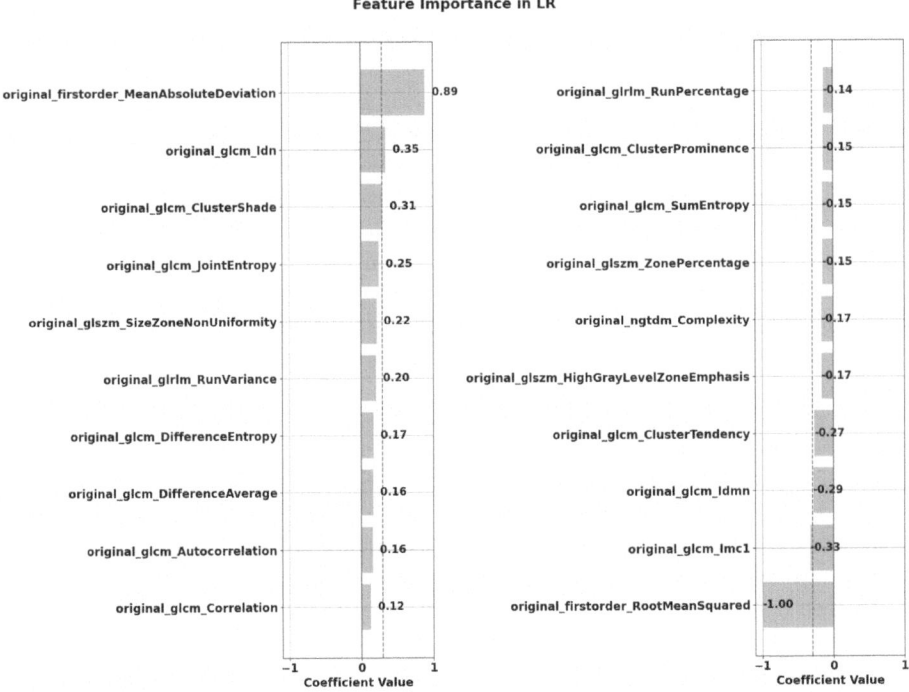

Fig. 5. Normalized radiomic features showing the highest importance (top 10 positive on the left, top 10 negative on the right), in terms of LR coefficients. The dashed red line represents a coefficient value of 0.3, the dashed green line a coefficient value of −0.3. (Color figure online)

Table 1. Comparing MS lesion detection performance between the original U-Net and its refined version using logistic regression (LR) relying on radiomic features from XAI maps. We report the number of true positives (TPs), false positives (FPs), false negatives (FNs), and the mean and confidence interval (CI) of F1 score and positive predictive value (PPV).

	U-Net only	U-Net + saliency [95% CI]
TPs	3050	2732
FPs	1818	763
FNs	789	1107
F1 score	0.7006	0.7450 [0.7358, 0.7547]
PPV	0.6265	0.7817 [0.7679, 0.7962]

4 Discussion

This work employed radiomics to extract features from XAI (saliency) maps generated for a DL semantic segmentation model. These features were fed to a linear model (i.e., LR) to discriminate between FP and TP predictions, and improve the classification score. Our main hypothesis was that XAI maps contained specific signatures that are distinctive of TP versus FP. As a first step of our investigation, we tried using only the minimum and maximum values of saliency to discriminate between TP and FP classes. In this way, the binary classifier could reach a higher precision but a lower recall, eventually resulting in a trade off where the F1 score did not improve. A similar trend was observed when trying to adjust the segmentation threshold at the U-Net output layer. The results in Table 1 show that using radiomics on saliency maps, it was possible to refine classification scores, improving the F1 score from 0.70 to 0.75 and the PPV from 0.63 to 0.78. Confidence intervals computed for the refined model are not including the performance values of the initial model, suggesting significance of the observed improvements.

In Sect. 3.1 we compared the maximum, minimum and mean values of XAI in the training and test set. According to this analysis, we found no evidence of domain shift between the two sets. The characteristic of having a slightly positive mean value was also preserved in both groups (TP and FP) and sets. This indicated that the radiomics model trained on saliency maps obtained on the training set will generalize to those of the test set.

In Sect. 3.2 we reported the features which contribute the most to discriminate between saliency maps from TP and FP examples. A strong positive coefficient for MAD reveals that the intensity variability with respect to the mean is higher for XAI maps of the TP class. This finding supports prior results obtained on maximum, minimum and mean values. A positive Inverse difference normalized (Idn) may indicate a more homogeneous texture surrounding voxels. A strong negative coefficient for RMS may describe saliency maps for the FP class as highly variable, and presenting more outliers. A negative Informational measure of correlation (Imc1) represents a higher tendency of neighbouring voxel pairs in FP cases to have similar values. Such findings suggest that saliency maps for TP examples may present a wider range of values (contrast between positive and negative regions), less outliers, and overall a more homogeneous texture.

This work has also some limitations. The application of this method is limited to identifying and ruling out FPs. A possible future improvement would be to extend the approach to FNs, and to refine the detection performance even further. In that case the issue would be to have FN candidates on the test set without using a ground truth. For this purpose, an estimation of the uncertainty [30,31] of the model's prediction could help to target possibly missed lesions. Moreover, this study explores the refinement of predictions from a single DL model. The impact of XAI on different models should be investigated, as we would expect the initial performance of the model to be relevant. In addition, it would be important to evaluate the performances of this method on saliency maps coming from an out of domain test set, or training and testing the model on multiple datasets. Though, this would also require XAI maps to be comparable for multi-centric data which, to our knowledge, has not been investigated yet. Nevertheless, it is important to remark that the MRI data used in this study were acquired with multiple scanners. Furthermore, investigating the which and how many radiomic features are required to achieve a desired performance would be of interest.

5 Conclusion

This work demonstrated that radiomic features extracted from XAI (saliency) maps generated for a DL semantic segmentation model can be used to improve the detection performance of a segmentation model by a large margin.

Acknowledgments. This work was supported by the Hasler Foundation with the project MSxplain number 21042, the Swiss National Science Foundation (SNSF) with the project 205320_219430, and the Swiss Cancer Research foundation with the project TARGET (KFS-5549-02-2022-R). We acknowledge access to the expertise of the CIBM Center for Biomedical Imaging, a Swiss research center of excellence founded and supported by CHUV, UNIL, EPFL, UNIGE and HUG.

Disclosure of Interests. The University Hospital Basel (USB) and the Research Center for Clinical neuroimmunology and Neuroscience (RC2NB), as the employers of Cristina Granziera, have received the following fees which were used exclusively for research support from Siemens, GeNeuro, Genzyme-Sanofi, Biogen, Roche. They also have received advisory board and consultancy fees from Actelion, Genzyme-Sanofi, Novartis, GeNeuro, Merck, Biogen and Roche; as well as speaker fees from Genzyme-Sanofi, Novartis, GeNeuro, Merck, biogen and Roche. Federico Spagnolo was an employee of F. Hoffmann-La Roche Ltd. The remaining authors have no competing interests to declare that are relevant to the content of this article.

References

1. Kołtuniuk, A., Pawlak, B., Krowczynska, D., Chojdak-Łukasiewicz, J.: The quality of life in patients with multiple sclerosis - association with depressive symptoms and physical disability: a prospective and observational study. Front. Psychol. **13**, 1068421 (2023). https://doi.org/10.3389/fpsyg.2022.1068421
2. Yang, J., et al.: Current and future biomarkers in multiple sclerosis. Int. J. Mol. Sci. **23** (2023). https://doi.org/10.3390/ijms23115877
3. Thompson, A., et al.: Diagnosis of multiple sclerosis: 2017 revisions of the McDonald criteria. Lancet Neurol. **17** (2017). https://doi.org/10.1016/S1474-4422(17)30470-2
4. Hemond, C.C., Bakshi, R.: Magnetic resonance imaging in multiple sclerosis. Cold Spring Harbor Perspect. Med. **8**, 5 (2018). https://doi.org/10.1101/cshperspect.a028969
5. Commowick, O., Comb'es, B., Cervenansky, F., Dojat, M.: Editorial: automatic methods for multiple sclerosis new lesions detection and segmentation. Front. Neurosci. **17** (2023). https://doi.org/10.3389/fnins.2023.1176625
6. Ma, Y., et al.: Multiple sclerosis lesion analysis in brain magnetic resonance images: techniques and clinical applications. IEEE J. Biomed. Health Inform. 1 (2022). https://doi.org/10.1109/JBHI.2022.3151741
7. Baselli, G., Codari, M., Sardanelli, F.: Opening the black box of machine learning in radiology: can the proximity of annotated cases be a way? Eur. Radiol. Exp. **4** (2020). https://doi.org/10.1186/s41747-020-00159-0
8. Spagnolo, F., et al.: How far MS lesion detection and segmentation are integrated into the clinical workflow? A systematic review. NeuroImage Clin. **39**, 103491 (2023). https://doi.org/10.1016/j.nicl.2023
9. Kobayashi, K., Alam, S.B.: Explainable, interpretable, and trustworthy AI for an intelligent digital twin: a case study on remaining useful life. Eng. Appl. Artif. Intell. **129**, 107620 (2024). https://doi.org/10.1016/j.engappai.2023.107620
10. Saranya, A., Subhashini, R.: A systematic review of explainable artificial intelligence models and applications: recent developments and future trends. Decis. Anal. J. **7**, 100230 (2023). https://doi.org/10.1016/j.dajour.2023.100230
11. Arun, N., et al.: Assessing the (un)trustworthiness of saliency maps for localizing abnormalities in medical imaging. Radiol.: Artif. Intell. **3** (2021). https://doi.org/10.1148/ryai.2021200267
12. Mahapatra, D., Poellinger, A., Reyes, M.: Interpretability-guided inductive bias for deep learning based medical image. Med. Image Anal. **81**, 102551 (2022). https://doi.org/10.1016/j.media.2022.102551
13. Smilkov, D., Thorat, N., Kim, B., Viégas, F., Wattenberg, M.: SmoothGrad: removing noise by adding noise. CoRR (2017)
14. Spagnolo, F., et al.: Instance-level quantitative saliency in multiple sclerosis lesion segmentation. arXiv (2024). https://doi.org/10.48550/ARXIV.2406.09335
15. Chattopadhay, A., Sarkar, A., Howlader, P., Balasubramanian, V.N.: Grad-CAM++: generalized gradient-based visual explanations for deep convolutional networks. In: 2018 IEEE Winter Conference on Applications of Computer Vision (WACV), pp. 839–847 (2018). https://doi.org/10.1109/WACV.2018.00097
16. Çiçek, O., Abdulkadir, A., Lienkamp, S.S., Brox, T., Ronneberger, O.: 3D U-Net: learning dense volumetric segmentation from sparse annotation. arXiv (2016). https://doi.org/10.48550/ARXIV.1606.06650

17. Raina, V., et al.: Tackling bias in the dice similarity coefficient: introducing ndsc for white matter lesion segmentation. In: 2023 IEEE 20th International Symposium on Biomedical Imaging (ISBI), pp. 1–5 (2023). https://doi.org/10.1109/ISBI53787.2023.10230755
18. Kofler, F., et al.: Blob loss: instance imbalance aware loss functions for semantic segmentation. arXiv (2022). https://doi.org/10.48550/ARXIV.2205.08209
19. Maier-Hein, L., et al.: Metrics reloaded: pitfalls and recommendations for image analysis validation. arXiv (2022). https://doi.org/10.48550/arXiv.2206.01653
20. Klein, S., Staring, M., Murphy, K., Viergever, M., Pluim, J.: Elastix: a toolbox for intensity-based medical image registration. IEEE Trans. Med. Imaging **29**, 196–205 (2009). https://doi.org/10.1109/TMI.2009.2035616
21. Shamonin, D., Bron, E., Lelieveldt, B., Smits, M., Klein, S., Staring, M.: Fast parallel image registration on CPU and GPU for diagnostic classification of Alzheimer's disease. Front. Neuroinform. **7**, 50 (2014). https://doi.org/10.3389/fninf.2013.00050
22. Tustison, N., et al.: N4itk: improved n3 bias correction. IEEE Trans. Med. Imaging **29**, 1310–1320 (2010). https://doi.org/10.1109/TMI.2010.2046908
23. van Griethuysen, J.J.M., et al.: Computational radiomics system to decode the radiographic phenotype. Can. Res. **77**(21), e104–e107 (2017). https://doi.org/10.1158/0008-5472.CAN-17-0339
24. Pedregosa, F., et al.: Scikit-learn: machine Learning in Python. J. Mach. Learn. Res. **12**, 2825–2830 (2011)
25. Ibrahim, A., et al.: Radiomics for precision medicine: current challenges, future prospects, and the proposal of a new framework. Methods **188**, 20–29 (2021). https://doi.org/10.1016/j.ymeth.2020.05.022
26. Annunziata, S., Treglia, G.: Editorial: radiomics and artificial intelligence in radiology and nuclear medicine. Front. Med. **10** (2023). https://doi.org/10.3389/fmed.2023.1216434
27. Elmahdy, M., Ronnie, S.: Radiomics analysis in medical imaging research. J. Med. Radiat. Sci. **70**(1), 3–7 (2023). https://doi.org/10.1002/jmrs.662
28. Ghezzo, S., et al.: External validation of a convolutional neural network for the automatic segmentation of intraprostatic tumor lesions on 68Ga-PSMA PET images. Front. Med. **10** (2023). https://doi.org/10.3389/fmed.2023.1133269
29. Disanto, G., et al.: The swiss multiple sclerosis cohort-study (SMSC): a prospective swiss wide investigation of key phases in disease evolution and new treatment options. PLoS One **11**(3) (2016). https://doi.org/10.1371/journal.pone.0152347
30. Nair, T., Precup, D., Arnold, D.L., Arbel, T.: Exploring uncertainty measures in deep networks for multiple sclerosis lesion detection and segmentation. Med. Image Anal. **59**, 101557 (2020). https://doi.org/10.1016/j.media.2019.101557
31. Molchanova, N., et al.: Structural-based uncertainty in deep learning across anatomical scales: analysis in white matter lesion segmentation. arXiv (2024). https://doi.org/10.48550/arXiv.2311.08931

Proceedings of the Embodied AI and Robotics for HealTHcare Workshop (EARTH 2024)

EndoGS: Deformable Endoscopic Tissues Reconstruction with Gaussian Splatting

Lingting Zhu[1], Zhao Wang[2], Jiahao Cui[3], Zhenchao Jin[1], Guying Lin[1], and Lequan Yu[1](✉)

[1] The University of Hong Kong, Hong Kong SAR, China
ltzhu99@connect.hku.hk, lqyu@hku.hk
[2] The Chinese University of Hong Kong, Hong Kong SAR, China
[3] Sun Yat-sen University, Guangzhou, China

Abstract. Surgical 3D reconstruction is a critical area of research in robotic surgery, with recent works adopting variants of dynamic radiance fields to achieve success in 3D reconstruction of deformable tissues from single-viewpoint videos. However, these methods often suffer from time-consuming optimization or inferior quality, limiting their adoption in downstream tasks. Inspired by 3D Gaussian Splatting, a recent trending 3D representation, we present **EndoGS**, applying Gaussian Splatting for deformable endoscopic tissue reconstruction. Specifically, our approach incorporates deformation fields to handle dynamic scenes, depth-guided supervision with spatial-temporal weight masks to optimize 3D targets with tool occlusion from a single viewpoint, and surface-aligned regularization terms to capture the much better geometry. As a result, EndoGS reconstructs and renders high-quality deformable endoscopic tissues from a single-viewpoint video, estimated depth maps, and labeled tool masks. Experiments on DaVinci robotic surgery videos demonstrate that EndoGS achieves superior rendering quality. Code is available at https://github.com/HKU-MedAI/EndoGS.

Keywords: Gaussian Splatting · Robotic Surgery · 3D Reconstruction

1 Introduction

Reconstruction of high-quality deformable tissues from endoscopic videos is a significant but challenging task, facilitating downstream tasks like surgical AR, education, and robot learning [4,26,27]. Earlier attempts [18,24,28,39,40] adopt depth estimation to achieve great success in endoscopic reconstruction, but these methods still struggle to produce realistic 3D reconstruction due to two key issues. First, non-rigid deformations with sometimes large movements, which require practical dynamic scene reconstruction, hinders the adaptation of those techniques. Second, tool occlusion happens in single-viewpoint videos, producing difficulties in learning affected parts with limited information.

While [12,17] have proposed frameworks combining tool masking, stereo depth estimation, and sparse warp field [7,21] for single-viewpoint 3D reconstruction, they are still prone to failure in the presence of dramatic non-topological deformable tissues changes. Neural Radiance Fields (NeRFs) [20] have shown great potentials in 3D representations, and methods based on variants of dynamic radiance field [6,23] have become representative works in deformable tissues reconstruction from videos. For example, EndoNeRF [29] follows the modeling of D-NeRF [23] to represent deformable surgical scenes as the combination of a canonical neural radiance field and a time-dependent neural displacement field, and LerPlane [33] factorizes six 2D planes for static field and dynamic field to accelerate optimization similar to [2,6].

Recently 3D Gaussian Splatting (3D-GS) [3,10,31] has been witnessed as a powerful representation that renders higher-quality results at a real-time level. Follow-up works [19,30,35,37] extend 3D-GS to represent dynamic scenes and achieve state-of-the-art performances on rendering fidelity and speed. To model dynamic representation of dynamic scenes, [19,35] formulate 4D Gaussians and assign extra parameters as attributes in the time dimension, and [30,37] apply MLPs to predict the deformation of the Gaussians, sharing the same rationale with dynamic NeRFs [22,23]. In this paper, we present EndoGS, a method based on surface-aligned Gaussian Splatting for deformable endoscopic tissues reconstruction with better rendering quality and better rendering speed.

To summarize, our main contributions are three-fold: **1)** We present the first Gaussian Splatting based method for deformable endoscopic tissues reconstruction. This is one of the first attempts [13] introducing Gaussian Splatting in the medical domain. **2)** We represent dynamic surgical scenes with the combination of static Gaussians and the deformable parameters in the time dimension, adopt depth-guided supervision with spatial-temporal weight masks for monocular optimization with tool occlusion, and combine surface-aligned regularization terms [8] to capture the much better geometry. **3)** We use the same input tool masks involved in the training and inference for comparison methods and make a clear and fair comparison, and experiments demonstrate our superior performances.

2 Method

2.1 Overview

In this paper, we introduce our method, referred to as EndoGS, which utilizes a deformable variant of 3D-GS to reconstruct 3D surgical scenes from a single-viewpoint video, estimated depth maps, and labeled tool masks. Specifically, given a stereo video with left and right frames $\{(\boldsymbol{I}_i^l, \boldsymbol{I}_i^r)\}_{i=1}^T$, where T is the total number of frames, our goal is to reconstruct 3D representations of the deformable tissues that render in high quality. We follow the approach of [29,32,33] by combining the extracted binary tool masks $\{\boldsymbol{M}_i\}_{i=1}^T$ and the depth maps $\{\boldsymbol{D}_i\}_{i=1}^T$ estimated from binocular captures for the left views. The pipeline of EndoGS is illustrated in Fig. 1. In this section, we first introduce the preliminary

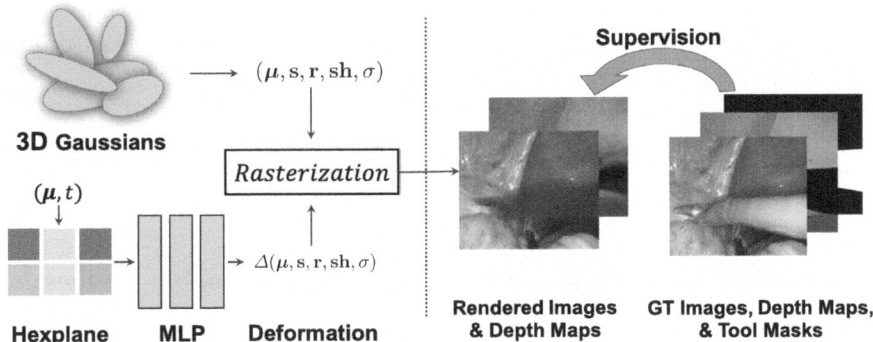

Fig. 1. The overview of our EndoGS pipeline. Given 3D Gaussians, we use the mean and the time as input to compute features by querying multi-resolution voxel planes. A single MLP is used to obtain the deformation of the Gaussians. With differentiable rasterization, the rendered images and depth maps are obtained and we use ground truth images, depth maps and the tool masks to provide the supervision.

of 3D Gaussian Splatting (Sect. 2.2). We then present the modeling of deformable tissues with a dynamic version of 3D-GS, which adopts a lightweight MLP to represent the dynamic field (Sect. 2.3). The training optimization of the Gaussian Splatting with the tool masks and the depth maps is introduced (Sect. 2.4). Finally, we discuss how to align Gaussians with the Surface (Sect. 2.5).

2.2 Preliminaries of 3D Gaussian Splatting

3D Gaussian Splatting (3D-GS) [10] offers the state-of-the-art solution for real-time novel view synthesis in multi-view static scenes. The 3D Gaussians with a 3D covariance matrix Σ and mean μ served as the rendering primitives in the form of point clouds:

$$G(x) = e^{-\frac{1}{2}(x-\mu)^T \Sigma^{-1}(x-\mu)}. \tag{1}$$

The 3D Gaussians can be projected onto 2D space and rendered for pixels: $\Sigma' = JW\Sigma W^T J^T$, where Σ' is the covariance matrix in the 2D plane, W denotes view transformation, and the Jacobian J is the affine approximation of the projective transformation. To enforce the positive semi-definiteness, Σ is parameterized as R: $\Sigma = RSS^T R^T$ with a scale S and rotation.

To render the color of the pixels p, point-based volume rendering is adopted:

$$C(p) = \sum_{i \in N} c_i \alpha_i \prod_{j=1}^{i-1}(1-\alpha_j), \tag{2}$$

$$\text{where } \alpha_i = \sigma_i e^{-\frac{1}{2}(p-\mu_i)^T \Sigma'^{-1}(p-\mu_i)}. \tag{3}$$

The c_i means the color of the Gaussians along the ray, μ_i denotes the coordinates, and σ_i denotes the opacity. And 3D-GS applies spherical harmonics to model the view-dependent color.

In total, the explicit 3D Gaussians are characterized by: position $\boldsymbol{\mu} \in \mathbb{R}^3$, scaling factor $\boldsymbol{s} \in \mathbb{R}^3$, rotation factor $\boldsymbol{r} \in \mathbb{R}^4$, spherical harmonic (SH) coefficients $\boldsymbol{sh} \in \mathbb{R}^k$ (k means number of SH functions), and opacity $\sigma \in \mathbb{R}$. Finally each Gaussian can be represented as $(\boldsymbol{\mu}, \boldsymbol{s}, \boldsymbol{r}, \boldsymbol{sh}, \sigma)$.

2.3 Gaussian Splatting Representations for Deformable Tissues

We represent a surgical scene as a 4D volume, where the deformation of the tissues involves time dimension. To this end, we introduce the Gaussian deformation to represent the time-varying motions and shapes, following the basic designs of [30]. The final goal is to learn the original representation of the 3D Gaussians $\{(\boldsymbol{\mu}, \boldsymbol{s}, \boldsymbol{r}, \boldsymbol{sh}, \sigma)\}$ as well as the Gaussian deformations $\{\Delta(\boldsymbol{\mu}, \boldsymbol{s}, \boldsymbol{r}, \boldsymbol{sh}, \sigma)\} = \{(\Delta\boldsymbol{\mu}, \Delta\boldsymbol{s}, \Delta\boldsymbol{r}, \Delta\boldsymbol{sh}, \Delta\sigma)\}$.

In Fig. 1, for each 3D Gaussian, we use the mean $\boldsymbol{\mu} = (x, y, z)$ and the time t to compute the deformation. We use six orthogonal feature planes to encode the spatial and temporal information [2,6,30,32,33]. To be specific, the multi-resolution HexPlane [2,6] consists of three space planes XY, XZ, YZ and three space-time planes XT, YT, ZT. The planes encode features $F \in \mathbb{R}^{h \times N_1 \times N_2}$, where h denotes the hidden dimension and N_1, N_2 stand for the plane resolution, and we utilize bilinear interpolation $\mathcal{B}$ to interpolate the four nearby queried voxel features. As a result, the voxel feature can be represented in the format of matrix element-wise multiplication with operation $\odot$:

$$f_{voxel}(\boldsymbol{\mu}, t) = \mathcal{B}(F_{XY}, x, y) \odot \mathcal{B}(F_{YZ}, y, z) \ldots \mathcal{B}(F_{YT}, y, t) \odot \mathcal{B}(F_{ZT}, z, t). \quad (4)$$

Then we employ a single MLP to update the Gaussian attributes and it merges all the information and decodes the deformation of the position, scaling factor, rotation factor, spherical harmonic coefficients, and opacity:

$$\Delta(\boldsymbol{\mu}, \boldsymbol{s}, \boldsymbol{r}, \boldsymbol{sh}, \sigma) = \text{MLP}(f_{voxel}(\boldsymbol{\mu}, t)). \quad (5)$$

2.4 Training Combined with Tool Masks and Depth Maps

Reconstructing from videos with tool occlusion poses a challenge and we follow former works [29,32,33] to use labeled tool occlusion masks to indicates the unseen pixels. Furthermore, we leverage spatiotemporal importance sampling strategy to indicate the crucial areas related to the occlusion issue. To be specific, the binary masks are denoted as $\{M_i\}_{i=1}^T$, where 0 stands for tissue pixels and 1 stands for tool pixels, and the importance maps $\{\mathcal{V}_i\}_{i=1}^T$ involve temporal statistics and are denoted as $\mathcal{V}_i = (1 - M_i) \odot \left(1 + \alpha \sum_{j=1}^T M_j / \left\|\sum_{j=1}^T M_j\right\|_F\right)$. We only optimize in the seen part by introducing the item $1 - M_i$. Meanwhile, the statistics of the mask frequencies normalized by the Frobenius norm along the temporal dimension provide the information of the uncertainty and allocate higher importance for tissue areas with higher occlusion frequencies. The parameter α is used to control the scaling strength. We use the L_1 loss with spatial masks, and thus the spatial supervision on i-th is

$$\mathcal{L}_{L1}(i) = |\boldsymbol{I}_i \odot \boldsymbol{\mathcal{V}}_i - \hat{\boldsymbol{I}}_i \odot \boldsymbol{\mathcal{V}}_i|, \tag{6}$$

where $\hat{\boldsymbol{I}}_i$ is the rendering image on i-th frame.

Monocular reconstruction provides limited information for 3D reconstruction and makes overfitting happen with single-viewpoint images [5]. To mitigate illness from single-viewpoint inputs, we introduce depth-guided loss with the estimated depth maps. The coarse stereo depth maps are obtained via STTRlight [14]. We adopt Huber loss $\mathcal{L}_D(i)$ for depth regularization following [33].

We adopt total variation (TV) losses in the spatial dimension and the temporal dimension to serve as the additional regularization. To prevent color drifts in unseen area, we use a spatial total variation item for areas with tool masks and it is denoted as $\mathcal{L}_{tv-spatial}(i) = \text{TV}(\hat{\boldsymbol{I}}_i \odot \boldsymbol{\mathcal{M}}_i)$. And we use the temporal total variation item $\mathcal{L}_{tv-temporal}$ in [30] to regularize the Hexplane optimization.

2.5 Surface-Aligned Gaussians

When reconstructing the region with limited 3D cues, especially for surrounding tool occlusion masks, noticeable artifacts on the surface are evident. [8] proposes a technique aimed at facilitating precise and rapid mesh extraction from 3D-GS.

To ensure tight integration of the Gaussians with the surface, surface alignment normalization is applied by controlling the density function of the Gaussians, which can be defined as $d(\boldsymbol{p}) = \sum_g \sigma_g \exp\left(-\frac{1}{2}(\boldsymbol{p} - \boldsymbol{\mu}_g)^T \boldsymbol{\Sigma}_g^{-1}(\boldsymbol{p} - \boldsymbol{\mu}_g)\right)$, where $\boldsymbol{p}$ denotes the position and g denotes the Gaussian.

If the Gaussians are aligned with the surface, we could have three assumptions. 1) The closest Gaussian $g^* = \arg\min_g \left\{(\boldsymbol{p} - \boldsymbol{\mu}_g)^T \boldsymbol{\Sigma}_g^{-1}(\boldsymbol{p} - \boldsymbol{\mu}_g)\right\}$ to the point $\boldsymbol{p}$ is likely to contribute much more than others to the density value $d(\boldsymbol{p})$. 2) To ensure the 3D Gaussians to be flat, every Gaussian g would have one of its three scaling factors close to zero. 3) Gaussians are opaque and we can encourage σ_i to be 1 with cross-entropy loss. Under these assumptions, the density can be approximated as $\bar{d}(\boldsymbol{p}) = \exp\left(-\frac{1}{2s_{g^*}^2}\langle \boldsymbol{p} - \boldsymbol{\mu}_{g^*}, \boldsymbol{n}_{g^*}\rangle^2\right)$, where s_{g^*} is the smallest value of s_{g^*} and $\boldsymbol{n}_{g^*}$ is the direction of the corresponding axis. Based on the approximated expression of $\bar{d}(\boldsymbol{p})$, we could find the zero-crossings of the Signed Distance Function and approximate the ideal distance function associated with the density function d as $f(\boldsymbol{p}) = \pm s_{g^*}\sqrt{-2\log(\bar{d}(\boldsymbol{p}))}$. We do not use the density loss in the implementation of [8] and refer to [8] for details of the approximation.

We use the regularization term on the ideal SDF $f(\boldsymbol{p})$ and an estimated $\hat{f}(\boldsymbol{p})$ that is the difference between the depth of $\boldsymbol{p}$ and the depth in the corresponding depth map at the projection of $\boldsymbol{p}$:

$$\mathcal{L}_{SDF} = \frac{1}{|\mathcal{P}|} \sum_{\boldsymbol{p} \in \mathcal{P}} |\hat{f}(\boldsymbol{p}) - f(\boldsymbol{p})|. \tag{7}$$

The estimated $\hat{f}(\boldsymbol{p})$ is defined as the difference between the depth of $\boldsymbol{p}$ and the depth in the corresponding depth map at the projection of $\boldsymbol{p}$. Meanwhile, we add a regularization term for normal direction:

$$\mathcal{L}_{norm} = \frac{1}{|\mathcal{P}|} \sum_{p \in \mathcal{P}} \left\| \frac{\nabla f(\boldsymbol{p})}{\|\nabla f(\boldsymbol{p})\|_2} - \boldsymbol{n}_{g^*} \right\|_2^2. \tag{8}$$

Besides, to encourage opaque Gaussians, we adopt cross-entropy loss for opacity regularization:

$$\mathcal{L}_{opacity}(i) = -\sum_{j}(\sigma + \Delta\sigma)_j \log(\sigma + \Delta\sigma)_j, \tag{9}$$

where $(\sigma + \Delta\sigma)_j$ denotes the j-th Gaussian's opacity in the i-th frame.

To sum up, our final optimization target at the i-th frame is:

$$\mathcal{L}(i) = \mathcal{L}_{L1}(i) + \lambda_D \mathcal{L}_D(i) + \lambda_{TV1} \mathcal{L}_{tv-spatial}(i) + \lambda_{TV2} \mathcal{L}_{tv-temporal} + \lambda_S \mathcal{L}_S(i), \tag{10}$$

where $\mathcal{L}_S(i) = \mathcal{L}_{SDF} + \mathcal{L}_{norm} + 0.5 \mathcal{L}_{opacity}(i)$ denotes the surface-aligned regularization. Hyperparameters λ_D, λ_{TV1}, λ_{TV2}, λ_S control the strength.

3 Experiments

3.1 Datasets and Evaluation Metrics

We evaluate our proposed method on the dataset from [29]: typical robotic surgery videos from 6 cases of DaVinci robotic data. The datasets are designed to capture challenging surgical scenes with non-rigid deformation and tool occlusion. We use standard image quality metrics, including PSNR, SSIM, and LPIPS. Since in evaluation the groundtruth pixels for unseen areas are missing, the tool masks are used to exclude unseen parts for computation and unlike [29,32,33], we do not count those pixels in PSNR. We also report the frame per second (FPS) to compare the rendering speed of the methods. Besides, while former works [29,32,33] adopt the different tool mask configurations in training and evaluation or compare methods under different configurations, we argue to train and evaluate in the same tool mask configurations to prevent meaningless pixels comparison, and compare methods the same tool occlusion masks.

3.2 Implementation Details

In our approach, we adopt the two-stage training methodology in [30] to model the static and deformation fields. In the first stage, we train 3D Gaussian models for the static field, while in the second stage, we focus on training the deformation field. We conduct 3,000 and 60,000 iterations for the first and second stages, respectively. The initial point clouds are estimated using COLMAP [25]. The importance maps scaling strength α is set to 30 and $\delta = 0.2$ for depth loss. Hyperparameters λ_D, λ_{TV1}, λ_{TV2}, λ_S are set to 0.5, 0.01, 1.0, 0.2. We train our models on an NVIDIA RTX 3090 GPU.

Table 1. Quantitative comparison on rendering quality and speed (standard deviation in parentheses).

Methods	PSNR ↑	SSIM ↑	LPIPS ↓	FPS↑
EndoNeRF [29]	35.112 (1.470)	0.936 (0.021)	0.066 (0.030)	<0.2
ForPlane [32]	36.427 (1.214)	0.947 (0.007)	0.058 (0.003)	~1.7
EndoGS w/o SA	37.603 (0.076)	0.964 (0.005)	0.036 (0.009)	~70
EndoGS (Ours)	**37.935 (0.088)**	**0.966 (0.003)**	**0.034 (0.001)**	~70

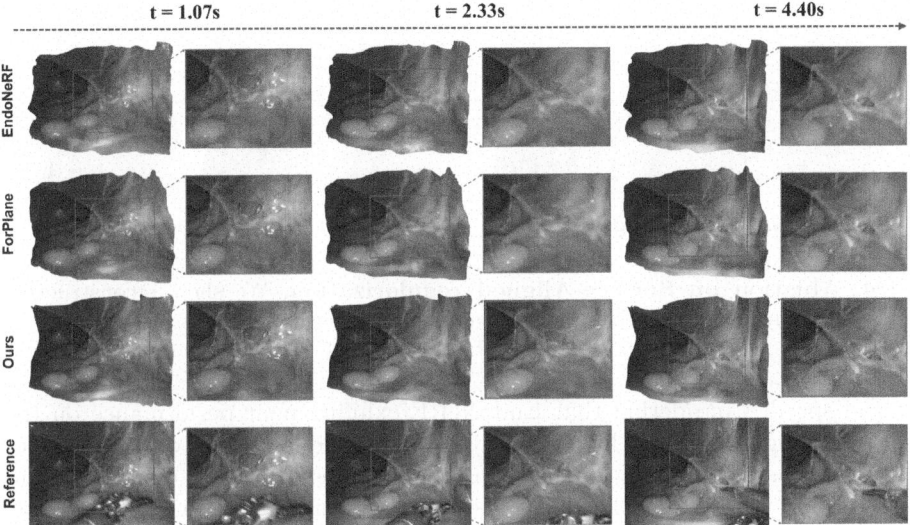

Fig. 2. Qualitative results on scene "traction" at different timesteps.

3.3 Results

We compare EndoGS against two methods, *i.e.*, EndoNeRF [29] and ForPlane [32] (an updated version of LerPlane [33]), due to their competitive quality. ForPlane is trained for 32k iterations. We use the same masks in training and evaluation for three methods and evaluate the rendering results on the same cropped zone where the lowest part of the videos that contain display patterns are removed.

Figure 2 presents a qualitative comparison on scene "traction" between EndoGS and competitive baselines. On the rendering quality, EndoGS clearly outperforms other methods. Tissues deformation occurs at different timesteps, and our method better reconstructs the deformation along the time. We also include the ablation results over the Surface-Aligned regularization which is denoted as SA in the table. Table 1 presents a quantitative comparison on the 6 videos, showcasing the superior performances of our method over the baseline methods in terms of various evaluation metrics related to rendering qual-

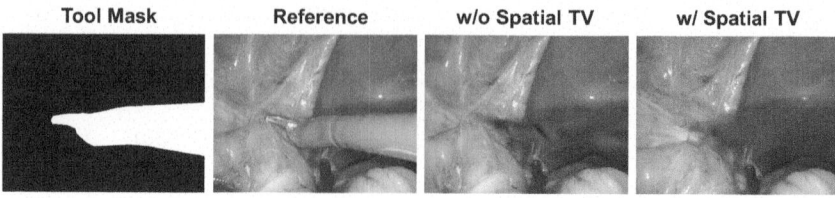

Fig. 3. Ablation on spatial TV loss. We show rendering frames w/ and w/o spatial TV loss on scene "cutting tissues twice".

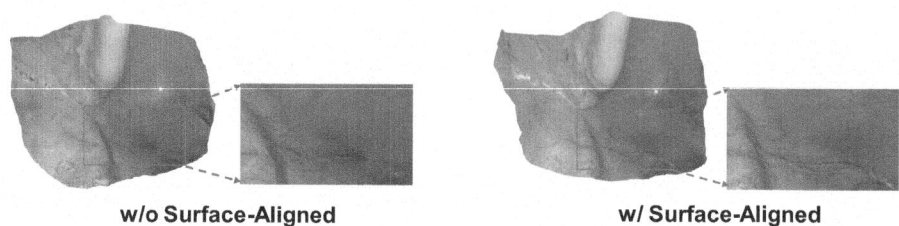

Fig. 4. Ablation on Surface-Aligned regularization. We show reconstruction results w/o and w/ Surface-Aligned regularization on scene "pulling soft tissues".

ity and speed. Considering that EndoNeRF exhibits poor performance on the first rendering frame, we also exclude the first frames from the evaluation process. In terms of rendering quality, EndoGS demonstrates a significant advantage, outperforming the other methods by a considerable margin. Furthermore, EndoGS benefits from the rendering efficiency of Gaussian Splatting, enabling it to achieve real-time rendering speeds. In contrast, the baseline methods struggle to maintain a high FPS rate, highlighting the superiority of EndoGS in this regard.

Ablation Analysis. In Fig. 3, we show the effectiveness of spatial Total Variation loss. While we optimize the Gaussians on seen pixels in frames with the tool masks, the lack of continuity leads to color drift in rendering results (frame w/o spatial TV). This phenomenon can be mitigated during the optimization with spatial TV loss. Table 1 and Fig. 4 present the quantitative and qualitative results over the effectiveness of Surface-Aligned regularization [8,41]. When reconstructing the surrounding of tool occlusion masks, noticeable artifacts on the surface are evident, which cause the rendered image to become blurred. It is shown that with Surface-Aligned regularization more details are preserved.

4 Conclusion

We present a method for deformable endoscopic tissue reconstruction based on surface-aligned Gaussian splatting, which achieves high-quality, real-time reconstruction from a single-viewpoint video, estimated depth maps, and labeled tool masks. Experiments on DaVinci robotic surgery videos demonstrate the superior quality of our method. However, there is limitation to 3D reconstruction from single-viewpoint videos, as it is an ill-posed problem that makes it infeasible for surgical downstream applications. For example, we lack 3D cues for tissues that are occluded by tools. Therefore, future work can focus on practical endoscopic reconstruction, and 3D tissue reconstruction with more surgical cameras is needed to facilitate realistic downstream tasks. We would also like to recommend readers referring to other concurrent and follow-up works [1,9,11,15,16,34,36,38].

Acknowledgement. This work was partially supported by the Research Grants Council of Hong Kong (T45-401/22-N and 27206123) and the National Natural Science Foundation of China (No. 62201483). We thank Med-AIR Lab CUHK for DaVinci robotic prostatectomy data.

References

1. Bonilla, S., Zhang, S., Psychogyios, D., Stoyanov, D., Vasconcelos, F., Bano, S.: Gaussian pancakes: geometrically-regularized 3D gaussian splatting for realistic endoscopic reconstruction. arXiv preprint arXiv:2404.06128 (2024)
2. Cao, A., Johnson, J.: Hexplane: a fast representation for dynamic scenes. In: CVPR (2023)
3. Chen, G., Wang, W.: A survey on 3D gaussian splatting. arXiv preprint arXiv:2401.03890 (2024)
4. Chen, L., Tang, W., John, N.W., Wan, T.R., Zhang, J.J.: Slam-based dense surface reconstruction in monocular minimally invasive surgery and its application to augmented reality. Comput. Methods Program. Biomed. (2018)
5. Chung, J., Oh, J., Lee, K.M.: Depth-regularized optimization for 3D gaussian splatting in few-shot images. arXiv:2311.13398 (2023)
6. Fridovich-Keil, S., Meanti, G., Warburg, F.R., Recht, B., Kanazawa, A.: K-planes: explicit radiance fields in space, time, and appearance. In: CVPR (2023)
7. Gao, W., Tedrake, R.: SurfelWarp: efficient non-volumetric single view dynamic reconstruction. arXiv:1904.13073 (2019)
8. Guédon, A., Lepetit, V.: SuGaR: surface-aligned gaussian splatting for efficient 3d mesh reconstruction and high-quality mesh rendering. arXiv:2311.12775 (2023)
9. Huang, Y., Cui, B., Bai, L., Guo, Z., Xu, M., Ren, H.: Endo-4DGS: distilling depth ranking for endoscopic monocular scene reconstruction with 4D gaussian splatting. arXiv preprint arXiv:2401.16416 (2024)
10. Kerbl, B., Kopanas, G., Leimkühler, T., Drettakis, G.: 3D gaussian splatting for real-time radiance field rendering. ACM Trans. Graph. **42**(4) (2023)
11. Li, C., et al.: EndoSparse: real-time sparse view synthesis of endoscopic scenes using gaussian splatting. arXiv preprint arXiv:2407.01029 (2024)
12. Li, Y., Richter, F., Lu, J., Funk, E.K., Orosco, R.K., Zhu, J., Yip, M.C.: SuPer: a surgical perception framework for endoscopic tissue manipulation with surgical robotics. RA-L (2020)
13. Li, Y., Fu, X., Zhao, S., Jin, R., Zhou, S.K.: Sparse-view CT reconstruction with 3D gaussian volumetric representation. arXiv:2312.15676 (2023)
14. Li, Z., et al.: Revisiting stereo depth estimation from a sequence-to-sequence perspective with transformers. In: ICCV (2021)

15. Liu, H., Liu, Y., Li, C., Li, W., Yuan, Y.: LGS: a light-weight 4D gaussian splatting for efficient surgical scene reconstruction. arXiv preprint arXiv:2406.16073 (2024)
16. Liu, Y., Li, C., Yang, C., Yuan, Y.: EndoGaussian: gaussian splatting for deformable surgical scene reconstruction. arXiv preprint arXiv:2401.12561 (2024)
17. Long, Y., et al.: E-DSSR: efficient dynamic surgical scene reconstruction with transformer-based stereoscopic depth perception. In: MICCAI (2021)
18. Lu, J., Jayakumari, A., Richter, F., Li, Y., Yip, M.C.: Super deep: a surgical perception framework for robotic tissue manipulation using deep learning for feature extraction. In: ICRA (2021)
19. Luiten, J., Kopanas, G., Leibe, B., Ramanan, D.: Dynamic 3D gaussians: tracking by persistent dynamic view synthesis. arXiv:2308.09713 (2023)
20. Mildenhall, B., Srinivasan, P.P., Tancik, M., Barron, J.T., Ramamoorthi, R., Ng, R.: NeRF: representing scenes as neural radiance fields for view synthesis. Commun. ACM **65**(1), 99–106 (2021)
21. Newcombe, R.A., Fox, D., Seitz, S.M.: DynamicFusion: reconstruction and tracking of non-rigid scenes in real-time. In: CVPR (2015)
22. Park, K., et al.: NeRFies: deformable neural radiance fields. In: ICCV (2021)
23. Pumarola, A., Corona, E., Pons-Moll, G., Moreno-Noguer, F.: D-NeRF: neural radiance fields for dynamic scenes. In: CVPR (2021)
24. Recasens, D., Lamarca, J., Fácil, J.M., Montiel, J., Civera, J.: Endo-depth-and-motion: reconstruction and tracking in endoscopic videos using depth networks and photometric constraints. RA-L (2021)
25. Schonberger, J.L., Frahm, J.M.: Structure-from-motion revisited. In: CVPR (2016)
26. Scott, D.J., Cendan, J.C., Pugh, C.M., Minter, R.M., Dunnington, G.L., Kozar, R.A.: The changing face of surgical education: simulation as the new paradigm. J. Surg. Res. (2008)
27. Shin, C., Ferguson, P.W., Pedram, S.A., Ma, J., Dutson, E.P., Rosen, J.: Autonomous tissue manipulation via surgical robot using learning based model predictive control. In: ICRA (2019)
28. Song, J., Wang, J., Zhao, L., Huang, S., Dissanayake, G.: Dynamic reconstruction of deformable soft-tissue with stereo scope in minimal invasive surgery. RA-L (2017)
29. Wang, Y., Long, Y., Fan, S.H., Dou, Q.: Neural rendering for stereo 3D reconstruction of deformable tissues in robotic surgery. In: MICCAI (2022)
30. Wu, G., Yi, T., Fang, J., Xie, L., Zhang, X., Wei, W., Liu, W., Tian, Q., Wang, X.: 4D gaussian splatting for real-time dynamic scene rendering. arXiv:2310.08528 (2023)
31. Wu, T., et al.: Recent advances in 3D gaussian splatting. Comput. Visual Media 1–30 (2024)
32. Yang, C., Wang, K., Wang, Y., Dou, Q., Yang, X., Shen, W.: Efficient deformable tissue reconstruction via orthogonal neural plane. arXiv:2312.15253 (2023)
33. Yang, C., Wang, K., Wang, Y., Yang, X., Shen, W.: Neural lerplane representations for fast 4D reconstruction of deformable tissues. arXiv:2305.19906 (2023)
34. Yang, S., Li, Q., Shen, D., Gong, B., Dou, Q., Jin, Y.: Deform3DGS: flexible deformation for fast surgical scene reconstruction with gaussian splatting. arXiv preprint arXiv:2405.17835 (2024)
35. Yang, Z., Yang, H., Pan, Z., Zhu, X., Zhang, L.: Real-time photorealistic dynamic scene representation and rendering with 4D gaussian splatting. arXiv:2310.10642 (2023)
36. Yang, Z., Chen, K., Long, Y., Dou, Q.: Efficient data-driven scene simulation using robotic surgery videos via physics-embedded 3d gaussians. arXiv preprint arXiv:2405.00956 (2024)

37. Yang, Z., Gao, X., Zhou, W., Jiao, S., Zhang, Y., Jin, X.: Deformable 3D gaussians for high-fidelity monocular dynamic scene reconstruction. arXiv:2309.13101 (2023)
38. Zhao, H., Zhao, X., Zhu, L., Zheng, W., Xu, Y.: HFGS: 4D gaussian splatting with emphasis on spatial and temporal high-frequency components for endoscopic scene reconstruction. arXiv preprint arXiv:2405.17872 (2024)
39. Zhou, H., Jagadeesan, J.: Real-time dense reconstruction of tissue surface from stereo optical video. TMI (2019)
40. Zhou, H., Jayender, J.: EMDQ-SLAM: real-time high-resolution reconstruction of soft tissue surface from stereo laparoscopy videos. In: MICCAI (2021)
41. Zhu, L., Wang, Z., Jin, Z., Lin, G., Yu, L.: Deformable endoscopic tissues reconstruction with gaussian splatting. arXiv preprint arXiv:2401.11535 (2024)

VISAGE: Video Synthesis Using Action Graphs for Surgery

Yousef Yeganeh[1,2], Rachmadio Lazuardi[1], Amir Shamseddin[1], Emine Dari[1], Yash Thirani[1], Nassir Navab[1,2,3], and Azade Farshad[1,2(✉)]

[1] Technical University of Munich, Munich, Germany
azade.farshad@tum.de
[2] Munich Center for Machine Learning, Munich, Germany
[3] Johns Hopkins University, Baltimore, USA

Abstract. Surgical data science (SDS) is a field that analyzes patient data before, during, and after surgery to improve surgical outcomes and skills. However, surgical data is scarce, heterogeneous, and complex, which limits the applicability of existing machine learning methods. In this work, we introduce the novel task of future video generation in laparoscopic surgery. This task can augment and enrich the existing surgical data and enable various applications, such as simulation, analysis, and robot-aided surgery. Ultimately, it involves not only understanding the current state of the operation but also accurately predicting the dynamic and often unpredictable nature of surgical procedures. Our proposed method, **VISAGE** (**VI**deo Synthesis using **A**ction **G**raphs for Surgery), leverages the power of action scene graphs to capture the sequential nature of laparoscopic procedures and utilizes diffusion models to synthesize temporally coherent video sequences. VISAGE predicts the future frames given only a single initial frame, and the action graph triplets. By incorporating domain-specific knowledge through the action graph, VISAGE ensures the generated videos adhere to the expected visual and motion patterns observed in real laparoscopic procedures. The results of our experiments demonstrate high-fidelity video generation for laparoscopy procedures, which enables various applications in SDS.

Keywords: Surgical Video Synthesis · Diffusion Models · Surgical Scene Graphs · Surgical Data Science

1 Introduction

Surgical data science (SDS) is an emerging field that focuses on the quantitative analysis of pre-, intra-, and postoperative patient data [18,26]; it can help to decompose complex procedures, train surgical novices, assess outcomes of actions, and create predictive models of surgical outcomes [13,16,17,22]. In recent years, there have been multiple works on surgical action recognition [24,25,30]. However, SDS faces several challenges, such as the scarcity and heterogeneity of surgical data, the variability and complexity of surgical processes, and the ethical and legal issues of data collection and sharing. To overcome these challenges, we introduce the novel task of surgical video generation, which aims to synthesize realistic and diverse videos of surgical procedures that can be used for various applications, such as simulation, analysis, and robot-aided surgery. Surgical video generation can provide a valuable solution to augment and enrich the real data, and to enable the exploration and evaluation of different surgical scenarios and techniques. Video generation [27] is a challenging task that aims to synthesize realistic and coherent video sequences from a given input, such as a text [14], an image [23], flow maps [35], or a video [31]. Video generation has been extensively studied in the computer vision and machine learning literature, and various methods have been proposed, such as generative adversarial networks (GANs) [21] and autoregressive models [34]. Bar *et al.*[2] propose conditioning video synthesis models on action graphs [11], while WALDO [21] introduces a framework for conditioning the model on segmentation and flow maps [10]. However, most of these methods suffer from limitations, such as mode collapse, blurriness, artifacts, and temporal inconsistency [36]. Moreover, most of these methods are not suitable for laparoscopic video generation, as they do not incorporate domain-specific knowledge and constraints, such as anatomy, surgical actions, and camera motion.

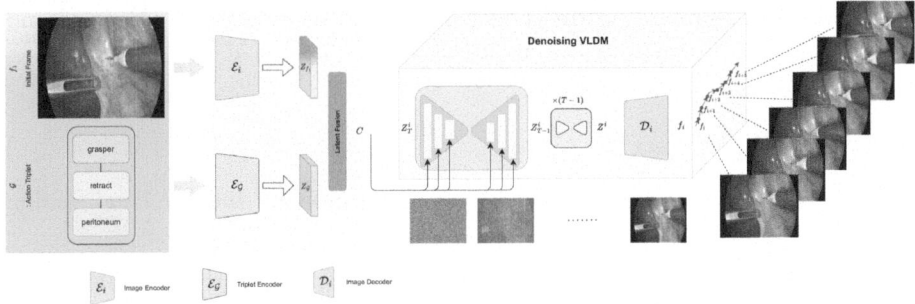

Fig. 1. VISAGE pipeline. The Video Latent Diffusion Model (VLDM) generates the future frames conditioned on the fused conditional features obtained from the input frame and the action graph.

In this work, we introduce the novel task of future video generation in laparoscopic surgery, which aims to generate realistic and diverse videos of laparoscopic procedures conditioned on a single frame and an action triplet, defining the action to be performed. For example, given a frame of a cholecystectomy (gallbladder removal) and a triplet of "cut", "cystic duct", and "clip", the task is to generate a video of the surgeon cutting the cystic duct and applying a clip. This task is challenging, as it requires modeling the complex dynamics and interactions of the surgical scene, as well as generating high-fidelity and temporally coherent video frames.

To address this task, we propose VISAGE (VIdeo Synthesis using Action Graphs for Surgery), which leverages the power of action scene graphs and diffusion models (Fig. 1). An action scene graph is a structured representation of the organs, the surgical tools, and their relations, which capture the sequential nature of the procedures [24]. Image generation [5,7,8,15,19,20,33] and manipulation [6,9] models conditioned on action scene graphs have been previously explored and showed promising outcomes in computer vision. Diffusion models are a class of generative models that can produce high-fidelity images and videos by reversing a Markov chain of Gaussian noise [12,29]. Recent advances in generative AI [1,37] have led to promising models in unconditional video synthesis in the field of computer vision [3,4]. By incorporating domain-specific knowledge through the action graph, VISAGE ensures the generated videos adhere to the expected visual and motion patterns observed in real laparoscopic procedures. Moreover, by using diffusion models, VISAGE avoids the common pitfalls of GANs, such as mode collapse and instability, and achieves state-of-the-art sample quality on the CholecT50 dataset [25]. To summarize, our main contributions are: (1) We introduce the novel task of future video generation in laparoscopic surgery, which has many potential applications and challenges. (2) We propose VISAGE, which conditions the diffusion model on action scene graphs for laparoscopic video generation. (3) We conduct extensive experiments on the CholecT50 dataset, and we demonstrate the effectiveness of our method both quantitatively and qualitatively, (4) We compare our method with several baselines and ablations and show it outperforms them in various metrics and qualitative evaluations.

2 Method

In this section, we describe the video generation pipeline and the conditioning of the diffusion model.

Definitions. We have a dataset p_{data} of videos and their corresponding action triplets $(s, p, o) \in \mathcal{G}$, such that $x, \mathcal{G} \sim p_{data}$, where $x \in \mathcal{R}^{K \times 3 \times H \times W}$ is a sequence of K frames in RGB format, with height and width H and W, and $\mathcal{G}$ is the set of sequential actions performed in the video defined by the (s, p, o) which are the *subject, object,* and *predicate,* respectively. The goal of the model is to generate the subsequent video frames $x_1, ..., x_K$ given $\mathcal{G}$ and x_0. The diffusion model utilized for video generation is denoted by g and parameterized by θ. The diffusion model comprises an image encoder and an action graph encoder denoted by $\mathcal{E}_I, \mathcal{E}_\mathcal{G}$, and a decoder denoted by $\mathcal{D}$.

2.1 Video Latent Diffusion Model

Latent Diffusion Models (LDMs) [29] are generative models based diffusion process. The process comprises a forward (noising) process and a reverse (denoising) process. In the forward process, a data sample x_0 is encoded into a latent representation z_0 using an encoder $\mathcal{E}$. Then Gaussian noise is gradually added over a series of steps, resulting in a sequence of noisier latent variables until a pure noise latent variable z_T is reached:

$$z_t = \sqrt{1 - \beta_t} z_{t-1} + \sqrt{\beta_t} \epsilon_t, \quad \epsilon_t \sim \mathcal{N}(0, I) \qquad (1)$$

where β_t is the noise schedule for timestep t. The reverse process starts from the noise latent variable z_T and iteratively denoises it to recover the original latent representation z_0. A neural network p_θ is used to predict the noise added at each step and subtract it, refining the latent variable at each timestep:

$$z_{t-1} = \frac{1}{\sqrt{1 - \beta_t}} \left(z_t - \frac{\beta_t}{\sqrt{1 - \alpha_t^2}} p_\theta(z_t, t) \right) \qquad (2)$$

where p_θ is trained to predict the noise ϵ_t, and α_t is a variance schedule. To extend the diffusion model to video data, we follow the same procedure as [4] and employ 3D convolutional layers, which can capture both spatial and temporal features of the video frames. Similar to [4], a temporal layer is inserted into the LDM [29] after each spatial layer.

2.2 Action Conditioned Video Generation

An action scene graph consists of nodes and edges, where each node represents an organ or a surgical tool, and each edge represents the performed action. To condition the diffusion model on the action scene graph, we use the graph encoder $\mathcal{E}_\mathcal{G}$ to encode the action scene graph into a latent vector h, which is then fused with the encoded initial frame from $\mathcal{E}_I$. The diffusion model is trained on a denoising objective of the form.

$$\mathbb{E}_{x, h, \epsilon, t} w_t \| \hat{x}_\theta(\alpha_t x + \sigma_t \epsilon, \mathcal{G}) - x \|_2^2, \qquad (3)$$

where $(x, \mathcal{G})$ are data-conditioning pairs, $t \sim \mathcal{U}([0, 1])$, $\epsilon \sim \mathcal{N}(0, I)$, and α_t, σ_t, w_t are functions of t that influence sample quality.

Conditioning. The diffusion model is conditioned on the action graph using the extracted feature embeddings h from $\mathcal{E}_\mathcal{G}$. We propose and evaluate two types of feature encoding for the graph. The first variation encodes the action graph using a learnable embedding layer, where the embeddings are learned implicitly through optimizing the video generation process. The second variation employs CLIP [28] text embeddings for the organ, the tool, and the action. Additionally, we fine-tune the CLIP text encoder using the image generation objective.

Feature Fusion. We propose two variations of feature fusion between the graph and image embeddings. The first variation introduces a linear layer that combines the latent features through concatenation. The second variant employs a cross-attention layer for the future fusion of the action graph conditioning and the image features.

Sampling Process. To generate a video conditioned on the frame x_0 and the triplet (s, p, o), we first encode the action scene graph into a latent vector $h =$

$\mathcal{E}_\mathcal{G}(s,p,o)$. We then initialize the noise sample z_T by adding Gaussian noise to the single frame and then apply the reverse process of the diffusion model to denoise z_T into z_0. At each timestep t, we use the fused latent vector z_t to condition the network g_θ on the action scene graph and the initial frame.

2.3 Data Preprocessing

The videos in CholecT50 [25] dataset consist of an average of 1.7K frames, which is larger than the number of frames our baseline models can process. Therefore, we need to divide the videos into *scenes*, which are smaller clips of the videos in the dataset. To be able to generate temporally consistent videos, generative video models are better trained on datasets that consist of videos that are also temporally consistent [3]. However, raw videos are prone to containing motion inconsistencies, such as jumps between scenes, which we will call *scene cuts*, and still videos with very little motion as *static scenes*. When trained on static scenes, the model might learn to predict little to no motion, or when trained on videos with scene cuts, the model might learn to predict jumps between frames. Therefore, we process the dataset before training to mitigate possible issues. Due to SVD's [3] limitation for the maximum number of frames to process for each video, which is 7, we fix 7 as the frame count of each scene. We obtain 7-framed scenes after applying the methods mentioned in the following sections, which filter the videos to eliminate scene cuts and static scenes.

Scene Cut Detection. To detect scene cuts, which are sudden changes in a sequence of images, we first use the PySceneDetect[1] library. PySceneDetect analyzes videos by comparing the neighboring frames for changes in intensity, brightness, and HSV color space between frames and can also look for fast camera movements. The threshold for the sensitivity in detection can be defined, which we set to 0.27 as suggested. It returns a list of frame IDs where a cut is detected, which is our rough start to divide a video. After the first division by PySceneDetect, we further divide the detected scenes into 7-framed portions, where we add another rule regarding the triplet annotations. We force that all frames in the 7-framed scene at least have one common triplet. This allows us to use the triplet information also as a cut detection method since a frame with no common triplet with other frames in the scene would mean a jump in the depicted motion. We also eliminate the scenes that include frames with empty triplet annotation, such as an undefined triplet or undefined elements for the predicate, instrument, or target.

Static Scene Detection. Static scenes in our videos occur in two ways: Scenes with little motion and scenes that are completely blacked out due to privacy. We detect the latter simply by looking at pixel intensities and eliminating scenes, including all-black frames. They can also be detected by the empty triplet check. The first type of static scene is harder to detect. As in [3], we tried to detect the static scenes by using optical flow to calculate a motion score; however, the scores

---

[1] https://github.com/Breakthrough/PySceneDetect.

did not represent the motion well enough to be used in detection. Therefore, the static scenes of the first type are detected by the empty triplets or triplet elements; for example, scenes where only the (target) organ is in the frame and no action is performed can be detected by checking the triplet annotations.

Table 1. Comparison to SOTA. Quantitative evaluation of video synthesis on CholecT50 [25].

Model	Input	FVD ($\downarrow$)	PSNR ($\uparrow$)	LPIPS ($\downarrow$)	SSIM ($\uparrow$)
CoDi [31]	Image + Triplet	6,944	9.8	0.82	0.31
WALDO [21]	Image + Seg. + Flow	3,413	11.6	0.72	0.34
LFDM [23]	Image + Triplet	1,957	12.0	0.54	**0.71**
SVD [3]	Image	3,870	14.8	0.51	0.47
SVD + FT [3]	Image	1,931	<u>18.2</u>	0.40	0.55
VISAGE-T (Ours)	Image + Triplet	**1,780**	18.1	0.39	<u>0.56</u>
VISAGE-I (Ours)	Image + Triplet	<u>1,875</u>	**18.3**	**0.38**	<u>0.56</u>

3 Experiments and Results

3.1 Experimental Setup

Dataset. For all the experiments, we use the CholecT50 Dataset [25], which is a laparoscopic video dataset of 50 videos for recognizing and localizing surgical action triplets. Each action triplet includes a predicate defining the action, an object (surgical instrument), and a target (organ), which are used as annotations of the individual frames in videos. A frame can be annotated by zero or up to 3 triplets. In addition, the surgical phase for each frame is annotated. There are a total of 100 triplets, 10 predicates, 6 instruments, 15 targets, and 7 phases.

Implementation Details. All our models were trained for 10,000 iterations using Adam Optimizer and a learning rate of 1e-5. We applied an L2 loss between the latent space of the generated 7-frames and their corresponding ground truth to guide the training process effectively.

Evaluation Metrics. We employ the common metrics in video generation for computer vision applications to assess the performance of our model and the baselines. Frechet Video Distance (FVD) [32] compares the probability distribution of generated videos with real videos. Peak Signal-Noise Ratio (PSNR) measures the fidelity of reconstruction. Learned Perceptual Image Patch Similarity (LPIPS) quantifies the perceived similarity between two videos. Structural Similarity Index Measure (SSIM) measures changes in structural information between original and generated videos.

Table 2. Ablation Study. Different condition encoding and fusion techniques. **Att.** stands for cross-attention fusion either with an image or the triplet as the query. **FT** stands for fine-tuning.

Conditioning	Fusion	FVD (↓)	PSNR (↑)	LPIPS (↓)	SSIM (↑)
–	–	1,931	18.2	0.40	0.55
Triplets	Linear	2,461	17.0	0.47	**0.67**
Triplets	Att. + I	2,299	17.4	0.45	**0.67**
CLIP	Linear	2,022	17.3	0.41	0.53
CLIP + FT	Linear	1,851	17.6	0.39	0.54
CLIP + FT	Att. + I	1,875	**18.3**	**0.38**	0.56
CLIP + FT	Att. + T	**1,780**	18.1	0.39	0.56

Baselines. We evaluated four distinct video generation architectures on the CholecT50 dataset [25], specifically WALDO [21], CoDi [31], Stable Video Diffusion (SVD) [3], and Latent Flow Diffusion Model (LFDM) [23]. The comparison among these models involved conducting inference procedures on each model, followed by a comprehensive assessment of the generated outputs through both qualitative and quantitative analyses. It is important to note that these models were originally trained on natural video datasets; thus, the application of these models to egocentric videos from laparoscopic cholecystectomy represents an out-of-distribution scenario relative to their training data. The selection of WALDO as one of the baseline models stemmed from its unique utilization of both flow maps and segmentation maps, effectively integrating high-level semantic information into the video generation process. CoDi was chosen due to its versatile nature, as it inherently supports various modalities such as text, audio, image, and videos, both as input and output. LFDM was included owing to its capability to synthesize scene flow, particularly for its ability to synthesize scene flow in the process of video generation, given an initial image and an action class label. Lastly, the inclusion of SVD was motivated by its training on rich and diverse datasets, coupled with its inherent capacity to model temporal consistency, making it a significant contender for benchmarking against other models in the context of video generation tasks.

3.2 Results

Quantitative Results. Table 1 shows the comparison of different SOTA architectures on the surgical video generation task. As it can be seen, LFDM [23] has the lowest FVD and, on the other hand, the highest SSIM among inference-only models. It also ranks high in PSNR and LPIPS. VISAGE achieves the best overall performance across all models except for SSIM. SSIM captures the structural similarity between the frames, while FVD compares the general distribution of the generated data compared to the real distribution. VISAGE improves the FVD by a large margin compared to the baseline models, demonstrating its ability to adhere to the real data distribution. It is noteworthy that, although more complex GAN-based models such as WALDO receive additional information such as the segmentation and the flow map, they fail in generating realistic samples and are prone to mode collapse.

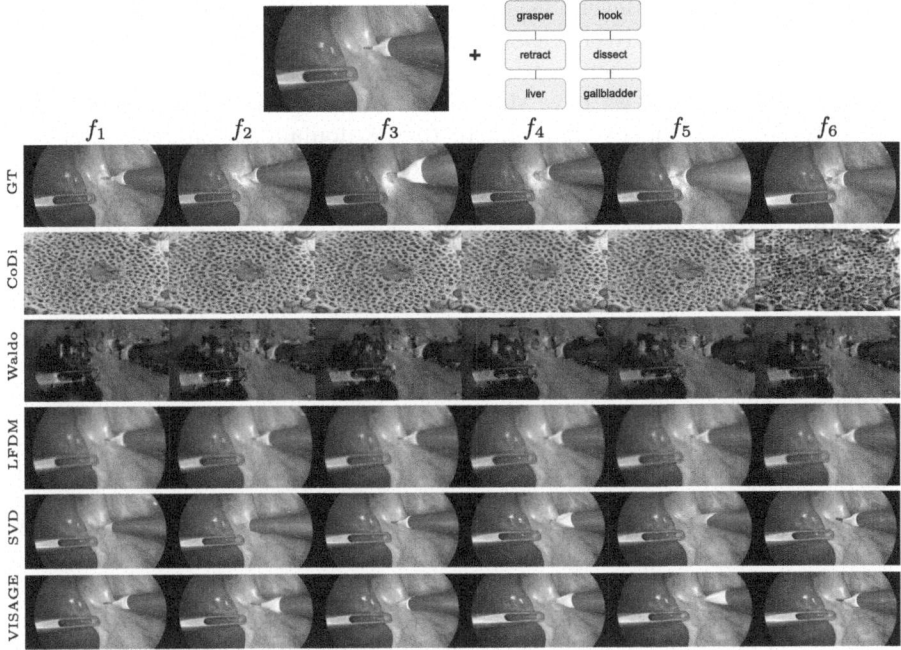

Fig. 2. Qualitative Results. Comparison of the SOTA models on video synthesis on CholecT50 [25].

Qualitative Results. Figure 2 demonstrates the qualitative comparison of the SOTA models compared to VISAGE. CoDi fails to generate realistic results, and Waldo suffers from artifacts in the generated samples. LFDM, SVD, and VISAGE were able to generate results resembling the real data. However, VISAGE generates the fine details, such as the tool tip, which is a key component of the surgery, with higher accuracy.

Ablation Study. We present an ablation study of the different components of VISAGE in Table 2. First, we compare conditioning the model on triplets using a learnable embedding layer versus using the CLIP text embeddings for the action triplet. The results show that utilizing CLIP embedding and further fine-tuning them with the image generation objective achieves the best overall performance. Next, we ablate the fusion of the graph and image embeddings using a linear layer and a cross-attention layer. It can be seen that the introduction of the cross-attention layer largely improves the video generation performance in both conditioning settings.

4 Conclusion

In this paper, we have presented a novel task of future video generation in laparoscopic surgery, which can benefit various aspects of surgical data science, such as simulation, analysis, and robot-aided surgery. We have proposed VISAGE, a generative model that leverages action scene graphs and diffusion models to synthesize realistic and diverse videos of laparoscopic procedures conditioned on a single frame and an action triplet. We have evaluated our method on the CholecT50 dataset, and we have shown that it can generate high-quality and temporally coherent videos that adhere to the domain-specific constraints of laparoscopic surgery. We have also compared our method with several baselines and ablations, and we have demonstrated its superiority in terms of various metrics and qualitative evaluations. Our work opens up new possibilities for future research on surgical video generation, such as incorporating more complex action sequences, improving the diversity and controllability of the generated videos, and exploring the applications of our method in surgical education and training.

References

1. Astaraki, M., et al.: AutoPaint: a self-inpainting method for unsupervised anomaly detection. arXiv preprint arXiv:2305.12358 (2023)
2. Bar, A., et al.: Compositional video synthesis with action graphs. In: Meila, M., Zhang, T. (eds.) Proceedings of the 38th International Conference on Machine Learning. Proceedings of Machine Learning Research, vol. 139, pp. 662–673. PMLR (2021). https://proceedings.mlr.press/v139/bar21a.html
3. Blattmann, A., et al.: Stable video diffusion: scaling latent video diffusion models to large datasets (2023)
4. Blattmann, A., et al.: Align your latents: high-resolution video synthesis with latent diffusion models. In: Proceedings of the IEEE/CVF Conference on Computer Vision and Pattern Recognition, pp. 22563–22575 (2023)
5. Chen, Y., Zhong, K., Wang, F., Wang, H., Zhao, X.: Surgical workflow image generation based on generative adversarial networks. In: 2018 International Conference on Artificial Intelligence and Big Data (ICAIBD), pp. 82–86. IEEE (2018)
6. Dhamo, H., et al.: Semantic image manipulation using scene graphs. In: Proceedings of the IEEE/CVF Conference on Computer Vision and Pattern Recognition, pp. 5213–5222 (2020)
7. Farshad, A., Musatian, S., Dhamo, H., Navab, N.: MIGS: meta image generation from scene graphs. In: BMVC (2021)
8. Farshad, A., Yeganeh, Y., Chi, Y., Shen, C., Ommer, B., Navab, N.: SceneGenie: scene graph guided diffusion models for image synthesis. In: Proceedings of the IEEE/CVF International Conference on Computer Vision, pp. 88–98 (2023)
9. Farshad, A., Yeganeh, Y., Dhamo, H., Tombari, F., Navab, N.: DisPositioNet: disentangled pose and identity in semantic image manipulation. In: 33rd British Machine Vision Conference 2022, BMVC 2022, London, UK, 21–24 November 2022. BMVA Press (2022). https://bmvc2022.mpi-inf.mpg.de/0340.pdf
10. Gao, R., Xiong, B., Grauman, K.: Im2Flow: motion hallucination from static images for action recognition. In: CVPR (2018)

11. Garg, S., Dhamo, H., Farshad, A., Musatian, S., Navab, N., Tombari, F.: Unconditional scene graph generation. In: Proceedings of the IEEE/CVF International Conference on Computer Vision, pp. 16362–16371 (2021)
12. Ho, J., Jain, A., Abbeel, P.: Denoising diffusion probabilistic models. Adv. Neural. Inf. Process. Syst. **33**, 6840–6851 (2020)
13. Holm, F., Ghazaei, G., Czempiel, T., Özsoy, E., Saur, S., Navab, N.: Dynamic scene graph representation for surgical video. In: Proceedings of the IEEE/CVF International Conference on Computer Vision, pp. 81–87 (2023)
14. Hu, Y., Luo, C., Chen, Z.: Make it move: controllable image-to-video generation with text descriptions. In: Proceedings of the IEEE/CVF Conference on Computer Vision and Pattern Recognition (CVPR) (2022)
15. Johnson, J., Gupta, A., Fei-Fei, L.: Image generation from scene graphs. In: CVPR (2018)
16. Köksal, Ç., Ghazaei, G., Holm, F., Farshad, A., Navab, N.: SANGRIA: surgical video scene graph optimization for surgical workflow prediction (2024). https://arxiv.org/abs/2407.20214
17. Maier-Hein, L., et al.: Surgical data science-from concepts toward clinical translation. Med. Image Anal. **76**, 102306 (2022)
18. Maier-Hein, L., et al.: Surgical data science for next-generation interventions. Nat. Biomed. Eng. **1**(9), 691–696 (2017)
19. Marzullo, A., Moccia, S., Catellani, M., Calimeri, F., De Momi, E.: Towards realistic laparoscopic image generation using image-domain translation. Comput. Methods Programs Biomed. **200**, 105834 (2021)
20. Mohamadipanah, H., Kearse, L., Wise, B., Backhus, L., Pugh, C.: Generating rare surgical events using cycleGAN: addressing lack of data for artificial intelligence event recognition. J. Surg. Res. **283**, 594–605 (2023)
21. Moing, G.L., Ponce, J., Schmid, C.: WALDO: future video synthesis using object layer decomposition and parametric flow prediction. In: ICCV (2023)
22. Murali, A., et al.: Latent graph representations for critical view of safety assessment. IEEE Trans. Med. Imaging (2023)
23. Ni, H., Shi, C., Li, K., Huang, S.X., Min, M.R.: Conditional image-to-video generation with latent flow diffusion models. In: Proceedings of the IEEE/CVF Conference on Computer Vision and Pattern Recognition, pp. 18444–18455 (2023)
24. Nwoye, C.I., et al.: Recognition of instrument-tissue interactions in endoscopic videos via action triplets. In: Medical Image Computing and Computer Assisted Intervention–MICCAI 2020: 23rd International Conference, Lima, Peru, 4–8 October 2020, Part III, pp. 364–374. Springer (2020)
25. Nwoye, C.I., et al.: Rendezvous: attention mechanisms for the recognition of surgical action triplets in endoscopic videos. Med. Image Anal. **78**, 102433 (2022)
26. Özsoy, E., Örnek, E.P., Eck, U., Czempiel, T., Tombari, F., Navab, N.: 4D-or: semantic scene graphs for or domain modeling. In: International Conference on Medical Image Computing and Computer-Assisted Intervention, pp. 475–485. Springer (2022)
27. Pan, J., et al.: Video generation from single semantic label map. In: Proceedings of the IEEE/CVF Conference on Computer Vision and Pattern Recognition (CVPR) (2019)
28. Radford, A., et al.: Learning transferable visual models from natural language supervision (2021)
29. Rombach, R., Blattmann, A., Lorenz, D., Esser, P., Ommer, B.: High-resolution image synthesis with latent diffusion models. In: Proceedings of the IEEE/CVF Conference on Computer Vision and Pattern Recognition, pp. 10684–10695 (2022)

30. Sharma, S., Nwoye, C.I., Mutter, D., Padoy, N.: Rendezvous in time: an attention-based temporal fusion approach for surgical triplet recognition. Int. J. Comput. Assist. Radiol. Surg. 1–7 (2023)
31. Tang, Z., Yang, Z., Zhu, C., Zeng, M., Bansal, M.: Any-to-any generation via composable diffusion. In: Thirty-seventh Conference on Neural Information Processing Systems (2023). https://openreview.net/forum?id=2EDqbSCnmF
32. Unterthiner, T., Van Steenkiste, S., Kurach, K., Marinier, R., Michalski, M., Gelly, S.: Towards accurate generative models of video: a new metric & challenges. arXiv preprint arXiv:1812.01717 (2018)
33. Venkatesh, D.K., et al.: Exploring semantic consistency in unpaired image translation to generate data for surgical applications. Int. J. Comput. Assist. Radiol. Surg. 1–9 (2024)
34. Weissenborn, D., Täckström, O., Uszkoreit, J.: Scaling autoregressive video models. In: International Conference on Learning Representations (2019)
35. Wu, Y., Gao, R., Park, J., Chen, Q.: Future video synthesis with object motion prediction. In: The IEEE Conference on Computer Vision and Pattern Recognition (CVPR) (2020)
36. Yan, W., Hafner, D., James, S., Abbeel, P.: Temporally consistent video transformer for long-term video prediction (2022)
37. Yeganeh, Y., Farshad, A., Navab, N.: Shape-aware masking for inpainting in medical imaging. arXiv preprint arXiv:2207.05787 (2022)

A Review of 3D Reconstruction Techniques for Deformable Tissues in Robotic Surgery

Mengya Xu[1,2], Ziqi Guo[1], An Wang[1], Long Bai[1,2], and Hongliang Ren[1,2,3(✉)]

[1] Department of Electronic Engineering, The Chinese University of Hong Kong (CUHK), Sha Tin, Hong Kong SAR, China
hlren@ee.cuhk.edu.hk
[2] CUHK Shenzhen Research Institute, Shenzhen, China
[3] Department of Biomedical Engineering, National University of Singapore, Singapore, Singapore

Abstract. As a crucial and intricate task in robotic minimally invasive surgery, reconstructing surgical scenes using stereo or monocular endoscopic video holds immense potential for clinical applications. NeRF-based techniques have recently garnered attention for the ability to reconstruct scenes implicitly. On the other hand, Gaussian splatting-based 3D-GS represents scenes explicitly using 3D Gaussians and projects them onto a 2D plane as a replacement for the complex volume rendering in NeRF. However, these methods face challenges regarding surgical scene reconstruction, such as slow inference, dynamic scenes, and surgical tool occlusion. This work explores and reviews state-of-the-art (SOTA) approaches, discussing their innovations and implementation principles. Furthermore, we replicate the models and conduct testing and evaluation on two datasets. The test results demonstrate that with advancements in these techniques, achieving real-time, high-quality reconstructions becomes feasible. The code is available at: https://github.com/Epsilon404/ surgicalnerf.

1 Introduction

Reconstruction of surgical scenes from stereo or monocular endoscopic video is a significant and complicated mission in robotic minimally invasive surgery, which could implement clinical applications such as augmented reality in surgical environments and precise surgical navigation [12,20]. However, the most challenging tasks not only lie in a large amount of consumption of computation time and resources but also exist in the endoscopic view with limited viewing directions and the dynamic scene with non-rigid deforming tissues, noticeable lighting variations, and surgical instruments occlusions [1,18,22].

After the emergence of NeRF [17], there has been an increasing number of studies focusing on implicit reconstruction techniques inspired by NeRF to

---
M. Xu and Z. Guo—Contributed equally to this work.

enhance its functionality and broaden its range of applications. Among them, EndoNeRF [22] sets the first precedent for applying it to robotic surgery by incorporating the neural radiance field for deformable tissue reconstruction to solve the above challenges. It utilizes an innovative ray sampling method that enhances the probability of casting the ray on pixels with high occluded frequency, aiming at avoiding the effects of occluding tools and removing them. Then, reconstruct the scene by integrating D-NeRF [19].

Since the first appearance of deformable tissue reconstruction, the number of works exceeding EndoNeRF significantly increased. EndoSurf [29] and Neural LerPlane [24] are two notable studies among them to reconstruct a smooth surface and significantly reduce the reconstruction time, respectively. From the result of NeuS [21], a signed distance function (SDF) works well in restoring a smoother surface than a density field in NeRF [17]. As a result, EndoSurf [29] was initiated to reconstruct smooth surfaces in a deformation surgical scene using the SDF. It employs three networks to accomplish the task: a deformation network converting points from observation space into canonical space, an SDF network precisely depicting the geometry of tissue surface, and a radiance network learning the color attributes of surface points. By incorporating these enhanced network structures, EndoSurf significantly improves reconstruction for deformable tissues. Meanwhile, enhancing training speed for real-time reconstruction during surgical procedures is crucial. To address this challenge, LerPlane [24] adopts a novel approach by dividing the 4D scene into two components: a static field that remains constant over time and a dynamic field that captures temporal changes. Each component is divided into multiple 2D planes: three planes represent spatial points in the static field. In comparison, another set of three planes captures temporal variations of spatial points within the dynamic field. This decomposition simplifies the projection process for each spatial point onto six 2D planes and facilitates the integration of features. Consequently, it reduces the complexity associated with deformation reconstruction, significantly reducing training time. This advancement offers promising prospects for achieving real-time reconstruction in robotic surgery.

Recently, 3D Gaussian Splatting [11] has taken a different route from NeRF in scene reconstruction. It represents the scene as explicit 3D Gaussians and directly projects them onto the 2D plane, known as differentiable splatting [28], to replace the complex volume rendering in NeRF. Therefore, 3D-GS has an observable 3D scene and a real-time rendering speed. Based on it, 4D Gaussians Splatting [23] imports time information to expand it to dynamic scenes. 4D-GS introduces a deformation field to predict the motion and variation of each 3D Gaussian at a specific time and splats 3D Gaussians to render the image.

In this work, we review 4 methods of surgical scene reconstruction, including EndoNeRF [22], EndoSurf [29], LerPlane [24] and 4D-GS [23], then reproduce their models and results, observe and evaluate their performance on not only the basic EndoNeRF dataset [22], also the additional StereoMIS dataset [7] and C3VD dataset [2]. Our contributions are:

- We evaluate the SOTA methods EndoNeRF, EndoSurf, LerPlane, and 4D-GS in terms of training time, GPU usage, and performance on three datasets.
- We compare the NeRF-based methods with Gaussian Splatting, which no work before us has investigated.
- We discover the domain gap between natural and surgical environments leads to a reduced generalization performance of 4D-GS when applying it to surgical scenes, which underscores the need for innovative approaches to address the challenge effectively.

2 Methodology

In this section, we first review the principles of two basic models, NeRF and 3D Gaussian Splatting in Sect. 2.1, and then introduce the implementation of the four methods in Sects. 2.2, 2.3, 2.4 and 2.5.

2.1 Preliminaries

NeRF: Neural Radiance Field. NeRF [17] utilizes a function F_Θ to map each spacial point location $\mathbf{x} = (x, y, z)$ and viewing direction $\mathbf{d} = (\theta, \phi)$ to the output point color and volume density $(\mathbf{c}, \sigma)$, i.e., $F_\Theta = (x, y, z, \theta, \phi) \mapsto (\mathbf{c}, \sigma)$. Then it defines a camera ray by $\mathbf{r}(t) = \mathbf{o} + t\mathbf{d}$, where the ray is emitted from $\mathbf{o}$ in the direction of $\mathbf{d}$ and reaches $\mathbf{r}(t)$. Finally uses the classical volume rendering [10] to predict the pixel color $\hat{C}(\mathbf{r})$ and depth $\hat{D}(\mathbf{r})$: $\hat{C}(\mathbf{r}) = \int_{t_n}^{t_f} T(t)\sigma(\mathbf{r}(t))\mathbf{c}(\mathbf{r}(t))dt, \hat{D}(\mathbf{r}) = \int_{t_n}^{t_f} T(t)\sigma(\mathbf{r}(t))tdt, T(t) = \exp(-\int_{t_n}^{t} \sigma(\mathbf{r}(s))ds)$.

3D Gaussian Splatting. Unlike NeRF, 3D-GS [11] represents a scene by explicit 3D Gaussian ellipsoids. Each 3D Gaussian has four attributes to be optimized: center point $\mathcal{X}$, covariance matrix Σ, opacity α, and color c. A 3D Gaussian can then be represented by: $G(X) = \exp(-\frac{1}{2}\mathcal{X}^T \Sigma^{-1} \mathcal{X})$. To render the image on novel views, it first computes the 2D covariance matrix $\Sigma' = JW\Sigma W^T J^T$ to be an attribute of the projected ellipse on the 2D plane, where J is the Jacobian matrix of projective transformation, and W is the viewing transformation. Then, a pixel color can be calculated with: $\hat{C} = \sum_i c_i \alpha_i \prod_{j=1}^{i-1}(1 - \alpha_j)$.

2.2 EndoNeRF: Endoscopic NeRF Reconstruction

To represent a deformable tissue scene, EndoNeRF [22] firstly uses the modeling process in D-NeRF [19] to build two fields: a static canonical field and a time-dependent deformation field. The canonical field follows the same function F_Θ as NeRF [17] in Sect. 2.1, while the deformation field G_Φ maps the location $\mathbf{x}$ in the canonical field and time t to the distance from the static $\mathbf{x}$ to the point $\mathbf{x}$ at time t. Thus, the color and density of one point $\mathbf{x}$ at a certain time t can be gained by $(\mathbf{c}, \sigma) = F_\Theta(\mathbf{x} + G_\Phi(\mathbf{x}, t), \mathbf{d})$.

Next is to sample rays on a randomly chosen frame. Following the uniform random sampling strategy in NeRF is not conducive to removing tool occlusion.

Therefore, EndoNeRF constructs importance maps $\mathcal{V}_i$ where i is the frame index to guide the casting of rays.

$$\mathcal{V}_i = \Lambda \otimes (\mathbf{1} - M_i), \Lambda = \left(1 + \frac{\sum_j M_j}{\|\sum_j M_j\|_F}\right), \hat{\mathcal{V}}_i = \frac{\mathcal{V}_i}{\|\mathcal{V}_i\|_F} \quad (1)$$

In Eq. 1, M_i is the tool mask of frame i where tool pixels are marked as 1, the constant Λ gives a higher importance on the tool occluded pixels, and $\otimes$ is element-wise multiplication. Then, by normalization, $\hat{\mathcal{V}}_i$ gives the probability mass function to sample rays where the probability of casting rays on tool pixels at this time frame i is zero.

The sampling point step leverages the estimated stereo depth to generate a Gaussian distribution sampling strategy, which samples more points near the surface of the tissue: $\delta(s; u, v, i) = \exp(-(s - \mathbf{D}_i(u, v))^2 / 2\xi^2)$. Here, s is the distance on the ray $\mathbf{r}(s)$ and $\mathbf{D}_i$ is the depth of pixel (u, v). Then, by classical volume rendering [10] as in NeRF, it predicts the color and depth to compute the loss function.

2.3 EndoSurf: Endoscope-Based Surface Reconstruction

The novelty of EndoSurf [29] is reconstructing the tissue surface and texture. It defines three neural fields: a deformation field $\mathbf{\Psi}_d$ for the deformable scene, an SDF field $\mathbf{\Psi}_s$ for the surface, and a radiance field $\mathbf{\Psi}_r$ for surface texture, to solve the problem. Similar with EndoNeRF [22], the deformation field maps a point $\mathbf{x}_o$ at time t to the displacement between $\mathbf{x}_o$ and its corresponding point in canonical space $\mathbf{x}_c$, i.e., $\Delta \mathbf{x} = \mathbf{\Psi}_d(\mathbf{x}_o, t)$, and $\mathbf{x}_c = \mathbf{x}_o + \Delta \mathbf{x}$. Inspired by NeuS [21], the SDF field takes canonical point $\mathbf{x}_c$ as input and takes the signed distance function ρ with a geometry feature vector $\mathbf{f}$ of the point as outputs, i.e., $(\rho, \mathbf{f}) = \mathbf{\Psi}_s(\mathbf{x}_c)$. Here ρ has to be positive when $\mathbf{x}_c$ is between the camera and the surface and otherwise negative. In this setting, the surface needed to be reconstructed is represented by $\mathcal{S} = \{\mathbf{x} | \mathbf{\Psi}_s(\mathbf{x}) = 0\}$, and one can calculate the surface normal $\mathbf{n}_c$ of a surface point $\mathbf{p}_c$ by the gradient: $\mathbf{n}_c = \nabla \mathbf{\Psi}_s(\mathbf{p}_c)$. For the radiance field, it outputs the pixel color $\mathbf{c}_c$ with input $(\mathbf{x}_c, \mathbf{v}_c, \mathbf{n}_c, \mathbf{f})$, where the parameters are spacial coordinates, the viewing direction, the surface normal, and the geometry feature vector.

With the predicted signed density function ρ_i and color $\mathbf{c}_i$ of sampled points $\mathbf{x}_i$ on ray $\mathbf{r}(h)$ at time t, it is able to conduct unbiased volume rendering [21] to estimate the ray color and depth:

$$\hat{\mathbf{C}}(\mathbf{r}(h)) = \sum_i \left(\prod_{j=1}^{i-1}(1-\alpha_j)\right) \alpha_i \mathbf{c}_i, \hat{\mathbf{D}}(\mathbf{r}(h)) = \sum_i \left(\prod_{j=1}^{i-1}(1-\alpha_j)\right) \alpha_i h_i \quad (2)$$

where $\alpha_i = \max\left(1 - \frac{1+\exp(-\rho_i/s)}{1+\exp(-\rho_{i+1}/s)}, 0\right)$ is the opacity of each point on the ray.

Ultimately, it sets the loss functions to optimize the rendered images and the SDF. The rendering loss is defined by $\lambda_1 \mathcal{L}_c + \lambda_2 \mathcal{L}_d$.

$$\mathcal{L}_c = \sum_{\mathbf{r}} \|M(\mathbf{r})(\hat{\mathbf{C}}(\mathbf{r}) - \mathbf{C}(\mathbf{r}))\|_1, \mathcal{L}_d = \sum_{\mathbf{r}} \|M(\mathbf{r})(\hat{\mathbf{D}}(\mathbf{r}) - \mathbf{D}(\mathbf{r}))\|_1 \quad (3)$$

Here M represents the tool mask and $\mathbf{C}$, $\mathbf{D}$ are ground truth color and depth. Then it optimizes the SDF field by four loss functions: the Eikonal loss [6], the SDF loss that requires the SDF outputs of surface points to be zero, the visible loss that generates a correct surface direction, and the smoothness loss that gives a smooth surface.

2.4 LerPlane: Linear Interpolation Plane

The reason why LerPlane [24] can rapidly reconstruct a surgical scene is the idea of decomposing the 4D scene into six explicit 2D planes similar to [5], which reduces the complexity from $O(N^4)$ to $O(N^2)$, and shrinks the neural network to a tiny MLP to accelerate the training. Specifically, it constructs two fields with three planes each to represent a deformable surgical scene. Three space planes XY, YZ, XZ form the static field, and three time-dependent planes XT, YT, ZT constitute the dynamic field. The total 6 planes are orthogonal to each other, resulting in a simple projection for a 4D point onto each plane.

To remove tool occlusion, a spatiotemporal importance sampling strategy is utilized for ray casting. With the tool mask $\boldsymbol{M}_i$ and input image $\boldsymbol{I}_i$ of the ith frame, a weight map $\mathbf{W}_i$ similar to the importance map of EndoNeRF [22] is generated by:

$$\mathbf{W}_i = \min[\frac{1}{3} \max_{j \in (i-n, i+n)} (\|\boldsymbol{I}_i \otimes \boldsymbol{M}_i - \boldsymbol{I}_j \otimes \boldsymbol{M}_j\|_1), \alpha] \otimes \boldsymbol{\Omega}_i, \boldsymbol{\Omega}_i = \beta \left(\frac{\boldsymbol{M}_i T}{\sum_{i=1}^{T} \boldsymbol{M}_i} \right) \quad (4)$$

where $\otimes$ is element-wise multiplication and hyperparameters α and β represent a lower bound and a balancing parameter respectively. Then, on the frequently occluded pixels, the $\boldsymbol{\Omega}$ value will be higher, leading to a higher probability of sampling rays on these pixels.

With the sampled ray and 4D point, the 2D features are extracted by projecting the point on six 2D planes and utilizing the bilinear interpolation method. Then fuse the six features into the final feature vector fed into the MLP, which estimates the color and density $(\mathbf{c}, \sigma)$, and renders the color and depth by volume rendering [10]. Optimizing the MLP and fields leverages not only the color and depth loss but also the total variation loss and smooth time loss that ensure the similarity of adjacent frames.

2.5 4D-GS: 4D Gaussian Splatting

Similar to the above methods of modeling deformable scenes, 4D-GS [23] is mainly aiming at optimizing a deformation field $\mathcal{F}$ to output the new states of 3D Gaussians in the space at a specific time t. Such a deformation field is separated into two parts in the implementation: multi-resolution neural voxels that extract the features on voxel planes and a tiny MLP that outputs the information of deformed 3D Gaussians by decoding the features.

Based on the fact that the 3D Gaussians with proximal space positions have similar states and that one 3D Gaussian will have akin features in adjacent timestamps, it utilizes a HexPlane module with multi-resolution to encode the information, including time t of all 3D Gaussians. Like the idea in LerPlane [24], the HexPlane module uses six 2D voxel planes with interpolation to extract and fuse features.

$$f = \bigcup \prod interp(R(i,j)), (i,j) \in \{(x,y), (y,z), (x,z), (x,t), (y,t), (z,t)\} \quad (5)$$

With the features in voxels, the required parameters, including the variation of location, rotation, scaling, opacity, and color, i.e., $(\Delta \mathcal{X}, \Delta r, \Delta s, \sigma, \mathcal{C})$, can be decoded by a tiny MLP. A new state of each 3D Gaussians is then represented by $\mathcal{S}' = \mathcal{F}(\mathcal{S}, t) = (\mathcal{X} + \Delta \mathcal{X}, r + \Delta r, s + \Delta s, \sigma, \mathcal{C})$, and the differential splatting [28] is exploited to render the final color $\hat{C} = \mathcal{G}(\mathcal{S}'|R, T)$ with the view-matrix $[R, T]$. Finally, it uses color reconstruction loss and total variation loss to optimize.

3 Experiments

3.1 Dataset Description

We evaluate the models on 3 public datasets, **EndoNeRF dataset** [22], **StereoMIS dataset** [7], and **C3VD** [2].

EndoNeRF dataset gives two endoscopic scenes generated from in-house DaVinci robotic surgery scenes. The video of each scene is captured by a single-viewpoint stereo camera. Each image has a resolution of 640 × 512, with a corresponding depth map and a binary mask of the surgical tool. The depth map is estimated by [14], and the tool mask is manually labeled in left camera images.

StereoMIS dataset is captured from the da Vinci Xi robotic surgery scenes. Each of the 11 scenes includes a stereo video from a single viewpoint and a set of binary tool masks. The video data is processed into left and right camera view image sets, with each image resolution 640 × 512.

C3VD is a colonoscopy 3D video dataset with totally 22 video sequences. The images have a resolution of 640 × 512 and the depth map is generated from optical images by a Generative Adversarial Network (GAN).

3.2 Implementation Details

We train and evaluate the models on the same platform with Ubuntu 20.04 and one RTX3090 GPU. We split the training data into train and test sets with the quantity ratio 7:1. Specifically, in the data sequence, after grouping 8 images, the first 7 images are added to the training set, and the last one is added to the testing set. We utilize the Depth Anything small-sized model [25] to generate a set of coarse depth maps for the StereoMIS dataset. We train each model until their respective convergence. For the EndoNeRF model, we train it in $100K$ iterations for about 5 h. For the EndoSurf model, we train it in $100K$ iterations for about 10 h. For the LerPlane model, we train it in $32K$ iterations for 12 min. For the 4D-GS model, we train it in $6K$ iterations for 5 min. The rest of the experimental settings retain the default values for each model. Finally, we use the image quality evaluation index to appraise the reconstruction performance of each model, including PSNR, SSIM, and LPIPS. These metrics present the similarity between synthesized and test set images, giving the quantitative results of the models on two datasets.

4 Results and Evaluation

We evaluate and compare the 4 models EndoNeRF [22], EndoSurf [29], LerPlane [24] and 4D-GS [23] on 3 datasets EndoNeRF [22], StereoMIS [7] and C3VD [2] using metrics of PNSR, SSIM and LPIPS, together with training time, inference time and GPU usage. We train each model until respective convergence. The evaluation and comparison are shown in Table 1 and Table 2. Figure 1 shows the visualization results.

Table 1. Quantitative Results of 4 models on 3 datasets. The ones in bold are the best value, and the underlined ones take second place. EndoNeRF and EndoSurf give better reconstruction results.

Models	EndoNeRF dataset [22]			StereoMIS dataset [7]			C3VD dataset [2]		
	PSNR↑	SSIM↑	LPIPS↓	PSNR↑	SSIM↑	LPIPS↓	PSNR↑	SSIM↑	LPIPS↓
EndoNeRF [22]	27.077	0.900	0.107	**31.511**	**0.832**	**0.190**	**36.759**	**0.886**	**0.214**
EndoSurf [29]	**34.795**	**0.945**	0.119	28.417	0.818	0.368	33.192	0.868	0.346
LerPlane [24]	34.643	0.922	**0.072**	17.526	0.741	0.379	16.914	0.845	0.348
4D-GS [23]	22.832	0.827	0.368	19.202	0.756	0.472	21.352	0.865	0.437

Table 2. Results for proof of real-time performance evaluation. 4D-GS consumes the shortest time and is closest to real-time rendering.

Models	Training Time	Inference Time	GPU Usage
EndoNeRF [22]	6 h	8585.3 ms	8 GB
EndoSurf [29]	10 h	33476.6 ms	19 GB
LerPlane [24]	12 min	601.3 ms	22 GB
4D-GS [23]	**5 min**	**18.3 ms**	**4 GB**

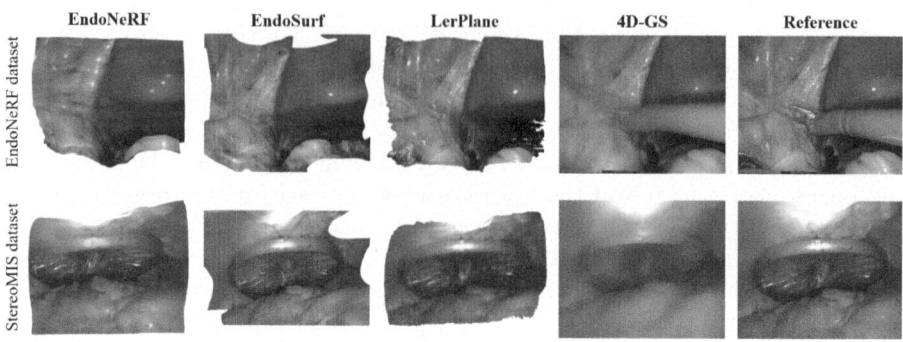

Fig. 1. Visualization Results of 4 models on 2 datasets. EndoNeRF, EndoSurf, and LerPlane on the first dataset give good 3D results. Still, LerPlane on the StereoMIS dataset cannot restore the original color, and 4D-GS presents poor performance on both endoscopic datasets.

From the experiment results, we can observe that (1) Training time: EndoSurf > EndoNeRF ≫ LerPlane > 4D-GS. The reason EndoNeRF and EndoSurf require more time is that they incorporate time information, which increases complexity. In contrast, the other two models employ a 2D plane representation, effectively reducing complexity and decreasing inference and training times. The inference time has the same trend as the training time, meaning that EndoNeRF and EndoSurf are difficult to use for real-time rendering, but LerPlane and 4D-GS have the potential for it. (2) GPU usage: LerPlane > EndoSurf > EndoNeRF > 4D-GS. EndoSurf consumes more GPU memory as it requires an additional field to locate the tissue surface. LerPlane's higher GPU usage may be attributed to the experiment's excessive multi-resolution setting and the subsequent large number of spatial points it generates. Reducing the number of explicit Gaussians and instead utilizing a smaller set of implicit points could potentially minimize GPU usage for 4D-GS. (3) Performances: The performance of LerPlane on the EndoNeRF dataset is comparable to that of EndoSurf, although it falls slightly short due to the inherent variability within the margin of error. LerPlane's ability to attain these results in a shorter time underscores the efficacy of its acceleration strategy. The disparate trends observed between the two datasets may be attributed to the distinct characteristics of the input data. Specifically, the EndoNeRF dataset presents a more deformable scene, whereas the StereoMIS and C3VD datasets exhibit less deformation. The subpar performance of LerPlane on the latter dataset likely arises from its inability to capture features within a more static scene context effectively.

5 Conclusion

In conclusion, this work summarizes and reviews the existing state-of-the-art models in surgical scene reconstruction. EndoNeRF introduces NeRF for the first endoscopic reconstruction, while EndoSurf restores a smooth surface, LerPlane dramatically increases training speed, and 4D-GS takes advantage of Gaussians to reconstruct the scene explicitly. 4D-GS performs worse on the surgical scene than the natural scene, implying the domain gap for transferring it directly to surgical scenes: (a) Due to the limited viewing direction, it cannot restore the initial Gaussians, (b) Surgical scenes with large deformations result in poor generalization, (c) Removing surgical tools also requires a sampling strategy similar to the previous models. We believe future studies will enable 4D-GS to achieve successful surgical scene reconstruction, closer to the purpose of real-time rendering. Meanwhile, a series of recent methodologies on endoscopic reconstruction related to GS and foundation models can be found at [3, 4, 8, 9, 13, 15, 16, 26, 27, 30, 31].

Acknowledgments. This work was supported by Hong Kong RGC CRF C4026-21G, RIF R4020-22, GRF 14211420 & 14203323, Shenzhen-Hong Kong-Macau Technology Research Programme (Type C) STIC Grant SGDX20210823103535014 (202108233000303) and the Key Project 2021B1515120035 (B.02.21.00101) of the Regional Joint Fund Project of the Basic and Applied Research Fund of Guangdong Province.

Disclosure of Interests. The authors have no competing interests to declare.

References

1. Batlle, V.M., Montiel, J.M., Fua, P., Tardós, J.D.: LightNeuS: neural surface reconstruction in endoscopy using illumination decline. In: International Conference on Medical Image Computing and Computer-Assisted Intervention, pp. 502–512. Springer (2023)
2. Bobrow, T.L., Golhar, M., Vijayan, R., Akshintala, V.S., Garcia, J.R., Durr, N.J.: Colonoscopy 3D video dataset with paired depth from 2D-3D registration. Med. Image Anal. 102956 (2023)
3. Cui, B., Islam, M., Bai, L., Ren, H.: Surgical-DINO: adapter learning of foundation models for depth estimation in endoscopic surgery. Int. J. Comput. Assist. Radiol. Surg. 1–8 (2024)
4. Cui, B., Islam, M., Bai, L., Wang, A., Ren, H.: EndoDAC: efficient adapting foundation model for self-supervised depth estimation from any endoscopic camera. arXiv preprint arXiv:2405.08672 (2024)
5. Fridovich-Keil, S., Meanti, G., Warburg, F.R., Recht, B., Kanazawa, A.: K-planes: explicit radiance fields in space, time, and appearance. In: Proceedings of the IEEE/CVF Conference on Computer Vision and Pattern Recognition, pp. 12479–12488 (2023)
6. Gropp, A., Yariv, L., Haim, N., Atzmon, M., Lipman, Y.: Implicit geometric regularization for learning shapes (2020)
7. Hayoz, M., et al.: Learning how to robustly estimate camera pose in endoscopic videos. Int. J. Comput. Assist. Radiol. Surg. **18**(7), 1185–1192 (2023)
8. Huang, Y., Cui, B., Bai, L., Guo, Z., Xu, M., Ren, H.: Endo-4DGS: distilling depth ranking for endoscopic monocular scene reconstruction with 4d gaussian splatting. arXiv preprint arXiv:2401.16416 (2024)

9. Huang, Y., Cui, B., Zhang, J., Bai, L., Ren, H.: Registering neural 4D gaussians for endoscopic surgery. arXiv preprint arXiv:2407.20213 (2024)
10. Kajiya, J.T., Von Herzen, B.P.: Ray tracing volume densities. ACM SIGGRAPH Comput. Graph. **18**(3), 165–174 (1984)
11. Kerbl, B., Kopanas, G., Leimkühler, T., Drettakis, G.: 3D gaussian splatting for real-time radiance field rendering. ACM Trans. Graph. **42**(4) (2023). https://repo-sam.inria.fr/fungraph/3d-gaussian-splatting/
12. Knappe, P., Gross, I., Pieck, S., Wahrburg, J., Künzler, S., Kerschbaumer, F.: Position control of a surgical robot by a navigation system. In: Proceedings 2003 IEEE/RSJ International Conference on Intelligent Robots and Systems (IROS 2003) (Cat. No. 03CH37453), vol. 4, pp. 3350–3354. IEEE (2003)
13. Li, C., et al.: EndoSparse: real-time sparse view synthesis of endoscopic scenes using gaussian splatting. arXiv preprint arXiv:2407.01029 (2024)
14. Li, Z., et al.: Revisiting stereo depth estimation from a sequence-to-sequence perspective with transformers. In: Proceedings of the IEEE/CVF International Conference on Computer Vision (ICCV), pp. 6197–6206 (2021)
15. Liu, H., Liu, Y., Li, C., Li, W., Yuan, Y.: LGS: a light-weight 4D gaussian splatting for efficient surgical scene reconstruction. arXiv preprint arXiv:2406.16073 (2024)
16. Liu, Y., Li, C., Yang, C., Yuan, Y.: EndoGaussian: gaussian splatting for deformable surgical scene reconstruction. arXiv preprint arXiv:2401.12561 (2024)
17. Mildenhall, B., Srinivasan, P.P., Tancik, M., Barron, J.T., Ramamoorthi, R., Ng, R.: NeRF: representing scenes as neural radiance fields for view synthesis. In: ECCV (2020)
18. Psychogyios, D., Vasconcelos, F., Stoyanov, D.: Realistic endoscopic illumination modeling for nerf-based data generation. In: International Conference on Medical Image Computing and Computer-Assisted Intervention, pp. 535–544. Springer (2023)
19. Pumarola, A., Corona, E., Pons-Moll, G., Moreno-Noguer, F.: D-NeRF: neural radiance fields for dynamic scenes. In: Proceedings of the IEEE/CVF Conference on Computer Vision and Pattern Recognition, pp. 10318–10327 (2021)
20. Qian, L., Wu, J.Y., DiMaio, S.P., Navab, N., Kazanzides, P.: A review of augmented reality in robotic-assisted surgery. IEEE Trans. Med. Robot. Bionics **2**(1), 1–16 (2019)
21. Wang, P., Liu, L., Liu, Y., Theobalt, C., Komura, T., Wang, W.: NeuS: learning neural implicit surfaces by volume rendering for multi-view reconstruction. In: NeurIPS (2021)
22. Wang, Y., Long, Y., Fan, S.H., Dou, Q.: Neural rendering for stereo 3D reconstruction of deformable tissues in robotic surgery. In: International Conference on Medical Image Computing and Computer-Assisted Intervention, pp. 431–441. Springer (2022)
23. Wu, G., et al.: 4D gaussian splatting for real-time dynamic scene rendering. arXiv preprint arXiv:2310.08528 (2023)
24. Yang, C., Wang, K., Wang, Y., Yang, X., Shen, W.: Neural lerplane representations for fast 4D reconstruction of deformable tissues. In: MICCAI (2023)
25. Yang, L., Kang, B., Huang, Z., Xu, X., Feng, J., Zhao, H.: Depth anything: unleashing the power of large-scale unlabeled data (2024)
26. Yang, S., Li, Q., Shen, D., Gong, B., Dou, Q., Jin, Y.: Deform3DGS: flexible deformation for fast surgical scene reconstruction with gaussian splatting. arXiv preprint arXiv:2405.17835 (2024)

27. Yang, Z., Chen, K., Long, Y., Dou, Q.: Efficient data-driven scene simulation using robotic surgery videos via physics-embedded 3D gaussians. arXiv preprint arXiv:2405.00956 (2024)
28. Yifan, W., Serena, F., Wu, S., Öztireli, C., Sorkine-Hornung, O.: Differentiable surface splatting for point-based geometry processing. ACM Trans. Graph. **38**(6), 1–14 (2019). https://doi.org/10.1145/3355089.3356513
29. Zha, R., Cheng, X., Li, H., Harandi, M., Ge, Z.: EndoSurf: neural surface reconstruction of deformable tissues with stereo endoscope videos (2023)
30. Zhao, H., Zhao, X., Zhu, L., Zheng, W., Xu, Y.: HFGS: 4D gaussian splatting with emphasis on spatial and temporal high-frequency components for endoscopic scene reconstruction. arXiv preprint arXiv:2405.17872 (2024)
31. Zhu, L., Wang, Z., Cui, J., Jin, Z., Lin, G., Yu, L.: EndoGS: deformable endoscopic tissues reconstruction with gaussian splatting. arXiv preprint arXiv:2401.11535 (2024)

SurgTrack: CAD-Free 3D Tracking of Real-World Surgical Instruments

Wenwu Guo[1], Jinlin Wu[1,2], Zhen Chen[1(✉)], Qingxiang Zhao[1], Miao Xu[1], Zhen Lei[1,2,3], and Hongbin Liu[1,2]

[1] Centre for Artificial Intelligence and Robotics (CAIR), HKISI-CAS, Beijing, China
chenzhen_ustc@163.com
[2] MAIS, Institute of Automation, Chinese Academy of Sciences, Beijing, China
[3] School of Artificial Intelligence, University of Chinese Academy of Sciences, Beijing, China

Abstract. Vision-based surgical navigation has received increasing attention due to its non-invasive, cost-effective, and flexible advantages. In particular, a critical element of the vision-based navigation system is tracking surgical instruments. Compared with 2D instrument tracking methods, 3D instrument tracking has broader value in clinical practice, but is also more challenging due to weak texture, occlusion, and lack of Computer-Aided Design (CAD) models for 3D registration. To solve these challenges, we propose the SurgTrack, a two-stage 3D instrument tracking method for CAD-free and robust real-world applications. In the first registration stage, we incorporate an Instrument Signed Distance Field (SDF) modeling the 3D representation of instruments, achieving CAD-freed 3D registration. Due to this, we can obtain the location and orientation of instruments in the 3D space by matching the video stream with the registered SDF model. In the second tracking stage, we devise a posture graph optimization module, leveraging the historical tracking results of the posture memory pool to optimize the tracking results and improve the occlusion robustness. Furthermore, we collect the Instrument3D dataset to comprehensively evaluate the 3D tracking of surgical instruments. The extensive experiments validate the superiority and scalability of our SurgTrack, by outperforming the state-of-the-arts with a remarkable improvement. The code and dataset are available at https://github.com/wenwucode/SurgTrack.

Keywords: Surgical Instruments · 3D Instrument Tracking · Signed Distance Field · Posture Memory Pool · Posture Graph Optimization

1 Introduction

Developing computer-assisted surgery systems can improve the quality of interventional healthcare for patients [1,4–7,14,25], offering significant benefits, such as reduced operational times and minimized risk of surgical complications. In particular, surgical navigation systems have become an indispensable component in modern surgery [2,13,15], and ascertain the exact positioning of surgical instruments by tracking distinctive sections of the tools. As a critical element of surgical navigation systems, including electromagnetic-based [18], optical-based [20], and vision-based systems [27]. Among these, vision-based systems have garnered considerable interest due to non-invasive, cost-effective, flexible, and not subject to line-of-sight limitations or electromagnetic disturbances [26,27].

The 3D tracking algorithm is essential in vision-based surgical navigation systems [20]. However, most existing methods of instrument tracking are based on object-tracking algorithms, detecting the region of interest object and corresponding matching the detected region across different frames. Early works [29] required markers of surgical instruments, and achieved instrument tracking by recognizing and matching markers across different frames. This method causes invasion of surgical instruments, lacking scalability. Later works [3] proposed marker-freed tracking methods, detecting instruments with handcraft visual features and then tracking instruments through the Kalman filter algorithm. Limited by the generalizability of handcraft visual features, these marker-freed methods did not perform well in real-world applications. Recently, Fathollahi et al. [9] proposed a highly accurate instrument tracking method, which introduces Yolo-v5 [12] to improve the accuracy of instrument detection and applies ReID [28] technology to improve the accuracy of cross-frame matching. However, these methods focused on developing 2D tracking of instruments, which can only perceive 2 degrees of freedom, which is not enough to provide sufficiently accurate information for surgical navigation.

Existing 2D tracking systems [29] are restricted to the x and y planes, accommodating in-plane rotations for a total of three degrees of freedom. In comparison, 3D object tracking approaches [17,19,22,23,30] match detected objects with pre-established computer-aided design (CAD) models to ascertain their 3D orientation. Represented through six degrees of freedom-spanning the x, y, and z axes, and including the rotational dimensions of pitch, yaw, and roll-this detailed spatial understanding is vital for vision-based navigational systems. However, the application of these 3D tracking methods to surgical environments is fraught with challenges. A primary challenge is the inaccessibility of CAD models for surgical instruments, as they are often proprietary due to patent protections. The absence of CAD models hinders most 3D tracking techniques in the realm of surgical instrument tracking. Additional obstacles are the low textural features and frequent occlusions of surgical instruments, which complicate their detection and sustained tracking.

Inspired by existing works [16,19,24], we design a novel 3D surgical instrument tracking method, named SurgTrack, which is capable of accurately tracking the 6 degrees of freedom of surgical instruments in real 3D space. To solve the problem of missing CAD models, we incorporate an Instrument Signed Distance Field (SDF) model generating the 3D representation of the surgical instrument with RGB-D video frames. We also propose an Instrument SDF model to further accurately learn the 3D shape and texture of instruments. Through Instrument SDF, SurgTrack completes the registration of 3D tracking without CAD models. To solve tracking problems caused by occlusion and weak textures, we apply a posture memory pool to provide historical tracking results as a reliable reference. We also utilize a posture graph optimization module to optimize the

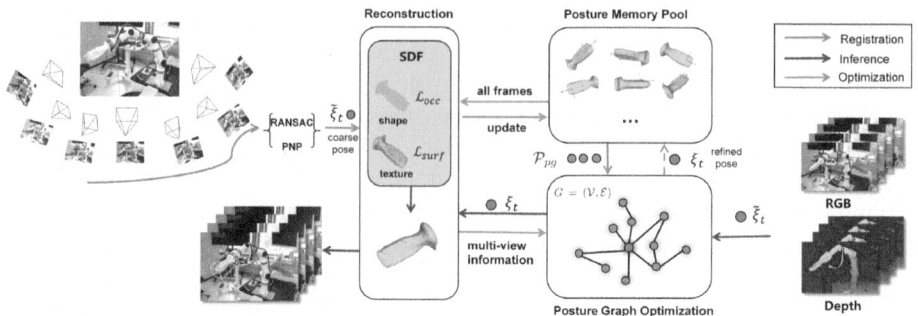

Fig. 1. The overview of our SurgTrack framework. Our SurgTrack comprises a registration stage and a tracking stage. (a) In the registration stage, the 3D model is reconstructed using the instrument SDF. (b) The tracking stage first uses RANSAC for rough pose estimation, and then performs pose optimization using posture memory pool and posture graph.

ongoing tracking results with historical references and ensure that occlusions and weak textures do not cause tracking interruptions.

Furthermore, to facilitate a comprehensive analysis and evaluation of our methods, we collect a 3D tracking dataset of surgical instruments, named Instrument3D. Our SurgTrack achieves a remarkable 3D tracking performance with the 88.82% ADD-S and the 12.85 reconstruction error. We also conduct experiments on the general 3D object tracking dataset HO3D to demonstrate the generalization and scalability of our SurgTrack.

2 Method

2.1 Overview of SurgTrack

An overview of our SurgTrack framework is shown in Fig. 1. To achieve CAD-free registration, we first model the 3D shape of the surgical instrument using SDF (Sect. 2.2). Then, we track the 6-DoF pose of the instruments through the Posture Memory Pool and Posture Graph Optimization (Sect. 2.3).

2.2 CAD-Free Instrument Registration

Instrument SDF Modeling. Given the 3D point cloud $\{v|v \in \mathbb{R}^3\}$ captured by a RGB-D camera, we adapt the Signed Distance Function (SDF) to model the 3D representation of the surgical instrument as follows:

$$S = \{v|\Psi(v) = 0\}, \tag{1}$$

where $\Psi(v) = 0$ represents the points on the surface of the instrument. Therefore, we can derive the 3D model of the instrument from point cloud data, eliminating the need for a pre-existing Computer-Aided Design (CAD) model. This 3D model facilitates the registration process for 3D tracking. However, the SDF methodology faces inherent limitations when dealing with complex scenarios, such as occlusions and low-texture regions.

Occlusion and Texture Optimization. To address this, we incorporate the occlusion constraint and shape constraint in the SDF model. For occlusions, we introduce a positive value δ to alleviate boundary ambiguities between background and instrument caused by partial occlusions:

$$\mathcal{L}_{occ} = \frac{1}{|V_{occ}|} \sum_{v \in V_{occ}} (\Psi(v) - \delta)^2. \tag{2}$$

For surfaces with weak textures, we consider points near the surface in the SDF modeling process, enabling our SurgTrack to better capture the surface geometry and handle areas with weak textures, as follows:

$$\mathcal{L}_{surf} = \frac{1}{|V_{surf}|} \sum_{v \in V_{surf}} (\Psi(v) + d_v - d_\Delta)^2. \tag{3}$$

In this way, the total loss function $\mathcal{L}$ is defined as follows:

$$\mathcal{L} = \alpha \mathcal{L}_{occ} + \beta \mathcal{L}_{surf}, \tag{4}$$

where α and β balance the contributions of the two components.

2.3 Instrument Tracking

Tracking Initialization. In the tracking stage, we estimate a coarse pose $\tilde{\xi}_t$ by matching the current frame and its adjacent frames with RANSAC algorithm as follows:

$$\tilde{\xi}_t = \arg\min_{R,t} \sum_i \|Rp_i + t - q_i\|^2. \tag{5}$$

In the above equation, RANSAC algorithm minimizes the distance between the reconstructed results p_i and their corresponding scene points q_i and estimates the coarse pose $\tilde{\xi}_t$. R and t represent the rotation and translation matrix.

Tracking Optimization. Following the initial rough pose estimation obtained using RANSAC, the pose $\tilde{\xi}_t$ serves as the initial estimate in the subsequent optimization phase. This pose is further refined by integrating the pose memory pool with the pose graph to improve accuracy and robustness. First, to address challenges such as long-term tracking drift, data loss, and occlusions, it is crucial to preserve the pose data from previous frames. We implement a posture memory pool $\mathcal{P}$ that stores this information as follows:

$$\mathcal{P} = \{(\xi_i, M_i) \mid i = 1, 2, \ldots, N\}, \tag{6}$$

where $\xi_i \in SE(3)$ represents the optimized pose of the ith frame, M_i contains the 3D point cloud data associated with the ith frame, and N is the number of keyframes currently stored in the posture memory pool.

With the initial pose $\tilde{\xi}_t$, we construct a posture graph using selected relevant frames from the posture memory pool. The selection is based on criteria such as the RANSAC matching threshold and frame overlap to ensure reliable references. Then, the posture graph is constructed as follows:

$$G = (\mathcal{V}, \mathcal{E}), \tag{7}$$

where the nodes $\mathcal{V}$ consist of the current frame $\mathcal{F}_t$ and the selected reference frames $\mathcal{P}_{pg}$, as $\mathcal{V} = \mathcal{F}_t \cup \mathcal{P}_{pg}$ with $|\mathcal{V}| = K + 1$.

Based on the posture graph, we refine the tracking results of the current frame through the following loss function, resulting in the final optimized pose $\xi_t \in SE(3)$:

$$\xi_t \leftarrow \arg\min_{\xi_t} \left(w_s \mathcal{L}_{\text{SDF}}(t) + \sum_{i \in \mathcal{V}, j \in \mathcal{V}, i \neq j} [w_f \mathcal{L}_{\text{3D}}(i,j) + w_p \mathcal{L}_{\text{2D}}(i,j)] \right), \tag{8}$$

where $\mathcal{L}_{\text{3D}}(i,j)$ is the 3D distance loss, $\mathcal{L}_{\text{2D}}(i,j)$ is the 2D projection loss, $\mathcal{L}_{\text{SDF}}(t)$ is the instrument SDF depth loss, and the scalar weights w_f, w_p, w_s are empirically set to 1. Specifically, the 3D distance loss $\mathcal{L}_{\text{3D}}$ is calculated as:

$$\mathcal{L}_{\text{3D}}(i,j) = \sum_{(p_m, p_n) \in C_{i,j}} \rho \left(\left\| \xi_i^{-1} p_m - \xi_j^{-1} p_n \right\|_2 \right). \tag{9}$$

This 3D distance loss measures the Euclidean distance between corresponding RGB-D features $p_m, p_n \in \mathbb{R}^3$, using the Huber loss function ρ to enhance the robustness of our SurgTrack.

On the other hand, the 2D projection loss $\mathcal{L}_{\text{2D}}$ is calculated as:

$$\mathcal{L}_{\text{2D}}(i,j) = \sum_{p \in I_i} \rho \left(\left| n_i(p) \cdot \left(T_{ij}^{-1} \pi_{D_j}^{-1} (\pi_j(T_{ij} p)) - p \right) \right| \right). \tag{10}$$

This 2D projection loss assesses the pixel-wise point-to-plane distance after projection and transformation, comparing node i to the plane in node j.

Finally, the instrument SDF depth loss $\mathcal{L}_{\text{SDF}}$ is calculated as follows:

$$\mathcal{L}_{\text{SDF}}(t) = \sum_{p \in I_t} \rho \left(\left| \Psi(\xi_t^{-1}(\pi_D^{-1}(p))) \right| \right). \tag{11}$$

This instrument SDF depth loss measures the distance between the current frame and the implicit surface defined by the Instrument SDF, where $\Psi(\cdot)$ is the signed distance function indicating proximity to the surface. Note that this loss is considered only after the initial training of the object field has converged.

In this way, the optimization strategy for our SurgTrack, starting from the rough pose $\tilde{\xi}_t$ and resulting in the final optimized pose $\xi_t \in SE(3)$, integrates 3D spatial information, instrument shape, and depth data from a single viewpoint to complete pose optimization, improving robustness against reflections, weak textures, and long-term tracking challenges.

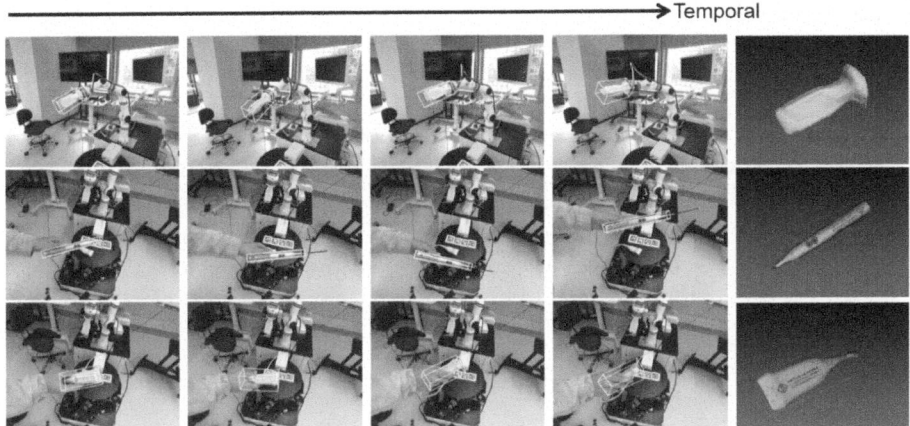

Fig. 2. Visualization on the Instrument3D dataset test samples. Our SurgTrack achieves causal 3D tracking and reconstruction of weakly textured surgical instruments for monocular RGB-D sequences.

3 Experiments

3.1 Experimental Settings

Datasets. We collect a 3D tracking dataset of surgical instruments in RGB-D videos, named Instruments3D. The Instruments3D dataset consists of 13 videos across 5 surgical instruments, including ultrasound bronchoscopes, flexible and rigid endoscopes, thoracoscopes, and ultrasound probes. The Instruments3D dataset presents RGB-D videos by capturing human hands manipulating YCB objects, recorded at close range using an Intel RealSense camera. The ground truth data is derived through multi-view registration. We also conduct experiments on the general object 3D tracking dataset, HO3D [10,11].

Evaluation Metrics. We follow the classical evaluation protocol of 3D object tracking [10,11]. We use the ADD and ADD-S as the accuracy metric of 3D tracking, with their values ranging from 0 to 1, where higher values signify better accuracy. We use the Chamfer Distance (CD) as a measure of reconstruction error, where a smaller value indicates a more precise reconstruction.

3.2 Comparison Results on Instrument3D and HO3D

Comparison on Instrument3D. The Instrument3D dataset presents a complex challenge due to the frequent occlusions and severe motion blur encountered during the manipulation of surgical instruments. Furthermore, the inherent characteristics of these instruments such as their weak texture, reflective surfaces, and slender profiles compound the difficulty. Despite these difficulties of the Instrument3D dataset, our SurgTrack maintains the capability of robust,

Table 1. Comparison of our SurgTrack with state-of-the-arts on the Instrument3D and HO3D datasets. The ADD and ADD-S are AUC percentages (0 to 0.1 m). Reconstruction is measured by Chamfer Distance (CD).

Dataset	Method	Pose		Reconstruction
		ADD-S (%) ↑	ADD (%) ↑	CD (cm) ↓
HO3D	NICE-SLAM [30]	22.29	8.97	52.57
	SDF-2-SDF [19]	35.88	16.08	9.65
	KinectFusion [17]	25.81	16.54	15.49
	DROID-SLAM [22]	64.64	33.36	30.84
	BundleTrack [23]	92.39	66.01	52.05
	SurgTrack	95.85	92.53	0.65
Instrument3D	Pixtrack [8]	60.59	45.13	-
	OnePose [21]	30.06	16.98	-
	SurgTrack	88.82	83.65	12.85

Table 2. Ablation study of our SurgTrack on the Instrument3D dataset.

Ablations	Pose		Reconstruction
	ADD-S (%) ↑	ADD (%) ↑	CD (cm) ↓
SurgTrack	88.82	83.65	12.85
w/o occlusion and texture optimization	76.39	62.09	35.52
w/o posture memory pool	75.65	47.14	-
w/o posture graph	77.23	42.36	15.60

long-term tracking in most cases, as shown in Fig. 2. The comparison results in Table 1 confirm the remarkable advantage of our SurgTrack over state-of-the-art 3D tracking methods.

Comparison on HO3D. As shown in Table 1 and Fig. 3, on the HO3D dataset, we achieve the best results compared with other tracking schemes. Our algorithm shows strong capabilities in both ADD-S and ADD. While BundleTrack matches our performance in ADD-S, it falls short in all other metrics where we excel significantly, and it also demands more than 300 rounds of training. This demonstrates the strong generalization ability of our method to general objects.

3.3 Ablation Study

To comprehensively evaluate our SurgTrack framework for 3D tracking of surgical instruments, we investigate the impact of each module. These modules include occlusion and texture Optimization, posture memory pool, and posture graph. As shown in Table 2, the occlusion and texture optimization is helpful for tracking optimization, which can increase ADD-S by 12.43% and ADD by 21.56%. When constructing the posture graph, selecting the most matching pose subset instead of randomly selecting can reduce the CD error by nearly 3 cm and

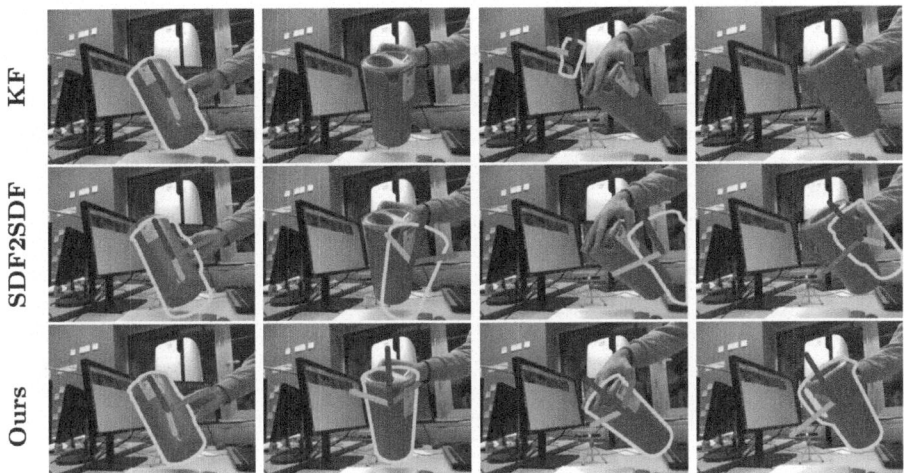

Fig. 3. The 3D tracking visualization of our SurgTrack and state-of-the-art methods (*i.e.*, KF and SDF-2-SDF) on the HO3D dataset.

increase the ADD by 41.29%. In this way, these comparisons further validate the effectiveness of our SurgTrack with tailored modules.

4 Conclusion

In this study, we collect a new multi-category surgical instrument 3D tracking data set, conduct a comprehensive study on 3D surgical instrument tracking, and propose a framework for 3D instrument tracking. We use Instrument SDF to generate the 3D representation of surgical instruments, achieving CAD-free 3D tracking registration. In the tracking stage, we use the posture memory pool and combine it with the posture graph for pose optimization, which greatly improves the 3D tracking accuracy. We also use the Instrument SDF to further improve the robustness to occlusion, weak texture, and long-term tracking. Experiments show that our method has significant superiority and scalability over public data sets and surgical instrument 3D tracking datasets.

Acknowledgments. This work was supported by the National Natural Science Foundation of China (Grant No. #62306313 and No. #62206280), and the InnoHK program.

Disclosure of Interests. The authors declare no competing interests.

References

1. Bai, L., et al.: EndoUIC: promptable diffusion transformer for unified illumination correction in capsule endoscopy. In: MICCAI. Springer (2024)

2. Van den Bempt, M., Liebregts, J., Maal, T., Berge, S., Xi, T.: Toward a higher accuracy in orthognathic surgery by using intraoperative computer navigation, 3D surgical guides, and/or customized osteosynthesis plates: A systematic review. J. Cranio-Maxillofac. Surg. **46**(12), 2108–2119 (2018)
3. Bouget, D., Allan, M., Stoyanov, D., Jannin, P.: Vision-based and marker-less surgical tool detection and tracking: a review of the literature. Med. Image Anal. **35**, 633–654 (2017)
4. Chen, Z., et al.: Surgical video captioning with mutual-modal concept alignment. In: MICCAI, pp. 24–34. Springer (2023)
5. Chen, Z., et al.: VS-assistant: versatile surgery assistant on the demand of surgeons. arXiv preprint arXiv:2405.08272 (2024)
6. Chen, Z., Zhai, Y., Zhang, J., Wang, J.: Surgical temporal action-aware network with sequence regularization for phase recognition. In: BIBM, pp. 1836–1841. IEEE (2023)
7. Chen, Z., et al.: ASI-Seg: audio-driven surgical instrument segmentation with surgeon intention understanding. In: IROS (2024)
8. Chidananda, P., Nair, S., Lee, D., Kaehler, A.: PixTrack: precise 6DoF object pose tracking using nerf templates and feature-metric alignment. arXiv preprint arXiv:2209.03910 (2022)
9. Fathollahi, M., et al.: Video-based surgical skills assessment using long term tool tracking. In: MICCAI, vol. 13437, pp. 541–550. Springer (2022)
10. Hampali, S., Rad, M., Oberweger, M., Lepetit, V.: Honnotate: a method for 3D annotation of hand and object poses. In: CVPR (2020)
11. Hampali, S., Sarkar, S.D., Rad, M., Lepetit, V.: Keypoint transformer: solving joint identification in challenging hands and object interactions for accurate 3D pose estimation. In: CVPR (2022)
12. Jocher, G.: Ultralytics/YOLOv5: v3.1 - bug fixes and performance improvements (2020)
13. Lehner, M., et al.: On-site cad templates reduce surgery time for complex craniostenosis repair in infants: a new method. Childs Nerv. Syst. **36**, 793–801 (2020)
14. Luo, X., Pang, Y., Chen, Z., Wu, J., Zhang, Z., Lei, Z., Liu, H.: SurgPlan: surgical phase localization network for phase recognition. In: ISBI. IEEE (2024)
15. Ma, L., Huang, T., Wang, J., Liao, H.: Visualization, registration and tracking techniques for augmented reality guided surgery: a review. Phys. Med. Biol. **68**(4), 04TR02 (2023)
16. Mildenhall, B., Srinivasan, P.P., Tancik, M., Barron, J.T., Ramamoorthi, R., Ng, R.: NeRF: representing scenes as neural radiance fields for view synthesis. In: ECCV (2020)
17. Newcombe, R.A., et al.: KinectFusion: real-time dense surface mapping and tracking. In: IEEE International Symposium on Mixed and Augmented Reality, pp. 127–136. IEEE (2011)
18. Shi, Y., Lin, L., Wu, W.: Research on the application of electromagnetic navigation technology in surgical robots. Chin. J. Med. Instrument. **47**(1), 26–31 (2023)
19. Slavcheva, M., Kehl, W., Navab, N., Ilic, S.: SDF-2-SDF registration for real-time 3d reconstruction from RGB-D data. Int. J. Comput. Vision **126**, 615–636 (2018)
20. Sorriento, A., et al.: Optical and electromagnetic tracking systems for biomedical applications: A critical review on potentialities and limitations. IEEE Rev. Biomed. Eng. **13**, 212–232 (2019)
21. Sun, J., Wang, Z., Zhang, S., He, X., Zhao, H., Zhang, G., Zhou, X.: OnePose: one-shot object pose estimation without cad models. In: CVPR, pp. 6825–6834 (2022)

22. Teed, Z., Deng, J.: Droid-SLAM: deep visual slam for monocular, stereo, and RGB-D cameras. In: NeurPS, vol. 34, pp. 16558–16569 (2021)
23. Wen, B., Bekris, K.: BundleTrack: 6D pose tracking for novel objects without instance or category-level 3D models. In: IROS, pp. 8067–8074. IEEE (2021)
24. Wen, B., et al.: BundleSDF: Neural 6-DoF tracking and 3D reconstruction of unknown objects. In: CVPR, pp. 606–617 (2023)
25. Xu, H., Wu, J., Cao, G., Chen, Z., Lei, Z., Liu, H.: Transforming surgical interventions with embodied intelligence for ultrasound robotics. In: MICCAI. Springer (2024)
26. Xu, L., et al.: Information loss challenges in surgical navigation systems: from information fusion to AI-based approaches. Inf. Fusion **92**, 13–36 (2023)
27. Yang, L., Etsuko, K.: Review on vision-based tracking in surgical navigation. IET Cyber-Syst. Robot. **2**(3), 107–121 (2020)
28. Ye, M., Shen, J., Lin, G., Xiang, T., Shao, L., Hoi, S.C.H.: Deep learning for person re-identification: a survey and outlook. IEEE Trans. Pattern Anal. Mach. Intell. **44**(6), 2872–2893 (2021)
29. Zhang, L., Ye, M., Chan, P., Yang, G.: Real-time surgical tool tracking and pose estimation using a hybrid cylindrical marker. Int. J. Comput. Assist. Radiol. Surg. **12**(6), 921–930 (2017)
30. Zhu, Z., et al.: Nice-slam: Neural implicit scalable encoding for slam. In: CVPR, pp. 12786–12796 (2022)

MUTUAL: Towards Holistic Sensing and Inference in the Operating Room

Julien Quarez[1]($\boxtimes$), Yang Li[1], Hassna Irzan[1], Matthew Elliot[1,2], Oscar MacCormac[1,2], James Knigth[2], Martin Huber[1], Toktam Mahmoodi[4], Prokar Dasgupta[1,3], Sebastien Ourselin[1], Nicholas Raison[1,3], Jonathan Shapey[1,2], and Alejandro Granados[1]

[1] Surgical & Interventional Engineering, King's College London, London, UK
{julien.quarez,alejandro.granados}@kcl.ac.uk
[2] Neurosurgery Department, King's College Hospital, London, UK
[3] Department of Urology, Guy's Hospital, London, UK
[4] Department of Engineering, King's College London, London, UK

Abstract. Embodied AI (E-AI) in the form of intelligent surgical robotics and other agents is calling for data platforms to facilitate its development and deployment. In this work, we present a cross-platform multimodal data recording and streaming software, MUTUAL, successfully deployed on two clinical studies, along with its ROS 2 distributed adaptation, MUTUAL-ROS 2. We describe and compare the two implementations of MUTUAL through their recording performance under different settings. MUTUAL offers robust recording performance at target configurations for multiple modalities, including video, audio, and live expert commentary. While this recording performance is not matched by MUTUAL-ROS 2, we demonstrate its advantages related to real-time streaming capabilities for AI inference and more horizontal scalability, key aspects for E-AI systems in the operating room. Our findings demonstrate that the baseline MUTUAL is well-suited for data curation and offline analysis, whereas MUTUAL-ROS 2, should match the recording reliability of the baseline system under a fully distributed manner where modalities are handled independently by edge computing devices. These insights are critical for advancing the integration of E-AI in surgical practice, ensuring that data infrastructure can support both robust recording and real-time processing needs.

Keywords: Multimodal data · Embodied AI · ROS 2 · Surgical data

---

J. Quarez and Y. Li—These two authors contributed equally to this work.

Supplementary Information The online version contains supplementary material available at https://doi.org/10.1007/978-3-031-77610-6_17.

© The Author(s), under exclusive license to Springer Nature Switzerland AG 2025
M. E. Celebi et al. (Eds.): MICCAI 2024 Workshops, LNCS 15274, pp. 178–188, 2025.
https://doi.org/10.1007/978-3-031-77610-6_17

1 Introduction

While Artificial Intelligence (AI) has traditionally operated within the digital realm, only recently have new methodologies been proposed to enable agents to interact within a physical environment. Embodied AI (E-AI), supported by the integration of sensors and actuators, allows digital systems to perceive, manipulate, and learn from the physical world [26,32]. Learning through interactions within an environment, known as embodied cognition [25,32], has garnered increasing interest over the years. This interest has shifted the field from conventional AI, which primarily relies on offline datasets and static environments [3], to artificial general intelligence, where AI can adapt to and overcome environmental changes [5]. E-AI holds significant promise for automating tasks prone to human error [5] and adapting to unforeseen events.

Surgery has seen early forms of E-AI through Robotic-Assisted Surgery (RAS) [17,20,30], meeting three out of the four paradigms of E-AI [25]: perception, action, and memory, while lacking continuous learning. RAS has been used to automate tasks of varying complexity, from simple gestures such as knot-tying [29] to entire procedures like knee arthroplasty [14]. Despite these advancements, we argue that surgeons will remain the core agents in the operating room (OR), with E-AI systems enhancing the precision of their technical skills and supporting their situational awareness and decision-making abilities (non-technical skills) to ensure a holistic approach to surgical practice. However, substantial integration of E-AI in the OR is still limited due to the lack of tools necessary to capture the environmental characteristics of the OR [27].

Capturing a holistic scene of the OR is a challenging endeavor [18]. The OR is a highly complex and dynamic environment, and introducing additional recording and streaming technologies can be disruptive [28]. Furthermore, domain expert knowledge is seldom captured during interventions in the OR and is typically limited to manual annotations provided retrospectively, which leads to the loss of valuable information. Moreover, while there has been a push to diversify the modalities captured in the OR, video and imaging remain the primary data sources for AI applications. A multimodal approach to data is expected to increase the understanding of an environment by processing different sources of information similarly to human cognition.

To enable the meaningful development of E-AI, we propose a distributed **mult**imodal s**u**rgic**al** data platform, MUTUAL, for sensing and inference in the OR. Our contributions are as follows: **1)** two multimodal platforms for efficient recording of data and distributed inference, **2)** integration of real-time expert knowledge and annotations, and **3)** comparative evaluation of both platforms and their demonstration on two clinical scenarios. Code and tutorial can be found on https://github.com/JK-rez/MUTUAL.git.

2 Related Work

Few platforms have been deployed and trialled in the OR to capture multimodal intraoperative surgical data, including the OR Black Box®, which continuously captures and synchronises several sources of intraoperative data [9], and the Multi-sensing AI Environment for Surgical Task and Role Optimisation (MAE-STRO) [24]. The OR Black Box® includes panoramic cameras, microphones, and anaesthesia monitors. In contrast, the MAESTRO platform integrates a wider array of modalities, such as depth cameras, laparoscopic cameras, eye trackers, and several wearable physiological sensors and functional neuroimaging sensors. These platforms support various downstream tasks, including measuring surgeon cognitive workload [8], automatic surgical check-listing [24], resource optimisation, and education [7]. Despite their advancements, these platforms face significant challenges in the context of E-AI. As surgical data recording becomes increasingly common, the variety and volume of recordings will escalate, necessitating robust connectivity, high Input/Output bandwidth, and abundant storage space for recording platforms. Additionally, if storage devices are not closely integrated with high-performance computing devices, transferring data for training E-AI becomes inefficient. The MAESTRO platform employs the Lab Streaming Layer (LSL) [1] for real-time data streaming. However, LSL is standalone software that only natively supports a limited set of recording devices and lacks integration with common E-AI systems, including robotic systems. Moreover, no multimodal surgical data platform has been rigorously assessed for surgical recording and streaming performance, which is a critical gap given the complex requirements of multimodal data handling.

Performance assessment for multimodal data recording and streaming systems is inherently complex. While substantial work exists in other domains, such as smart city Internet of Things, where platforms like FIWARE undergo load testing and scalability assessments [2], similar efforts are absent in the surgical domain. FIWARE's testing metrics include CPU and RAM usage, highlighting the need for analogous performance metrics in surgical data systems.

Few studies evaluate inference performance and resource consumption of AI models developed for surgical applications [15]. With the AI research community's focus on faster inference through methods including model optimisation such as pruning [22], hardware acceleration [4,10,19], and framework optimisation [12], there remains a lack of exploration into efficiently deploying AI, particularly E-AI, in the OR. Considerable research explores leveraging E-AI in surgical robotic systems [6,13,31] and virtual assistants [11,21]. For integrating a data platform with E-AI, the Robot Operating System 2 (ROS 2) [16] has been widely adopted across various domains. This widespread adoption motivates us to design our platform in ROS 2 to address the integration challenges and enhance the capabilities of surgical data platforms for E-AI applications.

In summary, a multimodal surgical data platform that supports a wide range of customisable devices, is performance-tested, and is distributed to enable close integration with E-AI is needed.

3 Methods

We propose MUTUAL (Multimodal Surgical Data Platform), a multi-process cross-platform software utilising open-source Software Development Kits

Table 1. Summary of modalities used in our study. While all modalities are included in the endoscopic study (eTPS), only the first two modalities are included in the RAS skills assessment scenario. When using MUTUAL-ROS 2 data is stored in rosbag files

Modality	Manufacturer	Resolution @(Hz)	Storage	Captured Content
ZED 2i	StereoLabs	1080p*2 @15	SVO	RGB-D and body tracking
RealSense	Intel	480p*2 @15	bag	RGB-D and hand pose
Force Sensor	ATI	@ 15	txt	Forces/torque (pantoms)
IMU	MBIENTLAB	@ 10	txt	Hand movement
PTZ	Panasonic	1080p @30	AVI	Overall and hands view
Endoscope	Karl Storz	1080p @30	AVI	Endoscopic video
OR Audio	Sennheise	N/A @$48*10^3$	WAV	Conversations
Expert Audio	HyperX	N/A @$48*10^3$	WAV	Expert commentary
Annotations	N/A	N/A	txt	OSATS and comments

(SDKs), FFmpeg and Shell scripts to capture multimodal surgical data. We also introduce MUTUAL-ROS 2 which extends MUTUAL for more native support for E-AI applications using ROS 2. A Graphical User Interface (GUI) is designed to facilitate the acquisition of expert knowledge alongside the data captured by these two platforms.

Data Modalities and Equipment: We demonstrate the performance of our proposed platform across multiple and diverse modalities (Table 1) captured simultaneously. These modalities are illustrative inputs that an agent would potentially need access to capture the knowledge of the environment at a given time. These modalities can be connected to laptops or edge computing devices in the OR and/or in a Control Room, a room adjacent to the OR used for monitoring surgical interventions by other clinical team members or by the surgical team during tele-operated interventions.

3.1 Multi-modal Platform Overview

MUTUAL (baseline): A Shell script is used to launch and manage the recording (Fig. 1). This script calls each of the device's SDKs as a separate process while recording their process IDs (PIDs). SDKs were modified to wait in an endless loop once all respective initialisation steps are performed. Every device has varying initialisation times after launch, allowing devices to "wait" for one another, is one way to ensure small differences in synchronisation. The Shell scripts check that all devices are initialised and ready to record before allowing the generation of the starting criterion through a terminal or Secure Shell (SSH) command. Once recording has started, the Shell script monitors device connectivity and error handling using the PIDs. The file sizes are also checked to make sure data is stored throughout. Error-catching protocols are incorporated in case a device fails due to a killed process or due to a file not increasing in size. Ignore the error, restart the concerned process, or intervene on the device are some of the options a user could consider. Recording are also contained in an endless loop, waiting for a stop criterion that will kill all processes and clean temporary files. A Python script is used to launch and manage all FFmpeg recordings in the control room. Once recording is triggered, a Python subprocess call will send a start criterion through an SSH command to the managing Shell script via the orchestration server. This allows for relatively synchronised recording between the two laptops used in the eTPS study. See Sect. 3.2. Once a stop button is clicked on the GUI, Python will kill all FFmpeg processes and send a stop criterion to the managing Shell script through the orchestration server. See supplementary material for overview of recording workflow.

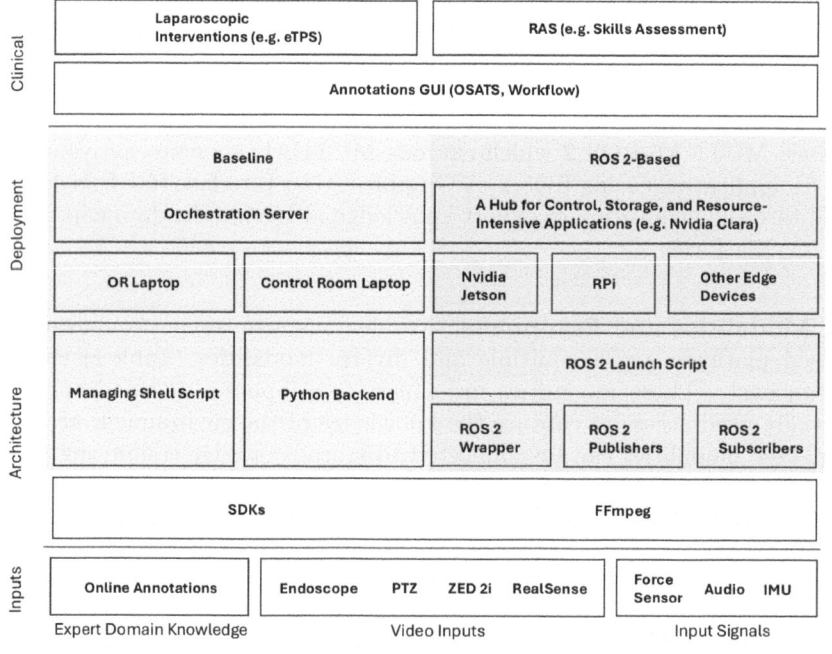

Fig. 1. Overview of MUTUAL and MUTUAL-ROS 2.

MUTUAL-ROS 2: MUTUAL was adapted to ROS 2 to investigate methods for further minimising start/stop latency, increasing horizontal scalability, adopting a unified storage format (rosbag2), and enabling real-time streaming for deploying E-AI applications. The building blocks of MUTUAL-ROS 2 are illustrated in Fig. 1. Using the publisher and subscriber mechanism to interact with data sources, we can leave the data publishers running and subscribe to them for any applications on any devices connected to the ROS 2 network.

Table 2. Start and stop latency and size of recording comparisons between platforms for the four assessed modalities running simultaneously, measured on the laptop

Metrics	Baseline	ROS 2 (Local)	ROS 2 (Networked)
Start/Stop Latency (ms)	639	142	1211
Size of Recording (10 min)(GB)	53	97	3.6

Expert Knowledge Acquisition and Input Orchestration GUI: A bottleneck towards the translation of AI models into the OR has been a lack of annotations [18]. Allowing for real-time annotations during a procedure removes much of the process's friction and facilitates the creation of quality datasets. Through the clinically tailored GUI, clinicians can start and stop recording, annotate workflow, assign skill levels (OSATS scores [23]), and write comments on how the procedure is being performed (see supplementary material).

3.2 Experimental Design

MUTUAL has been deployed for two real-world surgical data studies (Fig. 1 top) requiring multimodal data: **1)** a study for endoscopic Transsphenoidal Pituitary Surgery (eTPS) using phantom models in a mock OR at St Thomas' Hospital, London, UK, and **2)** a study for surgical skills assessment for RAS at Guy's Hospital, London, UK. The GUI was developed using the open-source version of PySimpleGUI. In our study, MUTUAL consists of two laptops (one in the mock OR and one in the control room interconnected through an orchestration server), whereas MUTUAL-ROS 2 consists of a laptop and an edge computing device. The performance metrics evaluated include CPU and RAM usage, start and stop latency, recording size, as well as sampling frequency. We record data from the first four modalities simultaneously, using the specification outlined in Table 1, running the experiment for ten minutes. The four chosen modalities are the ones deployed in the OR for the eTPS study as they are the most likely to be integrated into an edge computing device. All experiments are carried out with a laptop (CPU: i7-11800H @ 2.30G, RAM: 16 GB DDR4-3200) and a Nvidia Jetson Orin Nano 8GB developer kit to control the number of variables. The ROS 2 network router is the TP-Link BE9300 Tri-Band Router.

We compare the performance of MUTUAL and MUTUAL-ROS 2 platforms against a group of metrics. We monitor only the subscriber nodes that save incoming data into ROS 2 bags in the MUTUAL-ROS 2. The subscriber nodes in MUTUAL-ROS 2 offer the closest functionality to MUTUAL, and therefore, they are the only monitored processes. Additionally, the subscriber nodes on the laptop are initialised with either a local (laptop) or networked (Jetson) publisher to account for potential bandwidth limitations caused by either network conditions or ROS 2 middleware implementation. We refer to the two setups as "Local Sub" and "Networked Sub", respectively.

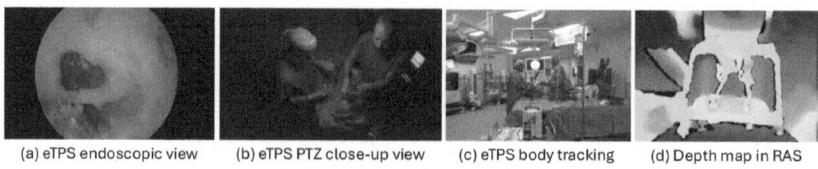

(a) eTPS endoscopic view (b) eTPS PTZ close-up view (c) eTPS body tracking (d) Depth map in RAS

Fig. 2. Sample data captured during eTPS and RAS skills assessment studies

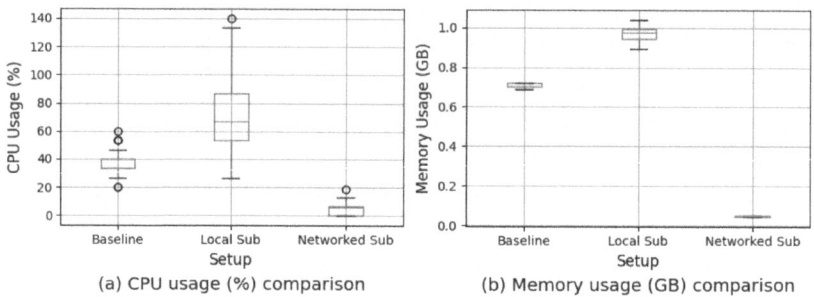

(a) CPU usage (%) comparison (b) Memory usage (GB) comparison

Fig. 3. CPU&RAM usage when recording four modalities on a laptop over 10 min. CPU usage (%) is expressed in per core capacity. *Baseline*: MUTUAL; *Local Sub*: MUTUAL-ROS 2 where publishers and subscribers are on the same machine; *Networked Sub*: MUTUAL-ROS 2 where publishers and subscribers are on different machines

4 Results

We demonstrate the modalities captured during our experiments during two clinical scenarios, i.e. eTPS and RAS skills assessment in Fig. 2. Under such clinical scenarios, MUTUAL can maintain the configured recording resolution throughout multiple one-hour recording sessions per day. The GUI used during the eTPS study allowed for annotations (workflow and OSATS scores), recording of commentary, and recording orchestration, giving full control to the clinical expert (see Supplemental material).

In relation to the comparison between MUTUAL and MUTUAL-ROS 2 over ten minutes, the ROS 2 Local Sub setup consumes the most resources (CPU and RAM usage) while the ROS 2 Networked Sub setup consumes the least resources; the difference between their median value is approximately 60% (Fig. 3). With the Networked Sub setup, the frequency of recording drops, especially for video modalities, where the recording frequency is approximately halved (see Table 3). MUTUAL is able to maintain the configured recording frequency over the 10-min period as expected. Furthermore, we observe that when running the Local Sub setup on the Jetson, the recording frequency increases compared to running the same setup on the laptop. As shown in Table 3, the recording frequency more than tripled for the RealSense device. The decrease in recording frequency with the Networked Sub setup is also reflected in the size of the recording, as illustrated in Table 2. The Local Sub configuration resulted in larger storage consumption even at a lower recording frequency compared to MUTUAL. With the Networked Sub configuration, it also takes more than eight times longer to discover all the topics for subscription and recording. As shown in Table 2, MUTUAL-ROS 2 with Local Sub setup offers the lowest start/stop latency.

Table 3. Recording frequencies in Hz

Modality @(Hz)	Baseline	Local Sub (Laptop/Jetson)	Networked Sub
ZED Cam Video @15	15	3.2/5.5	1.0
RealSense Cam Video @15	15	3.2/11.3	1.0
Force Sensor @15	15	14.9/15	14.5
IMU @10	10	9.9/9.9	9.6

5 Discussion

Capturing heterogeneous annotated surgical data is critical for developing E-AI methodologies into the OR. Furthermore, ensuring the real-time streaming of this data will facilitate large-scale integration of E-AI. Our proposed platform addresses both of these components effectively. Through our proposed platforms, we showcase how varied modalities can be seamlessly integrated into one to capture a holistic view of the OR. The designed GUI allowed clinical expertise to be captured in real-time, through clinical context via comments, audio recording and OSATS, data which has historically been lacking in the field. Even when AI models will eventually avoid manual annotations, expert knowledge could be used in real-time to validate such predictions.

MUTUAL was deployed successfully in two different environments. During the eTPS study, 24 one-hour data samples were recorded, whereas during the robotic-assisted training, 50 ten-minute samples were recorded. The platform setup took less than an hour in each scenario, and no modifications to the training setup were needed for deployment during RAS training.

MUTUAL baseline's performance meets the target configuration under the clinical use cases and the experiments. This makes it suitable for recording and dataset curation applications. Still, it lacks the streaming capability or horizontal scalability of MUTUAL-ROS 2, both of which are essential for deploying E-AI applications effectively in the OR. Although the framerate performance of MUTUAL-ROS 2 does not meet the configured recording criteria, it meets the inference rate for many currently AI models running inference on video at 1 Hz. Moreover, when running only one modality per device using the Jetson edge computing device, the framerate performance can reach the recording criteria with performance similar to MUTUAL, demonstrating the value of distributed inference. Lastly, MUTUAL does not provide a unified storage format and the same level of start/stop synchronisation achieved by the Local Sub version of MUTUAL-ROS 2.

Despite its competitive performance, our platform can still be further improved. Plug-and-play capabilities are needed for the platform, since a technician is still required to be present for device set up and initialisation. Moreover, the GUI is procedure-specific and requires expertise for adapting it to different clinical scenarios. Last, although the streaming performance of MUTUAL-ROS 2 has not been tested for inference we demonstrate how our platform can support edge computing devices in a distributed manner.

6 Conclusion

In this work, we propose two multimodal platforms, MUTUAL and MUTUAL-ROS 2, that are evaluated on two real-world clinical scenarios and compared against resource consumption, start/stop synchronisation, storage, and frequency. Both platforms provide a step towards holistic sensing and inference in the OR, empowering the development and deployment of E-AI, especially robotic E-AI applications. Through careful design choices, the platform allows seamless integration in varied environments and should allow increased data capture at the feature and expert knowledge levels.

Acknowledgments. This work is supported by core funding from the Wellcome/EPSRC Centre for Medical Engineering [WT203148/Z/16/Z], a grant award from The Royal College of Surgeons of England and the Saven Research and Development Programme, and the King's-China Scholarship Council PhD Scholarship programme (K-CSC). For the purpose of Open Access, the Author has applied a CC BY public copyright license to any Author Accepted Manuscript version arising from this submission. **Data Access.** No data is shared along with this manuscript.

Disclosure of Interests. The authors have no competing interests to declare that are relevant to the content of this article.

References

1. sccn/labstreaminglayer. https://github.com/sccn/labstreaminglayer. Accessed 20 June 2024
2. Araujo, V., Mitra, K., Saguna, S., ßhlund, C.: Performance evaluation of fiware: a cloud-based iot platform for smart cities. J. Parallel Distrib. Comput. **132**, 250–261 (2019)
3. Duan, J., Yu, S., Tan, H.L., Zhu, H., Tan, C.: A survey of embodied AI: from simulators to research tasks. IEEE Trans. Emerg. Top. Comput. Intell. **6**(2), 230–244 (2022)
4. Duarte, J., et al.: FPGA-accelerated machine learning inference as a service for particle physics computing. Comput. Softw. Big Sci. **3**(1), 13 (2019)
5. Goertzel, B.: Artificial general intelligence: concept, state of the art, and future prospects. J. Artif. Gen. Intell. **5**(1), 1–48 (2014)

6. Hao, R., Özgüner, O., Çavuşoğlu, M.C.: Vision-based surgical tool pose estimation for the da vinci® robotic surgical system. In: 2018 IEEE/RSJ International Conference on Intelligent Robots and Systems (IROS), pp. 1298–1305. IEEE (2018)
7. Inc, S.S.T.: Surgical Safety Technologies. https://www.surgicalsafety.com/. Accessed 20 June 2024
8. Jin, K., et al.: Identification of cognitive workload during surgical tasks with multimodal deep learning (2022)
9. Jung, J.J., Jüni, P., Lebovic, G., Grantcharov, T.: First-year analysis of the operating room black box study. Ann. Surg. **271**(1) (2020)
10. Karras, K., et al.: A hardware acceleration platform for ai-based inference at the edge. Circuits Syst. Signal Process. **39**(2), 1059–1070 (2020)
11. Kim, J.J.H., Um, R., Iyer, R.R., Theodore, N., Manbachi, A.: Design and Development of Smart Surgical Assistant Technologies: A Case Study for Translational Sciences. CRC Press, Boca Raton (2022)
12. Kim, S.Y., Lee, J., Kim, C.H., Lee, W.J., Kim, S.W.: Extending the onnx runtime framework for the processing-in-memory execution. In: 2022 International Conference on Electronics, Information, and Communication (ICEIC), pp. 1–4 (2022)
13. Leonard, S., Wu, K.L., Kim, Y., Krieger, A., Kim, P.C.: Smart tissue anastomosis robot (star): a vision-guided robotics system for laparoscopic suturing. IEEE Trans. Biomed. Eng. **61**(4), 1305–1317 (2014)
14. Liow, M.H.L., Chin, P.L., Pang, H.N., Tay, D.K.J., Yeo, S.J.: Think surgical tsolution-one®(robodoc) total knee arthroplasty. SICOT-J **3**, 63 (2017)
15. Liu, Y., et al.: Skit: a fast key information video transformer for online surgical phase recognition. In: 2023 IEEE/CVF International Conference on Computer Vision (ICCV), pp. 21017–21027. IEEE Computer Society, Los Alamitos, CA, USA (oct 2023)
16. Macenski, S., Foote, T., Gerkey, B., Lalancette, C., Woodall, W.: Robot operating system 2: design, architecture, and uses in the wild. Sci. Robot. **7**(66), eabm6074 (2022)
17. MacRae, C., Gilling, P.: How i do it: aquablation of the prostate using the aquabeam system. Can. J. Urol. **23**(6), 8590–8593 (2016)
18. Maier-Hein, L., Eisenmann, M.: Sarikaya: Surgical data science - from concepts toward clinical translation. Med. Image Anal. **76**, 102306 (2022)
19. Manor, E., Greenberg, S.: Custom hardware inference accelerator for tensorflow lite for microcontrollers. IEEE Access **10**, 73484–73493 (2022)
20. Miah, S., et al.: A prospective analysis of robotic targeted MRI-us fusion prostate biopsy using the centroid targeting approach. J. Robot. Surg. **14**(1), 69–74 (2019)
21. Mirchi, N., Bissonnette, V., Yilmaz, R., Ledwos, N., Winkler-Schwartz, A., Maestro, R.F.D.: The virtual operative assistant: an explainable artificial intelligence tool for simulation-based training in surgery and medicine. PLOS ONE **15**(2), e0229596 (2020). publisher: Public Library of Science
22. Molchanov, P., Tyree, S., Karras, T., Aila, T., Kautz, J.: Pruning convolutional neural networks for resource efficient inference (2017)
23. Niitsu, H., et al.: Using the objective structured assessment of technical skills (OSATS) global rating scale to evaluate the skills of surgical trainees in the operating room. Surg. Today **43**(3), 271–275 (2012)
24. Onyeogulu, T., et al.: Situation awareness for automated surgical check-listing in ai-assisted operating room (2022)
25. Paolo, G., Gonzalez-Billandon, J., Kégl, B.: Position: a call for embodied AI. In: Forty-first International Conference on Machine Learning (2024)

26. Pfeifer, R., Iida, F.: Embodied artificial intelligence: trends and challenges. Lecture notes in computer science, pp. 1–26 (2004)
27. Rivero-Moreno, Y., et al.: Autonomous robotic surgery: has the future arrived? Cureus (2024)
28. Rivkin, G., Liebergall, M.: Challenges of technology integration and computer-assisted surgery. J. Bone Joint Surg. **91**, 13–16 (2009)
29. Sazzad, F., Ler, A., Kuzemczak, M., Ng, S., Choong, A.M., Kofidis, T.: Automated fastener vs hand-tied knots in heart valve surgery: a systematic review and meta-analysis. Ann. Thorac. Surg. **112**(3), 970–980 (2021)
30. Wen, J., Yu, N., Long, X., Wang, X.: Robotic surgical systems in plastic and reconstructive surgery. Chin. Med. J. **137**(11), 1366–1368 (2023)
31. Yilmaz, N., Wu, J.Y., Kazanzides, P., Tumerdem, U.: Neural network based inverse dynamics identification and external force estimation on the da vinci research kit. In: 2020 IEEE International Conference on Robotics and Automation (ICRA), pp. 1387–1393. IEEE (2020)
32. Zhao, Z., Wu, Q., Wang, J., Zhang, B., Zhong, C., Zhilenkov, A.A.: Exploring embodied intelligence in soft robotics: a review. Biomimetics **9**(4), 248 (2024)

Proceedings of the Fifth MICCAI Workshop on Distributed, Collaborative and Federated Learning (DeCaF 2024)

Complex-Valued Federated Learning with Differential Privacy and MRI Applications

Anneliese Riess[1,2,3], Alexander Ziller[4], Stefan Kolek[5], Daniel Rueckert[4,6], Julia Schnabel[1,2,7], and Georgios Kaissis[1,4,6,8(✉)]

[1] Institute of Machine Learning in Biomedical Imaging, Helmholtz Munich, Neuherberg, Germany
[2] School of Computation, Information and Technology, Technical University of Munich, Munich, Germany
[3] Helmholtz AI, Helmholtz Munich, Oberschleißheim, Germany
[4] Artificial Intelligence in Healthcare and Medicine, Technical University of Munich, Munich, Germany
g.kaissis@tum.de
[5] Mathematical Foundations of AI, LMU Munich, Munich, Germany
[6] Department of Computing, Imperial College London, London, UK
[7] School of Biomedical Engineering and Imaging Sciences, King's College London, London, UK
[8] Institute for Diagnostic and Interventional Radiology, Technical University of Munich, Munich, Germany

Abstract. Federated learning enhanced with Differential Privacy (DP) is a powerful privacy-preserving strategy to protect individuals sharing their sensitive data for processing in fields such as medicine and healthcare. Many medical applications, for example magnetic resonance imaging (MRI), rely on complex-valued signal processing techniques for data acquisition and analysis. However, the appropriate application of DP to complex-valued data is still underexplored. To address this issue, from the theoretical side, we introduce the complex-valued Gaussian mechanism, whose behaviour we characterise in terms of f-DP, (ε, δ)-DP and Rényi-DP. Moreover, we generalise the fundamental algorithm DP stochastic gradient descent to complex-valued neural networks and present novel complex-valued neural network primitives compatible with DP. Experimentally, we showcase a proof-of-concept by training federated complex-valued neural networks with DP on a real-world task (MRI pulse sequence classification in k-space), yielding excellent utility and privacy. Our results highlight the relevance of combining federated learning with robust privacy-preserving techniques in the MRI context.

Keywords: Federated learning · Differential Privacy · Complex Numbers

1 Introduction

Complex-valued (CV) signal processing is becoming increasingly important in medicine and medical imaging tasks. For example, frequency-domain magnetic resonance imaging (MRI) data is acquired in the CV k-space; audio signals from speech or a patient's heartbeat can be represented as CV spectrograms and wearable or implanted biological sensors produce measurements which can be efficiently represented in the complex field. Moreover, many real-valued problems can be represented and solved in the complex domain, e.g. differential equations, which can be solved more efficiently by first taking their Fourier/Laplace transforms. In many of these examples, privacy preservation is paramount to protect patients and to furnish objective security guarantees, and is often mandated by ethical considerations and legal regulations [16].

Federated learning (FL) has been proposed to enable privacy-preserving data processing in medical imaging. Here, users contribute to training a joint model without sharing their private data, but rather only model updates (e.g. gradients) with a central server that coordinates the training. However, this decentralized approach alone does not suffice to prevent privacy violations, as prior works have shown that FL models are vulnerable to attacks which disclose sensitive information, such as data reconstruction attacks [4,12,14]. At the same time, FL does not provide a formal privacy guarantee that can objectively quantify the protection provided by this approach. These remarks underscore that, to be formally privacy-preserving, FL must be complemented by additional privacy technologies. Differential Privacy (DP) [10], a formal framework and set of techniques for deriving insights from sensitive databases while protecting the privacy of individuals who contributed their data, has established itself as the tool of choice in this regard. DP can be thought of as a "contract" between a data owner and a data processor that guarantees that the influence of any individual's data on the outcome of a computation and –by extension– any harm originating from the release of its results, is limited. However, while DP has been studied extensively in many sub-fields of AI, to our knowledge, it has yet not been sufficiently investigated in the context of CV data processing.

Our Contributions. We propose key theoretical and methodological innovations to enable the application of DP in federated CV neural networks (CVNNs). Concretely, we (1) introduce the complex-valued Gaussian mechanism and characterise its privacy properties in Sect. 3; (2) we generalise the fundamental algorithm of DP deep learning, DP stochastic gradient descent (DP-SGD) to CVNNs in Sect. 4; (3) we propose novel CVNN primitives (complex GroupNorm and ConjMish, a new activation function) and investigate their properties in Sect. 4; (4) finally, in a proof-of-concept medical imaging CV FL application in Sect. 5, we find that applying our methods yields excellent accuracy.

Related Work. CV signal processing workflows have witnessed increasing interest over the past few years. Arguably, biosensing [24] and magnetic resonance imaging analysis [6,20,29] are among the most relevant for privacy preservation, and have also seen increasing usage of AI tools. CVNNs have only recently gained significant traction, as automatic differentiation systems have –until recently– not natively supported CV gradients and due to the increased computational expense of CV operations. This has changed with the near-universal adoption of the Wirtinger calculus [19,30] in deep learning frameworks, and with the introduction of native (i.e. hardware-optimised) primitives for e.g. convolutions. So far, only a single other study has demonstrated the use of CVNNs in FL [33], and no studies before ours have addressed the biomedical domain or DP applications therein.

DP [9] has become a standard technique for privacy preservation in AI. Due to space constraints, for a detailed introduction to DP we refer to [7,10]. DP-SGD for real-valued NNs was introduced by [1]. Only a limited number of studies have examined DP in conjunction with CV data [5,11,13] or introduced techniques for privacy *accounting* using CV functional representations [18], however, to our knowledge, none have formalised a general framework to handle DP for CV tasks.

2 Preliminaries

Throughout the paper, we assume a standard FL setup with a *central server* and several *computation nodes*, but all introduced techniques apply equally to peer-to-peer FL topologies, swarm learning, etc. Moreover, we assume all parties to be *honest but curious*, such that computation nodes perform a local privatisation of their updates before submitting them to the central server; this is not a limitation as our techniques can be readily adapted to all other threat models. As is customary in DP literature, each node holds a set of sensitive records from a universe $\mathcal{X}$, called a database $\mathcal{D}$. From this, an adjacent database $\mathcal{D}'$ can be constructed by adding, removing or replacing the data of a single individual. We assume without loss of generality that individuals are unique throughout the federation. DP is typically realised by first executing a deterministic query function q over the database and then randomising its output by the addition of noise through a DP mechanism $\mathcal{M}$. The noise is calibrated to the query function's (global) (ℓ_p-)sensitivity induced by the p-norm ($p \in [1, \infty)$), which we denote by $\Delta_p(q)$. As the p-norm is also defined for CV vectors, we employ the same strategy to randomise the output of a CV query. In turn, we introduce the complex Gaussian mechanism (cGM) in Sect. 3, which serves as the CV counterpart to the Gaussian mechanism (GM), one of the most employed mechanism to achieve DP in real-valued settings.

Every CV function $q : \mathcal{X} \to \mathbb{C}^n$ can be written as:

$$q(\mathcal{D}) = q_{\Re}(\mathcal{D}) + \mathrm{i} \cdot q_{\Im}(\mathcal{D}), \qquad (1)$$

where $q_{\Re} : \mathcal{X} \to \mathbb{R}^n$ and $q_{\Im} : \mathcal{X} \to \mathbb{R}^n$ denote the real and imaginary parts of $q(\mathcal{D})$, respectively. Representation 1 is useful as many complex functions can be thought of as operators acting on the real and imaginary parts of a complex number separately and then "assembling" the result. However, we caution against equating CV networks to real-valued networks with two "channels" if the appropriate CV operations are not used, as this discards the information within the relationship between the real and imaginary part. Other differences between $\mathbb{C}$ and $\mathbb{R}^2$ call for distinctive treatment when handling tasks in $\mathbb{C}$. For instance, since the complex plane does not admit a natural ordering, the minimisation of CV functions is not defined. Hence, CVNNs use complex-to-real loss functions. Moreover, to obtain correct gradients for optimisation, we employ the Wirtinger calculus [19], which provides a CV gradient operator for real-valued loss functions in CVNNs. In particular, this serves as a base for our proposed CV counterpart to DP-SGD.

3 Theoretical Results

To characterise the privacy properties of CV mechanisms, we utilise the f-DP framework [7]. Relying on statistical hypothesis testing, f-DP interprets DP through a *trade-off function* T between the *Type I* and *Type II* statistical errors faced by a membership inference adversary trying to determine whether one of the adjacent databases contains the individual or not. A mechanism $\mathcal{M}$ satisfies f-DP if, for all pairs of adjacent databases $\mathcal{D}$ and $\mathcal{D}'$, $T(q(\mathcal{D}), q(\mathcal{D}'))(\alpha) \geq f(\alpha)$ holds $\forall \alpha \in [0,1]$ for some trade-off function f. Gaussian DP (GDP) is a specialisation of f-DP when the trade-off-function has the form $G_\mu := T(\mathcal{N}(0,1), \mathcal{N}(\mu, 1))$. In particular, $\mathcal{M}$ preserves μ-Gaussian DP (μ-GDP) if it preserves f-DP, for $f(\alpha) = G_\mu(\alpha) = \Phi(\Phi^{-1}(1-\alpha) - \mu)$, where α is the Type-I statistical error and Φ is the cumulative distribution function of the standard, real-valued normal distribution. In this light, we introduce our key CV additive noise mechanism:

Definition 1 (Complex Gaussian mechanism). *Let $q : \mathcal{X} \to \mathbb{C}^n$, $\mathcal{D} \in \mathcal{X}$, and $\psi \sim \mathcal{N}_\mathbb{C}(\mathbf{0}, \Gamma, C)$ denote the complex Gaussian distribution with location parameter $\mu = \mathbf{0} \in \mathbb{C}^n$, covariance matrix $\Gamma \in \mathbb{C}^{n \times n}$ and relation matrix $C \in \mathbb{C}^{n \times n}$. Then, the complex Gaussian mechanism (cGM) is defined as:*

$$\mathcal{M}(\mathcal{D}) = q(\mathcal{D}) + \psi. \tag{2}$$

We will consider the cGM when $\psi \sim \mathcal{N}_\mathbb{C}(\mathbf{0}, 2\sigma^2 \mathbf{I}_n, 2i\gamma \mathbf{I}_n)$. The cGM has variance σ^2 in the real and imaginary part of each coordinate and *total* variance $2\sigma^2$ per coordinate, as $\text{Var}(z) = \text{Var}(\Re(z)) + \text{Var}(\Im(z))$ holds for any random variable in $\mathbb{C}$. Moreover, the cGM marginals are *non-circular* complex Gaussian distributions whose real and imaginary components are correlated with correlation coefficient $\rho = \frac{\gamma}{\sigma^2}$. Whenever $\rho = 0$, we observe a special case: the *circular* cGM, whose marginals are circular complex Gaussian distributions. In turn, its real and imaginary components are i.i.d. scalar real-valued Gaussian distributions $\mathcal{N}(0, \sigma^2)$. We next characterize the privacy properties of the cGM:

Theorem 1. *Let $\mathcal{M}$ be the cGM with correlation coefficient $\rho \neq 1$ acting on a query function q. Then, $\mathcal{M}$ satisfies μ-GDP with:*

$$\mu = \sqrt{\frac{\Delta_2(q)^2}{\sigma^2(1-\rho^2)} + \frac{2|\rho|}{\sigma^2(1-\rho^2)} \Delta_2(q_\Re) \Delta_2(q_\Im)}. \tag{3}$$

Proof. The proof of Theorem 1 can be found in Appendix A. □

Note that 3 is monotonically increasing in $|\rho|$. Specifically, for $|\rho| \to 1$, $\mu \to \infty$ and the cGM becomes *blatantly non-private* We next turn to the circular case:

Corollary 1. *The circular cGM acting on q satisfies μ-GDP with $\mu = \Delta_2(q)/\sigma$.*

Proof. Follows from Theorem 1 by setting $\rho = 0$. □

Since the cGM (including the circular special case) satisfies μ-GDP, it inherits all of the properties of GDP, i.e. resilience to post-processing, group privacy, subsampling and composition. Additionally, one can provide (ε, δ) and Rényi-DP guarantees using the techniques presented in [7,22]. These results allow one to leverage available privacy accounting tools for real-valued DP to design DP workflows for CV tasks as demonstrated in Sect. 5.

Interestingly, Corollary 1 shows that choosing $\rho \neq 0$ can *never improve the privacy guarantee of the cGM*. Moreover, observe that the mean squared error (MSE) between $z \in \mathbb{C}$ and its perturbed version $z + \psi$, where ψ is a CV random variable drawn from a zero-centered distribution, satisfies:

$$\text{MSE}(z, z+\psi) = \mathbb{E}\left(||z-(z+\psi)||_2^2\right) = \text{Var}(\psi) = \text{Var}(\Re(\psi)) + \text{Var}(\Im(\psi)). \quad (4)$$

Hence, the MSE is independent of the correlation between the real and imaginary components of the CV noise, and consequently, there is no benefit from using correlated complex noise in terms of the introduced distortion. The circular cGM is thus in this sense *optimal* in terms of its privacy-utility trade-off.

4 Training CVNNs with DP

ζ-DP-SGD. Real valued DP-SGD [1] is a key technique to train deep NNs with DP. Recall that the key steps of DP-SGD are (1) clipping the ℓ_2-norm of the *per-sample* gradients to a pre-defined threshold, and (2) adding (real-valued) Gaussian noise calibrated to this threshold. Then, each training step leads to the release of a privatised gradient which is used to update the local node's weights, or is shared with the central server, e.g. for aggregation. To generalize DP-SGD to CVNNs and enable their federated training, we next introduce ζ-DP-SGD, presented in Algorithm 1. Recall from Sect. 2 that a complex-to-real loss function $\mathcal{L} : \mathbb{C}^n \mapsto \mathbb{R}^1$ is minimised in CVNNs. Using the Wirtinger calculus, we clip the ℓ_2-norm of the per-sample *conjugate gradient* [19], which represents the direction of steepest ascent in this setting:

$$\nabla \overline{\mathcal{L}} := 2\left(\frac{\partial \mathcal{L}}{\partial \overline{\theta}_1}, \ldots, \frac{\partial \mathcal{L}}{\partial \overline{\theta}_n}\right), \quad (5)$$

where $\overline{\boldsymbol{\theta}} = (\overline{\theta}_1, \ldots, \overline{\theta}_n)$ is the conjugate weight vector. The conjugate gradient is twice the conjugate Wirtinger derivative with respect to the weights [19], which results in parity with the real-valued case in terms of the effective learning rate.

Algorithm 1. ζ-DP-SGD

Require: Database with samples $\{z_1, \ldots, z_N\} \in \mathbb{C}^n$, neural network with loss function $\mathcal{L}$ and weight vector $\boldsymbol{\theta} \in \mathbb{C}^m$. Hyperparameters: learning rate η_t, noise variance σ^2, sampling probability $p = \frac{R}{N}$, gradient norm bound B, total steps T.
Initialize $\boldsymbol{\theta}_0$ randomly
for $t \in [T]$ **do**
  Draw a batch L_t with sampling probability p (e.g. using *Poisson* sampling)
  Compute per-sample conjugate gradient
  For each $i \in L_t$, compute $\overline{\boldsymbol{g}}_t(z_i) \leftarrow \nabla \overline{\mathcal{L}}(\boldsymbol{\theta}_t, z_i)$
  Clip conjugate gradient
  $\boldsymbol{g}_t(z_i) \leftarrow \overline{\boldsymbol{g}}_t(z_i) / \max\left(1, \frac{\|\overline{\boldsymbol{g}}_t(z_i)\|_2}{B}\right)$
  Apply the circular complex Gaussian Mechanism and average
  $\widetilde{\boldsymbol{g}}_t \leftarrow \frac{1}{R}\left(\sum_i \boldsymbol{g}_t(z_i) + \mathcal{N}_{\mathbb{C}}(\mathbf{0}, 2B^2\sigma^2 \mathbf{I}_m, \mathbf{0})\right)$
  Descend
  $\boldsymbol{\theta}_{t+1} \leftarrow \boldsymbol{\theta}_t - \eta_t \widetilde{\boldsymbol{g}}_t$
end for
Output updated neural network weight vector $\boldsymbol{\theta}_T$ and compute the privacy cost.

In particular, using the theoretical results in the previous section, each step of ζ-DP-SGD satisfies GDP, enabling us to utilise the composition and sub-sampling theorems of [7] to account for the total privacy cost of training a CVNN.

CVNN Primitives for ζ-DP-SGD Training. Many CVNN components such as complex convolutional and linear layers as well as split (e.g. $\mathbb{C}$ReLU [28]) and fully complex (e.g. Cardioid [29]) activation functions are compatible with ζ-DP-SGD. However, Batch Normalisation (BN) [15] and its CV implementation [28] are prohibited in DP as they "contaminate" the activations with information from other samples in the batch, leading to undefined *per-sample* (conjugate) gradients, which are required for a correct implementation.

To address this issue, BN is typically replaced with Group Normalisation (GN) [31] in DP NNs. Since a CV implementation of the GN layer is missing, we next introduce a novel **CV GN layer**. Recall that, while real vectors are normalised by subtracting the mean and dividing by the variance, in complex vectors the covariance between the real and imaginary components must also be considered. We address this by grouping the activations, and then *whitening* them group-wise. Similar to [28], we initialise the affine parameters of the GN layer to $\gamma = \frac{1}{\sqrt{2}} + \frac{1}{\sqrt{2}}i$ and to $\beta = \mathbf{0}$. An implementation of the whitening algorithm and of the GN layer can be found in Listing 4.1. Of note, the same approach can be used for Layer, Instance or weight normalisation [26], as our implementation is differentiable.

As an additional contribution, we introduce a novel **CV Mish activation function**. Recall that the real-valued Mish [23] is defined as: $\text{Mish}(x) := x \tanh\left(\log\left(e^x + 1\right)/x\right)$. For use with CVNNs, we define a *conjugate* version:

$$\text{ConjMish}(z) := (1 + i)\,\text{Mish}(\Re(z)) - (1 - i)\,\text{Mish}(\Im(z)). \tag{6}$$

Listing 4.1 PyTorch implementations of complex GN.

```
def whiten_single(vec):
    flat_vector = vec.flatten()
    centered = flat_vector - flat_vector.mean() # subtract mean to center the tensor
    stacked = torch.stack([centered.real, centered.imag])
    sigma = torch.cov(stacked) # compute covariance between real and imaginary.
    u_mat, lmbda, _ = torch.linalg.svd(sigma) # Compute 1/sqrt. of covariance matrix.
    w_mat = torch.matmul(
        u_mat, torch.matmul(torch.diag(1.0 / torch.sqrt(lmbda + 1e-5)), u_mat.T))
    result = torch.matmul(w_mat, stacked)
    return (result[0] + result[1] * 1j).reshape(vec.shape)

whiten_group = vmap(vmap(whiten_single)) #vmap over batch and group axis

class ComplexGroupNorm2d(nn.Module):
    def __init__(self, num_groups, num_channels):
        ... #initialise gamma and beta

    def forward(self, x):
        group_shape = (-1, self.groups, self.num_channels // self.groups) + x.shape[2:]
        x = x.reshape(group_shape) # split into groups
        x = whiten_group(x) # whiten each group
        x = x.reshape((-1, self.num_channels,) + group_shape[3:]) # reshape to original shape
        x = x * gamma + beta # affine operation
        return x
```

We empirically found ConjMish to drastically improve accuracy by up to 5% over the best previous alternatives (Cardioid [29], ModReLU or ℂReLU [28]). In contrast to Cardioid and ℂReLU, ConjMish has both a *magnitude thresholding* effect and "phase non-linearity" effect instead of merely "passing through" the phase. The latter seems to improve NN convergence, and could be of independent interest. We leave a detailed investigation to future work.

5 Experiments

We next demonstrate the experimental evaluation of our framework in the context of training federated CVNNs on a real-life medical dataset, where both, stringent privacy guarantees and high accuracy are desired. We selected the task of automated MRI pulse sequence classification, which is relevant for both, the automated curation of medical images for AI applications and for image retrieval tasks in clinical routine. Recent works have tackled this challenge using both supervised [21] and unsupervised [17] deep learning techniques. Contrary to the aforementioned works, we directly classify the MRI pulse sequence in k-space, that is, to *directly* classify the CV frequency-domain MRI data.

We utilised data from the *brain* sub-challenge of the Medical Segmentation Decathlon [2], consisting of 484 training records and 266 test records, which are partitioned such that one patient is only present in a single dataset. We instantiated an FL simulation using the Flower framework [3] which we augmented with a customised version of Opacus [32], and distributed the training records uniformly at random among 11 computation nodes to obtain an i.i.d. FL setting. Moreover, we uniformly distributed 110 randomly selected test records to each computation node to serve as a validation set. The rest of the test set remained at the central server and was used only to compute the final accuracy. Additionally, for comparison, we also trained the CVNN under centralised conditions. From each record, we extracted 20 centre slices for each of the four available pulse sequences: Fluid Attenuation Inversion Recovery (FLAIR), T1-weighted (T1w), T1-weighted with contrast agent (T1wGD) and T2-weighted (T2w). This resulted in a total dataset size of 38 720 training and 21 280 testing images, which we resized to 32 × 32 pixels, Fast Fourier transformed to simulate k-space (where we retained duplicated frequency components to obtain a representation with the same dimensions as the input), and normalised by whitening.

We used the model architecture from [8] consisting of three convolutional blocks with 32, 64 and 128 filters, CV GN and the ConjMish activation function (see Sect. 4) as well as average pooling layers. The classification layer of the network consisted of a single linear layer with 128 units. We trained the model using Adaptive Federated Averaging [25] for 500 epochs using the NAdam optimiser with a learning rate of 0.0002, which we decayed by 10× after 300 epochs, a fixed ℓ_2-norm bound of 1, 16 GN groups, an expected batch size of 24, and a target $\varepsilon \in [1, 3, 5, 8, 10]$ for $\delta = 0.001$, as well as non-privately ($\varepsilon = \infty$). All stated privacy guarantees are "per-patient", and all nodes participated in every round with one round per step. Table 1 summarises these results across 10 random seeds as well as the results from centralised learning as a reference. We note for completeness that the ε-parameter represents the *privacy budget* in DP, and higher values correspond to worse privacy guarantees for the individuals. Interestingly, the CVNN achieved an accuracy of nearly 90% at an ε-value of 3, with (at most) 1 to 2% of additional performance gained by diminishing the privacy guarantee. This indicates that, in the task we consider, relatively stringent (local) DP guarantees can be achieved in FL practically without any accuracy penalty, even compared to centralised learning.

Table 1. Accuracy in % (mean ± standard deviation) on the MRI test set across 10 random seeds for FL and centralised learning (CL).

ε	1	3	5	8	10	∞
FL	81.65 ± 1.03	87.98 ± 1.46	88.46 ± 1.37	89.08 ± 1.11	89.99 ± 0.70	90.12 ± 1.26
CL	82.85 ± 1.49	89.53 ± 1.89	89.31 ± 1.49	89.62 ± 1.06	90.33 ± 0.59	90.89 ± 1.41

6 Discussion

In this work, we investigated the application of DP techniques to CVNNs. We theoretically showed that the cGM naturally extends its real-valued counterparts to the complex domain, allowing for efficient privacy accounting. Moreover, we experimentally demonstrated a proof-of-concept for FL with DP in CVNNs and found that DP CVNN training is possible with strong privacy guarantees and excellent utility, a crucial combination in sensitive fields like healthcare.

We foresee several interesting avenues for future work: For one, the communication efficiency of CVNNs in FL is reduced to their nominally higher number of parameters (two real-valued floating point numbers per parameter). Thus, optimising e.g. mixed-precision techniques for such applications could reduce communication overhead. Moreover, network quantisation strategies tailored to CVNNs could further increase efficiency while maintaining high accuracy. Furthermore, we intend to explore additional CV mechanisms, such as the CV Laplace mechanism, in future studies.

In conclusion, we anticipate the adoption of CVNNs to increase in a variety of machine learning tasks through the broader availability of software tools and improved hardware support. In particular, since, in collaborative and federated learning, many such tasks concern sensitive data, we contend that integrating rigorous privacy techniques such as DP is essential for increasing trust by providing formal guarantees of model behaviour.

Acknowledgments. We are grateful to Dmitrii Usynin, Moritz Knolle, Reinhard Heckel, Rickmer Braren and Kerstin Hammernik for their contributions to previous versions of this work. GK received support from the German Federal Ministry of Education and Research and the Bavarian State Ministry for Science and the Arts under the Munich Centre for Machine Learning (MCML), from the German Ministry of Education and Research and the the Medical Informatics Initiative as part of the PrivateAIM Project, from the Bavarian Collaborative Research Project PRIPREKI of the Free State of Bavaria Funding Programme "Artificial Intelligence – Data Science", and from the German Academic Exchange Service (DAAD) under the Kondrad Zuse School of Excellence for Reliable AI (RelAI). This project was supported by the German Federal Ministry of Health on the basis of a decision by the German Bundestag, under the frame of ERA PerMed.

Disclosure of Interests. The authors have no competing interests to declare that are relevant to the content of this article.

A Proof of Theorem 1

Theorem 1. *Let $\mathcal{M}$ be the cGM with correlation coefficient $\rho \neq 1$ acting on a query function q. Then, $\mathcal{M}$ satisfies μ-GDP with:*

$$\mu = \sqrt{\frac{\Delta_2(q)^2}{\sigma^2(1-\rho^2)} + \frac{2|\rho|}{\sigma^2(1-\rho^2)} \Delta_2(q_\Re)\Delta_2(q_\Im)}. \tag{3}$$

Proof. Consider a membership inference adversary who observes a mechanism output $y = \mathcal{M}(q(\cdot)) \in \mathbb{C}^n$ and wants to assess whether y originated under $\mathcal{D}$ or $\mathcal{D}'$ based on this single observation. Moreover, assume the adversary is able to conduct a Neyman-Pearson optimal hypothesis test to distinguish $\mathcal{M}(q(\mathcal{D}))$ from $\mathcal{M}(q(\mathcal{D}'))$. The proof is thus reduced to a CV simple vs. simple binary hypothesis testing problem for the location parameter (i.e. mean) of a complex Gaussian distribution with equal covariance and relation matrix. Choosing the likelihood ratio as our test statistic leads to the optimal test design with the hypotheses:

$$\mathcal{H}_0 : y \sim \mathcal{N}_\mathbb{C}(q(\mathcal{D}), 2\sigma^2 \mathbf{I}_n, 2\mathrm{i}\gamma \mathbf{I}_n) \quad \text{and} \quad \mathcal{H}_1 : y \sim \mathcal{N}_\mathbb{C}(q(\mathcal{D}'), 2\sigma^2 \mathbf{I}_n, 2\mathrm{i}\gamma \mathbf{I}_n). \tag{7}$$

Now, we introduce some notation to ease reading of the remaining of the proof. Let $\tilde{z}$ denote the augmented vector constructed from $z \in \mathbb{C}^n$ in the following way:

$$\tilde{z} = \begin{bmatrix} z \\ \bar{z} \end{bmatrix} \in \mathbb{C}^{2n}, \tag{8}$$

where $\bar{z}$ is the element-wise complex conjugate of z. Moreover, let $C, \Gamma \in \mathbb{C}^{n \times n}$ be the diagonal matrices $\Gamma = 2\sigma^2 I_n$ and $C = 2\mathrm{i} \cdot \gamma I_n$. Then, the probability density functions (PDFs) $f_0(z)$ and $f_1(z)$ under $\mathcal{H}_0$ and $\mathcal{H}_1$, respectively, are:

$$f_0(z) = \frac{1}{\pi^n \sqrt{\det(\Gamma) \cdot \det(P)}} \exp\left(-\frac{1}{2}[\tilde{z} - \widetilde{q(D)}]^H \begin{bmatrix} \Gamma & C \\ \bar{C} & \bar{\Gamma} \end{bmatrix}^{-1} [\tilde{z} - \widetilde{q(D)}]\right),$$

$$f_1(x) = \frac{1}{\pi^n \sqrt{\det(\Gamma) \cdot \det(P)}} \exp\left(-\frac{1}{2}[\tilde{z} - \widetilde{q(D')}]^H \begin{bmatrix} \Gamma & C \\ \bar{C} & \bar{\Gamma} \end{bmatrix}^{-1} [\tilde{z} - \widetilde{q(D')}]\right),$$

where $P = \bar{\Gamma} - C^H \Gamma^{-1} C \in \mathbb{C}^{n \times n}$, and H denotes the complex conjugate transpose. These probability density functions (PDFs) $f_0(z)$ and $f_1(z)$ under $\mathcal{H}_0$ and $\mathcal{H}_1$, respectively, are used to compute the log likelihood ratio $L = \log\left(\frac{f_1(x)}{f_0(x)}\right)$. It is well-known that, for this problem, the log-likelihood ratio test statistic (i.e. privacy loss random variable) L is (real) Gaussian distributed [27]. In particular, the mean of L is $\frac{d}{2}$ under $\mathcal{H}_1$ and $-\frac{d}{2}$ under $\mathcal{H}_0$, and its variance is d under both hypotheses, where d is given by:

$$d = [\widetilde{q(D')} - \widetilde{q(D)}]^H \begin{bmatrix} \Gamma & C \\ \bar{C} & \bar{\Gamma} \end{bmatrix}^{-1} [\widetilde{q(D')} - \widetilde{q(D)}], \tag{9}$$

(we refer to Sect. 7 from [27] for more details). Moreover, it is also well-known that that the power of any such a test is monotonically increasing with d. Therefore, we seek to maximise d for all $\mathcal{D}, \mathcal{D}' \in \mathcal{X}$. Due to the specific form of the matrix above (see Eq. 9), after some algebraic manipulation, we can compute it explicitly:

$$\begin{bmatrix} \Gamma & C \\ \bar{C} & \bar{\Gamma} \end{bmatrix}^{-1} = \begin{bmatrix} \frac{\sigma^2}{2(\sigma^4 - \gamma^2)} \mathbf{I}_n & -\frac{\mathrm{i}\gamma}{2(\sigma^4 - \gamma^2)} \mathbf{I}_n \\ \frac{\mathrm{i}\gamma}{2(\sigma^4 - \gamma^2)} \mathbf{I}_n & \frac{\sigma^2}{2(\sigma^4 - \gamma^2)} \mathbf{I}_n \end{bmatrix}. \tag{10}$$

Using 10, we can rewrite d, and obtain:

$$d = \frac{\|q(\mathcal{D}) - q(\mathcal{D}')\|_2^2}{\sigma^2(1 - \rho^2)} \pm \frac{2|\rho|}{\sigma^2(1 - \rho^2)} (\Re(q(\mathcal{D}) - q(\mathcal{D}')))^T (\Im(q(\mathcal{D}) - q(\mathcal{D}'))). \tag{11}$$

Without loss of generality, the adversary can choose $\pm\rho$ to obtain the highest d. Moreover, using 11, we can compute an upper bound for d employing the sensitivity $\Delta_2(q)$ and the Cauchy-Schwarz inequality:

$$d \leq \frac{\Delta_2(q)^2}{\sigma^2(1-\rho^2)} + \frac{2|\rho|}{\sigma^2(1-\rho^2)} ||\Re(q(\mathcal{D}) - q(\mathcal{D}'))||_2 \cdot ||\Im(q(\mathcal{D}) - q(\mathcal{D}'))||_2 \quad (12)$$

$$\leq \frac{\Delta_2(q)^2}{\sigma^2(1-\rho^2)} + \frac{2|\rho|}{\sigma^2(1-\rho^2)} \Delta_2(q_\Re)\Delta_2(q_\Im) := \hat{d}. \quad (13)$$

No tighter bound than 13 can be computed without making assumptions on the query q or the databases $\mathcal{D}, \mathcal{D}'$. Thus, we can use $\hat{d}$ to compute the trade-off that bounds the worst-case scenario of the cGM:

$$f_{\sqrt{\hat{d}}}(\alpha) = \Phi\left(\Phi^{-1}(1-\alpha) - \sqrt{\hat{d}}\right), \quad (14)$$

where α is the Type-I statistical error and Φ is the cumulative distribution of the standard, real-valued normal distribution. To conclude, we note that 14 is the trade-off function of a (real-valued) $\sqrt{\hat{d}}$-GDP mechanism. □

References

1. Abadi, M., et al.: Deep learning with differential privacy. In: Proceedings of the 2016 ACM SIGSAC Conference on Computer and Communications Security, pp. 308–318 (2016)
2. Antonelli, M., et al.: The medical segmentation decathlon. arXiv preprint arXiv:2106.05735 (2021)
3. Beutel, D.J., et al.: Flower: a friendly federated learning research framework. arXiv preprint arXiv:2007.14390 (2020)
4. Boenisch, F., Dziedzic, A., Schuster, R., Shamsabadi, A.S., Shumailov, I., Papernot, N.: When the curious abandon honesty: federated learning is not private (2023)
5. Chatalic, A., Schellekens, V., Houssiau, F., De Montjoye, Y.A., Jacques, L., Gribonval, R.: Compressive learning with privacy guarantees. Inf. Infer. J. IMA **11**(1), 251–305 (2022)
6. Cole, E.K., Cheng, J.Y., Pauly, J.M., Vasanawala, S.S.: Analysis of deep complex-valued convolutional neural networks for MRI reconstruction. arXiv preprint arXiv:2004.01738 (2020)
7. Dong, J., Roth, A., Su, W.J.: Gaussian differential privacy. arXiv preprint arXiv:1905.02383 (2019)
8. Dörmann, F., Frisk, O., Andersen, L.N., Pedersen, C.F.: Not all noise is accounted equally: how differentially private learning benefits from large sampling rates. In: 2021 IEEE 31st International Workshop on Machine Learning for Signal Processing (MLSP), pp. 1–6. IEEE (2021)
9. Dwork, C., McSherry, F., Nissim, K., Smith, A.: Calibrating noise to sensitivity in private data analysis. In: Halevi, S., Rabin, T. (eds.) TCC 2006. LNCS, vol. 3876, pp. 265–284. Springer, Heidelberg (2006). https://doi.org/10.1007/11681878_14
10. Dwork, C., Roth, A., et al.: The algorithmic foundations of differential privacy. Found. Trends Theor. Comput. Sci. **9**(3–4), 211–407 (2014)

11. Fan, L., Xiong, L.: Adaptively sharing real-time aggregate with differential privacy. IEEE Trans. Knowl. Data Eng. (TKDE) **26**(9), 2094–2106 (2013)
12. Feng, S., Tramèr, F.: Privacy backdoors: stealing data with corrupted pretrained models (2024)
13. Fioretto, F., Mak, T.W., Van Hentenryck, P.: Differential privacy for power grid obfuscation. IEEE Trans. Smart Grid **11**(2), 1356–1366 (2019)
14. Fowl, L., Geiping, J., Czaja, W., Goldblum, M., Goldstein, T.: Robbing the fed: Directly obtaining private data in federated learning with modified models (2022)
15. Ioffe, S., Szegedy, C.: Batch normalization: accelerating deep network training by reducing internal covariate shift. In: International Conference on Machine Learning, pp. 448–456. PMLR (2015)
16. Jobin, A., Ienca, M., Vayena, E.: The global landscape of AI ethics guidelines. Nat. Mach. Intell. **1**(9), 389–399 (2019)
17. Kart, T., Bai, W., Glocker, B., Rueckert, D.: DeepMCAT: large-scale deep clustering for medical image categorization. In: Engelhardt, S., et al. (eds.) DGM4MICCAI/DALI -2021. LNCS, vol. 13003, pp. 259–267. Springer, Cham (2021). https://doi.org/10.1007/978-3-030-88210-5_26
18. Koskela, A., Jälkö, J., Honkela, A.: Computing tight differential privacy guarantees using FFT. In: International Conference on Artificial Intelligence and Statistics, pp. 2560–2569. PMLR (2020)
19. Kreutz-Delgado, K.: The complex gradient operator and the CR-calculus. arXiv preprint arXiv:0906.4835 (2009)
20. Küstner, T., et al.: CINENet: deep learning-based 3D cardiac CINE MRI reconstruction with multi-coil complex-valued 4D spatio-temporal convolutions. Sci. Rep. **10**(1), 1–13 (2020)
21. de Mello, et al.: Deep learning-based type identification of volumetric MRI sequences. In: 2020 25th International Conference on Pattern Recognition (ICPR). IEEE (2021). https://doi.org/10.1109/icpr48806.2021.9413120
22. Mironov, I.: Rényi differential privacy. 2017 IEEE 30th Computer Security Foundations Symposium (CSF) (2017)
23. Misra, D.: Mish: a self regularized non-monotonic activation function. arXiv preprint arXiv:1908.08681 (2019)
24. Peker, M.: An efficient sleep scoring system based on EEG signal using complex-valued machine learning algorithms. Neurocomputing **207**, 165–177 (2016)
25. Reddi, S., et al.: Adaptive federated optimization (2021). https://arxiv.org/abs/2003.00295
26. Salimans, T., Kingma, D.P.: Weight normalization: a simple reparameterization to accelerate training of deep neural networks. In: Advances in Neural Information Processing Systems, vol. 29 (2016)
27. Schreier, P.J., Scharf, L.L.: Statistical Signal Processing of Complex-valued Data: The Theory of Improper and Noncircular Signals. Cambridge University Press, Cambridge (2010)
28. Trabelsi, C., et al.: Deep complex networks. arXiv preprint arXiv:1705.09792 (2017)
29. Virtue, P., Yu, S., Lustig, M.: Better than real: complex-valued neural nets for MRI fingerprinting. In: 2017 IEEE International Conference on Image Processing (ICIP), pp. 3953–3957. IEEE (2017)
30. Wirtinger, W.: Zur formalen Theorie der Funktionen von mehr komplexen Veränderlichen. Math. Ann. **97**(1), 357–375 (1927)
31. Wu, Y., He, K.: Group normalization. In: Proceedings of the European Conference on Computer Vision (ECCV), pp. 3–19 (2018)

32. Yousefpour, A., et al.: Opacus: user-friendly differential privacy library in PyTorch. arXiv preprint arXiv:2109.12298 (2021)
33. Yu, H., Liu, Y., Chen, M.: Complex-valued neural network based federated learning for multi-user indoor positioning performance optimization. IEEE Internet Things J. (2024)

Enhancing Privacy in Federated Learning: Secure Aggregation for Real-World Healthcare Applications

Riccardo Taiello[1,2,3](✉), Sergen Cansiz[1], Marc Vesin[1], Francesco Cremonesi[1], Lucia Innocenti[1], Melek Önen[2], and Marco Lorenzi[1,3]

[1] Epione Research Project, Inria, Sophia Antipolis, Paris, France
{riccardo.taiello,marco.lorenzi}@inria.fr
[2] EURECOM, Sophia Antipolis, Paris, France
melek.onen@eurecom.fr
[3] Université Côte d'Azur, Nice, France

Abstract. Deploying federated learning (FL) in real-world scenarios, particularly in healthcare, poses challenges in communication and security. In particular, with respect to the federated aggregation procedure, researchers have been focusing on the study of secure aggregation (SA) schemes to provide privacy guarantees over the model's parameters transmitted by the clients. Nevertheless, the practical availability of SA in currently available FL frameworks is currently limited, due to computational and communication bottlenecks. To fill this gap, this study explores the implementation of SA within the open-source Fed-BioMed framework. We implement and compare two SA protocols, Joye-Libert (JL) and Low Overhead Masking (LOM), by providing extensive benchmarks in a panel of healthcare data analysis problems. Our theoretical and experimental evaluations on four datasets demonstrate that SA protocols effectively protect privacy while maintaining task accuracy. Computational overhead during training is less than 1% on a CPU and less than 50% on a GPU for large models, with protection phases tacking less than 10 s. Incorporating SA into Fed-BioMed impacts task accuracy by no more than 2% compared to non-SA scenarios. Overall this study demonstrates the feasibility of SA in real-world healthcare applications and contributes in reducing the gap towards the adoption of privacy-preserving technologies in sensitive applications.

Keywords: Federated Learning · Secure Aggregation · Healthcare Applications

1 Introduction

Federated Learning (FL) is a distributed machine learning paradigm that enables multiple clients to collaboratively train a global model without sharing their local datasets. While researchers have largely focused in developing FL theories and methods in a variety of applications, the deployment of FL in real-world scenarios is still challenging, particularly in terms of communication protocols, security, and customization bottlenecks.

A critical requirement for real-world applications of FL concerns the protection of the model's parameters shared by the clients during model aggregation. To this end, privacy-preserving methodologies such as Secure Aggregation (SA) [17] are currently under study, to guarantee that aggregated data shared among participants do not reveal individual contributions. Contrarily to other privacy-enhancing technologies like Differential Privacy (DP) [11], the privacy guarantees of SA rely on the security proofs of established cryptographic primitives [13,15].

On the practical side, while DP requires only minor adjustments to the federated aggregation process through the injection of noise to the model's parameters, implementing SA in production is more complex as it requires changes to the standard operational flow of the FL framework by incorporating new communication phases. As a result, the adoption of SA in currently available FL software frameworks is lagging behind. Existing SA solutions primarily target settings with a large number of clients, where hardware limitations can lead to protocol execution failures. Some preliminary solutions have been proposed in the framework FLOWER [4], which however introduce a non-negligible overhead. The approach provided by NVFLARE is simpler but suffers from a weak security model [21]. Finally SA in OPENFL [20] requires dedicated hardware solutions. Overall, the applications of these SA protocols in the cross-silo healthcare setting is suboptimal, due to the limited number of clients, and their general availability as compared to the cross-device setting.

To address these limitations, in this work we explore the implementation of SA schemes optimally customized for cross-silo healthcare applications. In particular, we study the two suitable categories of SA based on masking and additively homomorphic encryption [17]. We identify respectively LOW OVERHEAD MASKING [15] and JOYE-LIBERT [13] as the most relevant solutions for our application. These protocols are designed to protect individual updates from being exposed during the aggregation process.

This work is based on theoretical and experimental evaluation of these SA protocols within the Fed-BioMed framework [9]. In particular, we conducted a comprehensive comparison on four distinct medical datasets including medical images and tabular data: Fed-IXI [24], Fed-Heart [24], REPLACE-BG [1], and FedProstate [12]. We measured the computational resources required for training, encryption, and overall execution time. When training was performed on a CPU, we achieved a total computation overhead of less than 1%, while on a GPU, for larger machine learning models ($> 5M$ parameters), the overhead was less than 50%, with a protection phase that took less than 10 s. Furthermore, we analyzed the impact of SA on task accuracy, demonstrating that incorporating SA into Fed-BioMed affects accuracy by no more than 2% compared to non-SA scenarios. Overall this study demonstrates the feasibility of SA in real-world healthcare applications and contributes in reducing the gap towards the adoption of privacy-preserving technologies in sensitive applications.

2 Background

Federated Learning. As introduced by McMahan et al. [18], FL consists of a distributed machine learning paradigm where a group of clients, denoted as $\mathcal{U}$, collaboratively trains a global model with parameters $\boldsymbol{\theta} \in \mathbb{R}^d$, under the guidance of a FL server. One of the first and popular methods used to train a FL model is the FedAvg scheme [18]. With FedAvg, at each FL round denoted by τ, each client $u \in \mathcal{U}$ trains the model $\boldsymbol{\theta}_{u,\tau}$ on the private local data $\mathcal{D}_u$, for example through Stochastic Gradient Descent (SGD) [6]. Upon completion of the local training, each client forwards its updated model $\boldsymbol{\theta}_{u,\tau}$ to the server and the local dataset size $w_u = |\mathcal{D}_u|$. When the server receives the updated models from all participating clients, it proceeds to the weighted aggregation step:

$$\boldsymbol{\theta}_{\tau+1} \leftarrow \frac{\sum_{\forall u \in \mathcal{U}} w_u \boldsymbol{\theta}_{u,\tau}}{\sum_{\forall u \in \mathcal{U}} w_u}.$$

This iterative process continues until the global model $\boldsymbol{\theta}$ reaches some desired level of accuracy. The presence of a large number of FL clients significantly impacts the communication overhead. To mitigate this, instead of involving all clients in the training, at each FL round, the server selects a subset of clients (*client selection* [18]), denoted as $\mathcal{U}^{(\tau)} \subseteq \mathcal{U}$, with $|\mathcal{U}^{(\tau)}| = n$, and collects their parameters only for aggregation.

Secure Aggregation. SA [17] typically involves multiple *users* and a single *aggregator*. Each user possesses a private input, and the role of the aggregator is to calculate the sum of these inputs. A property of SA is that the aggregator learns nothing more than the aggregated sum, thereby preserving the privacy of individual user inputs.

SA has found significant applications in Federated Learning (FL), where it is used to securely aggregate the updated model parameters received from FL clients (aligned with the *user's* concept in SA) during each FL round, by instantiating an FL server (*aggregator* in the context of SA). The adoption of SA is motivated by the potential threats posed by adversaries having access to the client's updated model $\boldsymbol{\theta}_{u,\tau}$ which may infer information about its private dataset $\mathcal{D}_u$ [19,23]. Hence, the local models should remain confidential even against the FL server. SA in FL was first developed by Bonawitz et al. [5]. The protocol considered in that study faced two different challenges:

- *Threat models* defining the potential risks and behaviors that the security protocol is designed to protect against. The primary threat scenarios in SA include the honest-but-curious model where parties (server and clients) follow the protocol without tampering with the data but may attempt to infer additional information.
- *Client dropouts*, caused by factors such as connectivity issues or voluntary withdrawal, are common in real-world federated learning environments. Dropouts can significantly impact the computation and number of communication rounds of the SA protocol, as they often require the participation

of all selected clients within a training round. With communication rounds, we refer to the number of interactions required between the clients and the server to complete a particular phase of the protocol.

3 Related Works

In real-world deployments, only a few FL frameworks implement some form of SA: OPENFL [20], NVFLARE [21], and FLOWER [4].

FLOWER implements SECAGG+ [2], a masking-based protocol that ensures security in the honest-but-curious model. This protocol requires four communication rounds and uses Shamir's Secret Sharing to recover missing masks in case of client dropout, ensuring the server can complete the aggregation. Compared to the SA schemes here introduced in Fed-BioMed, Flower's approach is more costly in terms of communications, albeit accommodating for client dropout.

NVFLARE introduces an SA method that leverages the CKKS asymmetric homomorphic encryption scheme [8]. This threat model is considered weaker than typical state-of-the-art protocols because it requires clients to share a common secret key and assumes clients are honest. Clients protect their inputs using a public key, while the server, operating under the honest-but-curious model, aggregates these inputs and returns the aggregate to each client for decryption using the same secret key. This approach requires one communication round and allows client dropout.

OPENFL's use of Trusted Execution Environments (TEEs) represents a further step in sandboxing and securing local computations, but requires specific hardware which may not be available in typical FL studies involving hospitals.

4 Methods

In this section, we detail the implementation in Fed-BioMed of the two SA protocols, JOYE-LIBERT (JL) and LOW OVERHEAD MASKING (LOM). From this point on, we adopt the terminology of Fed-BioMed, where a client is referred to as a node.

A general overview of SA is depicted in Fig. 1, and a more detailed scheme is provided in Supplementary Fig. 3. An SA protocol comprises two phases: **setup** and **online**. The setup phase, illustrated in Fig. 1, is executed among all participating nodes in $\mathcal{U}$ before the FL training. This step ensures that all parties have the appropriate cryptographic material necessary to run the specific SA protocol.

The online phase, Fig. 1 is repeated during each FL round τ and consists of two steps: (i) *protect* and (ii) *aggregate*. In the *protection* step, each node protects its private local model using specific SA primitives and then sends the protected model to the server. In the *aggregation* step, the server receives the protected local models, computes the aggregate, and then decrypts it. To ensure the correct functioning of the cryptographic primitives, the locally-trained model vector of each node must be quantized beforehand.

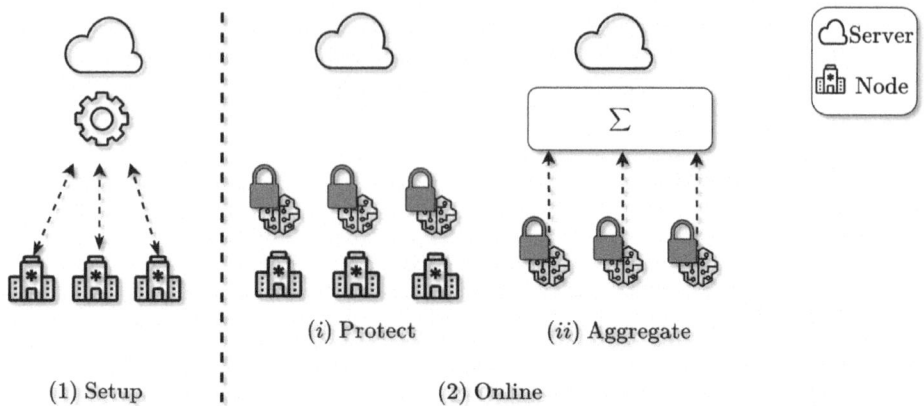

Fig. 1. Overview of Secure Aggregation phases.

Prerequistes. To perform FedAvg with SA, we first convert the node's local parameters $\theta_{u,\tau} \in \mathbb{R}^d$ into integers $\mathbb{Z}_{2^L}^d$, where L represents the maximum number of bits of the plaintext. This conversion is achieved by applying uniform quantization, defined as: $Q(\theta_{u,\tau}) = \left\lfloor \frac{2^L \cdot (\theta_{u,\tau} - \theta_{\min})}{(\theta_{\max} - \theta_{\min})} \right\rceil$. Here, $\lfloor \cdot \rceil$ denotes the standard rounding function. To ensure that real values are within a desired range, we apply a clipping function, $\text{clip}(x, \theta_{\min}, \theta_{\max}) = \min(\max(x, \theta_{\min}), \theta_{\max})$, where $\theta_{\min}$ and $\theta_{\max}$ are the lower and upper bounds, respectively.

To apply weighted averaging over the integers, we assume that $w_u \in \mathbb{Z}_{2^{W_u}}$, where W_u is the number of bits to represent the node's dataset size, and we define $W = \max(\{W_u\}_{\forall u \in \mathcal{U}})$.

The weighted local model is computed as $\boldsymbol{x}_{u,\tau} = Q(\theta_{u,\tau}) \cdot w_u$, resulting in $\boldsymbol{x}_{u,\tau} \in \mathbb{Z}_{2^{L+W}}^d$. To avoid overflow, we define $M = L + W + \log_2(n)$ as the maximum number of bits for sum computation. The aggregate $\boldsymbol{x}_{\tau+1} = (\sum_{u \in \mathcal{U}(\tau)} \boldsymbol{x}_{u,\tau}) \in \mathbb{Z}_{2^M}^d$ is then divided by $s = \sum_{u \in \mathcal{U}(\tau)} w_u$ and dequantized using the following formula: $\theta_{\tau+1} = Q^{-1}(\boldsymbol{x}_{\tau+1}) = \boldsymbol{x}_{\tau+1} \cdot \frac{(\theta_{\max} - \theta_{\min})}{2^L} + \theta_{\min}$.

In this context, we assume that quantization has been performed and omit the details of the dequantization process in the protocol explanation.

Joye-Libert

In Supplementary Fig. 3a, we illustrate the Joye-Libert (JL) implementation in Fed-BioMed. During the **setup** phase, the participating nodes $\mathcal{U}$ generate their private keys sk_u, and the server creates its server key sk_0 - which is the sum of the node keys - using Shamir Secret Sharing (SS) [22].

During the **online** phase, the protection and aggregation are applied as described in JL (Sect. 4 [13]). In the protection step, each node uses a private secret key sk_u at FL round τ with a one-time mask derived from sk_u and τ, to obtain a protected local model through modular exponentiation over a large moudulus N. Using the server key sk_0, the server can recover the aggregate of the nodes' private local models in clear.

Our JL implementation works with vectors; the protection and aggregation algorithms are applied element-wise. We use the element's index i to generate a unique FL round (need to guarantee a one-time mask) for each element in the vector. For instance, to protect $\boldsymbol{x}_{u,\tau}$, we execute protect and aggregate over the FL round $\tau||i$ and input $\boldsymbol{x}_{u,\tau}[i]$, where $\boldsymbol{x}_{u,\tau}[i]$ represents the i-th element of the vector $\boldsymbol{x}_{u,\tau}$.

The computation and communication of the protected local model is optimized by using vector encoding [16].

Software Details. SS is integrated into Fed-BioMed using MP-SPDZ library [14]. The modulus N is provided by the server, and the modular operations are performed using the GMPY2[1] Python library.

Low Overhead Masking

The second implementation, Low Overhead Masking (LOM) [15], which supports client selection, is depicted in Supplementary Fig. 3b. During the **setup** phase, all participating nodes $\mathcal{U}$ establish a pairwise secret $s_{u,v}$, such that $s_{u,v} = s_{v,u}$, with all nodes through the Diffie-Hellman Key Agreement (KA) [10], which will be used in the protect step.

In the **online** phase, during the *protection* step, a selected node $u \in \mathcal{U}^{(\tau)}$ runs the protect algorithm (Sect. 3.4 [15]). This algorithm protects the local model with a one-time mask derived through a Pseudo-Random Function (PRF) which uses the pairwise secret with the selected nodes $\mathcal{U}^{(\tau)}$ and the current FL round τ, and sends the protected local model to the server. The server then sums the protected local models and collects the final aggregate $\boldsymbol{x}_{\tau+1}$.

Software Details. Diffie-Hellman KA and PRF are implemented in the CRYPTOGRAPHY[2] Python library, with ECDH and the ChaCha20 [3] stream cipher, respectivelly. Distribution of the DH public key is assumed outside of Fed-BioMed, offline, or trough a Public Key Infrastructure.

5 Evaluation

In this Section we provide our theoretical and experimental evaluation of the two implemented SA protocols.

Complexity Analysis: JL's node computation is $O(d)$, independent of the number of selected nodes, but requires modular exponentiation, and node communication for vector encoding is $O(d \cdot 2 \cdot M)$ [16]. The server's computation is $O(n + d)$, involving n multiplications and d exponentiation [13].

---

[1] GMPY2: https://gmpy2.readthedocs.io/.
[2] CRYPTOGRAPHY: https://github.com/pyca/cryptography.

LOM's node computation is $O(nd)$, dependent on the number of selected nodes, using faster modular addition and PRF evaluation. The server's computation involves nd modular additions, and node communication is $O(d \cdot M)$ [15].

Experimental Evaluation: The experimental evaluation consists of tracking the computation time between JL and the LOM. We carried out the experiments by considering varying FL hyper-parameters represented by the number of total nodes n_{tot}, the number of selected nodes n, the number of FL rounds T, the number of local SGD steps e, the batch size b and the learning rate η. For SA, the hyper-parameters we explored were the number of bits input L, the number of bits weight W. Moreover, we fixed the aggregation number of bits $M = 32$ and the clipping range min and max. Finally, we report the hardware used to train ML model. We report all this information for each experiments in Table 1.

We use four medical datasets to evaluate the task accuracy of our SA implementations over the aggregated global model at each FL round, using a dedicated tasks-specific test set, and tracking the required computational resources for the nodes.

Table 1

SA	Time Train (s)	Time Enc. (s)	Time Tot. (s)
FedIXI ($d = 246K; n_{tot} = n = 3$)			
JL	68.10 ± 2.17	52.21 ± 0.85	121.48 ± 2.50
LOM	46.51 ± 1.39	0.62 ± 0.14	48.22 ± 1.03
FedHeart ($d = 258; n_{tot} = n = 4$)			
JL	0.24 ± 0.08	0.08 ± 0.01	0.68 ± 0.09
LOM	0.20 ± 0.09	> 0.01	0.59 ± 0.08
REPLACE-BG ($d = 256K; n_{tot} = 180; n = 18$)			
JL	N/A	N/A	N/A
LOM	53.72 ± 8.61	0.39 ± 0.06	57.42 ± 6.95
FedProstate ($d = 7.4M; n_{tot} = n = 4$)			
JL	N/A	> 300	> 300
LOM	7.65 ± 1.6	9.22 ± 0.38	23.86 ± 2.1

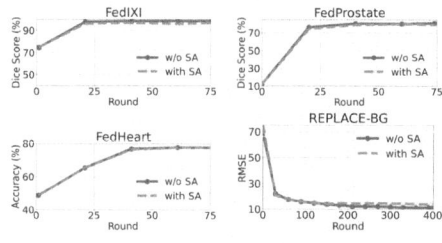

Fig. 2

Table 1 Comparison of node average computation time across different SA protocols using four medical datasets. Each dataset is characterized by the total number of nodes (n_{tot}), the number of selected nodes (n), and the size of the local model (d). Figure 2 Compare the task accuracy of the global model at each FedAvg aggregation with and without applying SA for FedIXI, FedProstate, FedHeart and REPLACE-BG. The SA is characterized by L bits for representing the local model, W bits for representing the maximum dataset size, and the specified maximum and minimum clipping range.

The four datasets are:

- Fed-Heart [24], providing patients' demography and clinical history from four hospitals. The task is to predict the clinical status of a patient (binary classification from tabular data). For FL training and testing we follow [24], and the target evaluation metric is the balanced accuracy.
- Fed-IXI [24], is composed by T1 and T2 brain magnetic resonance images (MRIs) from three hospitals. The task is supervised brain segmentation, and

ground truth segmentations are provided. For FL training and testing we follow [24], and the target evaluation metric is the dice score.
- REPLACE-BG dataset [1] was obtained from a cohort of 202 participants. The task is prediction of blood glucose levels for the subsequent hour based on data from the last three hours, including glucose levels, insulin boluses, and CHO content.
- FedProstate dataset [12] provides T2 MRIs of the whole prostate from three publicly available datasets, and the task is supervised prostate segmentation. We defined the splitting criteria into different clients, the pre-processing methods, and the FL training and testing parameters coherently with [12].

Supplementary Table 2 reports the dataset details, the FL and SA hyperparameters, and the hardware specific for model training across experiments. The code is publicly available[3].

In Table 1, we report the required node's computational resources comparing the two SA solutions. We present the average training time, encryption time, and total time. LOM consistently outperforms JL due to its faster underlying primitive (modular addition vs. modular exponentiation). Specifically, in all experiments where training runs on a CPU, LOM accounts for less than 1% of the total time. When a GPU (e.g., in FedProstate) is available, the overall encryption time is around 40% of the total time, considering a large input parameter dimension of $d = 7.4M$.

In Fig. 2, we display the task accuracy comparison with and without SA for FedIXI, FedProstate, FedHeart and REPLACE-BG. This figure demonstrates that incorporating SA in Fed-BioMed affects the accuracy by no more than 2% compared to the case without SA.

6 Conclusion and Future Works

We have demonstrated that SA can be effectively implemented within the Fed-BioMed framework to enhance privacy in federated learning. Our evaluations using four medical datasets show that both Joye-Libert and Low Overhead Masking protocols protect privacy while maintaining task accuracy. The computational overhead is minimal, making SA a viable option for real-world deployments. As part of future work, we plan to replace MP-SPDZ with a direct implementation of additive secret sharing within Fed-BioMed. We also aim to replace JL with a quantum-resistant SA [7] using the SHELL C++ library[4].

Acknowledgements. This work has been supported by the French government, through the 3IA Côte d'Azur Investments in the Future project managed by the National Research Agency (ANR) with the reference number ANR-19-P3IA0002, by the TRAIN project ANR-22-FAI1-0003-02, and by the ANR JCJC project Fed-BioMed 19-CE45-0006-01.

---

[3] GitHub code.
[4] SHELL library: https://github.com/google/shell-encryption/.

A Appendix

Prerequisites Security paramter λ.
Parties: Server, nodes $\mathcal{U}$ and selected nodes $\mathcal{U}^{(\tau)}$, s.t $|\mathcal{U}| = n_{tot}$ and $|\mathcal{U}^{(\tau)}| = n$.

Public Parameters:

- $(\perp, pp^{JL}) \leftarrow$ **JL.Setup**(λ)

Setup - Key Setup:

Node u:
1. $sk_u \xleftarrow{R} \mathbb{Z}_{N^2}$
2. $\{(v, [sk_u]_v)\}_{\forall v \in \mathcal{U}} \leftarrow$ **SS.Share**$(sk_u, t, \mathcal{U})$
3. Send $\forall v \in \mathcal{U} \setminus \{u\}, [sk_u]_v$
4. Receive $\{[sk_v]_u\}_{\forall v \in \mathcal{U} \setminus \{u\}}$
5. $[sk_0]_u \leftarrow \sum_{\forall v \in \mathcal{U}} [sk_v]_u$
6. Send $[sk_0]_u$ to Server

Server:
1. Collect $\{[sk_0]_u\}_{\forall u \in \mathcal{U}}$.
2. If $|\mathcal{U}| < t$, abort; otherwise, proceed.
3. $sk_0 \leftarrow$ **SS.Recon**$(\{[sk_0]_v\}_{\forall v \in \mathcal{U}}, t)$

Online - Protection (τ):

Node $u \in \mathcal{U}$:
1. $\boldsymbol{y}_{u,\tau} \leftarrow$ **JL.Protect**$(pp^{JL}, sk_u, \tau, \boldsymbol{x}_{u,\tau})$
2. Send $\boldsymbol{y}_{u,\tau}$ to Server.

Online - Aggregation (τ):

Server:
1. Collect $\{\boldsymbol{y}_{u,\tau}\}_{\forall u \in \mathcal{U}}$.
2. $\boldsymbol{x}_{\tau+1} \leftarrow$ **JL.Agg**$(pp, -sk_0, \tau, \{\boldsymbol{y}_{u,\tau}\}_{\forall u \in \mathcal{U}})$

(a) JL

Public Parameters:

- $(\perp, pp^{LOM}) \leftarrow$ **LOM.Setup**(λ)
- $(\perp, pp^{KA}) \leftarrow$ **KA.Param**(λ)

Setup - Key Setup:

Node $u \in \mathcal{U}$:
1. $(c_u^{SK}, c_u^{PK}) \leftarrow$ **KA.Gen**(pp^{KA})
2. Broadcast c_u^{PK}
3. Receive $\forall v \in \mathcal{U} \setminus \{u\}, c_v^{PK}$
4. $\forall v \in \mathcal{U} \setminus \{u\}$,
   $s_{u,v} \leftarrow$ **KA.Agree**$(pp^{KA}, c_u^{SK}, c_v^{PK})$

Online - Protection $(\tau, \mathcal{U}^{(\tau)})$:

Node $u \in \mathcal{U}^{(\tau)}$:
1. $\boldsymbol{y}_{u,\tau} \leftarrow$
   LOM.Protect$(pp^{LOM}, \{s_{u,v}\}_{\forall v \in \mathcal{U}^{(\tau)} \setminus u}, \tau, \boldsymbol{x}_{u,\tau})$
2. Send $\boldsymbol{y}_{u,\tau}$ to Server.

Online - Aggregation (τ):

Server:
1. Collect $\{\boldsymbol{y}_{u,\tau}\}_{\forall u \in \mathcal{U}^{(\tau)}}$.
2. $\boldsymbol{x}_{\tau+1} \leftarrow$ **LOM.Agg**$(pp^{LOM}, \{\boldsymbol{y}_{u,\tau}\}_{\forall u \in \mathcal{U}^{(\tau)}})$

(b) LOM

Fig. 3. SA protocols implemented in Fed-BioMed

Table 2. FL hyper-params: number of total nodes n_{tot}, the number of selected nodes n, the number of FL rounds T, the number of local SGD steps e, the batch size b, and the learning rate η. SA hyper-params: number of bits input L, number of bits weight W and clipping range max/min.

Dataset	FL Hyper-params					SA Hyper-params			Hardware spec.
	n_{tot}	n	T	e	b	η	L	W	max/min	
FedIIXI	3	3	75	10	2	1×10^{-3}	22	8	+20/−20	CPU
FedHeart	4	4	75	10	8	5×10^{-4}	15	17	+3/−3	CPU
REPLACE-BG	180	18	400	10	64	1×10^{-3}	13	15	+3/−3	CPU
FedProstate	4	4	75	6	8	1×10^{-3}	22	8	+2/−2	GPU

References

1. Aleppo, G., et al.: Replace-bg: a randomized trial comparing continuous glucose monitoring with and without routine blood glucose monitoring in adults with well-controlled type 1 diabetes. Diabetes Care **40**(4), 538–545 (2017)
2. Bell, J.H., Bonawitz, K.A., Gascón, A., Lepoint, T., Raykova, M.: Secure single-server aggregation with (poly) logarithmic overhead. In: Proceedings of the 2020 ACM SIGSAC Conference on Computer and Communications Security, pp. 1253–1269 (2020)
3. Bernstein, D.J., et al.: Chacha, a variant of salsa20. In: Workshop Record of SASC, vol. 8, pp. 3–5. Citeseer (2008)
4. Beutel, D.J., et al.: Flower: a friendly federated learning research framework. arXiv preprint arXiv:2007.14390 (2020)
5. Bonawitz, K., et al.: Practical secure aggregation for privacy-preserving machine learning, pp. 1175–1191. CCS '17, Association for Computing Machinery, New York, NY, USA (2017)
6. Bottou, L.: Stochastic learning. In: Bousquet, O., von Luxburg, U. (eds.) Advanced Lectures on Machine Learning, pp. 146–168. LNAI, vol. 3176. Springer Verlag, Berlin (2004). http://leon.bottou.org/papers/bottou-mlss-2004
7. Brakerski, Z., Vaikuntanathan, V.: Fully homomorphic encryption from ring-lwe and security for key dependent messages. In: Annual Cryptology Conference, pp. 505–524. Springer (2011)
8. Cheon, J.H., Kim, A., Kim, M., Song, Y.: Homomorphic encryption for arithmetic of approximate numbers. In: Advances in Cryptology–ASIACRYPT 2017: 23rd International Conference on the Theory and Applications of Cryptology and Information Security, Hong Kong, China, 3–7 December 2017, Proceedings, Part I 23, pp. 409–437. Springer (2017)
9. Cremonesi, F., et al.: Fed-biomed: open, transparent and trusted federated learning for real-world healthcare applications. arXiv preprint arXiv:2304.12012 (2023)
10. Diffie, W., Hellman, M.E.: New directions in cryptography. In: Democratizing Cryptography: The Work of Whitfield Diffie and Martin Hellman, pp. 365–390 (2022)
11. Dwork, C.: Differential privacy. In: International Colloquium on Automata, Languages, and Programming, pp. 1–12. Springer (2006)
12. Innocenti, L., et al.: Benchmarking collaborative learning methods cost-effectiveness for prostate segmentation. arXiv preprint arXiv:2309.17097 (2023)
13. Joye, M., Libert, B.: A scalable scheme for privacy-preserving aggregation of time-series data. In: Sadeghi, A.R. (ed.) Financial Cryptography and Data Security. Springer, Berlin Heidelberg (2013)
14. Keller, M.: Mp-spdz: a versatile framework for multi-party computation. In: Proceedings of the 2020 ACM SIGSAC Conference on Computer and Communications Security, pp. 1575–1590 (2020)
15. Kursawe, K., Danezis, G., Kohlweiss, M.: Privacy-friendly aggregation for the smart-grid. In: Privacy Enhancing Technologies: 11th International Symposium, PETS 2011, Waterloo, ON, Canada, 27–29 July 2011. Proceedings 11, pp. 175–191. Springer (2011)
16. Mansouri, M., Önen, M., Ben Jaballah, W.: Learning from failures: secure and fault-tolerant aggregation for federated learning. In: Proceedings of the 38th Annual Computer Security Applications Conference, pp. 146–158 (2022)

17. Mansouri, M., Onen, M., Jaballah, W.B., Conti, M.: SOK: secure aggregation based on cryptographic schemes for federated learning. Proc. Priv. Enhanc. Technol. **1**, 140–157 (2023)
18. McMahan, B., Moore, E., Ramage, D., Hampson, S., y Arcas, B.A.: Communication-efficient learning of deep networks from decentralized data. In: Proceedings of the 20th International Conference on Artificial Intelligence and Statistics. Proceedings of Machine Learning Research, vol. 54. PMLR (2017)
19. Nasr, M., Shokri, R., Houmansadr, A.: Comprehensive privacy analysis of deep learning: passive and active white-box inference attacks against centralized and federated learning. In: 2019 IEEE Symposium on Security and Privacy (SP) (2019)
20. Reina, G.A., et al.: Openfl: an open-source framework for federated learning. arXiv preprint arXiv:2105.06413 (2021)
21. Roth, H.R., et al.: Nvidia flare: federated learning from simulation to real-world. arXiv preprint arXiv:2210.13291 (2022)
22. Shamir, A.: How to share a secret. Commun. ACM (1979)
23. Shokri, R., Stronati, M., Song, C., Shmatikov, V.: Membership inference attacks against machine learning models. In: 2017 IEEE Symposium on Security and Privacy (SP) (2017)
24. Ogier du Terrail, J., et al.: Flamby: datasets and benchmarks for cross-silo federated learning in realistic healthcare settings. Adv. Neural Inf. Process. Syst. **35**, 5315–5334 (2022)

Federated Impression for Learning with Distributed Heterogeneous Data

Atrin Arya[1,2(✉)], Sana Ayromlou[1,2], Armin Saadat[1], Purang Abolmaesumi[1], and Xiaoxiao Li[1,2]

[1] Electrical and Computer Engineering Department, The University of British Columbia, Vancouver, BC V6T 1Z4, Canada
{atrinarya,s.ayromlou,xiaoxiao}@ece.ubc.ca
[2] Vector Institute, Toronto, ON M5G 0C6, Canada

Abstract. Standard deep learning-based classification approaches may not always be practical in real-world clinical applications, as they require a centralized collection of all samples. Federated learning (FL) provides a paradigm that can learn from distributed datasets across clients without requiring them to share data, which can help mitigate privacy and data ownership issues. In FL, sub-optimal convergence caused by data heterogeneity is common among data from different health centers due to the variety in data collection protocols and patient demographics across centers. Through experimentation in this study, we show that data heterogeneity leads to the phenomenon of catastrophic forgetting during local training. We propose `FedImpres` which alleviates catastrophic forgetting by restoring synthetic data that represents the global information as federated impression. To achieve this, we distill the global model resulting from each communication round. Subsequently, we use the synthetic data alongside the local data to enhance the generalization of local training. Extensive experiments show that the proposed method achieves state-of-the-art performance on both the BloodMNIST and Retina datasets, which contain label imbalance and domain shift, with an improvement in classification accuracy of up to 20%. The code is available at https://github.com/Atrin78/FedImpress.

Keywords: Federated Learning · Catastrophic Forgetting · Data Synthesis · Data Heterogeneity

1 Introduction

Deep learning models are widely utilized in medical imaging owing to their promising outcomes. However, these models are typically designed for centralized environments where all data are stored in a single database. Despite its benefits,

---

A. Arya and S. Ayromlou—These authors contributed equally.

Supplementary Information The online version contains supplementary material available at https://doi.org/10.1007/978-3-031-77610-6_20.

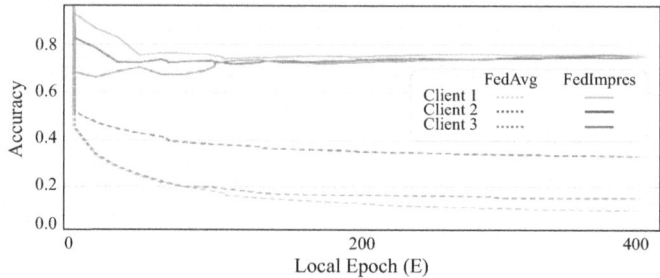

Fig. 1. Catastrophic forgetting occurs when server weights are overwritten during local training, causing a loss of previous knowledge. To investigate the effect of catastrophic forgetting during local training in FL, we conducted experiments on BloodMNIST using the same experimental settings described in Sect. 3. Specifically, we plot each client's local model accuracy over other clients' data during local training. The accuracy drops drastically using FedAvg; however, FedImpres maintains stable accuracy across clients.

centralizing data can be impractical for training purposes, *i.e.*, healthcare facilities are generally hesitant to disclose their patients' information due to issues of data privacy, transmission costs, and access rights [20]. Federated Learning (FL) presents a promising alternative, enabling multiple hospitals to leverage distributed data without sharing it. In each iteration, local models are initialized with the distributed server model. They are then trained on local data and send back their updates to the server for aggregation. However, conventional FL methods such as FedAvg [18] encounter performance degradation, when applied to non-IID (heterogeneous) data [10, 14].

Heterogeneity happens due to 1) label imbalance *i.e.*, various disease populations in different medical centers, and 2) domain shift, *i.e.*, various data acquisition settings in medical devices. Studies have been carried out to mitigate each of the mentioned heterogeneities independently. However, based on our experiments in Fig. 1, we show that both of these cases lead to a common issue called catastrophic forgetting, which has been usually overlooked in previous works. In FL, catastrophic forgetting [5] occurs when a model overwrites past aggregated knowledge with local data. As shown in Fig. 1, when observing a specific client during local training, the local model's accuracy on the other local datasets degrades since the server model's past aggregated knowledge is overwritten by the local heterogeneous data. In this work, we focus on solving the catastrophic forgetting issue in FL caused by label imbalance and domain shift.

Recent efforts in FL literature have mainly concentrated on improving local training on client side [9, 13, 16, 30]; and refining aggregation on the server side [15, 17, 25, 29]. Notably, client side enhancements have been reported to achieve better outcomes [13]. To improve client side training, two main categories of methodologies have been investigated: 1) *model-level* approaches, which refine model optimization strategies through techniques such as setting a prior on model weights [13] or gradient update corrections [10, 22]; and 2) *data-level* methods which aim to alleviate statistical heterogeneity among local data across clients by employing techniques like sharing statistical information [7, 21] or synthetic data generation [24,30]. Among them, model-level studies such as [22] and data-level studies such as [26] have directly tackled the issue of catastrophic forgetting in FL. In terms of addressing catastrophic forgetting, data-level approaches exhibit superior model agnosticity, which is advantageous in deep learning [5]. However, the generation of synthetic images with high fidelity that preserves the server model's information remains a persistent challenge.

In this paper, we propose a data-level approach, FedImpres, to mitigate catastrophic forgetting, caused by heterogeneous data in FL setting. To achieve this, after server aggregation in each FL iteration, we generate high-quality prototypical synthetic images by back-propagating on the server model's aggregated weights as a federated impression of global data. Furthermore, we add a model gradient-based constraint to this optimization to ensure that the synthesized data globally fits the entire latent distribution of the server model. We share the synthesized data with clients and perform weighted training on both local and synthesized data on the client-side. We have chosen to use FedAvg as the base method for aggregating the local models on the server-side for the sake of simplicity. However, it is important to note that our approach is also compatible with other model aggregation strategies.

2 Method

2.1 Problem Setting

The general FL setting aims to collaboratively train over a group of clients $\{C_1, C_2, ..., C_N\}$ and their respective local datasets, with N being the number of clients. The objective is to maintain high classification accuracy across all clients. Let $(x_i^n, y_i^n) \in \mathcal{X}_n$ represent an input image and its corresponding class label drawn from client n's dataset. We denote the weights of feature extractors as θ and that of classifiers as ϕ. In this setting, our goal is to have a model on the server that performs well on all clients by minimizing the following objective:

$$J(\theta_G, \phi_G) = \sum_{n=1}^{N} \mathbb{E}_{(x_i^n, y_i^n) \in \mathcal{X}_n} \ell(g(f(x_i^n; \theta_G); \phi_G), y_i^n), \tag{1}$$

with loss function ℓ which is cross-entropy (CE) loss, $\mathcal{L}_{CE}$, in our case, client number n, server model's feature extractor $f(; \theta_G)$ and its classifier $g(; \phi_G)$. Note that the local data cannot be shared due to privacy concerns. As a result, in each round r, we train models $\{f(; \theta_1^r), ..., f(; \theta_N^r)\}$ initialized by $f(; \theta_G^r)$ using their respective client's local dataset, and share their weights $\{\theta_1^r, ..., \theta_N^r\}$ with the server model to aggregate them into θ_G^{r+1}. A common strategy for aggregation is [18] simply averaging the weights of clients, which we will follow in our study.

2.2 Overview

As described in the introduction (Sect. 1), catastrophic forgetting during local training is one of the primary problems in heterogeneous FL. To develop a robust

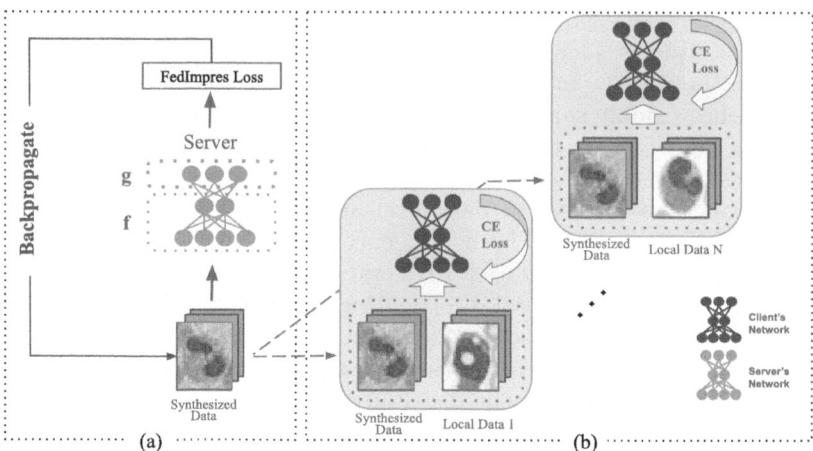

Fig. 2. Our proposed approach, FedImpres, aims to capture the global distribution learned by the aggregated server model and distill it into a dataset that can be shared with clients. The approach consists of two steps: a) First, we perform pixel-wise optimization by starting from unlabeled public data and using the server model's predicted pseudo-labels to backpropagate using Eq. ((4)). b) Second, to improve local training, we add the synthesized data as a regularizer to the local data using Eq. ((5)). This allows us to share the global distilled distribution with clients and leverage it to improve local training.

FL algorithm suitable for heterogeneous data, we need to address two fundamental challenges: 1) How to alleviate catastrophic forgetting in local training? This can be achieved by utilizing a united synthetic data as a regularizer in local client training to penalize catastrophic forgetting; 2) How to generate this synthetic dataset? We can synthesize data using the server model to capture a genuine federated impression for local training. The overall paradigm of our method is shown in Fig. 2. In the following sections, we will provide a detailed description of our proposed paradigm.

2.3 Federated Impression

Past methods like VHL [24] have proposed to use global synthetic data to improve FL on heterogeneous data. However, VHL's synthetic data does not preserve the server model's information useful for the targeted classification task during local training. Inspired by [2], to empower the global synthetic data to assist FL, we introduce an adaptive global data generation paradigm, which synthesizes data based on the server model in each communication round. Next, we aim to have not only high-fidelity data but also the **information-preserving property**, *i.e.*, training a model from scratch using synthesized data results in a model that performs similarly to the original server model. To obtain data with this characteristic, we optimize pixel values on the image space $v_1, v_2, ..., v_S \in \mathcal{V}$

CE loss of the server model. Additionally, to achieve the information-preserving property following [28], we add an equality constraint to the optimization process to ensure that the gradient of the server model's CE loss on $\mathcal{V}$ with respect to its weights θ_G^r is close to 0. Specifically, we aim to solve

$$\min_{\mathcal{V}} \sum_{(v_i,\hat{y}_i)\in\mathcal{V}} \mathcal{L}_{CE}(g(f(v_i;\theta_G^r);\phi_G^r),\hat{y}_i) \ \ s.t. \ \nabla_{(\theta_G^r,\phi_G^r)}\mathcal{L}_{CE}=0, \qquad (2)$$

where $\hat{y}_i$ is initialized with the prediction of the server model when given v_i. Since optimizing Eq. 2 is computationally expensive, according to [28], we solve the relaxed version of the optimization problem imposing the equality constraint on ϕ_G^r only

$$\min_{\mathcal{V}} \sum_{(v_i,\hat{y}_i)\in\mathcal{V}} \mathcal{L}_{CE}(g(f(v_i;\theta_G^r);\phi_G^r),\hat{y}_i) \ \ s.t. \ \nabla_{(\phi_G^r)}\mathcal{L}_{CE}=0, \qquad (3)$$

It's worth noting that such a relaxation does not steer us away from our ultimate goal of information-preserving property. Instead of generating precise images with this property, we aim to produce images whose latent representation would capture the exact global distribution of the server in the latent space. Next, we solve it using the augmented lagrangian formulation:

$$\max_{\Lambda} \min_{\mathcal{V}} \ L_{FedImpres} =$$

$$\sum_{(v_i,\hat{y}_i)\in\mathcal{V}} [\mathcal{L}_{CE}(g(f(v_i;\theta_G^r);\phi_G^r),\hat{y}_i) + tr(\Lambda^T \nabla_{\phi_G^r}\mathcal{L}_{CE}) + \frac{\rho}{2}||\nabla_{\phi_G^r}\mathcal{L}_{CE}||^2], \qquad (4)$$

where Λ is the lagrangian dual variable matrix for the equality constraint in Eq. (2) and ρ is the penalty hyperparameter. According to [28], we solve it approximately using an alternating direction method of multipliers (ADMM) [4]. After synthesizing this data as the federated impression, we pass it to all clients for local training. Note that we don't need any additional private data information to generate the synthetic dataset compared to general FL methods like [18].

2.4 Forgetting-Penalized Local Training

To train the local model for client n, we receive an optimized synthetic dataset $\mathcal{V}$ from the server at the beginning of each local training round. To prevent catastrophic forgetting during local training, we train the model on synthetic data in addition to the local data using the following

$$\min_{(\theta_n^r,\phi_n^r)} L_{local}(\theta_n^r,\phi_n^r) + \beta L_{global}(\theta_n^r,\phi_n^r); \qquad (5)$$

where L_{local} and L_{global} are CE loss over each client's local data and shared global data, respectively. Here, L_{global} basically used as a regularization term for improving the generalizability of local training over captured federated impression in the previous step. This approach preserves information from the server model due to the information-preserving property of the synthetic data. Note that as opposed to [28], we use the CE loss directly on the synthesized data to enforce the information-preserving property. It is also worth noting that merely replacing the global loss with another regularization that instead aims to decrease the distance between the local model's and the server model's weights directly, as done in [22], may not be optimal since it would limit the ability to capture local information.

3 Experiments

3.1 Datasets

We use two public medical image datasets to evaluate `FedImpres` on two typical heterogeneous settings for classification: label imbalance and domain shift:

BloodMNIST [1] is one of the datasets in the standard medical imaging benchmark, MedMNIST [27]. We chose this dataset over other modalities as it contains adequate classes (eight in total), which can better demonstrate `FedImpres` on imbalanced labels settings. The images in this dataset are padded to size 32×32.

Retina dataset [3,6,19,23] consists of retina images of size 256×256 gathered from four different sites, resulting in label imbalance and domain shift. We aim to solve the binary classification problem to detect Glaucomatous images from normal ones for this dataset. Samples and label distribution of both datasets for each client are provided in the supplementary material.

3.2 Experimental Settings

We conducted experiments to study label imbalance and domain shift among FL clients. For each experiment, we used three different alternatives of initialization for the synthesis step of `FedImpres`, *i.e.*, random noise, public natural images (CIFAR-10 [12]), and a public *unlabeled* medical dataset in a similar domain of local private data, which will be explained for each dataset separately. Note that obtaining unlabeled data from the same modality used for synthesis initialization is not a problem in the real world.

Data Heterogeneity: To simulate class imbalance, we used BloodMNIST. To replicate unlabeled medical data for synthesis initialization, we randomly selected 10% of the data that were mutually exclusive from all of the training data. Afterwards, we utilized Latent Dirichlet Analysis (LDA) [8,25] to divide the remaining data into eight clients for an eight-way classification. We set the partition parameter of LDA (α) to 0.01 and 0.005 to create moderate and severe imbalanced datasets. Subsequently, in a more practical evaluation, we carried out experiments on the Retina dataset, which encompasses data from four distinct domains with different demographic distributions and are naturally class-imbalanced. We employed data from one of the four sites as publicly accessible

Table 1. Classification accuracies on BloodMNIST and Retina dataset compared with the state-of-the-art methods. We reported `FedImpres` results using random, CIFAR-10 and medical unlabeled data of the same modality data as initialization. Although medical initialization performs overall better than CIFAR-10 and random, we still outperform baselines in most of the settings.

Dataset	BloodMNIST				Retina	
α	0.01		0.005		NA	
Local update epochs (E)	5	10	5	10	5	10
FedAvg [18]	83.1	82.4	39.0	37.6	55.7	52.0
FedProx [13]	82.8	83.1	35.1	34.9	68.2	61.9
VHL [24]	<u>84.9</u>	83.3	50.3	43.0	<u>80.8</u>	78.8
FedVSS [30]	82.9	82.8	38.1	36.7	62.3	68.3
FedCurv [22]	68.5	61.7	26.2	25.9	79.9	78.1
FedReg [26]	20.1	16.9	18.9	16.8	62.5	62.1
`FedImpres` (Random init)	83.9	82.6	52.6	51.4	78.1	<u>80.6</u>
`FedImpres` (CIFAR-10 init)	84.1	<u>83.6</u>	<u>60.2</u>	<u>53.8</u>	**81.5**	79.8
`FedImpres` (Medical init)	**94.2**	**93.1**	**70.2**	**65.1**	80.6	**81.1**

unlabeled data for synthesis initialization and performed binary classification on the remaining three datasets.

Implementation Details: We used a simple Convolutional Neural Network (CNN) for classification in all settings. The architecture is detailed in the supplementary. All models were implemented with PyTorch and trained on one NVIDIA Tesla V100 GPU with 16 GB of memory. Our implementation contains two stages of optimization in each communication round. 1) We freeze model weights for the image synthesis stage and use the SGD optimizer and optimize the batch of [11, 27] images for 5 ADMM epochs in BloodMNIST and Retina, respectively. 2) In local model training, we update local model weights again with the SGD optimizer. We fixed the total training epochs for 400 iterations and performed our experiments in two different settings. We reported our results for 80 and 40 communication rounds with local update epochs (E) of 5 and 10, warmed up with 15 and 10 rounds of FedAvg, respectively. Hyperparameters are detailed in the Supplementary.

3.3 Comparison with Baselines

We compared our results with common and state-of-the-art (SOTA) FL algorithms. Among common methods, we choose **FedAvg** [18] and **FedProx** [13] as two main baselines. FedProx solves performance degradation compared to FedAvg in the Non-IID setting by adding a regularization term for local training, which prevents divergence of local model weights from the server model. We also compare with SOTA FL methods that share similar ideas with ours by

Table 2. Classification accuracies reported on the Retina dataset comparing synthesizing with `FedImpres` (CE loss) (Eq. 2) vs. vanilla CE loss. In both cases, we initialize the synthesis step with random noise.

Dataset	Retina	
Local update epochs (E)	5	10
Data synthesis w CE loss	73.9	75.4
Data synthesis w FedImpres loss	**78.1**	**80.6**

adding global synthetic data or editing local training. **VHL** [24], which generates global virtual data using untrained StyleGAN [11] and does not update global virtual data during training. We also compare our results with **FedVSS** [30], which adversarially modifies local data using the server model to synthesize more general data for each client. Finally, we compare our results to SOTA methods **FedCurv** [22] and **FedReg** [26] that focus on tackling the issue of catastrophic forgetting in FL.

The results are illustrated in Table 1. Although medical initialization has the best results, we show that even with CIFAR-10 and noise initialization, we outperform SOTA in most experiments, and this proves the effectiveness of the synthesis step regardless of the initialization. In all of the experiments `FedImpres` improves FedAvg by a large margin. This can be particularly observed when the level of heterogeneity is higher with $\alpha = 0.005$ and the Retina dataset. Although FedProx was designed to have smoother local training by adding a penalty for divergence from the server model, this is harmful to severe heterogeneity due to a shortage in learning local data. Compared to VHL and FedVSS, we surpass them by virtue of our adaptive and unified synthesis data approach among clients, correspondingly. Although, FedCurv achieves close results to our method on Retina dataset, its performance degrades when facing label shift on the BloodMnist dataset. FedReg does not perform well on both datasets since it's not designed for architectures with batch normalization.

3.4 Ablation Studies

To assess the effect of our data synthesis algorithm, we consider another synthetic data generation variant adopted by our proposed method and study its performance on the Retina dataset, as it is a real-life dataset and has both label imbalance and domain shift. For this, we omit the constraint of globalizing data synthesized to distribution seized by the server model in Eq. (2) and optimize only with CE loss. For both methods, we use random noise to initialize data synthesis to omit any initialization bias. As shown in Table 2, the proposed `FedImpres` approach surpasses its other variant, showing the effectiveness of its data synthesis algorithm for data generation.

4 Conclusion

Previous FL approaches suffer from catastrophic forgetting in their local training due to the heterogeneity of the distributed data. This problem becomes more pronounced for clients dealing with medical data due to the heterogeneity caused by both domain shift and label imbalance across clients. To this end, we proposed a novel method called `FedImpres`, which uses the server model to generate synthetic data at each round to account for the server model's information in the local training and avoid forgetting. We demonstrated how this method could achieve superior performance for two benchmark medical datasets, particularly in highly heterogeneous cases. Moreover, the ablation section showed the data synthesis algorithm's effectiveness. It is worth noting the synthetic data-restoring method is efficient without training additional generative models. Furthermore, our proposed method shows the potential to be applied in many healthcare applications using data from multiple centers. We will explore integrating our research with other practical applications in the medical domain. This may involve testing our approach on various medical datasets and improving the pipeline to meet the preferred standards of clinical practice.

Acknowledgement. This work is supported in part through computational resources and services provided by Advanced Research Computing at the University of British Columbia, Natural Sciences and Engineering Research Council of Canada (NSERC), the Canadian Institutes of Health Research (CIHR), Compute Canada, and Vector Institute.

Disclosure of Interests. The authors have no competing interests to declare that are relevant to the content of this article.

References

1. Acevedo, A., Merino, A., Alférez, S., Molina, Á., Boldú, L., Rodellar, J.: A dataset of microscopic peripheral blood cell images for development of automatic recognition systems. Data Brief **30** (2020)
2. Ayromlou, S., Abolmaesumi, P., Tsang, T., Li, X.: Class impression for data-free incremental learning. In: Medical Image Computing and Computer Assisted Intervention–MICCAI 2022: 25th International Conference, Singapore, 18–22 September 2022, Proceedings, Part IV, pp. 320–329. Springer (2022)
3. Batista, F.J.F., Diaz-Aleman, T., Sigut, J., Alayon, S., Arnay, R., Angel-Pereira, D.: Rim-one dl: a unified retinal image database for assessing glaucoma using deep learning. Image Anal. Stereol. **39**(3), 161–167 (2020)
4. Boyd, S., Parikh, N., Chu, E., Peleato, B., Eckstein, J., et al.: Distributed optimization and statistical learning via the alternating direction method of multipliers. Found. Trends Mach. Learn. **3**(1), 1–122 (2011)
5. De Lange, M., et al.: A continual learning survey: defying forgetting in classification tasks. IEEE Trans. Pattern Anal. Mach. Intell. **44**(7), 3366–3385 (2021)

6. Diaz-Pinto, A., Morales, S., Naranjo, V., Köhler, T., Mossi, J.M., Navea, A.: Cnns for automatic glaucoma assessment using fundus images: an extensive validation. Biomed. Eng. Online **18**, 1–19 (2019)
7. Dinsdale, N.K., Jenkinson, M., Namburete, A.I.: Fedharmony: unlearning scanner bias with distributed data. In: Medical Image Computing and Computer Assisted Intervention–MICCAI 2022: 25th International Conference, Singapore, 18–22 September 2022, Proceedings, Part VIII, pp. 695–704. Springer (2022)
8. He, C., et al.: Fedml: a research library and benchmark for federated machine learning. arXiv preprint arXiv:2007.13518 (2020)
9. Jiang, M., Wang, Z., Dou, Q.: Harmofl: harmonizing local and global drifts in federated learning on heterogeneous medical images. In: Proceedings of the AAAI Conference on Artificial Intelligence, vol. 36, pp. 1087–1095 (2022)
10. Karimireddy, S.P., Kale, S., Mohri, M., Reddi, S., Stich, S., Suresh, A.T.: Scaffold: stochastic controlled averaging for federated learning. In: International Conference on Machine Learning, pp. 5132–5143. PMLR (2020)
11. Karras, T., Laine, S., Aila, T.: A style-based generator architecture for generative adversarial networks. In: Proceedings of the IEEE/CVF Conference on Computer Vision and Pattern Recognition, pp. 4401–4410 (2019)
12. Krizhevsky, A., Hinton, G., et al.: Learning multiple layers of features from tiny images (2009)
13. Li, T., Sahu, A.K., Zaheer, M., Sanjabi, M., Talwalkar, A., Smith, V.: Federated optimization in heterogeneous networks. Proc. Mach. Learn. Syst. **2**, 429–450 (2020)
14. Li, X., Huang, K., Yang, W., Wang, S., Zhang, Z.: On the convergence of fedavg on non-iid data. In: International Conference on Learning Representations (2020)
15. Li, X., Jiang, M., Zhang, X., Kamp, M., Dou, Q.: Fedbn: federated learning on non-iid features via local batch normalization. In: International Conference on Learning Representations (2021)
16. Liu, Q., Chen, C., Qin, J., Dou, Q., Heng, P.A.: FEDDG: federated domain generalization on medical image segmentation via episodic learning in continuous frequency space. In: Proceedings of the IEEE/CVF Conference on Computer Vision and Pattern Recognition, pp. 1013–1023 (2021)
17. Luo, K., Li, X., Lan, Y., Gao, M.: Gradma: a gradient-memory-based accelerated federated learning with alleviated catastrophic forgetting. In: Proceedings of the IEEE/CVF Conference on Computer Vision and Pattern Recognition, pp. 3708–3717 (2023)
18. McMahan, B., Moore, E., Ramage, D., Hampson, S., y Arcas, B.A.: Communication-efficient learning of deep networks from decentralized data. In: Artificial Intelligence and Statistics, pp. 1273–1282. PMLR (2017)
19. Orlando, J.I., et al.: Refuge challenge: a unified framework for evaluating automated methods for glaucoma assessment from fundus photographs. Med. Image Anal. **59**, 101570 (2020)
20. O'herrin, J.K., Fost, N., Kudsk, K.A.: Health insurance portability accountability act (hipaa) regulations: effect on medical record research. Ann. Surg. **239**(6), 772 (2004)
21. Shin, M., Hwang, C., Kim, J., Park, J., Bennis, M., Kim, S.L.: Xor mixup: privacy-preserving data augmentation for one-shot federated learning. In: Proceedings of the International Conference on Machine Learning (2020)
22. Shoham, N., et al.: Overcoming forgetting in federated learning on non-iid data. In: NeurIPS Workshop (2019)

23. Sivaswamy, J., Krishnadas, S., Joshi, G.D., Jain, M., Tabish, A.U.S.: Drishti-gs: retinal image dataset for optic nerve head (onh) segmentation. In: 2014 IEEE 11th International Symposium on Biomedical Imaging (ISBI), pp. 53–56. IEEE (2014)
24. Tang, Z., Zhang, Y., Shi, S., He, X., Han, B., Chu, X.: Virtual homogeneity learning: defending against data heterogeneity in federated learning. In: International Conference on Machine Learning, pp. 21111–21132. PMLR (2022)
25. Wang, H., Yurochkin, M., Sun, Y., Papailiopoulos, D., Khazaeni, Y.: Federated learning with matched averaging. In: International Conference on Learning Representations (2020)
26. Xu, C., Hong, Z., Huang, M., Jiang, T.: Acceleration of federated learning with alleviated forgetting in local training. In: International Conference on Learning Representations (2022). https://openreview.net/forum?id=541PxiEKN3F
27. Yang, J., et al.: Medmnist v2-a large-scale lightweight benchmark for 2d and 3d biomedical image classification. Scientific Data **10**(1), 41 (2023)
28. Yao, H., Guo, Y., Yang, C.: Source-free unsupervised domain adaptation with surrogate data generation. In: Proceedings of NeurIPS 2021 Workshop on Distribution Shifts: Connecting Methods and Applications (2021)
29. Yeganeh, Y., Farshad, A., Navab, N., Albarqouni, S.: Inverse distance aggregation for federated learning with non-iid data. In: Domain Adaptation and Representation Transfer, and Distributed and Collaborative Learning: Second MICCAI Workshop, DART 2020, and First MICCAI Workshop, DCL 2020, Held in Conjunction with MICCAI 2020, Lima, Peru, 4–8 October 2020, Proceedings 2, pp. 150–159. Springer (2020)
30. Zhu, W., Luo, J.: Federated medical image analysis with virtual sample synthesis. In: Medical Image Computing and Computer Assisted Intervention–MICCAI 2022: 25th International Conference, Singapore, 18–22 September 2022, Proceedings, Part III, pp. 728–738. Springer (2022)

A Federated Learning-Friendly Approach for Parameter-Efficient Fine-Tuning of SAM in 3D Segmentation

Mothilal Asokan, Joseph Geo Benjamin(✉), Mohammad Yaqub, and Karthik Nandakumar

Mohamed bin Zayed University of Artificial Intelligence (MBZUAI), Abu Dhabi, United Arab Emirates
{mothilal.asokan,joseph.benjamin,mohammad.yaqub, karthik.nandakumar}@mbzuai.ac.ae

Abstract. Adapting foundation models for medical image analysis requires finetuning them on a considerable amount of data because of extreme distribution shifts between natural (source) data used for pre-training and medical (target) data. However, collecting task-specific medical data for such finetuning at a central location raises many privacy concerns. Although Federated learning (FL) provides an effective means for training on private decentralized data, communication costs in federating large foundation models can quickly become a significant bottleneck, impacting the solution's scalability. In this work, we address this problem of 'efficient communication while ensuring effective learning in FL' by combining the strengths of Parameter-Efficient Fine-tuning (PEFT) with FL. Specifically, we study plug-and-play Low-Rank Adapters (LoRA) in a federated manner to adapt the Segment Anything Model (SAM) for 3D medical image segmentation. Unlike prior works that utilize LoRA and finetune the entire decoder, we critically analyze the contribution of each granular component of SAM on finetuning performance. Thus, we identify specific layers to be federated that are very efficient in terms of communication cost while producing on-par accuracy. Our experiments show that retaining the parameters of the SAM model (including most of the decoder) in their original state during adaptation is beneficial because fine-tuning on small datasets tends to distort the inherent capabilities of the underlying foundation model. On Fed-KiTS, our approach decreases communication cost (∼48× ↓) compared to full fine-tuning while increasing performance (∼6% ↑ Dice score) in 3D segmentation tasks. Our approach performs similar to SAMed while achieving ∼2.8× reduction in communication and parameters to be finetuned. We further validate our approach with experiments on Fed-IXI and Prostate MRI datasets. Our code is available at https://github.com/BioMedIA-MBZUAI/FLAP-SAM.

Keywords: Federated Learning · Foundation Model · 3D Medical Image Segmentation · Parameter-Efficient Fine-Tuning

Supplementary Information The online version contains supplementary material available at https://doi.org/10.1007/978-3-031-77610-6_21.

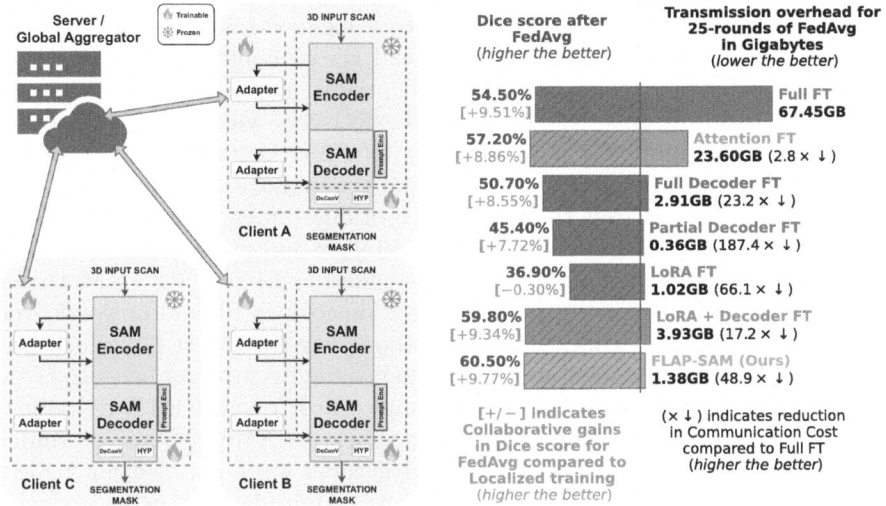

Fig. 1. (Left) The proposed FLAP-SAM framework and (Right). The comparison (in terms of Dice score(%), Collaborative gains(%) and Communication Cost(× ↓)) of our method against other fine-tuning methods on Fed-KITS2019 [26].

1 Introduction

Segmentation is one of the cornerstone tasks in modern medical image analysis for automated diagnosis and disease monitoring. While the advent of foundational models has pushed the boundaries of the state-of-the-art in many computer vision applications, such benefits are yet to transfer fully to the medical imaging domain [33]. For example, the Segment Anything Model (SAM) [14] has an excellent zero-shot generalization to new distributions and tasks involving natural images. However, the SAM model fails to generalize well across diverse medical imaging modalities due to the insurmountable distribution shifts [11]. Works like [6,10] highlight a substantial performance gap between the zero-shot inference and training on domain-specific medical images despite using various prompts in SAM. MSA [29] and SAM-Med2D [4] improve SAM by using tailored prompting techniques in 2D medical images. However, creating such prompts for each 2D slice of 3D data is labor-intensive.

The usual approach has been fine-tuning SAM for the target application using large task-specific datasets e.g., MedSAM [20]. For tasks with significant distribution shifts with limited data, the decoder block of SAM is fine-tuned while leaving the encoder untouched. In contrast to fine-tuning all parameters, parameter-efficient fine-tuning(PEFT) methods fine-tune only a minimal number of parameters using representative data such as prompt tuning [12] and low-rank adapters (LoRA) [9]. Several works [22,28,32] have employed LoRA for fine-tuning, resulting in superior performance in various 2D segmentation tasks. For 3d segmentation, [2] uses factor tuning (FacT) adapters [13] for training. However, accessing diverse medical data for such finetuning is not always feasible because relevant datasets specific to a medical task may not be available with any single entity. It is often spread across multiple institutions and cannot be shared due to privacy and confidentiality constraints [26]. While the data decentralization issue can be handled effectively with federated learning (FL) [16,21], the ginormous parameter size of SAM (~100M-700M) makes it impractical for FL as it imposes a substantial communication cost.

In this work, we uncover the importance of fine-tuning various components of SAM when adapted for 3D medical segmentation and propose **FLAP-SAM**, *a PEFT approach involving LoRA that is amenable to FL* (see Fig. 1). Moreover, high parameter efficiency reduces communication costs in FL and prevents overfitting in data-limited scenarios. With methods like MA-SAM [2], which uses FacT adapters for 3D segmentation, it is challenging to federate because of the tensor decomposition involved. Hence, we employ LoRA, which is FL-friendly, to customize SAM for 3D medical image segmentation. SAMed [32] uses a similar approach where LoRA and the entire SAM decoder are fine-tuned for 2D segmentation. Our approach selectively finetunes certain decoder parts, reducing parameters and communication costs.

2 Preliminaries

Overview of SAM: The architecture of SAM [14] can be decoupled into three major components: the *Image Encoder* (IE) to compute image embeddings, the *Prompt Encoder* (PE) to generate prompt embeddings, and the *Mask Decoder* (MD) that combines the image and prompt embeddings to generate segmentation masks as shown in Fig. 2. Utilizing ViT [5] as the backbone, IE extracts image features through a sequence of L transformer blocks. Meanwhile, PE takes various input prompts in the form of points, boxes, or masks and encodes them into prompt embeddings to aid in segmentation tasks. We operate SAM in the *fully automatic* mode, in which a regular grid of foreground points is presented as input prompts to the PE, thus eliminating the dependence on user-defined prompts. MD performs cross-attention between the image and prompt embeddings, employing transposed convolutional layers for up-scaling back to image dimension (UP) and a hyper multi-layer perceptron (HYP) to produce segmentation masks. Following [2], we use a slightly modified SAM mask decoder that has two additional transposed convolutional layers, which up-sample the feature maps by 16× to match the resolution of the input while ensuring improved discrimination of small anatomical structures or lesions in medical images [24].

For simplicity, let θ_{IE}, θ_{PE}, and θ_{MD} denote the parameters of IE, PE, and MD, respectively. Also, θ_{IE} can be further partitioned as θ_{IE-AT} and θ_{IE-NA}, where θ_{IE-AT} denotes the parameters of all the attention layers within IE and θ_{IE-NA} represents all the other parameters in IE not related to the attention layers. On the other hand, θ_{MD} can be partitioned as θ_{MD-TR}, θ_{MD-UP}, and θ_{MD-HYP}, where θ_{MD-TR} denotes the parameters of all the transformer blocks within MD (such as self-attention, cross-attention from tokens to image embeddings (t2i), and cross-attention from image embeddings to tokens (i2t)), $\theta_{\texttt{MD-UP}}$ denotes the parameters of the transposed convolutional layers used for upscaling, and $\theta_{\texttt{MD-HYP}}$ represents the parameters of HYP.

PEFT Formulation: The most straightforward approach to adapt a SAM model for a downstream task is to fine-tune all its parameters, including $\theta_{\texttt{IE}}$, $\theta_{\texttt{PE}}$, and $\theta_{\texttt{MD}}$. This full fine-tuning (FullFT) strategy requires more memory footprint to store a copy of all the updated parameters and often leads to overfitting when the data is severely limited. Recent works have shown that fine-tuning only the attention layers of a transformer encoder is sufficient for good adaptation [27]. This approach is called attention fine-tuning (AttnFT), where only $\theta_{\texttt{IE-AT}}$ and $\theta_{\texttt{MD}}$ are updated. Typically, the attention-related parameters of a transformer encoder constitute one-third of its overall parameters. Thus, AttnFT leads to some improvement in parameter efficiency and generally provides good performance on downstream tasks. Another common approach is to freeze the image encoder and fine-tune the entire mask decoder. This is because the cross-attention layers in the decoder focus on specific patches in the image embeddings corresponding to the prompts and transform them into segmentation predictions [31]. We call this approach DecFT, where $\theta_{\texttt{MD}}$ is updated. It is also possible to freeze all the parameters and fine-tune only the output layers, namely, UP and HYP. This approach is analogous to linear probing in classification tasks, which we refer to as partial decoder fine tuning (PDecFT). Since only a small fraction of parameters, namely, $\theta_{\texttt{MD-UP}}$, and $\theta_{\texttt{MD-HYP}}$ are updated, PDecFT has high parameter efficiency but usually provides only sub-optimal performance.

LoRA Adapters: Low-rank adaptation [9] is a promising PEFT technique widely used for adapting foundation models to downstream tasks. Each attention layer within a transformer block has four weight (projection) matrices W_q (query), W_k (key), W_v (value), and W_o (output), where each $W \in \mathbb{R}^{d \times d'}$. The core idea of LoRA is to constrain the modifications to a pre-trained weight matrix W to a linear update matrix ΔW, which can be further constrained using a low-rank decomposition, i.e., $\Delta W = BA$, where $B \in \mathbb{R}^{d \times r}, A \in \mathbb{R}^{r \times d'}$ and the rank $r \ll \min\{d, d'\}$. This approach effectively reduces the parameter space while preserving the essential information needed for adaptation. W is frozen during fine-tuning, and only A and B matrices are updated. For input x, the output $\tilde{x}$ is computed as follows:

$$\tilde{x} = (W + \alpha \Delta W)x = Wx + \alpha \Delta W x = Wx + \alpha BAx, \qquad (1)$$

where α is a scale parameter. Following [9], we employ LoRA only to the projection matrices W_q and W_v in all the Γ attention layers of IE and MD. Let $\theta_{\texttt{LoRA}}$ represent the set of all LoRA parameters, where $\theta_{\texttt{LoRA}} = \{A_q^\ell, A_v^\ell, B_q^\ell, B_v^\ell\}_{\ell=1}^{\Gamma}$. When only the LoRA parameters are updated during fine-tuning, we refer to this case as LoRAFT. While this approach also has good parameter efficiency, it typically results in sub-optimal performance for segmentation tasks. To improve this, in SAMed [32], both the decoder and LoRA are fine-tuned. Here, $\theta_{\texttt{MD}}$

and θ_{LoRA} parameters are updated together, and we represent this approach as LoRADecFT.

Federated Learning: In an FL system, K clients can collaboratively train a global model with parameters Θ. The goal is to solve the following optimization problem:

$$\min_{\Theta \in \mathbb{R}^T} \frac{1}{K} \sum_{k=1}^{K} \mathcal{L}_k^{seg}(\Theta), \tag{2}$$

where $\mathcal{L}_k^{seg}(\Theta) = E_{x \sim \mathcal{D}_k}[\mathcal{L}_k^{seg}(\Theta; x)]$ is the loss function of the kth client ($k \in [1, K]$), $\mathcal{D}_k$ represents the data distribution of the kth client, and $T = |\Theta|$ is the number of parameters that need to be learned. Note that if the distributions $\mathcal{D}_i$ and $\mathcal{D}_j$ are different for clients i and j, the scenario is referred to as non-iid (not independent and identically distributed). A widely used method for solving the optimization problem is FedAvg [21]. At each round, the server broadcasts the global model to each client. Then, all clients conduct local training on their data and send back the updated model to the server. Finally, the server updates the global model as a weighted average of these local model updates. The server update at round n in FedAvg can be formulated as follows:

$$\Theta^{n+1} = \sum_{k=1}^{K} \alpha_k \Theta_k^n, \tag{3}$$

where Θ_k^n denotes the local model of kth client in round n and α_k is the weight assigned for each client.

3 Proposed FLAP-SAM Approach

We aim to efficiently and effectively adapt the SAM for medical image segmentation tasks using limited data distributed across multiple entities. Based on this consideration, we propose to update both θ_{LoRA} as well as the final decoder output layers $\theta_{\text{MD-UP}}$ and $\theta_{\text{MD-HYP}}$. This leads to the proposed fine-tuning for SAM, a hybrid of PDecFT and LoRAFT, as shown in Fig. 2. Though there is a marginal increase in the number of parameters compared to LoRAFT, the proposed approach performs well because FLAP-SAM provides enough flexibility to be effectively fine-tuned. Moreover, since almost all the parameters of the original foundation model are retained without modification, its inherent capabilities remain unaffected. Another benefit is its memory efficiency, and the small parameter size of the proposed adapter makes it possible to learn them collaboratively via FL while greatly reducing communication costs.

When aggregating LoRA parameters (θ_{LoRA}), the kth client sends $\{A_{q,k}^{\ell}, A_{v,k}^{\ell}, B_{q,k}^{\ell}, B_{v,k}^{\ell}\}_{\ell=1}^{\Gamma}$ to the server. The server first needs to reconstruct $\Delta W_{q,k}^{\ell} = B_{q,k}^{\ell} \cdot A_{q,k}^{\ell}$ and $\Delta W_{v,k}^{\ell} = B_{v,k}^{\ell} \cdot A_{v,k}^{\ell}$ for each ℓ and k, then performs FedAvg as shown in Eq. (3) to get the aggregated global weight matrices ΔW_q^{ℓ} and

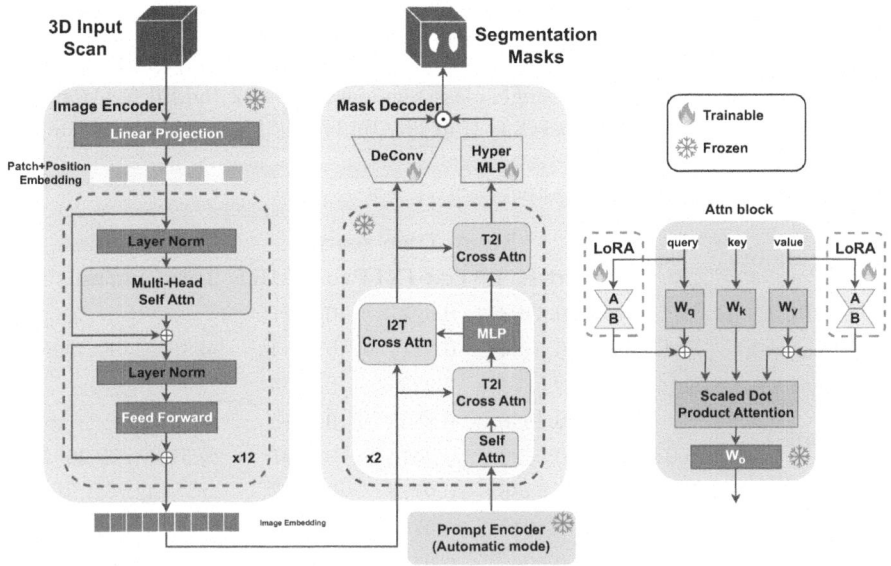

Fig. 2. Architecture of the proposed plug-and-play adapter. Only the decoder output layers and LoRAs are fine-tuned, while the remaining parameters in SAM are frozen.

ΔW_v^ℓ of each attention layer ℓ. Finally, the server applies singular value decomposition to decompose the aggregated matrices back to global LoRA parameters $\{A_q^\ell, B_q^\ell, A_v^\ell, B_v^\ell\}_{\ell=1}^{\Gamma}$, which are sent back to the clients. We refer to this federated learning of plug-and-play SAM adapter as FLAP-SAM.

4 Experiments

Datasets: We utilize **Fed-KITS2019**, a 6-client federated version of the KiTS19 dataset from FLamby [26], which was created from the Kidney Tumor Segmentation Challenge 2019 in CT scans [7,8]. Each client's train/test split is 9/3, 11/3, 9/3, 9/3, 12/4, and 24/6. The preprocessing pipeline comprises intensity clipping (5th and 95th percentile of image intensities of each client were calculated) followed by z-scale normalization, where we subtract the mean and divide by the standard deviation of the image intensities. **Fed-IXI**, extracted from the Information eXtraction from Images - IXI database [23,25] of brain T1 MRIs from 3 hospitals (Guys, HH, and IOP) contains 249/62, 145/36 and 59/15 train/test splits respectively. In a preprocessing step, min-max normalization was applied to each scan and padded with zeros in the axial plane (final shape $83 \times 64 \times 64$). **Prostate MRI** is a multi-site segmentation dataset proposed by Liu *et al.* [18], comprises prostate T2-weighted MRI data from six different data sources (*i.e.*, Site A to F) of the three publicly available datasets: NCI-ISBI13 dataset [1], I2CVB dataset [15] and PROMISE12 dataset [17]. Each site

Table 1. Comparison on all datasets for different fine-tuning methods. ‡— FL setting of MA-SAM is not feasible since decomposing FacT tensors after aggregation is not possible; a centralized score is provided for performance comparison in 3D segmentation. ∗∗ — Parameter counts for single class segmentation task (add $0.134M$ params for each additional class). The baseline (full fine-tuning) is highlighted in Blue and our method in Pink.

Experiments	Setting	Mean Dice score			Trainable/ Total params**
		Fed-KiTS	Fed-IXI	Prost.MRI	
FullFT (baseline) $\{\theta_{IE}, \theta_{PE}, \theta_{MD}\}$	Local	0.4493	0.9777	0.8421	90.399M/90.399M (100%)
	Federated	0.5444	0.9811	0.9084	
	Centralized	0.5274	0.9834	0.8955	
AttnFT $\{\theta_{IE-AT}, \theta_{MD}\}$	Local	0.4838	0.8848	0.6315	29.575M/90.399M (32.7%)
	Federated	0.5724	0.9674	0.8797	
	Centralized	0.5486	0.9774	0.8957	
DecFT $\{\theta_{MD}\}$	Local	0.4213	0.9750	0.8200	3.768M/90.399M (4.2%)
	Federated	0.5068	0.9771	0.8101	
	Centralized	0.5179	0.9789	0.8587	
LoRAFT $\{\theta_{LoRA}\}$	Local	0.3717	0.9728	0.8386	1.368M/91.767M (1.5%)
	Federated	0.3687	0.9777	0.8578	
	Centralized	0.5242	0.9798	0.8893	
LoRADecFT (SAMed)[20] $\{\theta_{LoRA}, \theta_{MD}\}$	Local	0.5053	0.9829	0.8929	5.270M/91.767M (5.8%)
	Federated	0.5987	0.9836	0.8949	
	Centralized	0.6100	0.9852	0.9039	
PDecFT $\{\theta_{UP}, \theta_{HYP}\}$	Local	0.3764	0.9678	0.7890	0.344M/90.399M (0.4%)
	Federated	0.4536	0.9693	0.7017	
	Centralized	0.4793	0.9711	0.8008	
FLAP-SAM (ours) $\{\theta_{LoRA}, \theta_{UP}, \theta_{HYP}\}$	Local	0.5069	0.9829	0.8845	1.712M/91.767M (1.9%)
	Federated	0.6046	0.9834	0.8867	
	Centralized	0.5980	0.9851	0.9044	
MA-SAM‡[2]	Centralized	0.6023	0.9707	0.9125	28.667M/115.298M (25%)

has 30, 30, 19, 13, 12, 12 MRI scans of patients respectively and were randomly divided into train($\approx 80\%$) and test($\approx 20\%$) sets. Since they were acquired with varying imaging protocols and contain heterogeneous data distributions, we normalized each site to zero mean and unit variance to reduce the intensity variance among different sites. We resized it to 224×224 in the axial plane.

Implementation Details: We follow the input format and data augmentation as described in [2], conducting all experiments using the "vit_b" version of

SAM on an NVIDIA A100-SXM4-40GB GPU. The input to the model is of size $(N \times H \times W)$, which consists of every set of N consecutive slices ($N = 5$). In LoRA, we initialize matrix A from a random Gaussian distribution while setting matrix B to zero and rank to 32. The fine-tuning process employs a hybrid segmentation loss, combining cross-entropy loss and Dice loss as $\mathcal{L}^{seg} = \alpha \mathcal{L}^{CE} + \beta \mathcal{L}^{Dice}$, with weighting factors $\alpha = 0.2$ and $\beta = 0.8$ following [32]. The training utilizes the Adam optimizer with a batch size of 32. We compare federated learning with localized (using client-owned data alone) and centralized (all data pooled) settings. We test each site data separately for all fine-tuning strategies, and the results are tabulated in Table 1.

Table 2. Average Dice score across local test data in the federated setting on Fed-KiTS19 dataset. (Left) different rank values of LoRA; (Right) different low-rank adapter methods.

LoRA rank	Mean Dice	Trainable / Total params	Adapter	Mean Dice	Trainable / Total params
32	0.605	1.846M/91.901M	LoRA	0.605	1.846M/91.901M
16	0.599	1.162M/91.217M	DoRA	0.592	1.846M/91.901M
4	0.600	0.649M/90.704M	MoLE	0.603	4.583M/94.637M

4.1 Results and Discussion

Our proposed FLAP-SAM method achieves 6% absolute improvement in Dice score compared to the FullFT approach, with a ~49× reduction in communication overhead on Fed-KITS. Due to the small size of the dataset, the FullFT approach easily results in overfitting, highlighting the importance of using PEFT methods in limited data settings [3]. The Attention fine-tuning (AttnFT) only achieves half of our improvement (2.8% less than FLAP-SAM) and still incurs ~17× more communication cost than our method. Both LoRAFT and PDecFT are more efficient but have lower Dice scores than our method. The LoRADecFT achieves an equivalent dice score to our method, but our method is ~2.8× more efficient regarding parameters and communication. We conduct ablation on the rank parameter of LoRA in FL, and the results are shown in Table 2. We observe that a lower LoRA rank significantly reduces the trainable parameters with a marginal degradation in the Dice score. We also conduct experiments with other low-rank adapters like DoRA [19] and MoLE [30], which only show marginal performance differences among the adapters.

We also benchmark FLAP-SAM against MA-SAM [2], which uses a 3D adapter along with FacT for fine-tuning. We perform this comparison only in the centralized setting because the decomposition of ΔW back to FacT-Tensor-Train or FacT-Tucker formats [13] after federated aggregation is not straightforward. Although MA-SAM produces comparable results to our method (see Table 1) in a centralized setting, it uses 28.7M trainable parameters (~16× more than our method). This validates our choice of using LoRA, which is both parameter-efficient and FL-friendly.

5 Conclusion

In this work, we have tackled adapting a foundational segmentation model (SAM) for 3D medical image segmentation by incorporating an effective PEFT strategy. We critically analyze the LoRA adapter's impact and various SAM components to make the fine-tuning for dense 3D segmentation tasks amenable to FL. Our approach simultaneously addresses data scarcity, overfitting, and communication overhead challenges, resulting in a practical and cost-efficient solution. Our current work analyses various fine-tuning methods in the context of FedAVG [21]; an interesting future direction would be studying the effects of various federated optimization strategies on low-rank adapters for datasets with considerable distribution shifts.

References

1. Bloch, N., et al.: NCI-ISBI 2013 challenge: automated segmentation of prostate structures. Cancer Imaging Arch. **370**(6), 5 (2015)
2. Chen, C., et al.: MA-SAM: modality-agnostic SAM adaptation for 3D medical image segmentation. arXiv preprint: arXiv:2309.08842 (2023)
3. Chen, G., Liu, F., Meng, Z., Liang, S.: Revisiting parameter-efficient tuning: are we really there yet? In: Proceedings of the 2022 Conference on Empirical Methods in Natural Language Processing, pp. 2612–2626 (2022)
4. Cheng, D., Qin, Z., Jiang, Z., Zhang, S., Lao, Q., Li, K.: Sam on medical images: A comprehensive study on three prompt modes. arXiv preprint: arXiv:2305.00035 (2023)
5. Dosovitskiy, A., et al.: An image is worth 16x16 words: transformers for image recognition at scale. In: ICLR (2021)
6. He, S., Bao, R., Li, J., Grant, P.E., Ou, Y.: Accuracy of segment-anything model (SAM) in medical image segmentation tasks. arXiv preprint: arXiv:2304.09324 (2023)
7. Heller, N., et al.: The state of the art in kidney and kidney tumor segmentation in contrast-enhanced CT imaging: results of the KiTs19 challenge. Med. Image Anal., 101821 (2020)
8. Heller, N., et al.: The KiTs19 challenge data: 300 kidney tumor cases with clinical context, CT semantic segmentations, and surgical outcomes. arXiv preprint: arXiv:1904.00445 (2019)
9. Hu, E.J., et al.: LoRA: low-rank adaptation of large language models. In: ICLR (2022)
10. Huang, Y., et al.: Segment anything model for medical images? Med. Image Anal. **92**, 103061 (2024)
11. Huix, J.P., Ganeshan, A.R., Haslum, J.F., Söderberg, M., Matsoukas, C., Smith, K.: Are natural domain foundation models useful for medical image classification? In: Proceedings of the IEEE/CVF Winter Conference on Applications of Computer Vision, pp. 7634–7643 (2024)

12. Jia, M., et al.: Visual prompt tuning. In: ECCV, pp. 709–727. Springer (2022)
13. Jie, S., Deng, Z.H.: FacT: factor-tuning for lightweight adaptation on vision transformer. In: Proceedings of the AAAI Conference on Artificial Intelligence, vol. 37, pp. 1060–1068 (2023)
14. Kirillov, A., et al.: Segment anything. In: ICCV, pp. 4015–4026 (2023)
15. Lemaître, G., Martí, R., Freixenet, J., Vilanova, J.C., Walker, P.M., Meriaudeau, F.: Computer-aided detection and diagnosis for prostate cancer based on mono and multi-parametric MRI: a review. Comput. Biol. Med. **60**, 8–31 (2015)
16. Li, T., Sahu, A.K., Zaheer, M., Sanjabi, M., Talwalkar, A., Smith, V.: Federated optimization in heterogeneous networks. Proc. Mach. Learn. Syst. **2**, 429–450 (2020)
17. Litjens, G., et al.: Evaluation of prostate segmentation algorithms for MRI: the promise12 challenge. Med. Image Anal. **18**(2), 359–373 (2014)
18. Liu, Q., Dou, Q., Heng, P.A.: Shape-aware meta-learning for generalizing prostate MRI segmentation to unseen domains. In: MICCAI (2020)
19. Liu, S.Y., et al.: DoRA: weight-decomposed low-rank adaptation. arXiv preprint: arXiv:2402.09353 (2024)
20. Ma, J., He, Y., Li, F., Han, L., You, C., Wang, B.: Segment anything in medical images. Nat. Commun. **15**(1), 654 (2024)
21. McMahan, B., Moore, E., Ramage, D., Hampson, S., y Arcas, B.A.: Communication-efficient learning of deep networks from decentralized data. In: Artificial Intelligence and Statistics, pp. 1273–1282. PMLR (2017)
22. Paranjape, J.N., Nair, N.G., Sikder, S., Vedula, S.S., Patel, V.M.: AdaptiveSAM: towards efficient tuning of SAM for surgical scene segmentation. arXiv preprint: arXiv:2308.03726 (2023)
23. Pérez-García, F., Sparks, R., Ourselin, S.: TorchIO: aPpython library for efficient loading, preprocessing, augmentation and patch-based sampling of medical images in deep learning. Comput. Methods Programs Biomed. **208**, 106236 (2021)
24. Ronneberger, O., Fischer, P., Brox, T.: U-net: convolutional networks for biomedical image segmentation. In: MICCAI 2015: 18th International Conference, Munich, Germany, 5-9 October 2015, Proceedings, Part III 18, pp. 234–241. Springer (2015)
25. Team, B.D.: IXI-dataset. https://brain-development.org/ixi-dataset/
26. Ogier du Terrail, J., et al.: FLamby: datasets and benchmarks for cross-silo federated learning in realistic healthcare settings. In: Advances in Neural Information Processing Systems, vol. 35, pp. 5315–5334 (2022)
27. Touvron, H., Cord, M., El-Nouby, A., Verbeek, J., Jégou, H.: Three things everyone should know about vision transformers. In: European Conference on Computer Vision, pp. 497–515. Springer (2022)
28. Wang, A., Islam, M., Xu, M., Zhang, Y., Ren, H.: SAM meets robotic surgery: an empirical study in robustness perspective. arXiv preprint: arXiv:2304.14674 (2023)
29. Wu, J., et al.: Medical SAM adapter: adapting segment anything model for medical image segmentation. arXiv preprint: arXiv:2304.12620 (2023)
30. Wu, X., Huang, S., Wei, F.: MoLE: mixture of LoRA experts. In: The Twelfth International Conference on Learning Representations (2023)
31. Xie, W., Willems, N., Patil, S., Li, Y., Kumar, M.: SAM fewshot finetuning for anatomical segmentation in medical images. In: Proceedings of the IEEE/CVF Winter Conference on Applications of Computer Vision, pp. 3253–3261 (2024)
32. Zhang, K., Liu, D.: Customized segment anything model for medical image segmentation. arXiv preprint: arXiv:2304.13785 (2023)
33. Zhang, S., Metaxas, D.: On the challenges and perspectives of foundation models for medical image analysis. Med. Image Anal. **91**, 102996 (2024)

Probing the Efficacy of Federated Parameter-Efficient Fine-Tuning of Vision Transformers for Medical Image Classification

Naif Alkhunaizi^{ID}, Faris Almalik^{ID}, Rouqaiah Al-Refai^{ID},
Muzammal Naseer^{ID}, and Karthik Nandakumar^{(✉)ID}

Mohamed Bin Zayed University of Artificial Intelligence, Abu Dhabi, UAE
{naif.alkhunaizi,faris.almalik,rouqaiah.al-refai,muzammal.naseer,
karthik.nandakumar}@mbzuai.ac.ae

Abstract. With the advent of large pre-trained transformer models, fine-tuning these models for various downstream tasks is a critical problem. Paucity of training data, the existence of data silos, and stringent privacy constraints exacerbate this fine-tuning problem in the medical imaging domain, creating a strong need for algorithms that enable collaborative fine-tuning of pre-trained models. Moreover, the large size of these models necessitates the use of parameter-efficient fine-tuning (PEFT) to reduce the communication burden in federated learning. In this work, we systematically investigate various federated PEFT strategies for adapting a Vision Transformer (ViT) model (pre-trained on a large natural image dataset) for medical image classification. Apart from evaluating known PEFT techniques, *we introduce new federated variants of PEFT algorithms* such as visual prompt tuning (VPT), low-rank decomposition of visual prompts, stochastic block attention fine-tuning, and hybrid PEFT methods like low-rank adaptation (LoRA)+VPT. Moreover, we perform a *thorough empirical analysis* to identify the optimal PEFT method for the federated setting and understand the impact of data distribution on federated PEFT, especially for out-of-domain (OOD) and non-IID data. The key insight of this study is that while most federated PEFT methods work well for in-domain transfer, there is a substantial accuracy vs. efficiency trade-off when dealing with OOD and non-IID scenarios, which is commonly the case in medical imaging. Specifically, every order of magnitude reduction in fine-tuned/exchanged parameters can lead to a 4% drop in accuracy. Thus, the choice of the initial model is critical for the effectiveness of federated PEFT - rather than starting with general vision models, it is preferable to use medical foundation models (if available) learned using in-domain medical image data. Code: https://github.com/Naiftt/PEFT.

Keywords: Vision Transformers · Parameter-Efficient Fine-tuning · Out-of-Domain Transfer · Federated Learning

---

Supplementary Information The online version contains supplementary material available at https://doi.org/10.1007/978-3-031-77610-6_22.

© The Author(s), under exclusive license to Springer Nature Switzerland AG 2025
M. E. Celebi et al. (Eds.): MICCAI 2024 Workshops, LNCS 15274, pp. 236–245, 2025.
https://doi.org/10.1007/978-3-031-77610-6_22

1 Introduction

Transformer models pre-trained on large-scale data can serve as a foundation for a wide range of downstream tasks [2]. While many general vision foundation models are available [8,23], developing generic medical foundation models is a challenge due to the diversity of imaging modalities and limited availability of well-annotated data [33]. Consider the scenario where a healthcare organization wants to learn transformer models for a range of medical image classification tasks such as chest x-ray disease classification [9,22], melanoma classification [5,24], and tumor categorization [6,18]. There are two main challenges in this problem setting. Firstly, the organization may not have sufficient training data for each task to learn task-specific models from scratch. This can be addressed by fine-tuning a model that is pre-trained on a large-scale, independent dataset (transfer learning) for the task(s) at hand [32]. Secondly, storing a separate model for each task is inefficient due to the large size of transformer models. Parameter-efficient fine-tuning (PEFT) methods such as subset fine-tuning [27], adapter [4], low-rank adaptation (LoRA) [15], and prompt tuning [16] can mitigate this problem by fine-tuning only a small number of parameters for each task and storing the base model along with minimal task-specific parameters. Most PEFT methods exploit the inherently modular transformer architecture (characterized by a sequence of identical self-attention blocks processing a set of tokens).

In some medical imaging applications, even fine-tuning of pre-trained models may not be feasible when a hospital has data only from a few patients. However, a consortium of hospitals may be willing to collaborate to realize PEFT. This introduces the additional challenge of privacy because healthcare data is often regulated by strict privacy guidelines (e.g., GDPR, HIPAA), and it is not possible to pool data from multiple healthcare institutions centrally to enable machine learning. Federated learning (FL) [20] can enable multiple entities to train a model collaboratively without sharing raw data. However, regular exchange of parameters in FL can become a communication burden, especially if the models are large. Hence, the combination of FL and PEFT is an ideal solution that can effectively solve multiple issues (paucity of data, storage of multiple large models, communication cost, and data privacy) simultaneously [34].

In this work, we consider a Vision Transformer (ViT) [8] model pre-trained on natural images as an illustrative example and explore federated PEFT in a cross-silo setting (with a small number of clients), aiming to answer the following questions: **(i)** Which PEFT method works well in conjunction with FL and provides the best accuracy vs. efficiency trade-off? **(ii)** Can federated PEFT transfer well for out-of-domain (OOD) and non-IID (independent, identically distributed) data encountered in medical image analysis? To the best of our knowledge, this is the first study that attempts to systematically study various PEFT strategies for ViTs within the FL framework. Our main contributions are:

1. **New federated variants of PEFT methods**: We are the first to investigate visual prompt tuning (VPT) and low-rank decomposition of visual prompts (DVPT) in a federated setting. We also introduce a new federated

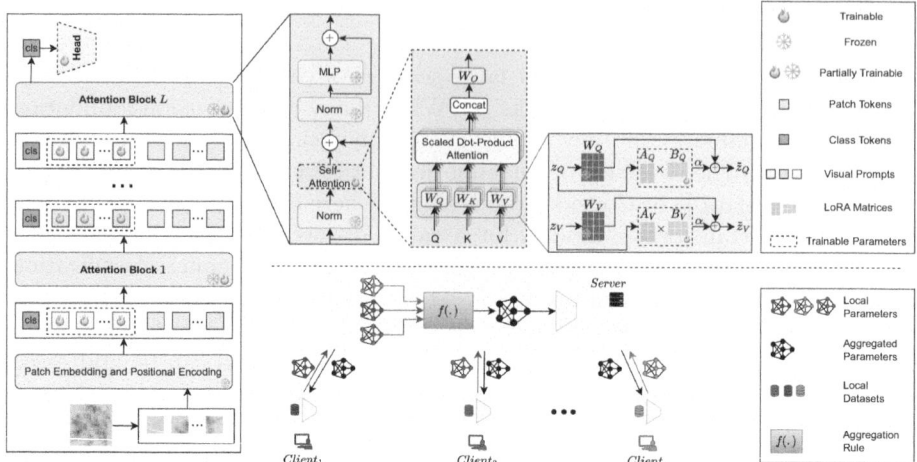

Fig. 1. Adaptation of Vision Transformer (ViT) model using federated PEFT methods. Only the parameters marked as *trainable* are exchanged between the clients and the server, while the frozen parameters are not communicated.

subset fine-tuning approach called stochastic block attention (SBA). Finally, we also consider hybrid methods such as combining LoRA with VPT.

2. **Analysis of federated PEFT methods**: We demonstrate that there is indeed a substantial trade-off between parameter efficiency and model accuracy in federated PEFT, especially for *out-of-domain tasks with non-IID client distributions*. Hence, one must proceed with caution when adapting a general vision model for medical image classification using federated PEFT.

2 Background and Related Work

Vision Transformer (ViT): A pre-trained ViT [8] can be considered as a feature extractor $\mathcal{V}_\Psi$ that maps a given input image $\mathbf{x}$ into a d-dimensional feature vector $\mathbf{f} \in \mathbb{R}^d$, where Ψ denotes the complete set of ViT parameters. For image classification, a classification head $\mathcal{H}_\eta$ is typically trained to learn the mapping between $\mathbf{f}$ and the class label $y \in \{1, 2, \cdots, K\}$, where K is the number of classes and η represents the parameters of the head $\mathcal{H}$. A ViT divides the $\mathbf{x}$ into S non-overlapping patches and a linear patch embedding layer $\mathcal{E}_\Lambda$ (with parameters Λ) is used to project each patch into $\mathbb{R}^d$, resulting in $\mathcal{T}_0 = \{\mathbf{t}_1, \cdots, \mathbf{t}_S\}$ *patch tokens*. Additionally, a learnable *class token* ($\tilde{\mathbf{t}}_0 \in \mathbb{R}^d$) is prepended to the sequence of patch tokens to assimilate the information as the tokens pass through L transformer blocks (denoted by $\mathcal{G}_{\psi_\ell}$). The operations of each transformer block in a ViT can be represented as $\{\tilde{\mathbf{t}}_\ell, \mathcal{T}_\ell\} = \mathcal{G}_{\psi_\ell}(\{\tilde{\mathbf{t}}_{\ell-1}, \mathcal{T}_{\ell-1}\})$, $\ell \in [1, L]$. The class token output by the Lth (last) block (i.e., $\tilde{\mathbf{t}}_L$) can be considered as the final feature representation $\mathbf{f}$. Each transformer block, in turn, consists of three types of parameters (Fig. 1) - ϕ_ℓ denotes the layer normalization parameters of the ℓth

block, θ_ℓ denotes the weight matrices of the multi-head self-attention (MHSA) layer of the ℓth block, and ω_ℓ represents the parameters of the multi-layer perceptron (MLP) of the ℓth block. For convenience, let $\Phi = \{\phi_\ell\}_{\ell=1}^L$, $\Theta = \{\theta_\ell\}_{\ell=1}^L$, and $\Omega = \{\omega_\ell\}_{\ell=1}^L$ denote the collection of normalization, MHSA, and MLP parameters of all the L blocks, respectively. Similarly, $\psi_l = \{\phi_\ell, \theta_\ell, \omega_\ell\}$ denote the set of all parameters of the ℓth block. Thus, ViT parameters can be summarized as $\Psi = \{\Lambda, \Phi, \Theta, \Omega\} = \{\Lambda, \psi_1, \cdots, \psi_L\}$ and ViT operations can be summarized as $\tilde{\mathbf{t}}_L = \mathcal{V}_\Psi(\mathbf{x}) = \mathcal{G}_{\psi_L}(\cdots(\mathcal{G}_{\psi_1}(\{\tilde{\mathbf{t}}_0, \mathcal{E}_\Lambda(\mathbf{x})\})))$. Since training a ViT from scratch requires a large dataset due to the lack of inductive bias [19], fine-tuning has been the de-facto approach to adapt pre-trained ViTs for downstream tasks [3].

Parameter-Efficient Fine-Tuning (PEFT): PEFT methods achieve efficient adaptation of large pre-trained models [12,14,15] by learning only a limited number of parameters. *Linear probing* learns only the head parameters η and it represents the lower bound for all PEFT methods. In contrast, *full fine-tuning* involves updating all the ViT parameters (Ψ) in addition to the head (η). *Subset fine-tuning* methods fine-tune only a chosen subset of the pre-trained model parameters such as the last few layers of the network (e.g., [13]) or the MHSA layer within each ViT block (e.g., [27]). *Visual Prompt Tuning (VPT)* [16] introduces a set of R learnable visual prompts before each ViT block, represented by $\mathcal{P}_v = \{\mathcal{P}_{v_\ell}\}_{\ell=1}^L \in \mathbb{R}^{L \times R \times d}$. The operations of each transformer block in a visually prompted ViT can be represented as $\{\tilde{\mathbf{t}}_\ell, \_, \mathcal{T}_\ell\} = \mathcal{G}_{\psi_\ell}(\{\tilde{\mathbf{t}}_{\ell-1}, \mathcal{P}_{v_\ell}, \mathcal{T}_{\ell-1}\})$, $\ell \in [1, L]$. During fine-tuning, only the prompts $\mathcal{P}_v$ are updated and the ViT parameters are unchanged. *Low-Rank Adaptation (LoRA)* [15] injects trainable low-rank matrices in parallel to the attention layer [14] while keeping the pre-trained model weights frozen. The MHSA parameters of a block ℓ can be considered as a collection of four weight matrices denoted as $\theta_\ell = \{\mathbf{W}_{O,\ell}, \mathbf{W}_{Q,\ell}, \mathbf{W}_{K,\ell}, \mathbf{W}_{V,\ell}\}$. In LoRA, the updates to $\mathbf{W}_{Q,\ell}$ and $\mathbf{W}_{V,\ell}$ are decomposed into a pair of low rank matrices $\mathbf{A} \in \mathbb{R}^{r \times d}$ and $\mathbf{B} \in \mathbb{R}^{d \times r}$, where r represents the rank of the two matrices. Let $z_{*,\ell}$ and $\tilde{z}_{*,\ell}$ be the input and output, respectively, of an attention layer in the ℓth block. Then, LoRA operations can be summarized as:

$$\begin{aligned} \tilde{z}_{Q,\ell} &= \mathbf{W}_{Q,\ell} z_{Q,\ell} + \alpha \mathbf{B}_{Q,\ell} \mathbf{A}_{Q,\ell} z_{Q,\ell}, \\ \tilde{z}_{V,\ell} &= \mathbf{W}_{V,\ell} z_{V,\ell} + \alpha \mathbf{B}_{V,\ell} \mathbf{A}_{V,\ell} z_{V,\ell}. \end{aligned} \quad (1)$$

Here, $\mathcal{A} = \{\mathbf{A}_{Q,\ell}, \mathbf{A}_{V,\ell}\}_{\ell=1}^L$ and $\mathcal{B} = \{\mathbf{B}_{Q,\ell}, \mathbf{B}_{V,\ell}\}_{\ell=1}^L$ are the only learnable parameters, and α is a fixed scalar. Recently, PEFT methods have also been studied in the FL context. While textual prompt learning via FL was proposed in [11,31], a FL extension to LoRA was proposed in [1].

3 Federated Parameter-Efficient Fine-Tuning Methods

Problem Statement: We assume that a ViT feature extractor $\mathcal{V}_{\Psi_0}$ that is already pre-trained on a large independent dataset is available at the server. The goal of the server is to collaborate with the C clients to fine-tune the pre-trained ViT feature extractor $\mathcal{V}_{\Psi_0}$ and learn the task-specific classification head $\mathcal{H}_\eta$ in a federated fashion while *maximizing task-specific performance* and *minimizing the number of parameters that are tuned and exchanged*. The server initializes η as η_0 and broadcasts both Ψ_0 and η_0 to all the clients before the collaboration begins. At the end of T collaboration rounds, the objective is to obtain Ψ_T and η_T, which are fine-tuned for the specified task. By minimizing the number of parameters that are tuned and exchanged, we seek to reduce both the communication costs between the clients and the server as well as the memory footprint required to store the task-specific parameters.

Vanilla Federated Learning (FedAvg): [20] Given an appropriate per-client loss function $\mathcal{L}^{(c)}(\Psi, \eta)$, the global loss function is defined as:

$$\mathcal{L}(\Psi, \eta) = \sum_{c=1}^{C} \frac{N^{(c)}}{N} \mathcal{L}^{(c)}(\Psi, \eta), \quad (2)$$

where $N = \sum_{c=1}^{C} N^{(c)}$ and $N^{(c)}$ is the number of training samples available at client $c \in [1, C]$. Starting from (Ψ_0, η_0), $\mathcal{L}(\Psi, \eta)$ is iteratively minimized over T collaboration rounds. At the start of round t, client parameters are initialized as: $\Psi_{t-1}^{(c)} = \Psi_{t-1}$ and $\eta_{t-1}^{(c)} = \eta_{t-1}$, $\forall t \in [1, T]$. In round t, the clients obtain:

$$\Psi_t^{(c)}, \eta_t^{(c)} = \underset{\Psi, \eta}{\arg\min} \; \mathcal{L}^{(c)}(\Psi, \eta). \quad (3)$$

At the end of round t, the server aggregates the client parameters as:

$$\Psi_t = \sum_{c=1}^{C} \frac{N^{(c)}}{N} \Psi_t^{(c)}, \quad \eta_t = \sum_{c=1}^{C} \frac{N^{(c)}}{N} \eta_t^{(c)}. \quad (4)$$

The above formulation can be considered as the federated version of full fine-tuning. For federated linear probing, only η is updated and $\Psi_T = \Psi_0$.

3.1 Proposed Variants of Federated PEFT Methods

Federated Subset Fine-Tuning: Inspired by [27], we unfreeze *all* MHSA parameters across all the L blocks and fine-tune Θ in a federated fashion. Henceforth, we refer to this method as **all blocks attention (ABA)** with $\{\Theta, \eta\}$ being the only trainable parameters. The optimization formulation for ABA is $\min_{\Theta, \eta} \mathcal{L}(\Psi = \{\Lambda, \Phi, \Theta, \Omega\}, \eta)$.

In the ABA method, clients must fine-tune and communicate the parameters of L MHSA layers, which is roughly a third of the parameters involved in full fine-tuning. To further improve parameter efficiency, we propose **stochastic block attention (SBA)**, which requires updating parameters of only a *single* MHSA layer in each collaboration round. Specifically, the server randomly samples a block ℓ^* in each round, where $\ell^* \in [1, L]$, and unfreezes its corresponding MHSA weights θ_{ℓ^*}. Then, all clients learn $\{\theta_{\ell^*}, \eta\}$ collaboratively as $\min_{\theta_{\ell^*}, \eta} \mathcal{L}(\Psi, \eta)$.

The SBA method involves learning only a fraction ($1/L$) of the ABA parameters in each round, resulting in better communication efficiency. However, SBA

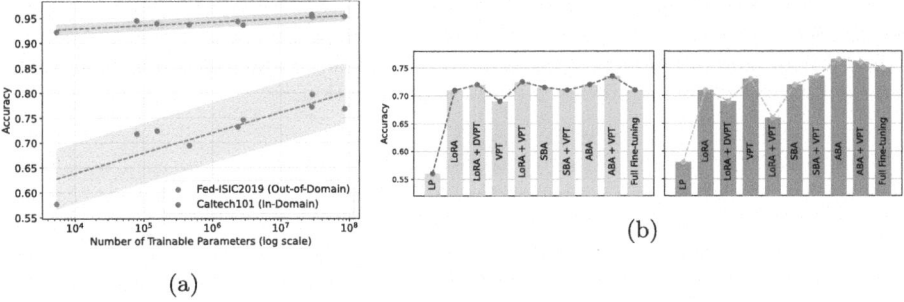

Fig. 2. (a) Accuracy vs. efficiency trade-off of various federated PEFT methods (Full Fine-tuning to LoRa shown in Table 1). The trade-off is more pronounced for OOD transfer (Fed-ISIC2019) compared to in-domain transfer (CalTech101). (b) Accuracy of federated PEFT methods on Fed-ISIC2019 with only 5 clients (excluding client 4), when (**Left**) base model is fine-tuned first with in-domain data (client 4 data) and (**Right**) base model is pre-trained using natural images. Clearly, the in-domain base model shows less performance variability.

requires the same storage as ABA because all the MHSA layers get updated over different rounds. In both ABA and SBA, FedAvg is used for aggregation.

Federated VPT: When VPT is used, the augmented ViT parameters can be denoted as $\mathcal{V}_{[\Psi,\mathcal{P}_v]}$ and the objective is $\min_{\mathcal{P}_v,\eta} \mathcal{L}([\Psi,\mathcal{P}_v],\eta)$, where the visual prompts are again aggregated through FedAvg. To further reduce the number of exchanged parameters, clients can decompose the locally learned prompts [30] into low-rank matrices using singular value decomposition (SVD) [17]. We refer to this technique as **Decomposed Visual Prompts (DVPT)**, where the prompts from all transformer blocks are concatenated to obtain a $(LR \times d)$ matrix, which is decomposed as $\mathcal{A}_{vp} \in \mathbb{R}^{LR \times r_v}$ and $\mathcal{B}_{vp} \in \mathbb{R}^{r_v \times d}$. Here, r_v denotes the rank of visual prompt decomposition matrices $\mathcal{A}_{vp}$ and $\mathcal{B}_{vp}$.

Federated LoRA: When LoRA is used, the augmented ViT parameters can be denoted as $\mathcal{V}_{[\Psi,\mathcal{A},\mathcal{B}]}$ and the objective function is $\min_{\mathcal{A},\mathcal{B},\eta} \mathcal{L}([\Psi,\mathcal{A},\mathcal{B}],\eta)$. In federated LoRA, the server: (i) reconstructs back the weight update matrices sent by the clients as $\Delta \mathbf{W}_{Q,\ell}^{(c)} = \mathbf{B}_{Q,\ell}^{(c)} \mathbf{A}_{Q,\ell}^{(c)}$ and $\Delta \mathbf{W}_{V,\ell}^{(c)} = \mathbf{B}_{V,\ell}^{(c)} \mathbf{A}_{V,\ell}^{(c)}$, (ii) performs FedAvg based on these reconstructed matrices $\Delta \mathbf{W}_{Q,\ell}^{(c)}$ and $\Delta \mathbf{W}_{V,\ell}^{(c)}$, and (iii) applies SVD to the aggregated matrices to obtain the new global weight update matrices $\mathbf{B}_{Q,\ell}$, $\mathbf{A}_{Q,\ell}$, $\mathbf{B}_{V,\ell}$, and $\mathbf{A}_{V,\ell}$, which are sent back to the clients, where $\ell \in [1, L]$. Thus, federated LoRA provides communication efficiency for both the clients and the server, as well as involves less trainable parameters. The number of trainable parameters in LoRA is directly related to the rank r. Finally, another key area of investigation in this work is understanding the impact of integrating multiple PEFT methods in federated settings to adapt pre-trained ViTs.

Table 1. Benchmarking of different approaches for federated fine-tuning of ViT. The number of exchangeable parameters (measured in *millions*) associated with each method is highlighted. Each experiment was repeated three times using different seeds, with the table reporting the mean and standard deviation.

Method	Parameters	Exchangeable Parameters (↓)		Balanced Accuracy (↑)			
		Number	Percentage (%)	HAM10000 (IID)	Fed-ISIC2019 (non-IID)	Caltech101 (IID)	Flowers102 (IID)
Centralized	Ψ, η	-	-	0.805 ± 0.011	0.786 ± 0.015	0.964 ± 0.003	0.966 ± 0.006
CentralizedVPT	$\mathcal{P}_v, \eta$	-	-	0.781 ± 0.008	0.746 ± 0.021	0.944 ± 0.002	0.966 ± 0.006
Full Fine-tuning	Ψ, η	86.0	100	0.791 ± 0.025	0.768 ± 0.046	0.956 ± 0.004	0.970 ± 0.004
ABA + VPT	$\Theta, \eta, \mathcal{P}_v$	28.815	33.5	**0.812 ± 0.019**	**0.797 ± 0.001**	0.946 ± 0.006	0.940 ± 0.002
ABA	Θ, η	28.354	32.97	0.812 ± 0.024	0.772 ± 0.013	**0.958 ± 0.001**	**0.969 ± 0.001**
SBA + VPT	$\theta_i^*, \eta, \mathcal{P}_v$	2.829	3.29	0.792 ± 0.016	0.746 ± 0.014	0.942 ± 0.009	0.938 ± 0.009
SBA	θ_i^*, η	2.368	2.75	0.782 ± 0.009	0.732 ± 0.009	0.948 ± 0.005	0.962 ± 0.002
LoRA + VPT	$\mathcal{A}, \mathcal{B}, \mathcal{P}_v, \eta$	0.613	0.71	0.784 ± 0.018	0.729 ± 0.014	0.937 ± 0.006	0.947 ± 0.005
VPT	$\mathcal{P}_v, \eta$	0.466	0.54	0.789 ± 0.002	0.694 ± 0.013	0.939 ± 0.002	0.939 ± 0.005
LoRA + DVPT	$\mathcal{A}, \mathcal{B}, \mathcal{A}_{vp}, \mathcal{B}_{vp}, \eta$	0.231	0.27	0.772 ± 0.022	0.724 ± 0.011	0.940 ± 0.004	0.946 ± 0.008
LoRA	$\mathcal{A}, \mathcal{B}, \eta$	0.152	0.18	0.770 ± 0.011	0.718 ± 0.004	0.949 ± 0.003	0.963 ± 0.006
PromptFL	$\mathcal{P}_t$	0.026	0.03	0.384 ± 0.005	0.389 ± 0.003	0.929 ± 0.002	0.814 ± 0.006
Linear Probing	η	0.005	0.006	0.714 ± 0.012	0.577 ± 0.015	0.924 ± 0.003	0.929 ± 0.011
Local	Ψ, η	0.0	0.0	0.674 ± 0.019	0.291 ± 0.028	0.607 ± 0.068	0.458 ± 0.009

4 Results and Discussion

Datasets: We conducted experiments on Fed-ISIC2019 [26], HAM10000 [28], Caltech101 [10], and Flowers102 [21] datasets. While the first two datasets are from the medical imaging domain (OOD), the latter two correspond to in-domain scenarios. Fed-ISIC2019 also has non-IID data distribution.

Implementation Setup: We use the ImageNet [7] pre-trained ViT-B/16 model from timm library [29], with $L = 12$ blocks, $d = 768$, and $S = 196$ patches. We use normal distribution with $\mu = 0$ and $\sigma = 0.1$ for LoRA initialization, with $r = 4$ and $\alpha = 2$. For VPT, we set $R = 50$. For DVPT, we experimented with different rank values and set the rank r_v to 8. We run FL for $T = 200$ collaboration rounds, employing an SGD optimizer with a learning rate of 10^{-2}, and a batch size of 32 using cross-entropy loss. We set the number of clients to $C = 6$ and allow parameter exchange in every round. All experiments were implemented using PyTorch 2.1.0 and Nvidia A100 GPU. For more details on the datasets and experimental set-up, please refer to the supplementary material.

Results: Results are summarized in Table 1, where the methods are divided into three groups. The first two rows correspond to centralized training, where data from all clients gets pooled at one location (violating privacy constraints). This setting serves as a useful reference to understand the impact of FL. The middle group of methods exchange parameters related to the ViT in a federated setting. Among these methods, federated full fine-tuning of ViT (in yellow) is used as the baseline to assess the various PEFT methods. The third group (last three rows) corresponds to the case where no ViT parameters are exchanged.

Which Federated PEFT Method Provides the Best Accuracy vs. Efficiency Trade-Off? While the performance of ABA is comparable to the baseline across all datasets, SBA achieves good performance only on IID datasets and has a noticeable degradation in Fed-ISIC2019. Due to the non-IID nature of Fed-ISIC2019, the stochastic block selected at each round might lead to divergence in the training process in certain rounds. A similar trend was observed with VPT, LoRA, and linear probing. *While most federated PEFT methods work well for the IID scenario*, easily achieving up to three orders of magnitude decrease in the exchangeable parameters at a marginal cost to accuracy, *they exhibit sub-optimal performance when there is statistical heterogeneity across clients*.

Can Federated PEFT Transfer Well for OOD Tasks? Our main finding is that there is a trade-off between parameter efficiency and model accuracy in federated PEFT. While this trade-off is *marginal for in-domain tasks* (approximately 0.5% decrease in accuracy for every order of magnitude reduction in the number of parameters fine-tuned/exchanged), this trade-off becomes *substantial for out-of-domain tasks with non-IID client distributions* (approximately 4% decrease in accuracy for every order of magnitude reduction as shown in Fig. 2a). Therefore, ABA is the best approach for OOD transfer, though it has less parameter efficiency. While existing wisdom is that PEFT can be achieved without compromising on model accuracy [25], we have demonstrated that the above claim is true only for in-domain tasks. For further validation, we first fine-tune the pre-trained ViT on client 4 of Fed-ISIC2019 and attempt to again fine-tune this new "pre-trained" model using the remaining 5 clients in a federated manner. Note that after the first fine-tuning, the classification head is discarded, but the feature extraction model is already familiar with the medical imaging domain. So, the second federated PEFT stage can be considered as in-domain transfer. As depicted in Fig. 2b (Left), there is little difference among the federated PEFT methods in this scenario, proving that they perform equally well for in-domain transfer. However, when the original "pre-trained" model is plugged back and collaboratively fine-tuned with the same 5 clients (excluding client 4), we observe significant variability in the accuracy (Fig. 2b (Right)).

Can a Combination of PEFT Methods Further Improve Performance? We experimented with different combinations of PEFT methods by using ABA, SBA, and LoRA in conjunction with VPT. Note that since both attention fine-tuning (ABA and SBA) and LoRA attempt to update the attention weights, it does not make sense to combine them. The results show that *combining VPT with attention fine-tuning is beneficial for OOD transfer, while it hurts in-domain transfer*. This finding is confirmed by observing a similar trend when comparing the LoRA+VPT method with LoRA. Furthermore, combining LoRA with DVPT improves parameter efficiency by 3× while yielding almost similar results.

Comparison with PromptFL: Federated learning of *text prompts* led to drastic performance degradation, particularly for OOD tasks (HAM10000 and Fed-ISIC2019), highlighting the relative superiority of federated VPT over PromptFL.

5 Conclusion

This work probed the efficacy of various federated PEFT methods to adapt pre-trained vision transformers for medical image classification, focusing on achieving optimal performance while minimizing communication costs. Through extensive experimentation, we show that PEFT methods exhibit limited efficacy when applied to heterogeneous and out-of-domain datasets across participating clients. Hence, we recommend that *it is preferable to start fine-tuning with in-domain medical foundation models* (if available), rather than models pre-trained on natural images. Our findings also highlight the robustness of visual prompts over text prompts, especially when the task does not involve natural images.

References

1. Babakniya, S., et al.: SLoRA: federated parameter efficient fine-tuning of language models. In: NeurIPS Workshop (2023)
2. Bommasani, R., et al.: On the opportunities and risks of foundation models. arXiv:2108.07258 (2022)
3. Carion, N., et al.: End-to-end object detection with transformers. In: ECCV, pp. 213–229 (2020)
4. Chen, S., et al.: AdaptFormer: adapting vision transformers for scalable visual recognition. In: NeurIPS, pp. 16664–16678 (2022)
5. Cirrincione, G., et al.: Transformer-based approach to melanoma detection. Sensors **23**(12) (2023)
6. Dai, Y., Gao, Y., Liu, F.: TransMed: transformers advance multi-modal medical image classification . Diagnostics **11**(8) (2021)
7. Deng, J., et al.: ImageNet: a large-scale hierarchical image database. In: CVPR, pp. 248–255 (2009)
8. Dosovitskiy, A., et al.: An image is worth 16x16 words: transformers for image recognition at scale. In: ICLR (2021)
9. Duong, L.T., et al.: Detection of tuberculosis from chest X-ray images: boosting the performance with vision transformer and transfer learning. Expert Syst. Appl. **184** (2021)
10. Fei-Fei, L., Fergus, R., Perona, P.: One-shot learning of object categories. IEEE Trans. Pattern Anal. Mach. Intell. **28**(4), 594–611 (2006)
11. Guo, T., et al.: PromptFL: let federated participants cooperatively learn prompts instead of models - federated learning in age of foundation model. IEEE Trans. Mob. Comput. (2023)
12. He, J., et al.: Towards a unified view on visual parameter-efficient transfer learning. In: ICLR (2022)
13. He, K., et al.: Masked autoencoders are scalable vision learners. In: CVPR, pp. 16000–16009 (2022)
14. He, X., et al.: Parameter-efficient model adaptation for vision transformers. In: AAAI, pp. 817–825 (2023)
15. Hu, E.J., et al.: LoRA: low-rank adaptation of large language models. In: ICLR (2022)
16. Jia, M., et al.: Visual prompt tuning. In: ECCV, pp. 709–727 (2022)
17. Klema, V., Laub, A.: The singular value decomposition: its computation and some applications. IEEE Trans. Autom. Control **25**(2), 164–176 (1980)

18. Lu, M., et al.: Smile: sparse-attention based multiple instance contrastive learning for glioma sub-type classification using pathological images. In: MICCAI Workshop on Computational Pathology, pp. 159–169 (2021)
19. Lu, Z., et al.: Bridging the gap between vision transformers and convolutional neural networks on small datasets. In: NeurIPS, pp. 14663–14677 (2022)
20. McMahan, B., et al.: Communication-efficient learning of deep networks from decentralized data. In: AISTATS, pp. 1273–1282 (2017)
21. Nilsback, M.E., Zisserman, A.: Automated flower classification over a large number of classes. In: ICVGIP, pp. 722–729 (2008)
22. Okolo, G.I., Katsigiannis, S., Ramzan, N.: IEViT: an enhanced vision transformer architecture for chest X-ray image classification. Comput. Methods Programs Biomed. **226** (2022)
23. Radford, A., et al.: Learning transferable visual models from natural language supervision. In: ICML. pp. 8748–8763 (2021)
24. Sarker, M.M.K., et al.: TransSLC: skin lesion classification in dermatoscopic images using transformers. In: Medical Image Understanding and Analysis, pp. 651–660 (2022)
25. Sun, G., et al.: Conquering the communication constraints to enable large pre-trained models in federated learning. arXiv:2210.01708 (2022)
26. Terrail, J.O., et al.: FLamby: datasets and benchmarks for cross-silo federated learning in realistic healthcare settings. In: NeurIPS (2022)
27. Touvron, H., et al.: Three things everyone should know about vision transformers. In: ECCV, pp. 497–515 (2022)
28. Tschandl, P., Rosendahl, C., Kittler, H.: The HAM10000 dataset, a large collection of multi-source dermatoscopic images of common pigmented skin lesions. Sci. Data **5**(11) (2018)
29. Wightman, R.: PyTorch image models (2019)
30. Xiao, Y., et al.: Decomposed prompt tuning via low-rank reparameterization. In: Findings of EMNLP (2023)
31. Yang, F.E., Wang, C.Y., Wang, Y.C.F.: Efficient model personalization in federated learning via client-specific prompt generation. In: ICCV, pp. 19159–19168 (2023)
32. Zamir, A.R., et al.: Taskonomy: disentangling task transfer learning. In: CVPR, pp. 3712–3722 (2018)
33. Zhang, S., Metaxas, D.: On the challenges and perspectives of foundation models for medical image analysis. Med. Image Anal. **91** (2024)
34. Zhuang, W., Chen, C., Lyu, L.: When foundation model meets federated learning: motivations, challenges, and future directions. arXiv:2306.15546 (2023)

FedGS: Federated Gradient Scaling for Heterogeneous Medical Image Segmentation

Philip Schutte[1], Valentina Corbetta[2,3,4], Regina Beets-Tan[2,4], and Wilson Silva[2,3(✉)]

[1] University of Amsterdam, Amsterdam, The Netherlands
[2] Department of Radiology, The Netherlands Cancer Institute, Amsterdam, The Netherlands
[3] AI Technology for Life, Department of Information and Computing Sciences, Department of Biology, Utrecht University, Utrecht, The Netherlands
w.j.dossantossilva@uu.nl
[4] GROW School for Oncology and Developmental Biology, Maastricht University Medical Center, Maastricht, The Netherlands

Abstract. Federated Learning (FL) in Deep Learning (DL)-automated medical image segmentation helps preserving privacy by enabling collaborative model training without sharing patient data. However, FL faces challenges with data heterogeneity among institutions, leading to suboptimal global models. Integrating Disentangled Representation Learning (DRL) in FL can enhance robustness by separating data into distinct representations. Existing DRL methods assume heterogeneity lies solely in style features, overlooking content-based variability like lesion size and shape. We propose FedGS, a novel FL aggregation method, to improve segmentation performance on small, under-represented targets while maintaining overall efficacy. FedGS demonstrates superior performance over FedAvg, particularly for small lesions, across PolypGen and LiTS datasets. The code and pre-trained checkpoints are available at the following link: https://github.com/Trustworthy-AI-UU-NKI/Federated-Learning-Disentanglement.

1 Introduction

Recently, the field of Deep Learning (DL)-automated medical image segmentation has begun to shift towards a Federated Learning (FL) paradigm, primarily motivated by the need to guarantee stringent privacy standards [19,21]. FL offers a promising approach by enabling collaborative model training, alternating local computation and periodic communication, without sharing patient data [23].

P. Schutte and V. Corbetta—These authors contributed equally.

Supplementary Information The online version contains supplementary material available at https://doi.org/10.1007/978-3-031-77610-6_23.

© The Author(s), under exclusive license to Springer Nature Switzerland AG 2025
M. E. Celebi et al. (Eds.): MICCAI 2024 Workshops, LNCS 15274, pp. 246–255, 2025.
https://doi.org/10.1007/978-3-031-77610-6_23

Despite the clear advantage of not requiring data sharing, implementing FL can be challenging due to variations in data statistics among different learners. When data is uniformly distributed among participating institutions, simple methods such as iteratively aggregating clients' model parameters via a weighted average approach (i.e., Federated Averaging (FedAvg) [14]) have been shown to produce effective global models, achieving performance metrics comparable to their centralised counterparts [11]. However, heterogeneous data distributions, which naturally arise in FL environments, pose challenges in the collaborative training process. This often results in clients overfitting to local data and underperforming on cases less represented among the clients, thus rendering parameter averaging an ineffective aggregation approach [15]. Several works have extended FedAvg to enhance robustness against client drift (*i.e.*, the state of a locally trained model drifts away from the state of the optimal global model) and address data heterogeneity. FedProx [10] introduces a proximal term to local training objectives to mitigate client drift. SCAFFOLD [7] uses variance reduction for this purpose. MOON [9] employs contrastive learning between representations from the global model and prior local models to address client drift.

A promising alternative approach involves integrating Disentangled Representation Learning (DRL) into the federated model architecture. The objective of DRL is to disentangle the underlying generative factors of the input data into distinct representations. DRL has been effectively employed in centralized settings for medical image segmentation, enhancing robustness to data heterogeneity in multi-center data [12]. However, the integration of DRL in FL has been explored by only a few studies [2,13]. Specifically, these studies implement Content Style Disentanglement (CSD), which separates content (e.g. anatomical structctures) from style (e.g. intensity). Then, only the content representation, assumed to be shared and consistent across centers, is employed in downstream tasks (e.g., classification, segmentation), thereby addressing data heterogeneity.

However, CSD relies on the assumption that data heterogeneity is embedded within style features, which encode variations in acquisition protocols, scanning machines, and settings. This assumption is not universally valid, as heterogeneity among clients can also stem from the content of the images. Indeed, the size and shape of the target segmentation significantly influence the difficulty of the segmentation task. The variability in the complexity of target segmentations among different clients can lead to underrepresentation of challenging samples, consequently diminishing their contribution to the aggregated global model. In lesion segmentation, lesions may present different sizes, unevenly distributed across centers (e.g., a specialized cancer institute may lack small early-stage tumors in its dataset). Smaller lesions are typically more challenging to detect, representing the cases where clinicians would benefit most from DL segmentation models [16]. Early detection of small lesions is critical; for example, small colorectal polyps are difficult to identify but are crucial in clinical practice due to their potential for growth and malignant transformation [6]. Accurate detection and management of these polyps are essential for colorectal cancer prevention [17].

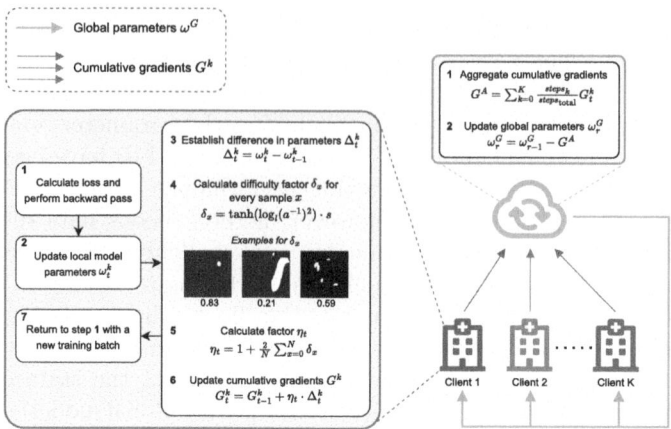

Fig. 1. Overview of the FedGS aggregation method. The segmentation masks depicted in the Figure come from the PolypGen dataset.

We propose a novel FL aggregation method, Federated Gradient Scaling (FedGS), which enhances segmentation performance on samples that are challenging due to their limited size and availability. Our key contributions are the following:

1. FedGS enhances segmentation performance on small-sized, under-represented segmentation targets while maintaining overall segmentation efficacy.
2. We apply FedGS to two segmentation models, one based on UNet [20] and a state-of-the-art CSD model, called SDNet [4], demonstrating the effectiveness of our aggregation strategy.
3. We show improved segmentation performance compared to FedAvg, particularly for small lesions, using our proposed approach on two public lesion segmentation datasets, Polypgen [1] and LiTS [3] highlighting the robustness of our method in addressing client data heterogeneity.

2 Methodology

Figure 1 provides an overview of FedGS. FedGS is inspired by FedNova [22], which normalizes local gradients to address inconsistencies caused by varying numbers of iterations due to differing client sample sizes. Unlike FedNova, which focuses on correcting client inconsistencies and normalizing gradients, FedGS aims to enhance segmentation performance on challenging (i.e., small lesions) targets by scaling the gradients originating from these difficult samples.

2.1 FedGS Overview

In FedGS, every client k maintains a cumulative gradient G_t^k, where t is the latest training iteration. After every client k has completed its training round, the server aggregates K cumulative gradients G_t^k of final training iteration T to obtain the aggregated cumulative gradient G^A. The aggregation is performed with weighted averaging based on the number of iterations completed by each client:

$$G^A = \sum_{k=0}^{K} \frac{\text{steps}_k}{\text{steps}_{\text{total}}} G_t^k \qquad (1)$$

The server then updates its global model parameters ω_r^G for training round r using the formula $\omega_r^G = \omega_{r-1}^G - G^A$.

During each iteration t during training round r, client k performs a standard training step which involves computing the local loss function and performing backward propagation to obtain gradient g_t. The local model parameters ω_t^k are then updated with learning rate α, $\omega_t^k = \omega_{t-1}^k - \alpha \cdot g_t$. The cumulative gradient G_t^k is updated with the difference in local model parameters, $\Delta_t^k = \omega_t^k - \omega_{t-1}^k$, scaled by a factor η_t, resulting in the following update rule:

$$G_t^k = G_{t-1}^k + \eta_t \cdot \Delta_t^k \qquad (2)$$

The factor η_t is based on the estimated segmentation difficulty of the input images X in the training batch.

It is important to note that FedGS does not rescale the gradients used to update the local model parameters ω_t^k. FedGS exclusively alters the gradients stored in the cumulative gradients, thus it does not affect the training and convergence of the local models during a training round; it only influences the aggregation of the local models at the end of a training round.

2.2 Small Lesion Classification and Difficulty Estimation

The factor η_t is based on the estimated difficulty of the segmentation targets present in the training batch of iteration t. If the batch contains at least one image of a small lesion, it receives a factor $\eta_t > 1$. If no image in the batch contains a small lesion, it receives no additional scaling, thus $\eta_t = 1$. We constrain η_t to a minimum of 1 to prevent decreasing gradients, which would undesirably reduce the total magnitude of the accumulated gradients G^A and lead to slower convergence of the global model.

To calculate η_t, we determine a difficulty factor $\delta_x \in [0, 1)$ for each image x in the training batch based on corresponding mask $m^x \in \{0,1\}^{H \times W}$ as follows:

$$\delta_x = \tanh(\log_l(a^{-1})^2) \cdot s$$

$$\text{where } a^{-1} = \frac{m_H^x \cdot m_W^x}{\sum_{i,j} m^x[i,j]} \text{ and } s = \begin{cases} 1, & \text{if } a^{-1} \geq \tau \\ 0, & \text{otherwise} \end{cases} \qquad (3)$$

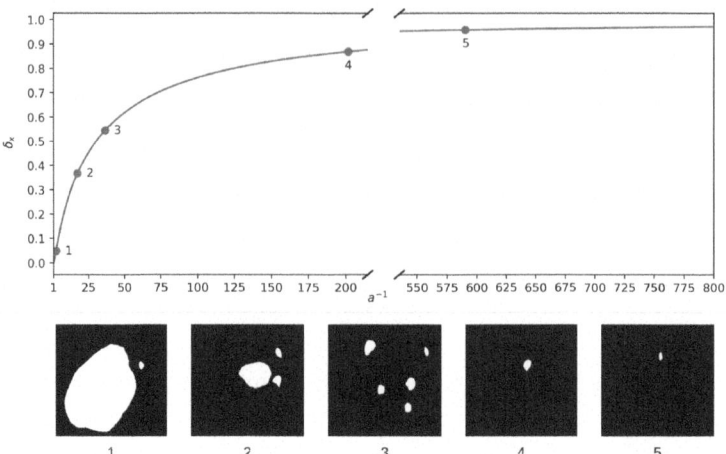

Fig. 2. Plot of Eq. 3 that calculates the difficulty factor δ_x for images with the inverse area a^{-1} as input. Additionally, five images from PolypGen that contain small polyps are shown in the graph. These images vary greatly in their total mask area and thus illustrate how the estimated difficulty changes based on a^{-1}.

Equation 3 shows that we use the inverse relative area a^{-1} of mask m^x to compute δ_x. This is because the inverse relative area naturally captures the overall segmentation difficulty of the lesions present in the mask. If a^{-1} is equal to or greater than a predefined threshold τ, then the mask contains a small lesion and s is set to 1. To calculate δ_x based on a^{-1}, we combine the *tanh* function with $\log_l^2$, transforming a^{-1} to a logarithmic scale and restricting the p_x values between 0 and 1. The base l of $\log_l^2$ is chosen based on the overall scale of a^{-1}. The methods for obtaining a^{-1}, and the values of τ are fine-tuned for the specific segmentation task at hand. Subsection 3.2 details the process for the selected datasets. We have determined that $l = 100$ is an appropriate setting for PolypGen, while $l = 1000$ is more suitable for LiTS due to the significantly larger scale of a^{-1}. Figure 2 illustrates how $\tanh(\log_l(a^{-1})^2)$ responds to different magnitudes of a^{-1} for $l = 100$ using samples from PolypGen, aiding in visualizing the behaviour of δ_x. Noticeably, the increase of δ_x rapidly decelerates as a^{-1} becomes higher. This is a desirable behaviour, as it is evident from the five images that changes in mask absolute area are substantially greater at lower ranges of a^{-1} than at higher ranges. There is a significant reduction in mask area from example 1 to 2, whereas the change between examples 4 and 5 is much less drastic.

Finally, η_t is computed by combining the difficulty factors δ_{x_i} of images x_i in the training batch of size N according to the following equation:

$$\eta_t = 1 + \frac{2}{N} \sum_{x=0}^{N} \delta_{x_i} \qquad (4)$$

For images without small lesions, $\delta_x = 0$. Therefore, these images do not affect the value of η_t. Equation 4 shows that we sum all difficulty factors δ_{x_i} and scale the sum down by $\frac{N}{2}$. We intentionally use a sum operation instead of averaging, because we want the number of small lesion samples in a batch to influence the final value of η_t. For example, a batch with three small lesion samples will have a significantly higher η_t than a batch with only one small lesion sample, assuming that all small lesion samples have a similar δ_x value.

3 Experiments

3.1 Model Architectures

We apply FedGS in FL training of two DL models: UTNet [5] and a modified SDNet [4], enhanced with a self-attention mechanism (SD-UTNet).

UTNet. Qu et al. [18] showed that self-attention-based architectures enhance FL performance on heterogeneous data. We selected UTNet, a hybrid transformer architecture that integrates transformer encoders and decoders into the UNet model [20].

SD-UTNet. SDNet is a state-of-the-art CSD network for medical imaging that disentangles center-invariant content from center-variant style in input images. We modified SDNet by replacing its UNet backbone with UTNet, creating the hybrid transformer CSD network, SD-UTNet.

For detailed architecture, we refer the reader to the original publications. An ablation study (Table 1, Supplementary Material) shows significant segmentation performance improvement with the introduction of self-attention.

3.2 Datasets

PolypGen. PolypGen is a publicly available dataset, which contains colonoscopy data collected from 6 different centers, encompassing diverse patient populations. Our analysis focuses on single frame samples, resulting in a total of 1537 images. The datasets of centers 1–5 are used for the training and validation of the global federated models, while Center 6 is kept separate for testing.

Small Polyp Classification. First, we need to compute the relative inverse area a^{-1} of the ground truth segmentation masks m to identify whether they contain at least one small polyp. To achieve this, we apply a blob detector [8] on m to locate the center points of the polyps. The blob detector includes a visual module that identifies regions in the image that stand out from the background. In cases where a small polyp is attached to a larger polyp, the blob detector alone is insufficient. Thus, we perform an erosion operation on the mask before applying the blob detector to separate attached polyps. Finally, for the center point with the lowest estimated scale, we use its estimated size to compute a^{-1}. If the inverse area exceeds the threshold τ, the blob is classified as small polyp. For PolypGen, we set $\tau = 150$, based on the dataset authors' description [1]. This classification reveals that in all 6 centers, small samples are a minority class, as shown in the histogram in Fig. 1(a) of the Supplementary Material.

LiTS. LiTS [3] is a liver tumor segmentation dataset with 131 Computed Tomography (CT) scans. We perform the experiments in 2D by extracting slices with non-empty tumor masks from the 3D volumes and saving them as 2D images, clipping Hounsfield Units (HU) values to the range $[-200, 200]$. We divided the scans into five centers: centers 1–4 each with 27 scans (24 for training, 3 for validation), and center 5 with 23 scans for testing.

Small Tumor Classification. In classifying the small tumors, we notice that liver tumors cover a significantly smaller image area on average than the polyps from PolypGen. Consequently, the scale of a^{-1} is higher than for PolypGen. Therefore, we choose base $l = 1000$. Moreover, the threshold is set $\tau = 1000$, with small tumors comprising around 20% of all samples, as can be seen in the histogram in Fig. 1(b) of the Supplementary Material. Finally, we exclude the blob detection step used in small polyp classification. Instead, we compare a^{-1} of the entire mask against τ. This approach prevents misclassification caused by small blobs that appear as small tumors in 2D slices but are actually part of a larger tumor when viewed in 3D across adjacent slices. By excluding blob detection, we prevent these masks from being incorrectly classified as "small."

Pre-processing. All images are resized to 512 × 512 pixels. PolypGen images are normalized using ImageNet mean and standard deviation, while LiTS images are normalized with a mean of 0 and standard deviation of 1. Augmentations applied with a 0.5 probability include horizontal and vertical flips, and random rotations up to 90°. Additionally, for PolypGen, color jitter is applied with a 0.3 probability.

Table 1. FedGS segmentation performance compared against FedAvg for SD-UTNet and UTNet on PolypGen and LiTS. The highest score per metric for each model is highlighted in **bold**. Equivalent scores are underlined. Results for PolypGen are reported with the standard deviation across the 5 folds.

Model	FL Method	PolypGen			LiTS		
		DiceS	DiceL	Dice	DiceS	DiceL	Dice
SD-UTNet	FedAvg	0.43±0.04	<u>0.77±0.01</u>	0.72±0.01	0.4266	**0.6336**	**0.6041**
	FedGS	**0.44 ± 0.03**	<u>0.77±0.01</u>	**0.73 ± 0.01**	**0.4806**	0.6189	0.5991
UTNet	FedAvg	0.39±0.02	**0.77 ± 0.01**	**0.72 ± 0.02**	0.4287	**0.6561**	**0.6237**
	FedGS	**0.41 ± 0.03**	0.76±0.01	0.71±0.01	**0.4499**	0.6390	0.6120

3.3 Training Setup

Both models are trained for 500 epochs (100 rounds of 5 epochs of local training) for PolypGen and 300 epochs (60 rounds of 5 epochs of local training) for LiTS. For PolypGen, we perform 5-fold cross-validation, saving the best checkpoint for each fold. We then evaluate each checkpoint on the test set and report the average performance of the five models. Due to time and computational constraints, 5-fold cross-validation was not feasible for LiTS; however, the large size of the testing set provides sufficiently representative results. We use a batch size of 4 for both datasets and the AdamW optimizer with a learning rate α of 0.0001. SD-UTNet is trained using the original implementation's loss functions, while UTNet is trained with Dice loss. We train both models using our aggregation strategy, FedGS, and also FedAvg for comparative analysis.

3.4 Results

Model performance is assessed by the Dice Score. This metric is divided into three components: total Dice Score (Dice), DiceS (computed only on lesions classified as small), and DiceL (computed on the remaining lesions). Empty masks are excluded from the computation of DiceS and DiceL. Results are reported in Table 1. We observe that FedGS generally enhances performance for smaller lesions (DiceS) across both datasets. For larger lesions (DiceL) and overall Dice, FedGS exhibits performance that is consistent with or marginally better or worse than FedAvg. The improvement in DiceS is more pronounced on the LiTS dataset. This discrepancy is likely because samples in PolypGen containing a large polyp and at least one small polyp are classified as small, as illustrated in Fig. 2, whereas in LiTS, all samples classified as small exclusively contain small lesions. Consequently, the stable performance on large polyps may account for the smaller improvement observed. Figure 2 in the Supplementary Material corroborates our findings qualitatively. Table 2 of the Supplementary Material shows that FedGS introduces a marginal training runtime overhead of 5.6% to 13.4% compared to FedAvg, justified by significant improvements in segmentation performance, especially for small and under-represented lesions.

4 Conclusion

We have introduced a novel aggregation strategy, FedGS, designed to address heterogeneity arising from varying and under-represented sizes of the segmentation targets. FedGS has demonstrated its effectiveness in enhancing segmentation performance for small polyps and tumors while maintaining overall segmentation quality. Our results indicate that the gradient scaling approach of FedGS is particularly effective for datasets with high variability in mask size, such as PolypGen, as well as for datasets characterized by significantly smaller mask sizes, such as LiTS. Compared to other FL aggregation strategies, such as those introduced in Sect. 1, or techniques like oversampling and class weighting for minority classes during training, FedGS offers the advantage of leaving local training processes unaffected, thereby simplifying implementation. This approach reduces complexity by avoiding the need for additional modifications or hyperparameter tuning during local training. It maintains scalability, as the standard local training process can be uniformly applied across all clients regardless of their number. Additionally, it enhances global model performance by focusing improvements on the aggregation strategy, addressing challenges like class imbalance and client drift without altering local training dynamics. Although our evaluation of FedGS has been confined to medical image segmentation, we believe that FedGS holds potential for successful application in other imaging tasks and even beyond the imaging domain. This potential is contingent upon the ability to estimate the difficulty of the data with respect to the downstream task.

Acknowledgements. Research at the Netherlands Cancer Institute is supported by grants from the Dutch Cancer Society and the Dutch Ministry of Health, Welfare and Sport. The authors would like to acknowledge the Research High Performance Computing (RHPC) facility of the Netherlands Cancer Institute (NKI).

References

1. Ali, S., et al.: A multi-centre polyp detection and segmentation dataset for generalisability assessment. Sci. Data **10**(1), 75 (2023)
2. Bercea, C.I., Wiestler, B., Rueckert, D., Albarqouni, S.: Feddis: disentangled federated learning for unsupervised brain pathology segmentation. arXiv preprint arXiv:2103.03705 (2021)
3. Bilic, P., et al.: The liver tumor segmentation benchmark (LiTS). Med. Image Anal. **84**, 102680 (2023)
4. Chartsias, A., et al.: Disentangled representation learning in cardiac image analysis. Med. Image Anal. **58**, 101535 (2019)
5. Gao, Y., Zhou, M., Metaxas, D.N.: UTNet: a hybrid transformer architecture for medical image segmentation. In: de Bruijne, M., et al. (eds.) MICCAI 2021. LNCS, vol. 12903, pp. 61–71. Springer, Cham (2021). https://doi.org/10.1007/978-3-030-87199-4_6
6. Ignjatovic, A., East, J., Suzuki, N., Vance, M., Guenther, T., Saunders, B.: Optical diagnosis of small colorectal polyps at routine colonoscopy (detect inspect characterise resect and discard; discard trial): a prospective cohort study. Lancet Oncol. **10**(12), 1171–8 (2009). https://doi.org/10.1016/S1470-2045(09)70329-8
7. Karimireddy, S.P., Kale, S., Mohri, M., Reddi, S., Stich, S., Suresh, A.T.: Scaffold: stochastic controlled averaging for federated learning. In: International Conference on Machine Learning, pp. 5132–5143. PMLR (2020)
8. Kong, H., Akakin, H.C., Sarma, S.E.: A generalized Laplacian of gaussian filter for blob detection and its applications. IEEE Trans. Cybern. **43**(6), 1719–1733 (2013)
9. Li, Q., He, B., Song, D.: Model-contrastive federated learning. In: Proceedings of the IEEE/CVF Conference on Computer Vision and Pattern Recognition, pp. 10713–10722 (2021)
10. Li, T., Sahu, A.K., Zaheer, M., Sanjabi, M., Talwalkar, A., Smith, V.: Federated optimization in heterogeneous networks. Proc. Mach. Learn. Syst. **2**, 429–450 (2020)

11. Li, W., et al.: Privacy-preserving federated brain tumour segmentation. In: Suk, H.-I., Liu, M., Yan, P., Lian, C. (eds.) MLMI 2019. LNCS, vol. 11861, pp. 133–141. Springer, Cham (2019). https://doi.org/10.1007/978-3-030-32692-0_16
12. Liu, X., Sanchez, P., Thermos, S., O'Neil, A.Q., Tsaftaris, S.A.: Learning disentangled representations in the imaging domain. Med. Image Anal. **80**, 102516 (2022)
13. Luo, Z., Wang, Y., Wang, Z., Sun, Z., Tan, T.: Disentangled federated learning for tackling attributes skew via invariant aggregation and diversity transferring. arXiv preprint arXiv:2206.06818 (2022)
14. McMahan, B., Moore, E., Ramage, D., Hampson, S., y Arcas, B.A.: Communication-efficient learning of deep networks from decentralized data. In: Artificial Intelligence and Statistics, pp. 1273–1282. PMLR (2017)
15. Mora, A., Bujari, A., Bellavista, P.: Enhancing generalization in federated learning with heterogeneous data: a comparative literature review. Future Gener. Comput. Syst. (2024)
16. Nair, T., Precup, D., Arnold, D.L., Arbel, T.: Exploring uncertainty measures in deep networks for multiple sclerosis lesion detection and segmentation. Med. Image Anal. (2020). https://doi.org/10.1016/j.media.2019.101557
17. Pickhardt, P., et al.: Assessment of volumetric growth rates of small colorectal polyps with CT colonography: a longitudinal study of natural history. Lancet Oncol. **14**(8), 711–20 (2013). https://doi.org/10.1016/S1470-2045(13)70216-X
18. Qu, L., et al.: Rethinking architecture design for tackling data heterogeneity in federated learning. In: Proceedings of the IEEE/CVF Conference on Computer Vision and Pattern Recognition, pp. 10061–10071 (2022)
19. Rieke, N., et al.: The future of digital health with federated learning. NPJ Digiit. Med. **3**(1), 119 (2020)
20. Ronneberger, O., Fischer, P., Brox, T.: U-Net: convolutional networks for biomedical image segmentation. In: Navab, N., Hornegger, J., Wells, W.M., Frangi, A.F. (eds.) MICCAI 2015 Part III. LNCS, vol. 9351, pp. 234–241. Springer, Cham (2015). https://doi.org/10.1007/978-3-319-24574-4_28
21. Van Panhuis, W.G., et al.: A systematic review of barriers to data sharing in public health. BMC Public Health **14**(1), 1–9 (2014)
22. Wang, J., Liu, Q., Liang, H., Joshi, G., Poor, H.V.: Tackling the objective inconsistency problem in heterogeneous federated optimization. Adv. Neural. Inf. Process. Syst. **33**, 7611–7623 (2020)
23. Zhang, C., Xie, Y., Bai, H., Yu, B., Li, W., Gao, Y.: A survey on federated learning. Knowl.-Based Syst. **216**, 106775 (2021)

Correction to: Medical Image Computing and Computer Assisted Intervention – MICCAI 2024 Workshops

M. Emre Celebi⬤, Mauricio Reyes⬤, Zhen Chen⬤, and Xiaoxiao Li⬤

Correction to:
M. E. Celebi et al. (Eds.): *Medical Image Computing and Computer Assisted Intervention – MICCAI 2024 Workshops*, LNCS 15274, https://doi.org/10.1007/978-3-031-77610-6

In the older version of this chapter, the affiliation of the volume editor M. Emre Celebi was incorrect. This has been corrected.

The updated version of this book can be found at
https://doi.org/10.1007/978-3-031-77610-6

© The Author(s), under exclusive license to Springer Nature Switzerland AG 2025
M. E. Celebi et al. (Eds.): MICCAI 2024 Workshops, LNCS 15274, p. C1, 2025.
https://doi.org/10.1007/978-3-031-77610-6_24

Author Index

A
Abhishek, Kumar 24, 45
Abolmaesumi, Purang 215
Alkhunaizi, Naif 236
Almalik, Faris 236
Al-Refai, Rouqaiah 236
Andrearczyk, Vincent 121
Arya, Atrin 215
Asokan, Mothilal 226
Atad, Matan 79
Ayromlou, Sana 215

B
Bach Cuadra, Meritxell 121
Bai, Long 157
Bamberg, Fabian 79
Beets-Tan, Regina 246
Benjamin, Joseph Geo 226
Bette, Stefanie 79

C
Cagol, Alessandro 89
Canas, Liane S. 35
Cansiz, Sergen 204
Chen, Xinjie 89
Chen, Zhen 168
Chung, Minjae 110
Chung, Yunsung 14
Corbetta, Valentina 246
Cremonesi, Francesco 204
Cuadra, Meritxell Bach 89
Cui, Jiahao 135

D
Dari, Emine 146
Dasgupta, Prokar 178
de Mortanges, Aurélie Pahud 59
De Santi, Lisa Anita 69
Depeursinge, Adrien 89, 121
Ding, Zhengming 14

E
Elliot, Matthew 178

F
Farshad, Azade 146

G
Gal, Yarin 99
Gordaliza, Pedro M. 89
Graf, Robert 79
Granados, Alejandro 178
Granziera, Cristina 89, 121
Guo, Wenwu 168
Guo, Ziqi 157

H
Hamarneh, Ghassan 24, 45
Hamm, Jihun 14
Huber, Martin 178
Hunecke, Florian 79

I
Inel, Oana 59
Innocenti, Lucia 204
Irzan, Hassna 178

J
Jin, Zhenchao 135

K
Kaissis, Georgios 191
Kawahara, Jeremy 24
Kim, Ganghyun 110
Kim, Yujin 110
Kirschke, Jan S. 79
Knigth, James 178
Kolek, Stefan 191
Kroencke, Thomas 79

L
Lazuardi, Rachmadio 146
Lei, Zhen 168
Li, Xiaoxiao 215

Li, Yang 178
Lin, Guying 135
Liu, Hongbin 168
Lorenzi, Marco 204
Lu, Po-Jui 89
Luo, Haozhe 59

M
MacCormac, Oscar 178
Mahil, Satveer K. 35
Mahmoodi, Toktam 178
Melie-Garcia, Lester 121
Modat, Marc 35
Moeller, Hendrik 79
Molchanova, Nataliia 89, 121
Müller, Henning 89
Murray, Benjamin A. K. 35

N
Nandakumar, Karthik 226, 236
Naseer, Muzammal 236
Nauta, Meike 69
Navab, Nassir 146
Nicolson, Angus 99
Niendorf, Thoralf 79
Noble, J. Alison 99

O
Ocampo-Pineda, Mario 89, 121
Önen, Melek 204
Ourselin, Sebastien 35, 178
Ozbulak, Utku 110

P
Paetzold, Johannes C. 79
Pischon, Tobias 79
Pohl, Soeren 79
Positano, Vincenzo 69

Q
Qiu, Linwei 3
Quarez, Julien 178

R
Raison, Nicholas 178
Ren, Hongliang 157
Reyes, Mauricio 59
Riess, Anneliese 191
Rueckert, Daniel 79, 191

S
Saadat, Armin 215
Scheschenja, Michael 69
Schlötterer, Jörg 69
Schmidt, Carsten 79
Schnabel, Julia 191
Schutte, Philip 246
Seifert, Christin 69
Shamseddin, Amir 146
Shapey, Jonathan 178
Silva, Wilson 246
Smith, Catherine H. 35
Spagnolo, Federico 121
Starck, Sophie 79

T
Taiello, Riccardo 204
Tan, Wei R. 35
Thirani, Yash 146

V
Vesin, Marc 204

W
Wang, An 157
Wang, Janet 14
Wang, Ke 3
Wang, Zhao 135
Weigel, Matthias 89
Wessendorf, Joel 69
Won, Jong Bum 110
Wu, Jinlin 168

X
Xie, Fengying 3
Xu, Mengya 157
Xu, Miao 168

Y
Yaqub, Mohammad 226
Yeganeh, Yousef 146
Yu, Lequan 135

Z
Zhang, Yilan 3
Zhao, Qingxiang 168
Zhu, Lingting 135
Ziller, Alexander 191

The manufacturer's authorised representative in the EU is Springer Nature Customer Service Centre GmbH, Europaplatz 3, 69115 Heidelberg, Germany. If you have any concerns regarding our products, please contact ProductSafety@springernature.com

Printed and bound by CPI Group (UK) Ltd, Croydon, CR0 4YY

26/03/2026

02078962-0009